Britain and the World

English-speaking countries

Independent Commonwealth members (mostly English-speaking)

1974 Year of founding as an independent state

Learning English

Green Line 6
Ausgabe Bayern

Unterrichtswerk für Gymnasien

von

Werner Beile, Alice Beile-Bowes,
Rosemary Hellyer-Jones,
Peter Lampater, Raimund A. Mader,
Noreen O'Donovan, Alan Posener,
Dieter Prankel, Helmut Reisener,
Rolf W. Roth und Alexander Saccaro

Ernst Klett Verlag
Stuttgart Düsseldorf Leipzig

Learning English - Green Line 6
Ausgabe Bayern
für Klasse 10 an Gymnasien

von

Prof. Dr. Werner Beile und Alice Beile-Bowes M. A., Wuppertal und Iserlohn;
Rosemary Hellyer-Jones M. A., Ehingen (Donau); Peter Lampater, Ehingen (Donau);
Raimund A. Mader M. A., Eschenbach i. d. Oberpfalz;
Noreen O'Donovan B. A., Pforzheim; Alan Posener, Berlin;
Dieter Prankel, Dillingen; Dr. Helmut Reisener Dipl.-Päd., Lüneburg;
Rolf W. Roth M. A., Idar-Oberstein; Dr. Alexander Saccaro, Freiburg

Beratende Mitarbeit:

Rachel Baron Schuhbeck, München;
Prof. Dr. Gerhard F. Strasser, Pennsylvania State University, University Park, Pennsylvania;
Gernot Wirsing, Würzburg

Visuelle Gestaltung:

Christian Dekelver, Weinstadt (Illustrationen, Karten, Layout)
Klett-Kartographie/Krüger (Karten)

Begleitender Tonträger zu diesem Band:

1 Kompakt-Kassette für Schüler und Lehrer, mit Lektionstexten, Ausspracheübungen, Hörverstehenstexten und Liedern.
Beide Seiten besprochen, Klettnummer 583970.

Begleitende Software zu diesem Band:

1 Vokabel-Training mit Übungen und Lernzielkontrollen zu Green Line 6.
Klettnummer 130470 (Windows/CD-ROM)

1 Grammatik-Training mit Übungen und Lernzielkontrollen zu Green Line 6.
Klettnummer 130469 (Windows/CD-ROM)

Die Texte, auf die sich die Hörverstehensaufgaben beziehen, sind auf der Kassette (Klettnummer 583970) und im Lehrerbuch (Klettnummer 583930) verfügbar.

1. Auflage A 1 8 7 6 5 | 2006 2005 2004

Alle Drucke dieser Auflage können im Unterricht nebeneinander benutzt werden, sie sind untereinander unverändert. Die letzte Zahl bezeichnet das Jahr dieses Druckes.

Internetadresse: http://www.klett-verlag.de

Redaktion: Peter Cole M. A.; Redaktionsdienst ETS, Stuart Amor, Stuttgart;
Lektorat Projekte, Gaby Bauer-Negenborn M. A., Starnberg

Umschlag: Dieter Gebhardt, Asperg
Druck: Ludwig Auer GmbH, Donauwörth. Printed in Germany.
ISBN 3-12-583900-9

9 783125 839007

Inhaltsverzeichnis

Zeichenerklärung

⟨ ⟩ Stücke in Winkelklammern sind fakultativ.

Das Stück ist auf Kassette (Klettnummer 583970) verfügbar.

Weist auf die Hörverstehenstexte hin.

Übungen, die den Schülern erlauben über sich und ihre eigene Situation zu sprechen.

Wiederholungsübungen

WORD POWER Wortschatzübungen

UNIT 1

A Britannia rules the waves

The British Empire

This is a map of the British Empire, 'upon which the sun never set'. At its height it included a quarter of the world's population, from Canada to the Falkland Islands and from Jamaica to New Zealand.

1 A first look at the British Empire

What do you know? What does the map tell you? What can you guess?

1. Which country is the greatest distance from London, the centre of the Empire?
2. Which colony had the largest population?
3. Where did the British find a cold, hot, wet or dry climate?
4. Why did the British have a small army, but the biggest navy in the world?
5. Link the following products to where they came from in the Empire:
   tea, wheat, gold, wool, timber, oil, beef.
6. Where would you have settled? Why?

The Empire through the centuries

The Empire started with the first settlement at Jamestown, North America, in 1607 and officially ended in 1931 when it was changed into the Commonwealth of Nations or simply the Commonwealth.

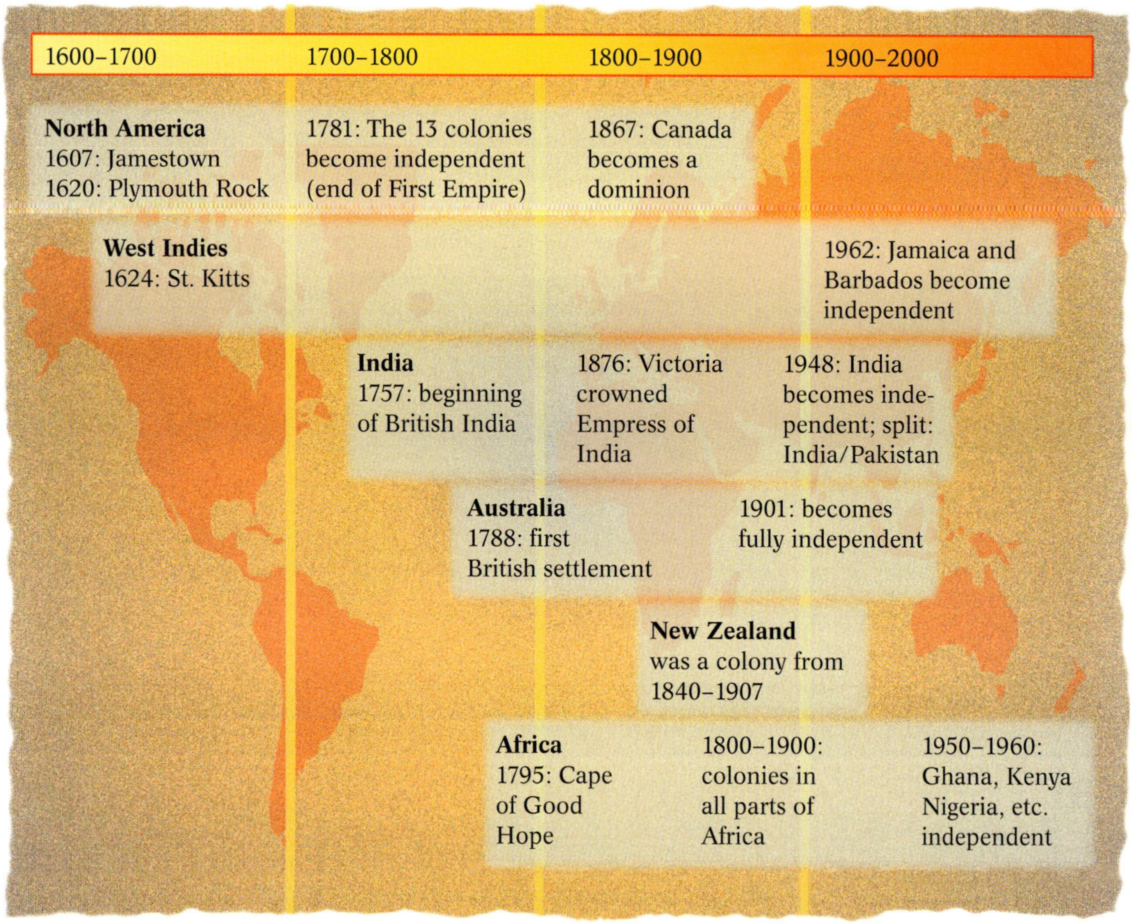

In 1585, the first English colony outside Europe was founded on Roanoke Island, North Carolina, but was wiped out by some mysterious disaster. Moreover, the Spaniards and the French had already started a number of trading posts in North America. The English, however, were able to do more than the others within the space of 150 years. Neither the Spaniards to the south nor the French to the north and west could stop them from becoming the masters of North America. The whole situation changed, however, with the American Revolution.

Nevertheless, Britain retained Canada and most of the West Indies. Furthermore, the British became the rulers of India and began to build up a Second Empire in the East. Both Australia and New Zealand were conquered and settled by the British. Thus it was not surprising that Britain took the biggest part of Africa in the 19th century. Yet in the 20th century colonialism became unpopular, especially with the people. Consequently, Britain had to give up most of her colonial territories. All the same, Britain's former colonies have kept some of their British culture after becoming independent. After all, most of them are still members of the Commonwealth.

2 Getting the facts

1. Why can we say that Britain had a bad start as a colonial power?
2. How long did it take the English to become the most powerful force in North America?
3. Did Britain lose all her territory in North America after the War of Independence?
4. Which word in the text tells us there were already people living in Australia and New Zealand when the British arrived?
5. In what form does the Empire still exist?

§1 **3 Connecting the facts**

§2 The text on the Empire consists of single sentences presenting facts. These facts are logically connected. The basic function of connectors is to show that the ideas are either flowing in the same direction (+) or going the opposite way (–). *Reread the text and write down all the connectors you can find. Then decide which box each of them belongs to. Give reasons for your decisions.*

Example: 1. In 1585, the first English colony outside Europe was founded on Roanoke Island, **but** was wiped out by some mysterious disaster. (–)
2. **Moreover,** the Spaniards and the French had already started a number of trading posts in North America. (+)

continues in the same direction (+)	turns in the opposite direction (–)
'Moreover' continues the idea of the sentence before. England had a bad start because there were already two strong powers in North America.	'But' changes the direction, as the English colony was wiped out.

§1 **4 Captain Cook**

§2 *Put in the missing connectors. Decide which connector best supports the ideas in the text.*

all the same	moreover	furthermore	yet	on the other hand	but
however	though	nevertheless	consequently	and	both

In 1768, Captain James Cook was sent on a journey round the world. … he made a lot of discoveries, he did not find a shorter passage around the American continent. … he was more successful in other parts of the world. He explored the coasts of … Australia … Tasmania. … Cook was not the first European to sail around Australia. He did, …, rediscover the Sandwich Islands. …, he found a medicine against scurvy.
…, Cook drew accurate maps. …, sailing in the Indian and Pacific Oceans became a lot easier. … the most immediate result of his journey was the first British settlement in Australia. … Cook didn't live to tell his story. … he will always be remembered as one of the greatest British explorers.

B The white man's burden?

Bringers of civilization

Before the 19th century colonialism was simply a question of money. The king gave private companies the right to do business in certain areas. Thus the journey of the Mayflower was paid for by the Virginia Company. Thanks to the Industrial Revolution, Britain became the workshop of the world and the colonies served as its market.

In the 19th century Europeans and North Americans were beginning to see themselves not only as wealthier and more powerful than Orientals or Africans, they also began to look upon them as second-class people. They felt it their duty to raise the cultural level of the 'barbarians'. The Americans said it was their 'manifest destiny' to make the Native Americans leave their homes as the new Americans moved west. The British said that the Anglo-Saxons had a mission to civilize the world. Therefore the Europeans and Americans demanded that China open her ports to white traders. They said it was important that everybody be christianized. They proposed that Africa be divided and insisted that every nation follow the path of European 'civilization'.

Lord Palmerston, Her Majesty's Prime Minister (1848): "Our duty is not to enslave, but to set free; and I may say without any boast that we stand at the head of moral, social, and political civilization. Our task is to lead the way and direct the march of other nations." (Ronald Hyam, *Britain's Imperial Century,* 1976)

1 Comprehension

1. What words did Palmerston use to make it clear that the Empire was not selfish?
2. What does the use of the phrase 'set free' (l. 13) mean?
3. What British institutions stood for moral, social and political civilization?
4. 'March' here is a military word. What was the role of the British on that march?
5. Project: The claim that the Europeans were bringers of civilization is questionable. Draw up a list of the 'gifts' of European 'civilization' under the headings *technology, politics, philosophy*, and *religion*. Decide which of the individual items brought real progress and which of them were harmful. Summarize your findings in about 80 words.

§4 2 Language and style

The subjunctive is not used very often in English. This means, however, that it has a very strong effect when it is used. The subjunctive after expressions of request or advice sounds especially formal and official. The sentences on the left use the subjunctive, the ones on the right are less formal. It would be a bit less formal to use 'should + infinitive' in place of the subjunctive. *Complete the sentences where needed.*

1. They insisted that every nation follow the path of European 'civilization'.
2. We request that the last person out switch off the lights.
3. I propose that Mr Nelson Mandela …
4. I insist that Tom leave our company.
5. I demand that we …
6. It is important that you …

1. They wanted every nation to follow the path of European 'civilization'.
2. Tell the last one out …
3. I think Nelson Mandela ought to become Secretary-General of the UN.
4. Tom …
5. Give us independence!
6. You simply have to be punctual!

The Roman Empire – the British Empire

Aeneas, who founded Rome, is given the following mission:

"Roman, remember that you shall
rule the nations by your authority,
for this is to be your skill:
to create peace and civilization."

Virgil (70–19 BC), Roman poet: *Aeneid,* VI 851 ff.

The British nation is addressed in the following lines:

"Take up the White Man's burden
Send forth the best ye breed
Go, bind your sons to exile
To serve your captives' need."

Rudyard Kipling (1865–1936), British author, poet: *The White Man's Burden*

Above there are two quotations, one by Virgil, a poet of the Roman Empire, and the other by Kipling, who wrote about the British Empire. *You may need your dictionary to find out the meaning of the words you don't know. Answer these questions:*
a) What is the main mission of the Roman Empire?
b) What does Britain do to 'serve their captives', i.e. to help the native population of her colonies?

The following text is an excerpt from Rudyard Kipling's 'Jungle Book'. *Use your dictionary to look up the words you can't guess from the context.*

Civilization as a chain of command: Servants of the Queen

The Viceroy is watching a parade of his troops in the company of a visiting Afghan chief.

The rain began to fall again, and for a while it was too misty to see what the troops were doing. They had made a big half-circle across the plain, and were spreading out into a line. That line grew and grew and grew till it was three-quarters of a mile long from wing to wing – one solid wall of men, horses, and guns. Then it came on straight toward the Viceroy and the Amir, and as it got nearer the ground began to shake, like the deck of a steamboat when the engines are going fast.
Unless you have been there you cannot imagine what a frightening effect this steady movement of troops has on the spectators, even when they know it is only a parade. I looked at the Amir. Up till then he had not shown any sign of astonishment or anything else. But now his eyes began to get bigger and bigger, and he picked up the reins on his horse's neck and looked behind him. For a minute it seemed as though he were going to draw his sword and cut his way out through the English men and women in the carriages at the back. Then the troops stopped dead, the ground stood still, the whole line saluted, and thirty bands began to play all together. That was the end of the parade. …
Then I heard an old grey-haired Central Asian chief, who had come down with the Amir, asking questions of an Indian officer.
"Now," said he, "in what manner was this wonderful thing done?"
And the officer answered, "An order was given, and they obeyed."
"But are the beasts as wise as the men?" said the chief.
"They obey, as the men do. Mule, horse, elephant, or ox, he obeys his driver, and the driver his sergeant, and the sergeant his lieutenant, and the lieutenant his captain, and the captain his major, and the major his colonel, and the colonel his brigadier commanding three regiments, and the brigadier the general, who obeys the Viceroy, who is the servant of the Empress. Thus it is done."
"Would it were so in Afghanistan!" said the chief, "for there we obey only our own wills."
"And for that reason," said the native officer, twirling his moustache, "your Amir whom you do not obey must come here and take orders from our Viceroy."
(Adapted from *The Jungle Book* by Rudyard Kipling)

3 Working with the text

1. Complete the sentences in this summary of the above excerpt.

   A few hundred artillery and cavalry … spread into a straight … and move towards a group of … . With clockwork … they stop and … . Then a sergeant explains to an … that … is the key to what they have just seen.

2. 'Size', 'precision' and 'power' combine to have a frightening effect on the visitors. Collect expressions that go with these three words.
3. What is the key to the troops' precision?
4. The chain of command: What is the lowest link? Who is at the top? If the chain continued, who would logically be above the Empress?
5. In a different passage Kipling describes the Amir's bodyguard as "savage men and savage horses who had never seen a military camp or a locomotive before in their lives". In the light of the above story, what are the differences between a civilized nation and a society that is not civilized?

§4 4 The subjunctive

a) Kipling's Afghan chief expresses the wish that Afghanistan might be as civilized as the British Empire using the words, "Would (= I wish) it were so in Afghanistan!" 'Were' is the only form which still shows that what looks like the past tense in wishes is in reality an old subjunctive. *Turn the facts on the left into phrases beginning with 'I wish …'.*

1. Afghanistan is poor.
2. The British have conquered India.
3. Queen Victoria is dead.
4. The natives have no political rights.
5. Germany didn't return Southwest Africa.
6. The English didn't give home rule to the Irish.

1. I wish Afghanistan were rich.
2. I wish …
3. …

b) In the 19th century the European powers simply divided up Africa. To avoid conflict among the Europeans, Bismarck suggested a meeting in Berlin (1884/85). Below are some notes a British politician might have taken during an interview with Bismarck. *Use the words from the box and turn the information into a report to Prime Minister Gladstone.*

Example: 1. Bismarck demands that the UK accept German Southwest Africa.

demand order insist request propose suggest

1. Das Vereinigte Königreich erkennt Deutsch-Südwestafrika an.
2. Deutschland behält Südwestafrika.
3. Deutschland verzichtet auf Betschuana (Bechuana).
4. England verhandelt mit den Buren (Boers).
5. Der Suezkanal (Suez Canal) ist für alle Nationen offen.
6. Frankreich setzt die Kolonialisierung von Algerien (Algeria) und Tunesien (Tunisia) fort.
7. Europa bringt moderne Regierungsformen nach Afrika.
8. Das Sklaventum wird verboten.
9. Das Treffen findet in Berlin statt.
10. Belgien wird eingeladen.

Leadership: "Send forth the best ye breed"

Read this text without using your dictionary. Try to guess the meaning of the words you don't know from the context.

Public school
In Britain, a prestigious fee-paying independent school. Some English public schools (for example Eton, Harrow, Rugby, Winchester) are ancient foundations, originally intended for poor male scholars; others developed in the 18th–19th centuries. Among those for girls are Roedean and Benenden. Many public schools are coeducational in the sixth forms, and some boys' schools now admit girls at 13. Some discipline (less than formerly) is in the hands of senior boys and girls (prefects).

Originally, British public schools stressed a classical education, character training and sports, but the curriculum is now closer to state education, though generally with a wider range of subjects offered and a lower pupil-to-teacher ratio.

Character-building

The future leaders of the nation and the Empire received the kind of education that set character above academic knowledge: sports and games played a very important part in the lives of public school boys. Their teachers believed that through sports their pupils would learn to fight for their aims, but respect the rules. Fairness was seen as the most important law. In 1867 a government commission examined education in eight of the most famous British public schools. The commission's report said:

"His (the public school boy's) intellectual education must certainly be accounted[1] a failure[2], though there may be no fault[3] to find with his principles, character, or manners. ... It is not easy to estimate[4] the degree in which the English people are indebted[5] to these schools for the qualities on which they pique[6] themselves most – for their capacity[7] to govern others and control themselves, their aptitude[8] for combining freedom with order, their public spirit[9], their vigour[10] and manliness[11] of character, ..., their love of healthy sports and exercise."

---

[1] [ə'kaʊnt] *bewerten;* [2] ['feɪljə] *Versagen;* [3] [fɔ:lt] *Fehler;* [4] ['estɪmeɪt] *beurteilen;* [5] [ɪn'detɪd] *verpflichtet sein;* [6] [pi:k] *sich viel auf etw. einbilden;* [7] [kə'pæsətɪ] *(geistige) Fähigkeit;* [8] ['æptɪtju:d] *Begabung;* [9] ['spɪrɪt] *Geist;* [10] ['vɪgə] *Stärke;* [11] ['mænlɪnɪs] *Männlichkeit*

The age of Empire – the birth of modern sports

Cricket: The most English of all sports – a game that can last up to five days. Its rules are so difficult that you have to grow up with the game to play it well.
Rugby: Rugby was born when in 1823 a boy at Rugby School picked up the ball and ran with it while playing football.
Tennis: Tennis was introduced by Major Walter Wingfield at a Christmas party in Wales, 1873.
Boxing: After the formulation of the Queensberry Rules in 1867 by the Marquess of Queensberry, fighting with gloves became the accepted way to fight in the latter part of the 19th century.

Can you find five words or phrases in the commission's report which express that people with these characteristics would make good colonial masters?

Example: Even in difficult situations they would be able to keep themselves under control.

C The black man's burden

Don't kick the butler

George Orwell, the famous British writer, served with the police in Burma from 1922–28. There he wrote his 'Burmese Days'. The setting of the following excerpt is an outpost in colonial Burma in the 1920s. Verrall, who has just arrived in Burma, has accepted an invitation to the officers' club, where he is joined by Ellis, a senior member of the club.

Verrall kept his promise and was at the club that evening. He arrived a little earlier than the others, and he had made his presence felt before being in the place five minutes. As Ellis entered the club the old butler darted out of the card-room. There were tears rolling down his cheeks.

"Sir! Sir!"

"What the devil's the matter now!" said Ellis.

"Sir! Sir! New master been beating me, sir!"

"What?"

"*Beating* me, sir!" His voice rose on the 'beating' with a tearful long wail – 'be-e-e-eating!'

"Beating you? Do you good. Who's been beating you?"

"New master, sir. Military police sahib. Beating me with his foot, sir – *here*!" He rubbed his behind.

"Hell!" said Ellis.

He went into the lounge. Verrall was reading the *Field*, and invisible except for his trouser-ends and two shiny shoes. He did not trouble or stir at hearing someone else come into the room. Ellis halted.

"Hey, you – what's your name – Verrall!"

"What?"

"Have you been kicking our butler?"

Verrall's unfriendly blue eye appeared round the corner of the magazine, like the eye of a crab looking round a rock.

"What?" he repeated shortly.

"Have you been kicking our bloody butler?"

"Yes."

"Then what the hell do you mean by it?"

"Beggar gave me his lip. I sent him for a whisky and soda, and he brought it warm. I told him to put ice in it, and he wouldn't – talked some bloody nonsense about saving the last piece of ice. So I kicked his bottom. Serve him right."

Ellis turned quite grey. He was furious. The butler was a piece of club property and not to be kicked by strangers. But what most angered Ellis was the thought that Verrall quite possibly suspected him of being *sorry* for the butler – in fact disapproving of the kick *as such*.

"Serve him right? I dare say it bloody well did serve him right. But what the hell's that got to do with it? Who are *you* to come kicking our servants?"

"Nonsense, my good chap. Needed kicking. You've let your servants get out of hand here."

"You cheeky young fellow, what's it got to do with *you* if he needed kicking? You're not even a member of this club. It's our job to kick the servants, not yours."

(Adapted from *Burmese Days* by George Orwell)

1 Comprehension

1. Write a summary of the above excerpt in two or three sentences.
2. In what way do Ellis and Verrall have the same view of natives?
3. "But what most angered Ellis was the thought that Verrall quite possibly suspected him of being *sorry* for the butler – in fact disapproving of the kick *as such*." What does this sentence tell us about the situation of whites who thought of natives as people?

2 Close reading

1. The description of the butler contains some 'funny' ideas that are based on his not being British. Can you identify two of them (language, behaviour)?
2. As Orwell didn't mean to write a comedy, which of the following could be a logical description of what he wanted to do?
   a) If the readers also think foreigners are funny, they will realize that – like the two colonial officers – they are in danger of thinking that foreigners are stupid.
   b) He wants us to see the officers as racists.
   c) 'Burmese Days' is a sad novel, so he needs to cheer up the readers now and then.
3. How does Orwell make it clear right from the beginning that Ellis does not want to help the butler?
4. The two officers do not speak in complete sentences. This is typical of their class. They also use swear-words. Pick out a few examples of both.

3 Essay writing

"Power tends to corrupt, and absolute power corrupts absolutely. Great men are almost always bad men." (Lord J. E. Acton, English historian, 1887)

Write an essay of about 200 words on this quotation and the relation of these words to the excerpt from George Orwell's 'Burmese Days'. First make notes on what you want to write. Then plan your essay, giving it an introduction, a main part, and an ending.

4 Language and social status

As you saw in the above excerpt, language is a mirror of social relationships. We don't just pass on information, we also show our relationship to the person we are talking to. Thus people might

- use very relaxed language with their friends,
- use fairly informal language with their parents,
- try to speak correct English or German at school,
- be very polite at a job interview,
- and use 'old-fashioned' formal language at the Royal Garden Party.

Levels of style are characterized by vocabulary from slang (very relaxed) to old-fashioned expressions (formal), grammar from half-sentences like "Got your ticket?" (very relaxed) to subjunctives like "I demand that you return (!) the ticket!" (very formal), and pronunciation from careless like "Arentcha tired?" (informal) to very careful "Are you not tired?" (very formal). *Explain the sentences below in this way. Give a short reason. You could also guess who is talking to whom.*
Example: 1. Be at the station at eight o'clock, will you?

(informal – the speaker is not very polite – possibly: master – servant)

1. Can you be at the station at eight o'clock?
2. Would you be so kind as to be at the station at eight o'clock, James?
3. It is absolutely vital that everybody follow the doctor's instructions.
4. Mr and Mrs Smith request the pleasure of your company at their wedding party.
5. Got a ciggy (= cigarette) for me?
6. I propose that the staff manager be informed immediately of the problem.
7. Leave me alone, will you?
8. May God be with you!
9. The manager insisted that Mr Jones be given the job of talking to our Japanese partners.

The end of the Empire

In 1919 the idea of self-determination for all nations was decided at Versailles. It was the beginning of the end of the British Empire. There were problems in much of the Empire during the 1930s, although especially in India, where Mahatma Gandhi led a campaign of 'civil disobedience' against British rule. World War II (1939–45) was the beginning of the end of the former colonial empires, mainly because it destroyed the idea upon which their existence depended. India got total independence in 1947/48; Sudan, Ghana and Malaya in the 1950s, and much of the rest of Africa in the 1960s. By 1970 the former British colonies in the West Indies were either independent or linked to Britain only by their own choice. Rhodesia said it was independent in 1965, but Britain didn't accept this. Finally, a London conference agreed on legal independence of Rhodesia under black rule, and the new state of Zimbabwe was born in 1980.
By 1973, when Britain joined the EEC, only a few small colonies remained, most of which were moving toward independence. Some did not want to end their colonial status. Gibraltar and Hong Kong, for example, felt they risked being taken over by Spain and China if Britain left them. However, the British Empire as a whole has largely disappeared, to be replaced by the Commonwealth of Nations.

5 Let's build castles in Spain, but let's not be too serious about it!

Start with the second part of the sentence.

Example: 1. <u>If the Americans had stayed in the Empire</u>, the Queen would be President of the United States.

1. If King George had treated the Americans better, <u>they would have stayed in the Empire</u>.
2. If World War I had not broken out, Ireland would have become an independent nation 80 years ago.
3. If Britain still had its Empire, millions of British people would live in the colonies.
4. If there had been less crime in London, the English would not have needed Australia for their prisoners.
5. If Nelson Mandela were a racist, he would not work with the whites.
6. If George Orwell hadn't hated colonialism, he would have remained a police officer in Burma.
7. If fewer people from Commonwealth countries lived in Britain, it would be less multicultural.

§5 6 It helps to know German

There are grammar structures you don't have to learn when you are German. A good example is the inverted conditional clause. Like the subjunctive of request it is formal, but for that very reason it has a strong effect when it is used. *Translate the following sentences into German.*

1. Had Orwell known colonialism, he wouldn't have gone to Burma.
2. Should Nigeria leave the Commonwealth, the price of oil will go up in the UK.
3. Had the British educational system not been changed, the Empire would have collapsed much earlier.
4. Should Australia put an end to the monarchy, its relationship to Britain will change.
5. Had the people of Quebec been less proud of their culture, French would have died out in Canada a long time ago.
6. Had Rhodesia not given up white rule in 1979, there might still be apartheid in South Africa.

D The Commonwealth and multicultural Britain

Use your dictionary to find out the meaning of the words you don't know. Remember you don't have to know every word to understand the main ideas.

The legacy of the Empire in the former colonies

The British built cities like New Delhi or Sydney where before their arrival there had been a wilderness. They drained swamps, irrigated deserts and built roads and bridges. Most important, they left behind the railways: India, not a very rich country, has one of the densest networks of railways in the world.

They also set an example of incorrupt government. British officials were not always very clever or competent, but they had a reputation for being honest and fair-minded. Even today this spills over into a world-wide respect for the BBC.

And they left behind a common British culture. On this point visiting businessmen, writers, soldiers, scientists and diplomats are all agreed. Nigeria is Nigerian and Jamaica is Jamaican, but like practically every former colony they are unmistakably British. The same uniforms, the same moustaches, the tea parties on the lawn, the same sports. In fact, there is hardly a game or sport from mountaineering to boxing, from lawn tennis to golf which the British did not first develop and then export to their old colonial partners.

The most important legacy, however, is the English language. In most former colonies English is the official language because the different language groups couldn't agree on any native language.

(Adapted from *The Imperial Dream* by Sir George A. Grierson)

1 Working with the text

a) *Read the text and answer the questions:*

1. What role did the British play in the development of the infrastructure in their former colonies?
2. How did the ideas of public school education influence these countries?
3. Why do former colonies have a British 'feeling' about them?
4. For what practical reason did most former colonies choose English as their official language?

b) *Use an encyclopedia and find out more information about the Commonwealth. Then answer the questions in more detail.*

Dropped goal?

You will understand the main ideas of the story without using your dictionary.

Colin lived and breathed rugby. He would sing ‘Sospan fach’ at internationals in Cardiff Arms Park and dreamed of playing for Wales one day. In this respect he was like thousands of other Welsh teenage boys, but there were two differences. He was a candidate for the Welsh schoolboys’ team. And he was black!

His Nigerian-born parents – his father was a successful GP – sometimes worried that his enthusiasm for rugby might affect his grades, but Colin was a bright boy who was generally expected to do very well in his A-levels.

His classmates at Duffryn, a large, well-run comprehensive in Newport, were proud of him and Mr Watkins, the coach of the school’s rugby XV, considered him God’s gift to Duffryn. It is true there were a few skinheads who hated him, but 16-year-old Colin was a big, strong lad who had big, strong friends on the rugby team. There was no denying it: he was a lucky young fellow by any standard.

Then something happened that changed his outlook on life forever: he fell in love. It was like a bolt out of the blue. He was sitting in an English literature class doing his best to concentrate on Mr Williams explaining the wonders of Shakespeare’s poetry when the door opened and a beautiful girl walked in. She was accompanied by ‘Goldfinger’, the chain-smoking headmaster, who introduced her to the class. “This is Lynne Davies. Her family has moved to Newport from Penarth. Her dad is the new manager of Stratton’s Electronics and I’m delighted her parents have chosen Duffryn. I’m sure you will make her feel welcome.” Andy Jones, Colin’s neighbour, was also his best friend, but now Colin wished him on the moon to make room for Lynne. Alas, Andy didn’t vanish into thin air and so Lynne found a seat next to Philip Gray, who instantly became Colin’s second candidate for a trip to the moon. He had fancied girls before, but this was different. Even in Duffryn’s somewhat dull school uniform – grey skirt, white blouse and navy-blue blazer – Lynne looked glamorous. When she told the teacher in her beautiful voice that ‘Shall I compare thee to a summer’s day’ was her favourite poem because she felt that “Shakespeare must have been madly in love to create such beautiful images”, Colin immediately decided to learn the sonnet by heart, just in case! He didn’t get a chance to recite Shakespeare; he didn’t even find the courage to ask her out for an ice-cream. Instead he spent the next few days moping, neglecting both his studies and his training. In a practice match against the second XV he only scored one single try. The coach looked rather worried after the game, but his star player just mumbled something about a cold and pushed past him.

“Hi, Colin. That was a lovely try. I hope you’ll score another one like that against Hartridge next week!” It was Lynne’s voice. She had been waiting for him. Colin was so flustered he just managed to stammer: “Ah well! Bit of an off day! I’ll do better next week! Didn’t know you were interested in rugby. See you.” Lynne liked rugby! No more sonnets! He was on cloud nine.

The following day everybody was surprised at the way Colin threw himself into the training session and Mr Watkins breathed a sigh of relief.

The big day arrived. As the two teams walked onto the pitch amid cheers, Lynne gave Colin the thumbs-up, but he didn’t need any encouragement. Outplaying everyone else he ran in five tries, kicked four penalty goals and scored two dropped goals. Duffryn thrashed their rivals by 35 points. Colin was the man of the match and the ‘South Wales Argus’ described him as one of the finest prospects in Welsh rugby. However, this was nothing compared to what happened two days later. Lynne phoned him. “Are you free on Saturday night? We are having a house-warming party. Dad told me I could invite friends from school. Mind you, it’ll probably be a bit formal. Maybe you should wear a suit.”

Colin’s heart was in his mouth when on Saturday night he rang the brightly polished brass bell of the splendid house. A servant wearing white gloves opened the door.

“Would you care to wait in the lounge, sir?” His voice was perfectly polite, but Colin didn’t like the arrogant droop of his mouth. After a while

Lynne appeared, took him by the hand and led him towards a brightly lit room filled with people in evening dress. "Dad used to play rugby at university. I'm sure he'll be delighted to meet you. And so will Mum." She pulled him towards a lady in a black silk dress who was talking to a man in a dinner jacket. "Mum, Dad, this is Colin." Mrs Davies raised her eyes and smiled a smile that froze when she focused on the young man. "Hello, Colin, I'm pleased to meet you," but her face told a different story. Embarrassed he stammered "Er ... Thank you ... er ... for inviting me! I really ..." He was interrupted by Mr Davies's even frostier welcome. "How do you do? Enjoy yourself. There is a buffet over there and you can get drinks from the servants." Hardly bothering to smile he waved vaguely in the direction of the buffet. Then he turned abruptly away to talk to a middle-aged man about the stock market. Colin felt his stomach tighten. Lynne tried to make the best of a bad start. "There are so many guests Mum and Dad have to look after!" They picked up a few sandwiches at the buffet and Colin even managed to seize a glass of orange juice from the servant's tray. "Let's meet some of my friends," Lynne suggested, steering him towards a group of young people with Swiss skiing suntans.

"Hello, folks," she warbled. "This is Colin, a friend of mine. We hope he'll be selected for the Welsh schoolboys' team." A tall, fair-haired young man eyed him languidly: "Yes, they'll do anything to win, won't they," he said in a snobbish voice.

Everybody fell silent. As the insult sank in Colin felt a rage welling up he had never felt before. He was painfully aware that all those beautiful people were staring at him. Some of them looked embarrassed, others were scrutinizing him with amused curiosity, while the rude young man looked pleased with himself. Finally Lynne broke the silence. "Look, James, that was completely uncalled for!" At this point Colin couldn't control his anger any longer. He clenched his fist breaking the glass of orange juice he was holding in his hand. The glass cracked and the orange juice spilt on the floor. Then blood started dripping from his hand onto the carpet. "My God! Your hand's bleeding!" Lynne cried. Colin didn't feel any pain. He turned to James: "I should wring your flipping neck!" Then he stormed out of the house. As he stepped into the garden Lynne cried out: "I'm sorry, Colin, I'm really sorry," but he ignored her. It was only when he was alone in the dark street that tears began to stream down his cheeks.

The next Monday there was a letter in the post: to Mr Colin Adinlawo from the Welsh selectors. ...

(By *Peter Rinkdale*)

2 Summary writing

In a summary you reduce an original to its main ideas, so you have to read the whole text before you can decide what the main points are.

Example: A black teenage boy finds out that his prestige as a rugby star doesn't protect him from racist insults.

If you want to write a 20-word summary, it might look like the above example. A 150-word summary should be less general. The following set of tips and questions will help you with the process of writing a summary of 'Dropped Goal?'.

a) *Collect the ideas and events that should be in your summary. Write them down in short sentences without linking them. Do one paragraph at a time. Don't write your final summary yet. You will probably be able to connect some of the paragraphs in one sentence. You may also find that some of the ideas come up more than once in the original. Read your notes several times before writing your summary.*

b) *Complete the sentences below after reading paragraphs I-VIII one at a time.*
I (ll. 1-7): Colin, a black Welsh teenage boy, is a candidate for ...
II (ll. 8-21): He is a ... pupil and very ...
III (ll. 22-59): a) He ... with Lynne, a new pupil ... b) He is too ... to ask her out.
IV (ll. 60-71): It turns out that Lynne ... rugby.
V (ll. 72-87): a) Colin ... b) Lynne ...
VI (ll. 88-128): a) At the Davieses' party ... b) Lynne's parents ... c) A friend of Lynne's ...
VII (ll. 129-150): a) Colin tries to control ... b) He breaks ... and ... c) He tells James what he thinks of him and ... d) Out in the street he ...
VIII (ll. 151-153): The next Monday ...
c) *Now you can write the summary. You may use the 'signpost' phrases between the gaps or choose expressions of your own. Try to write less than 180 words.*

3 Close reading

1. Find two expressions in the text that show how important rugby is to a large number of Welsh people.
2. How do you know that Lynne's parents are wealthy? List all the points that you can find in the story.
3. What do you understand by the phrase 'dropped goal'?
4. The following sentences use images to make the text less matter-of-fact. Replace the marked expressions with different phrases: a) Philip Gray *became* Colin's *second candidate for a trip to the moon*. b) He was *on cloud nine*. c) Duffryn *thrashed* their rivals.
5. Throughout the party Colin felt very unhappy. Collect the words or phrases expressing his feelings.

4 Expressing your opinion

1. Why do you think the headmaster is pleased Lynne has enrolled at Duffryn?
2. Who are the two most unpleasant characters in the story? Give reasons for your opinion.
3. Do you find Colin's reaction to the situation appropriate? What would you have done in his place?
4. Lynne obviously hadn't told her parents that Colin was black. Why can this be seen as an optimistic element in the story?
5. Is 'Dropped goal?' a realistic story? Why?/Why not?
6. The story ends with the letter from the Welsh selectors. How could it go on? Work out two different possible endings for 'Dropped goal?'.
7. There are quite a few British citizens of Nigerian origin. Can you explain why? Find some background information in an encyclopedia and explain the historical situation to your class.
8. Colin's parents didn't return to their home country because of the civil war in Biafra (1967-70). Look at the map and find at least three more Commonwealth countries where there have been civil wars since they became independent. Can you think of reasons for these wars?

⟨5 Listening comprehension: The multicultural forum⟩

Jim is interested in politics. So he decided to start a forum on multicultural Britain.
Listen to the cassette. Then answer the questions.

1. Which of the six speakers find Britain's multiculturalism a problem?
2. What examples does Jack give of the importance of Africans and Asians in British society?
3. What mistakes does Fiona point out in John's statement about 'non-Brits'?
4. What relationship does Philip see between Asians and Africans and the employment situation?
5. Does Bridget think the heyday of the British Empire were the 'good old days'? What examples does she give?
6. Describe the career of Ravi's father since he came to Britain in 1974?

A With God on its side

UNIT 2

Oh the history books tell it
They tell it so well
The cavalries charged
The Indians fell
The cavalries charged
The Indians died
Oh the country was young
With God on its side.
(Bob Dylan)

It is hard to say exactly when the first Native Americans arrived on the North American continent. Some came as early as 20,000 or even 40,000 years ago. Most, however, moved into North America about 12,000 years ago when the climate began to warm up after the last Ice Age. After settling on the American continent, Native American tribes developed cultures with political, social, religious and economic institutions. The coming of the Europeans to North America, however, changed the land and its people. Relocation, wars and diseases meant death for millions of Native Americans. The Native American population of North America was reduced from about 10 or 12 million in 1500 to about half a million in 1900.
Before emigrating to the new continent, many of the early pioneers had suffered hardship and persecution in their home countries, and were prepared to suffer hardship in the wilderness in the hope of a better life, or at least of more freedom. After arriving on the new continent, these people wanted to find land in the West and to settle there as farmers. However, they did not understand the Native Americans' use of the land. For the European settlers, the best use of land was for farming. Rather than hunting animals for meat and skins as the Native Americans did, they preferred to raise cattle, sheep, and pigs.

The following quotations show some of the differences between the Native Americans and the European settlers. *You may need your dictionary to look up some of the new words.*

... the average Indian of the woods and prairies is a being who does little credit to human nature. As I traveled through the area which forms the reservation of the Delawares, Potawatamies, etc., being the best cornlands on earth, and saw their owners sitting around the doors of their huts in the middle of the planting season I could not help saying, "These people must die out – there is no help for them. God has given this earth to those who will cultivate it, and it is vain to struggle against His righteous decree."
(From *An Overland Journey from New York to San Francisco in the Summer of 1859* by Horace M. Greeley)

... My culture did not prize the hoarding of private possessions, in fact, to hoard was a shameful thing to do among my people. The Indian looked on all things in nature as belonging to him and he expected to share them with others and to take only what he needed. (From *Brotherhood and Understanding* by Chief Dan George)

Differences about land ownership and the use of the land became a principal source of conflict between the European settlers and the Native Americans.

1. *Can you explain how ownership of land was seen by the Native Americans and the European settlers?*
2. *God is mentioned both in Bob Dylan's song and in Horace M. Greeley's quotation. Why did the settlers believe that taking away the land from the Native Americans was right?*

Jacob

Jack Schaefer wrote a lot of stories about the American West. In 'Jacob', he describes how a white boy from a small town in Montana met a famous Nez Percé Native American chief. This was sometime in the late 1870s. The Native American's name was Big-Deer-That-Walks-the-High-Places, but the whites called him Jacob.
Trouble started when white settlers began looking for land in Jacob's valley in Idaho, and the Native Americans pushed them out. Then the government suggested moving the Native Americans – there were about 700 of them – to a reservation; the whites thought the land was "too good for Indians because they didn't use it properly". But Jacob and his people did not want to leave their land.
When the government sent soldiers into the valley, the Native Americans escaped to the mountains. The soldiers followed them and there was fighting for four months, but the Indians did not give up. In the end they were beaten – not by the government and its soldiers, but by the winter. When the Native Americans began to die of cold and hunger, Jacob at last agreed to move to a reservation with his people. There were now about 300 of them left, and they were all loaded on a special train. On its way to Native American territory, the train had to pass through that small town in Montana ...
Try to get the meaning of the text without using your dictionary. You can guess the words you don't know from the context.

"The only good Indian is a dead Indian," my father always said. Yes. There were men who really said things like that. And believed them. My father was one.
Naturally we boys believed it too, because we heard it all the time. We never saw any fighting Indians in our little town, but I imagined them big and fierce and dangerous.
Well, when the day came for that train full of Indians to pass through our town, we boys wanted to see it. Anyway, we waited all afternoon, but the train didn't come. My father was a signalman and had to be there before the train arrived, so when he was called in the middle of the night, I got up and asked if I could go with him.
"Fool kid," he said, "excited about Indians all the time. It'll do you good to see what they're really like. Thieving, smelly things."
So I went with him. He went off to his signal, and I waited on the platform.

In about twenty minutes the train arrived. I was shaking inside as if I had some kind of fever. There wasn't much light in the train, and I couldn't see through the windows. When I went nearer, a soldier – a captain – stepped down from the first coach.
"Jee-sus," he said. "Why does everyone want to stare at them? Even kids. – All right. Go on in, take a look."
I was scared now.
"Go on," he said. "They don't eat boys. Only girls. Only at lunchtime." And I suddenly knew he was making a joke, and it would be all right, and I went up the steps and looked in.

Indians. Fighting Indians. The fighting Nez Percés who had led United States soldiers a bloody chase through the mountains of three states. The big and fierce redmen who had fought bravely against many times their own number of better armed soldiers (it had been about one brave to six or seven soldiers). And they weren't big and they weren't fierce at all. They were huddled figures on the coach seats, braves and squaws and young ones all the same, all dusty and tired. There was no room in me for any feeling except disappointment. There wasn't a hint of danger anywhere around.

I wanted to see everything, so I walked through the coach and looked all around me. And those Indians acted as if I wasn't there at all. Those that were awake. They knew I was there. I could tell that. A feeling. But they wouldn't look at me. They seemed to be far away in a place all their own and they weren't going to let me into it.

Full of disappointment, I went into the next coach and through it and to the third coach and on to the last. Each was the same. Soldiers asleep, and the huddled figures of the Indians on the coach seats. And then, at the end of the last coach, I saw him.
He had a seat to himself, and the headdress with its red feathers hung above his seat. I stopped and stared at him, and the low light from the lantern near him shone on his dark brown face.
I stared at him, and I felt empty inside. Even Jacob wasn't big or fierce. He wasn't as big as my father. He was short. And his face was quiet and – well, peaceful. I stared at him, and suddenly I felt ashamed and I hurried to the back of the coach to leave the train.

From outside I could just see Jacob through the window of the last coach. He was standing up. And then he came out onto the platform. All kinds of wild feelings went through my mind, but I couldn't move. Then I realized he wasn't going to do anything. He didn't even see me. He stood quietly on the platform and looked back along the double line of the track, towards the light of my father's signal lantern. I stayed where I was and watched him.
He did not move. Now I realized that he was looking far past the light of my father's signal lantern. Far on, where the lonely track ran into the horizon. He was looking back along the iron trail that was taking him and his people away from their valley. The iron trail that was taking them to an unknown place where they would no longer be themselves but only some among many other tribes, all dependent on a government that would soon forget them.

It wasn't an Indian I saw there any more. It was a man. It wasn't Jacob, the tamed chief that even kids could stare at. It was Big-Deer-That-Walks-the-High-Places and he was big, really big, and he was meant to walk the high places.

(From *Jacob* by Jack Schaefer)

1 Comprehension

a) *Can you finish these sentences?*

1. The boy who tells the story imagined that the Nez Percé Native Americans looked wild and dangerous, although he …
2. In those days a lot of whites believed that …
3. The boy went to the station with his father for …
4. On seeing the Native Americans in the train, he felt … because …
5. The boy had imagined that Jacob would look … but actually …
6. The boy hurried to get off the train because …
7. When Jacob came onto the platform, the boy thought at first that he was looking at … but really …

b) *Can you answer the following questions?*

1. "The only good Indian is a dead Indian." Why do you think so many of the European settlers believed this?
2. "It'll do you good to see what they are really like." Go through the text and say how the boy's feelings towards Native Americans develop and change during the story.
3. The boy feels that the Native Americans on the train are "far away in a place all their own …" (l. 50). Can you explain what he means?
4. Compare 'typical' Native Americans from films with the Native Americans we meet in Jack Schaefer's story.

§6 2 The early settlers

The first colonists had moved west across the Atlantic to a new continent. On arriving there, they stopped looking back to Europe. In the West, it seemed, there was room for everybody …
a) *Put the right parts of the sentences together.* b) *Use one of the following prepositions and a gerund instead of the subordinate clause:* before, on, after, in spite of, for.

Most settlers were very grateful to the Native Americans …
… new hardship awaited them.
… many of them settled there as farmers.
… many settlers suffered hardship in their home countries.
… they were surprised how hard it was to survive in the wilderness.

§6 3 The plains

The central part of North America is a world of grasslands called the 'Prairie Belt'. Before the European settlers came, humans had not made much of a difference in the plains. The Native Americans were hunters who followed the great herds of buffalo. *Rewrite the following sentences using gerunds.*

Example: 1. Before making the plains their home, the forefathers of the Native Americans crossed the Bering Strait into Alaska.

1. The forefathers of the Native Americans had crossed the Bering Strait into Alaska. They made the plains their home. (before)
2. After they had reached Alaska, they spread through the Americas. (after)
3. When the first Native Americans arrived, they found a land of beauty. (on)
4. Although they shared the plains as a common home, each tribe developed its own way of life. (in spite of)
5. Even though they didn't speak a common language, the different tribes could still communicate. (without)
6. The different tribes communicated. They used sign language. (by)
7. The buffalo was very important. It fed and clothed the Native Americans. (for)
8. They sometimes used their horses to pay for goods. They didn't pay with money. (instead of)
9. They used their horses not only for hunting but also for carrying things. (as well as)

4 The American Heartland

Translate the following text into German, using your dictionary if necessary.

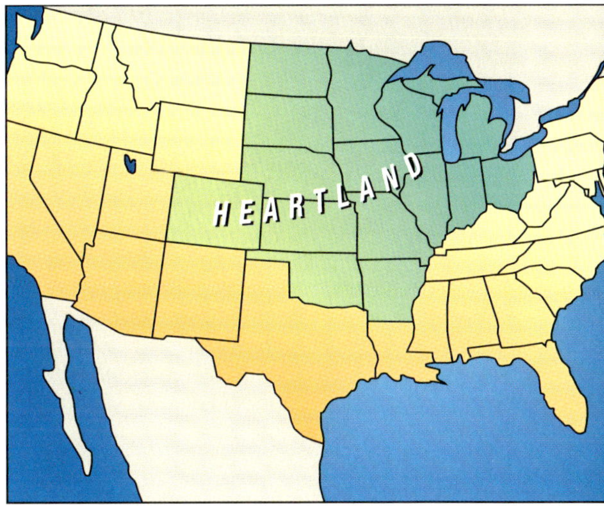

The Heartland of the North American continent is shaped like a triangle, with the Great Lakes along the top. It is almost impossible to see what the original face of the land looked like, since on settling there, the white man began to change it completely. Turned into farmland or built over with busy cities, towns and industrial plants, very little wilderness is left. The people in the Heartland developed and cultivated it over the last two centuries. The settlers were assisted by others. The beaver, for instance, has probably had more influence on the landscape of the area than any other animal. Beavers build dams which stop erosion and make the land even more fertile. The Heartland, which was formed by an ice cap, is one of the most interesting parts of the country. Some evidence of the Ice Age is clearly visible in the form of low hills. Side by side with these signs of an earlier age are the great cities and fertile farms of the people who chose the land and changed it.

5 Native American humor

A white man was introduced to an old chief in New York City. Since he liked the old man, the white man invited him out to dinner. The old chief hadn't eaten a good steak for a long time and accepted. He finished one steak in no time and still looked hungry. So the white man offered to buy him another steak. While they were waiting for the steak, the white man said: "Chief, I sure wish I had your appetite." "I don't doubt it, white man," the chief said. "You took my salmon and my buffalo. You took everything I had except my appetite and now you want that. Aren't you ever going to be satisfied?"

B Opening up the West

> We go eastward to realize history, and ...
> we go westward as into the future ...
> (Henry David Thoreau)

It all started with the first colonists moving west across the Atlantic to a new continent. When in 1776 the thirteen British colonies declared their independence from Britain, people stopped looking back to Europe, and began to look west – the opening up of the West began.

Settlers looking for new land left the original colonies. They moved west along the rivers, and through the mountains. First they crossed the Appalachian Mountains, then having crossed the Mississippi River, they finally reached the area today known as the Midwest. A few years later the whole western part of the U.S. had been settled. With more and more people coming to these territories, new states were created and became part of the Union. By about 1890 the settlement of the West had been completed.

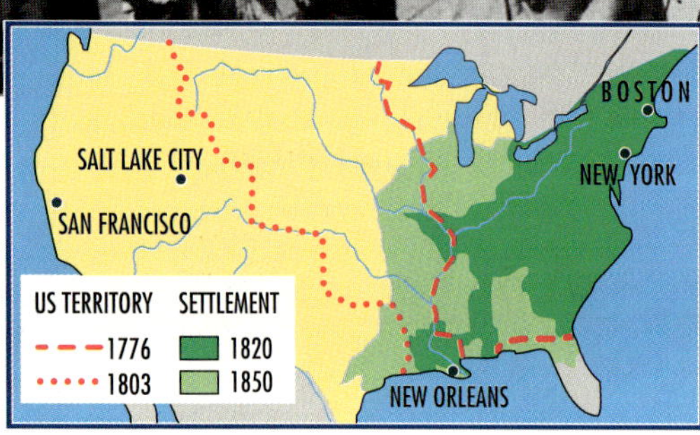

The frontier

Historians describe the American frontier as an imaginary line dividing areas with more than two people per square mile from those with fewer people – in other words the frontier was the border between settled and unsettled land.

The frontier experience, the opening and settlement of new lands to the west, continuing for more than two hundred years, had a great influence on the American character. Above all it supported the spirit of independence; while cultivating the wild land, people were completely independent of any form of government: the frontierspeople went ahead of governments, not behind them. It also made Americans more willing 'to get up and go' somewhere else looking for something better. Even today, Americans easily move from one part of the country to another.

America's 'manifest destiny'

The movement westward was not always peaceful, to put it mildly. However, Americans of the 19th century strongly believed that they were following God's will when they settled the U.S. territory all the way across the continent. They thought that America was the 'Promised Land' which God had given them to cultivate and to civilize. People believed that it was America's 'manifest destiny', her mission, to save 'living space' for future generations of immigrants, so that they could live in a land of freedom and democracy. Of course, there were also economic reasons prompting the movement westward. Americans were promised cheap land, and the West came to be seen as a land of golden opportunities. That's why the United States was not satisfied with half the continent, it wanted the other half as well.

In 1803 the U.S. got the chance to buy all the land between the Mississippi and the Rocky Mountains – the Louisiana Territory – from France. Napoleon Bonaparte had decided to sell Louisiana to the young American nation for $15 million rather than to lose it to the British who were ready to fight for it. So, the area of the United States was doubled. Other large areas of land were bought as well. Florida had once belonged to the Spanish. Alaska was sold by Russia for some $7 million.

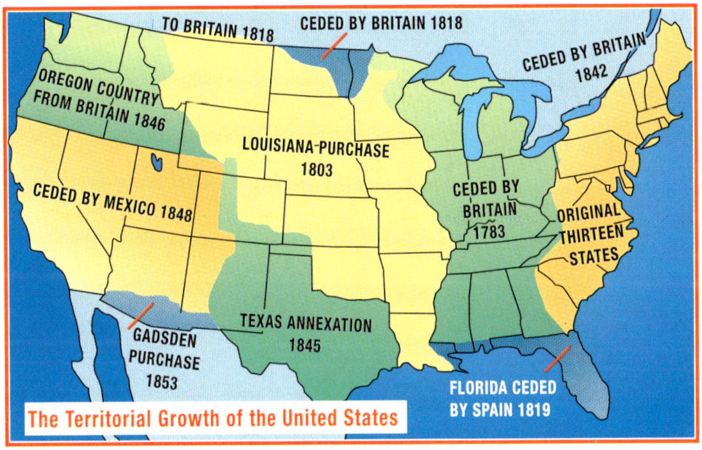

The Territorial Growth of the United States

Texas, which belonged to Mexico, was another area that attracted American interest. The Texans declared their independence from Mexico in 1836, and in 1845 Texas became the 28th U.S. state. Problems with Mexico concerning the border led to the Mexican War of 1846–48. The Americans were successful in this war and in 1848 New Mexico, California and the land in between became part of the United States.

The first transcontinental railroad

Plans for a transcontinental railroad had already begun in the first half of the 19th century. However, track construction was difficult and expensive. But it was also a fact that America's growing industrial economy needed new ways of transportation to reach the settlements far to the west. Thousands of miles of the plains, deserts, and mountains of the western United States had to be crossed.

In 1863, two railroad companies, the Central Pacific and the Union Pacific, finally started to put down tracks. From California, the Central Pacific pushed east; from Nebraska, the Union Pacific worked its way west. Central Pacific employed some 7,000 Chinese immigrants, while the Union Pacific workers were mainly Irish. On May 10, 1869, the two lines met at Promontory, Utah. An 'iron road' now connected the two 'halves' of the nation.

This led to the settlement of large areas in the Midwest, the South and the West. New towns developed along the tracks, and many of these towns grew into wealthy cities. Millions of immigrants reached the new territories with the help of the railroad. One can say that most of the states joining the Union in the 19th century owed their growth to the railroads.

1 Comprehension

a) 1. Look at a map of the United States and name some of the places American settlers had to pass through on their way to the Pacific.
2. What do you understand by 'frontier spirit'? Do you think that this spirit influenced the American character?
3. 'Space' is sometimes called America's new frontier. Does this make sense?
4. What were the main reasons for the American movement westward?
5. What role did the railroad play in opening up the American West?
6. Use your own words to explain Thoreau's quotation at the beginning of the text.

b) The passage about America's 'manifest destiny' shows the point of view of the European settlers. Rewrite the first part of this passage (ll. 37–45) from a Native American point of view.

§7 2 New England

Rewrite the following sentences using participle constructions.

Example: 1. Six states in the northeastern corner of the United States form a region long known as New England.

1. Six states in the northeastern corner of the United States form a region that has long been known as New England.
2. The first Europeans who settled in the area were the Puritans.
3. The Puritans, who suffered religious persecution, came from England.
4. Much of the land which covers the area is not very good for farming.
5. Many of the farms which were built by the early settlers were left empty when their owners moved west.
6. New Englanders, who are often called Yankees, made the area an industrial region.
7. Many of the old towns which were rebuilt some time ago show what life was like in the past.

§7 3 Voices from the frontier

Life on the frontier was often very hard, but most frontierspeople were ready to suffer hardship in the wilderness. This is what some of them said. *Rewrite their statements in a more formal way using participle constructions.*

Example: "Before going west I had worked as a teacher in Boston."

Jim: "Before I went west I had worked as a teacher in Boston."
Josh: "I often work as a guide since I know the area from my time as a trapper."
Lee: "After I had crossed the Appalachians, I traveled some of the way by riverboat."
Meredith: "I like it out here because my sons can grow up with the country."
Gordon: "When I came here I had to fight off Indians who were trying to save their hunting grounds."
Daniel: "I didn't really feel free until I had crossed the Mississippi."
Orville: "I've tried to find gold ever since I came here but had no luck."
Zachary: "While I was hunting in the forests, I met many Indians who were friendly and helpful."

§7 4 Railroads

The world's first railroad began running in England in 1825. Not long after that, business people were building railroads in America. Yet at the beginning there were many problems.

a) *Connect meaningful pairs of sentences by using words like:* since, as, because, when, while.

Example: Since each railroad line had its own cars, the cars of one line couldn't be used on the tracks of the other.

Each railroad line had its own cars.	Railroad companies could build bigger trains.
Many lines only had a single track.	Engineers didn't manage to stop at the stations.
Few railroad lines ran more than fifty miles.	Passengers could hardly breathe.
Iron rails were used in the beginning.	There was a danger of accidents.
Steel rails lasted far longer.	The cars of one line couldn't be used on the tracks of the other.
Smoke from the locomotive got into the cars.	Rails had to be replaced every few years.
Brakes didn't work properly.	People couldn't get very far with one line.

b) *Now use 'with + participle' instead of a subordinate clause.*

Example: With each railroad line having its own cars, the cars of one line couldn't be used on the tracks of the other.

⟨5 Listening comprehension: With God on our side⟩

In this song, one of the most famous American songwriters of the sixties and seventies, Bob Dylan, deals with American political ideas about land and other people.

First listen to his song then read the questions. Listen to the recording again taking notes to help you with the answers.

1. What do you get to know about the singer in this song?
   a) Where does he come from?
   b) What does he tell you about his early education?
2. How does he describe the men who died in the Civil War?
3. What does he have to say about the Second World War and the Germans?
4. What has he been taught about the Russians?
5. According to the singer, what is the most terrible thing that might happen?
6. With whom does he compare the Americans?
   What does he mean by this comparison?

C Slavery

In 1619, the first Africans to be shipped from Africa to North America arrived in Virginia, twelve years after the first settlers had come. But it was another half century before slaves were brought in large numbers. By 1690 there were slaves in all the English colonies. When the revolutionary war (1775–1783) against England broke out, all 13 colonies permitted slavery by law.
The reason why slavery was introduced in the New World was simple. If a farmer brought free people with him to work his land, these workers would not stay with him when they could easily get land for themselves. In order to find a solution to this problem, Africans, who – unlike Europeans – were not protected by law, were made slaves.
After the American Revolution, it was mainly on the large plantations in the South that slaves were used. By 1830 cotton had become the nation's most important export. Cotton needed a lot of people to work in the fields, so the last thing the white plantation owners wanted to do was to abolish slavery. While 'King Cotton' ruled in the South, the North was developing its industries.

In his novel 'Roots', Alex Haley, an African-American author, describes the life of six generations of African-Americans. He starts with Kunta Kinte, the sixteen-year-old boy who had once lived in Africa and who was brought to the slave markets of the New World – and who told his children about his life in Africa. This information was passed from one generation to the next. At the end of the line there is Alex Haley's own father, a professor and a former student of Cornell, one of America's most respected universities … 'Roots' is one of the books to read if you want to know something about the first Africans arriving in America.
First read the text without using your dictionary. Then read it once again and look up the words you need to get the details.

… One cold afternoon Kunta was on his way across one of the fields to help another man repair a fence when what looked like salt began to fall from the sky. When he bent down to pick some of it up, it was cold to his touch – and even colder when he licked it off a finger with his tongue. He didn't know what to make of it when he heard the blacks nearby exclaiming, "Snow!" and guessed that was what they called it.

By the time he had reached the other side of the field, the 'snow' had stopped and even begun to melt away. Kunta nodded silently to his black partner, who was waiting by the broken fence. After a while they reached a place almost hidden by tall grass, and as the other man hacked some of it down with the long knife he carried, Kunta looked to the nearest wood. He knew that the 'oberseer' was keeping watch in another field that day. Kunta worked busily, to give the other man no suspicion of what was in his mind. But his breath came tensely as he stood looking down on the head of the man bent over his work. The knife had been left a few steps behind them where the cutting of the grass had stopped.

With a silent prayer to Allah, Kunta put his hands together, lifted them high, and brought them down across the back of the man's neck with all the violence of which his body was capable. The man broke down with a sound as if he had been hit by an ax. Taking up the long knife, Kunta suppressed the impulse to stab him, and went running toward the woods. He felt as if he were running in a dream, as if this weren't really happening at all.

Kunta was prepared to live in the woods as the animals did. He had learned many things about this strange land by now, together with what he already knew from Africa. He would capture rabbits and cook them over a fire that wouldn't smoke. By nightfall, Kunta knew that he had run a good distance. Only when it was completely dark did he allow himself to stop. As he lay there in the darkness, he listened carefully for the sound of dogs. But there was nothing but stillness all around him. Was it possible? Was he really going to make it this time?

Just then he felt a cold fluttering on his face. 'Snow' was falling again! Soon he was covered by whiteness as far as he could see. Silently it fell, deeper and deeper, until Kunta began to fear he was going to be buried in it; he was already freezing. He wondered what to do. Should he look for better cover? In the end he couldn't stop himself from jumping up.

He had run a good way when he stumbled and fell; when he looked back he saw with horror that his feet had left a trail in the snow so deep that a blind man could follow him. He knew that the morning was not far away. The only thing to do was to put more distance between himself and the men chasing him. He tried to increase his speed, but he had been running most of the night, and needed a rest. The sky was beginning to lighten in the east when he heard the distant baying of the dogs. He ran like a hunted leopard, but the barking grew louder and louder, and finally, when he looked back over his shoulder, he saw them coming nearer and nearer.

The men couldn't be far behind. Kunta kept on running, but soon he heard the men on horses crashing through the brush behind him. Then there was a shot, and another – and he felt a flashing pain in his leg. Let them kill me, thought Kunta; I will die as a man should. Then another shot hit the same leg, and it smashed him down like a giant fist. He saw the 'oberseer' and another white man coming up toward him and he was about to jump up and force them to shoot him again, but the wounds in his leg wouldn't let him rise.

The other man held a gun at Kunta's head as the 'oberseer' jerked off Kunta's clothing until he stood naked in the snow, the blood trickling down his leg turning the whiteness at his feet red. Then both men tied him facing a large tree, with his wrists bound on the other side.

The lash began cutting into the flesh across Kunta's shoulders, with the 'oberseer' grunting and Kunta shuddering under the force of each blow. After a while Kunta couldn't stop himself from screaming with the pain, but the beating went on and on until his body pressed against the tree. He couldn't be sure, but the next thing Kunta knew he had the feeling he was falling. Then he felt the coldness of the snow against him and everything went black …

1 Comprehension

a) 1. What is Alex Haley's novel about?
   2. Try to sum up the events described in the passage above in not more than five sentences.
   3. From whose point of view is the story told? Why is this important for creating excitement?
   4. 'Snow' plays a very important role in this passage. Try to describe its role in the different parts of the text.
   5. Compare this passage of 'Roots' with 'Jacob'. What is similar and what is different?

b) 1. The year is 1766 and you are working for a newspaper in a southern state. Write a short article for the local pages in which you inform your readers about the events described in the passage of Haley's novel.
   2. Then try to report the events from a different point of view. This time someone who is strongly against slavery and who happens to be at the plantation when Kunta tries to run away writes a letter to his or her friend describing what happened.

§8 2 Another way to say it

§9 a) *How does the author say these things in the text?*

- Kunta worked busily so that he didn't give the other man any … (l. 38)
- He wondered what he should do. (l. 54)
- The only thing which he could do was to put … (ll. 60/61)

b) *Rewrite the following sentences using infinitives instead of subordinate clauses.*

1. Most of the people who became slaves in America were Africans.
2. If you want to know about the life of the early slaves, Alexander Haley is the author you should read.
3. Another novel about slavery which one should read is Harriett Beecher Stowe's 'Uncle Tom's Cabin'.
4. Her novel was one of the most famous ones that influenced Northerners against slavery.
5. When Abraham Lincoln once met Ms. Beecher Stowe, he wondered what he should say to her.
6. He thought about what joke he could make, and finally said, "So this is the little woman who made this big war" in order to show her his respect.

§10 3 Alex Haley

Use the passive in the following sentences.

1. When he was a young boy, his parents told him a lot about family history.
2. Later his mother advised him to write it down as a novel.
3. Alex Haley asked her and a lot of other people to support his project and most of them were helpful.
4. A friend from Henning, Tennessee, taught him how to use material from libraries all over the world.
5. After several interviews, an editor from a famous magazine gave him the opportunity to publish his book.
6. Alex sent him the first draft of his novel.
7. This editor, Murray Fisher, offered Alex help with the production of the book.
8. He showed him, for example, how to develop a storyline.

D Abraham Lincoln and the American Civil War

"I'm naturally anti-slavery. If slavery is not wrong, nothing is wrong ..."
(Abraham Lincoln, 1864)

a) The Civil War began in 1861. People often think that the war was fought to abolish slavery. The slavery question, however, was not the only problem between the North and the South to cause the war. There was more to it: the North had developed into a rich industrial region, while the South had remained an agricultural area based on the slave system and 'King Cotton'.

As time passed, more and more of the new states in the West became members of the Union. Their political and economic views were very similar to those of the North. This, however, meant that the balance of power within the U.S. government could not be kept up. People in the southern states therefore felt that the government of the United States of America was no longer fairly representing the South and its style of life, which included slavery. For them, the only step to take was to leave the Union and to start a new one. Northern leaders realized that this meant there would be no national government anymore and the United States would collapse. For them nothing else remained to be done but to go to war.

One of the most famous figures of the Civil War was Abraham Lincoln. He had been elected as the United States' 16th President only three months before the states of the Deep South decided to leave the Union. Lincoln was the candidate of a new political group called the Republican Party, which had been created a few years earlier by people who were against slavery. He was mainly supported by the people of the North, not by those of the South – but still he was elected. This was the final reason for the South to break away from the United States.

Lincoln was popular not only because of his practical common sense but also because he seemed to be fair and honest. He was called 'Honest Abe', and he was thought of as a hero by later generations of Americans. The Civil War caused terrible destruction in the South. Cities and farms lay in ruins. And more Americans were killed in this war than in any other, before or since. Lincoln realized that he had "to bind up the nation's wounds", but he didn't live long enough to do so. On April 14, 1865, only five days after the Union won the war, he was killed by John Wilkes Booth, a man who supported the South.

b) During the war, the President did not have much time to sit in Washington writing long documents. Most of the time he traveled around the country and talked to his soldiers. On November 19, 1863, he arrived at Gettysburg in Pennsylvania, where a cruel battle had been fought a few months before. Lincoln dedicated part of the battlefield as a national war cemetery. There he gave one of the most famous speeches in American history, the Gettysburg Address:

Fourscore and seven years ago our fathers brought forth on this continent a new nation, conceived in liberty, and dedicated to the proposition that all men are created equal.

Now we are engaged in a great civil war, testing whether that nation, or any nation so conceived and so dedicated can long endure. We are met on a great battlefield of that war. We have come to dedicate a portion of that field as a final resting place for those who here gave their lives that that nation might live. It is altogether fitting and proper that we should do this.

But, in a larger sense, we cannot dedicate – we cannot consecrate – we cannot hallow – this ground. The brave men, living and dead, who struggled here, have consecrated it far above our poor power to add or detract. The world will little note nor long remember what we say here, but it can never forget what they did here. It is for us, the living, rather, to be dedicated here to the unfinished work which they who fought here have thus far so nobly advanced. It is rather for us to be here dedicated to the great task remaining before us – that from these honored dead we take increased devotion to that cause for which they gave the last full measure of devotion; that we here highly resolve that these dead shall not have died in vain; that this nation, under God, shall have a new birth of freedom; and that government of the people, by the people, for the people, shall not perish from the earth.

Look up the words you don't know in your dictionary and translate Lincoln's speech into German.

1 Understanding and discussing the speech

1. Where and for what reason did Abraham Lincoln make this speech?
2. a) What did Lincoln think the world would forget?
   b) What would the world remember?
3. a) Which word might be called the keyword of this address?
   b) Explain the different meanings the word has in this text.
   c) Why do you think Lincoln made this speech at Gettysburg?
4. Look at the famous words at the end: What is meant by "government of the people, by the people, for the people"?
5. A reporter of the British newspaper 'The Times' said of Lincoln's address: "Anything more dull and commonplace would not be easy to produce." The 'Chicago Tribune' told its readers: "The remarks of President Lincoln will live among the annals of man." a) Explain this difference of opinion.
   b) Who do you agree with?

§ 10 2 Further information

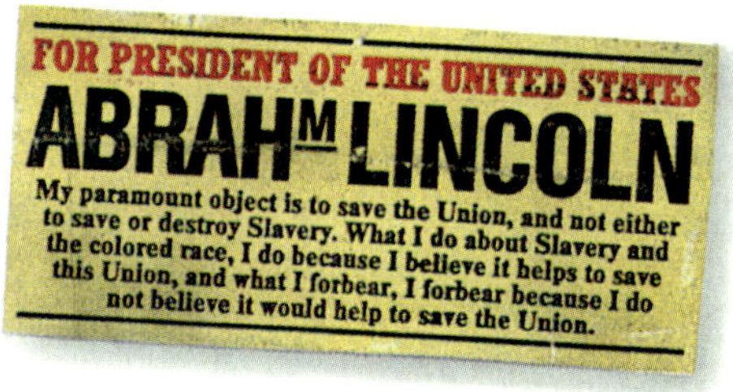

Use passive forms to complete these sentences.

1. Gettysburg … (to remember) for two things: the battle which … (to fight) there, and the speech which … (to give) by Abraham Lincoln.
2. At the time, Lincoln's speech … (to see) as a statement of what the North was fighting for.
3. By the time the South stopped fighting, almost a million soldiers … (to kill).
4. After Lincoln's death, plans … (to introduce) to bring the South back into the Union.
5. Slavery … (to abolish) officially through the 13th Amendment to the Constitution, but still, African-Americans … (not to accept) by many people as equal.
6. The time following the war … (to call) the time of 'Reconstruction'.

3 Reconstruction

Complete the sentences with grammatical and meaningful words.

In December 1865, Congress signed the 13th … to the U.S. Constitution, abolishing slavery. … slaves were now free; and the 14th Amendment … them citizens of the United States. But … were still second-class citizens. The separation … blacks and whites in public places … common. More than that, southern whites, … their civilization was lost and finding no … way to stop the course of …, turned to other means. Soon violence … more and more commonplace. Many whites … the former plantation owners and ex-Confederate … joined the Ku Klux Klan, a secret organization … just after the war. The Klan's … was to control elections and to … the Republican Party in the South. The … tried to keep African-American people out of … life. Teachers of African-American children … murdered, and sometimes African-Americans were killed … because they could read and write. … horse-riding Klansmen attacked and murdered … leaders and Republicans as well. … 1871, when a law was passed against the …, it had less influence. Still, … was a long way to go … the African-Americans were to have equal … .

UNIT 3

A A nation of immigrants

a) Ethnic roots

With the exception of the Native Americans, all Americans have ancestors who during the last 400 years immigrated into what today is the U.S.A. In colonial times, the number of people who came was quite small. In the 19th century, however, the number of people trying to find a new home in the U.S. increased. Most of them came from Europe, but at that time immigration from other continents had already begun. Today, more than 100 different ethnic or racial groups live in the U.S. There is hardly any group that cannot be found there.

The ethnic mix shows up in the population figures that are published by the U.S. Census Bureau every ten years. When the 1990 census was held, about 58 million of the 248 million Americans said they had at least one German ancestor. The next largest group are Americans whose forefathers came from England (about 41 million), closely followed by people with Irish ancestors (nearly 38 million). Another 24 million people reported African roots. About 14 million Americans have ancestors who came from Italy; there are also lots of people of Mexican (about 11.5 million), Scandinavian (about 10 million), French (about 10 million) and Polish (about 9 million) origin. Another one and a half million reported Chinese roots; about one million have Japanese ancestors and about 850,000 are of Cuban background.

b) The U.S. – a racial and ethnic mix

The ethnic mix has again been increasing during recent years. Between 1981 and 1990 alone more than nine million immigrants came to America, many of them illegally. Most of the new immigrants came from Mexico or from Asian countries, increasing the number of the minority groups already present in the U.S.A. Thus cities like Miami already have a Spanish-speaking majority. Hispanics, i.e. people who speak Spanish as their first language, are expected to become the largest group in the Los Angeles area by the year 2000. If these trends continue, whites who aren't of Hispanic origin – at the moment about 70 per cent of the total population – may become a minority by 2056.

The increased numbers of immigrants have deeply changed the face of America. They have changed its towns, its food, clothes and music, its entire way of life. There have long been Chinatowns in American cities, but now there are Little Havanas, Mexicos, Koreatowns and Little Saigons all over the country. For a Spanish-speaking person who wants to travel through the Southwest of the U.S.A. there is no need to know English. In Chicago's South Side, newspapers are offered in three languages: in Polish for the older generation, in English for the second generation of Polish Americans and in Spanish for its newer Mexican-American members. Schools have many immigrants, too. When Public School 217, a neighborhood elementary in Brooklyn, New York, informed the parents that a picture day would be held, the notice was translated into five languages; it should, however, have been translated into 26!

c) Dream and reality

The American Dream hasn't come true for all immigrants. Many had to discover that life in the U.S. can be difficult and that there is a lot of poverty in one of the richest countries of the world. If official figures can be trusted, about one in ten whites lives below the poverty line; for Hispanics the figure is about one in four and for African-Americans – though not counted as real immigrants – even one in three.
Naturally there are differences in incomes, too. While the average family income in 1990 was about $36,000 for whites, Hispanics only earned about $21,000 and African-Americans even less (about $20,000).
Unemployment figures are much lower for whites than for all other minorities living in the U.S.

1 Where they came from

1. When did large numbers of immigrants begin to arrive?
2. Where did most people come from in the 19th century?
3. What is the difference between immigration in the 19th century and present-day immigration?
4. Which are the largest groups of immigrants in the past and today?
5. What is typical of the U.S. population today?
6. What is the difference between an ethnic and a racial group?

2 A graph

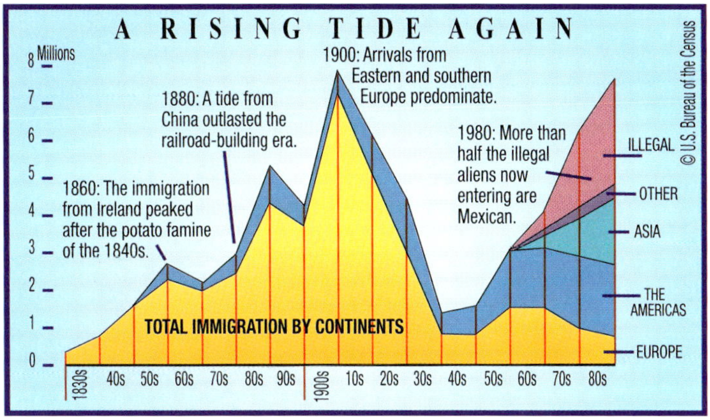

a) *Collect all the information from the graph about*
- the peak years of immigration,
- immigration from the different continents,
- changes in the origin of the immigrants,
- present-day immigration into the U.S.

b) *Rewrite 'Ethnic roots' (part a) and add the information given in the graph.*

3 Why they came

a) *Find out the reasons that made the following groups of people leave their home country.*
b) *Write a short report saying why people immigrated to the U.S.*

potato famines (1848–50)
political persecution after failed revolutions in Europe (1848)
slavery
poverty and unemployment as a result of the Industrial Revolution
the building of the railroads (1860–1880)
pogroms in Russia/Holocaust in Europe
the wars in Korea and Vietnam
change of government in Cuba
continuing discrimination against Puritans
revolution in Hungary

nearly 200,000 Chinese workers
more than 600,000 Cubans
about two million Irish
reasons for Jewish immigrants
one of the reasons for immigrants from England
new home for about 40,000 people
why many Africans were taken to America
made people leave their countries, too
led to a new immigration from Asian countries
millions of Europeans

4 Further discussion

1. Collect all the facts that have led to the growing changes in the American population. Are there any other facts not mentioned so far which may play a role, too?
2. An American magazine has talked about the 'browning of America'. Can you explain what is meant?
3. The U.S. has turned into a multicultural and multiracial society today. Can you think of the 'good' and the 'bad' sides of such a society? Think of at least three arguments for each side.
4. What do you think about immigration? Should people stay where they are or should they be allowed to move into the country of their choice? Give reasons.

OVER TO YOU

5. Do you like living in a multicultural society? Why?/Why not?
6. Organize a discussion in your class on the following question: Should Germany be allowed to follow the American example?
7. Are there any people you know who have immigrated into Germany? Why did they come?
8. Can you imagine leaving your country? Why?/Why not?

5 Promises and dreams

On their way to the New World many immigrants passed the Statue of Liberty. If they passed it near enough, they could read the following lines on the Statue:

Give me your tired, your poor,
Your huddled masses[1] yearning[2] to breathe free,
The wretched refuse[3] of your teeming[4] shore.
Send these, the homeless, tempest-tossed[5] to me.
I lift my lamp beside the golden door.

[1]['hʌdld 'mæsɪz] *zusammengekauerte Massen;* [2][jɜ:n] *sich sehnen;* [3]['retʃɪd 'refju:s] *armseliger Abschaum;* [4][ti:m] *wimmeln;* [5]['tempɪst 'tɒst] *vom Sturm herumgestoßen*

1. What do these lines say about the people who came to America? 2. How is America described in them? 3. What promise do these lines contain? What dreams of the immigrants can be seen in these lines?

6 The American Dream

You may have already heard of the American Dream – a dream shared by many immigrants.
a) *Write a short essay about the American Dream. Use words like 'moreover', 'furthermore', 'nevertheless', 'thus', etc. to connect your sentences.* b) *Try to find out why many immigrants believed in this dream and what was new about it.*

land of opportunity
a country where you can make it
place of new beginnings
lead a new life
easy to become rich
a chance for everyone
no social limits
it's up to you to make your dream come true
be yourself
no unfair traditions
land of milk and honey
make the most of your ability
a place where life is better

7 Dreams and reality

"Before we arrived, we believed that all the streets in America were paved with gold; when we arrived we saw that there were no streets at all and that we were expected to pave them."

This is an old immigrant joke that describes the experience of many immigrants. *Have a closer look at the quotation before answering questions 2 and 3.*

1. What was the immigrant experience like?
2. What did many immigrants often discover when they entered the U.S.?
3. What other problems did they often have?

B Prejudices

a) What do many white Americans think about the new immigration? If you ask people, this is what you are likely to hear:

They already get too much from the government. I hope they won't get my job, too.

If they keep on coming in such numbers, this won't be our country any more.

Well, look at our schools. I'm sure it won't help our kids if there is nobody who understands English any more.

Well, I can't find anything negative about immigration. I suppose they came for the same reasons that our grandparents came here. What would you do if you had no job, no money, no place to go to? I'm sure you would do the same.

I love going to other countries; but this is still America and not Cuba or Vietnam.

I happen to know some of them; they seem to take everything they can get and we have to pay for it.

I can understand why they come, but I'm afraid we can't take them all.

There are enough minorities here already. And what's the result of it all? A lot of problems, and taxes going up. If you ask me, I …

b) A recent opinion poll published in an American magazine seems to confirm these views.
This is what Americans think about immigration:

Opinion Poll

Was immigration a good thing or a bad thing for this country in the past?

59%	Good thing
31%	Bad thing

Is immigration a good thing or a bad thing for this country today?

29%	Good thing
60%	Bad thing

1 Comprehension

1. Sum up what many Americans think about immigration. What do they criticize, what do they fear?
2. As you see from the opinion poll, many Americans think that immigration in the past was something positive. Can you explain why?
3. What do you think made Americans change their minds?

2 Talking points

1. What is a prejudice? What is it based on? Try to give a definition.
2. Many views people have are based on or influenced by prejudices. Prejudices about foreign countries and foreigners are particularly common. Do you know any of these prejudices?
3. What opinions expressed in part a) seem to be based on prejudices?
4. What can be done about prejudices? Are there any solutions?
5. There are both negative and positive prejudices. Germans, for example, often think of themselves as very hard-working people. What dangers are there in such commonly held opinions?
6. Have you ever thought about the question of national identity? What makes a German a German or an American an American? Try to explain what you think is characteristic of the 'German identity'.

3 Stop immigration!

When at the beginning of this century the U.S. government began to limit immigration, the following cartoon appeared in the 'Washington Post':

1. What does this cartoon express? Compare its attitude towards immigration with the one expressed in the lines written on the Statue of Liberty.
2. Can you guess why many Americans wanted to limit immigration then?
3. What are the fears today? Are these fears justified, in your opinion?
4. Why are we not likely to see a black or Korean president in the near future?
5. Find out what you have to do to be able to immigrate to the U.S. today. Does the cartoon still characterize the present situation?

§11 4 An immigrant story

Chanrithy Ouk was born in 1971 in Battant, Cambodia's second-largest city. As his father had a good job, a good and peaceful future seemed to lie ahead of him. But in 1975 the Khmer Rouge won the war against the Cambodian government. As his father had worked for the government, Chanrithy was taken away from his parents and put in a child labor camp. Conditions were very hard there. He cried for days and days. In 1979, the camp was attacked by soldiers from Vietnam. As it was dark and there was much fighting, Chanrithy was able to run away. Somehow he managed to cross the border and found himself in a refugee camp in Thailand. He stayed there for three years, hoping to hear from his family again. He obviously wanted to return to his home. But things turned out differently. The Red Cross helped him find his father, who was living in New York. So Chanrithy was allowed to emigrate. When he got off the plane in New York, three men walked towards him. One of them was crying. Chanrithy knew that it was his father. In New York, Chanrithy went to school for the first time in his life. Though he had problems, he managed to adapt. Later he went to university, studying International Law.

a) *Read Chanrithy's story. Then express how certain the following ideas are by connecting them with these expressions:*

happen to	seem to/appear to	(be) likely to	(be) sure to/certain to

1. The Red Cross did not think they would be ... find Chanrithy's father, but incredibly they managed it.
2. It was very lucky that Chanrithy ... be at the border at exactly the right time, and was able to cross.
3. With his background, Chanrithy is ... to understand and help other immigrants with their problems.
4. After a very difficult life, Chanrithy ... be very happy these days.

b) *Translate each sentence into German. Remember to use German adverbs for the expressions above.*

§11 5 More verbal expressions for German adverbs

a) 'To be fond of' and 'to enjoy' are always used with a gerund; 'to like', 'to love', 'to hate' are used with the gerund if they express a habit or something general. *Work with a partner and agree on seven activities you like or dislike.*

Example: 1. We both enjoy walking in the snow.  2. We hate ... 

b) The gerund is also used with 'to go on', 'to keep on', 'to continue'. *Replace the words in the first box with 'it snows', 'I'm tired', 'I'm not hungry', etc. and think of suitable words for the second box.*

Example: When [my alarm clock rings] it's difficult to go on/keep on/continue [sleeping].

c) 'I hope', 'I'm afraid', 'I suppose' (+ 'that'-clauses) are also translated into German using adverbs. *Translate these sentences:*

1. I hope Chanrithy can help a lot of other immigrants.
2. I'm afraid that many children didn't find their parents after the war.
3. I suppose Chanrithy's father is very proud of him.

C School systems

The American school system

88% of all American children go to public schools. These schools are free and open to all students. So nearly all children from one neighborhood go to the same school. Though there are different kinds of schools for different age levels, students are not divided up into different types of schools as they are in many parts of Germany.

As all kinds of students go to American high schools, they offer many different courses including health education and keyboarding. Students are, however, not entirely free in their choice. They have to take certain courses that are compulsory for all students. These courses are usually English, math, natural sciences, social studies (history, geography and civics) and physical education.

What a student takes largely depends on what he or she wants to do after high school. Students wishing to go on to college or to university need to choose subjects like foreign languages, higher level math and science courses.

For each course students choose, they get credits. If they want to graduate, i.e. to finish high school successfully, they need a certain number of credits. Much emphasis is put on extracurricular activities, particularly on sports. Playing on the school's team or being elected team captain is very important to many young Americans. Matches between schools are big events in the life of a school; they are attended by teachers, students and parents, and they are reported on in the local media.

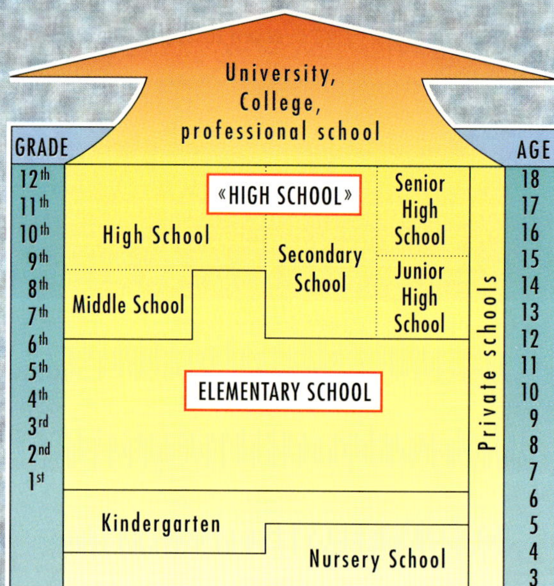

PERIOD	MO.	TUE.	WED.	THUR.	FRI.
1	English				
2	Geometry				
3	Spanish I				
4	Health Education				
	Lunch break				
5	Science				
6	Drama				
Extra-curricular	cheer-leader practice	School Magazine editors' meeting	/	church volunteers (hospital visits)	/

The British school system

After primary school most British schoolchildren go to comprehensive schools. During the first year, classes are of mixed ability, but from the second year on, they are usually divided into three different ability groups for academic subjects. The fourth and fifth years prepare pupils for the GCSE (General Certificate of Secondary Education) exam, which most of them take at the age of 16.
After this, pupils in ability groups I and II usually leave school and look for work, those in ability group III stay at school for two more years to take A-level (Advanced level) exams in two or three subjects of their choice. Young people who want to go to university need good A-levels in three subjects.
About 6% of British schoolchildren live in areas where there are no comprehensive schools. In these areas, about one in five pupils go to grammar schools (a type of school similar to the German *Gymnasium*), and the rest go to secondary schools where courses are similar to those for ability groups I and II at the comprehensives.
There are quite a large number of independent schools in Britain. Many of them are boarding schools. They include the famous public schools, some of which were founded several hundred years ago. Eton, Winchester and Harrow are probably the best-known fee-paying public schools.

1. BRITISH SCHOOLS

Type of school	Attended by
State comprehensive schools	approx. 87%
State grammar schools and secondary modern schools	approx. 6%
Independent schools (fee-paying), including public schools	approx. 7%

2. THE EXAMINATION SYSTEM

Age	Form	Exams
18		
17	Upper 6th	A-level exams
16	Lower 6th	
15	5th	GCSE exams
14	4th	school exams, usually twice a year
13	3rd	
12	2nd	
11	1st	

1 Talking points

1. What do you think is typical of the American school system? And what of the British?
2. What is good about them? Where might there be problems? Give examples from the texts.
3. Compare the American school system to the British and German system. What is similar, what is different? Use expressions like 'on the one hand', 'on the other hand', 'moreover', 'furthermore', 'in comparison with', 'in contrast to', etc.
4. Find out from the texts what is similar to the German *Gesamtschule, Gymnasium, Realschule, Realschulabschluß, Abitur* in the American and in the British school system.
5. Lots of German pupils would like to go or actually go to an American high school. Can you imagine why they want to go there?
6. Would you like to go there? Why?/Why not?

§ 12 2 Six months in the U.S.A. *Put in the correct forms of 'need/needn't'.*

Naturally I was quite nervous before leaving. There were still lots of things that ... to be done. You know, when leaving for a six-month stay, you ... a lot of things. You can't simply phone your Mom and tell her to send you what you ... have. So it's better to take everything you ... along with you. But as always happens when I go somewhere, I packed too many things this time, too. For example, I ... taken my school books with me; I ... them over there, because I had to buy new ones. I ... all of my warm clothes either. And I ... have worried so much before leaving. Most people understood my English and it was only during the first weeks I ... some help at school.

A critical view

During recent years, American high schools have been criticized. The following speech was given by Elizabeth Dole, a government official, to teachers and principals. *Use your dictionary to find out the meaning of the words you don't know.*

I know that you are familiar with the statistics. But let me briefly share some with you, as they define the size and scope of our problem.

- 25 percent of our young people – perhaps as many as one million students a year – drop out of high school. And of those who do graduate, a very disturbing number can't read their diplomas.
- 70 percent of all high school seniors can't write a basic letter seeking employment.
- 60 percent can't correctly add up their own lunch bills.
- Additionally, at least 20 million and possibly as many as 40 million adults experience substantial literacy problems.

Ladies and gentlemen, there is no doubt that this state is a challenge to the very foundation on which America is based. A dream has pervaded this country for over two hundred years. A dream that is etched in our culture and in our national conscience. A dream that any American could, through hard work and dedication, rise to the top and succeed in building a better life for himself and his children. And for millions of Americans this dream has come true. But now we are in danger of losing sight of this dream. For if you do not possess the basic skills required to survive in today's world, then you cannot get into the system, you cannot get a job, you cannot succeed, and you will spend a lifetime on the outside looking in.

3 Literacy problems

1. What problems are mentioned in Elizabeth Dole's speech and where do they occur?
2. Why does she consider these problems as a challenge to life in the U.S.A. and particularly to the American Dream?
3. Where do problems occur for an individual who doesn't have the basic skills?
4. What problems may there be for the economic situation of a country if school education falls below a certain level?
5. Why are basic skills like reading and writing so important in an industrialized country? Were they less important in the past? Why?/Why not?
6. You meet a middle-aged person who cannot read or write. This person, for reasons of time, money or embarrassment, does not want to go back to school. Give at least three arguments for the importance of doing this, and for each argument think of a counter-argument. Try to convince the person.

4 Talking about school

Read the texts on the school systems again and give definitions of the following words and phrases:

college   high school   to graduate   an academic subject   a graduate
public school   social studies   extracurricular activities   a grade
interschool games   credits   university   an elective   comprehensive school

Example: A college is an institution where students can go after high school. It offers programmes which usually take four years and which lead to a bachelor's degree in the arts or sciences.

High school kids at work

At least three-quarters of high school kids work part-time during the school year. They work in shops, restaurants and fast food places and of course, they babysit. The almost non-stop opening hours in the U.S. mean that there is always demand for part-time workers. Many teenagers work as many as 25-30 hours a week and earn more than $250 a month. They spend their money on luxuries that now seem to be things teenagers need like cars, stereo and video equipment, clothes and their social life. Few give anything to their family's budget. Working so many hours doesn't leave much time for hobbies and sports.

And what about school work? "I don't have to do any homework to get good grades," says Greg, who works in a local supermarket and has three cars and a girlfriend to spend his money on. However, his friend Todd admits that working from 7.00 p.m. to midnight is hard when you have a test the next day.

The school day ends earlier here than in Britain. This allows American teenagers to spend a large amount of time on doing pretty mindless work in order to have the money to buy things they want. It also brings them some economic independence from their parents and a taste of the working world.

(From *Early Times*, a British newspaper for teenagers)

5 Looking at the text

1. What does the text tell you about the 'free time activities' of many American teenagers, the jobs they do, the time and hours they work, the money they earn, the way they spend it, the problems at school, the advantages of these activities?
2. Can you connect this text with what you've heard about the performance of many American students?
3. What does this article tell you about many American schools?
4. Would it be possible for you to work 25 to 30 hours in your free time?
5. Do you think it's good to have a "taste of the working world" in this way? Give reasons.
6. Find out how many pupils in your class work after school. Use the questions in 1. and write an article for your school magazine.

〈6 Listening comprehension: The rabbits that caused all the trouble〉

Listen to the fable by James Thurber. Then answer the questions.

1. Why didn't the wolves like the rabbits?
2. What three disasters did the wolves blame on the rabbits?
3. The explanations for these disasters always start with "It is well-known …". Why is the passive used and what's wrong with the reasoning?
4. Why did the rabbits decide not to run away to a desert island?
5. What made it easy for the other animals to give the rabbits advice?
6. A fable helps us to think critically about a truth, or a cliché. Summarize the lesson of this fable by adding a 'because'-clause after the moral.

7 The mongoose[1] and the cobras[2]

These pictures give you the plot of another Thurber fable. *Translate them into writing. Find a good headline, the right register and a good moral.*

[1]['mɒŋgu:s] *Mungo;* [2]['kəʊbrə] *Kobra*

8 On an uninhabited island

There was a long silence after Jack stopped speaking, and I could see that each of us was thinking about our situation. For my part, I cannot say I was very pleased with my thoughts. I knew that we were on an island, because Jack had said so, but whether it was inhabited or not I did not know.
"Do you know what I think?" said Peterkin. "This is the best thing that ever happened to us. We've got an island all to ourselves. You shall be King, Jack! Ralph Prime Minister, and I shall be ..."
"... the fool," interrupted Jack.
"No," said Peterkin, "I have no title at all. I shall just accept an important job in the government. You see, I'm fond of earning a lot of money and having nothing to do."
"But to be serious," said Jack, "we are really in an uncomfortable position. If this is an uninhabited island, we shall have to live very much like wild beasts."

(From *The Coral Island* by R. M. Ballantyne)

a) *Answer the questions*

1. What situation do the boys find themselves in?
2. What do they have to decide?
3. What 'jobs' do they choose for themselves?
4. What reasons do they give for their choice?
5. What idea of democracy do the boys have in this extract from Ballantyne's 'The Coral Island'?
6. Can you see any symbolic meaning in the last sentence in connection with this?

b) *Democratic discussion*

The boys in the above text are talking about how to organize themselves on the island.
Write and act short dialogues in which two or three people are arguing about how to organize a holiday trip/a class party/a sports day, etc. Make conflicting suggestions and find a democratic compromise.

D In a ghetto school

The following text is an excerpt from Tom Wolfe's 'The Bonfire of the Vanities' (1987). Peter Fallow, an Englishman, is writing for a New York newspaper. Asked to write a story about a hit-and-run accident in which a black boy is badly injured, he tries to collect additional information by calling the boy's teacher. You will understand the main ideas of the text without using a dictionary.

On Peter Fallow's desk was a telephone directory for Nassau County, Long Island. He had never heard of Nassau County nor of Hewlett, which was in Nassau county, too, but somewhere in the town of Hewlett a telephone was ringing, and he desperately wanted it to be answered. Finally, after seven rings, it was.

"Hello?" Out of breath.

"Mr. Rifkind?"

"Yes ..." Out of breath and wary.

"This is Peter Fallow of the New York 'City Light'."

"Don't want any."

"Excuse me? I do hope you'll forgive me for ringing you up on a Saturday afternoon."

"You hope wrong. I subscribed to the 'Times' once. Actually I got it about once a week. Either somebody always took it from the front door before I left the house or it was soaking wet or it was never delivered."

"No, I'm a journalist, Mr. Rifkind. I write for 'The City Light'."

"Well, okay," said Mr. Rifkind, "go ahead."

"Actually, I'm calling to inquire about one of your students, a young Mr. Henry Lamb."

"Henry Lamb. Doesn't ring a bell. What's he done?"

"Oh, he hasn't done anything. He's been seriously injured. I was told he was a student in your English class."

"Who told you that?"

"His mother. I had quite a long talk with her. She's a very nice woman and very upset."

"Henry Lamb ... Oh, yes, I know who you mean. Well, that's too bad."

"What I would like to find out, Mr. Rifkind, is what kind of student Henry Lamb is."

"What kind?"

"Well, would you say he was an outstanding student?"

"Where are you from, Mr. – I'm sorry, can you tell me your name again?"

"Fallow."

"Mr. Fallow. I gather you're not from New York."

"That's true."

"Then there's no reason why you should know anything about Colonel Jacob Ruppert High School in the Bronx. At Ruppert we have comparative terms, but outstanding isn't one of them. The range runs more from cooperative to life-threatening." Mr. Rifkind began to chuckle. "Don't say I said that."

"Well, how would you describe Henry Lamb?"

"Cooperative. He's a nice fellow. Never gives me any trouble."

"Would you describe him as a good student?"

"Good doesn't work too well at Ruppert, either. It's more, does he attend class or doesn't he?"

"Did Henry Lamb attend class?"

"As I recall, yes. He's usually here. He's very dependable. He's a nice kid, as nice as they come."

"Was there any part of the curriculum he was particularly good – or, let me say, adept at, anything he did better than anything else?"

"Not particularly."

"No?"

"It's difficult to explain, Mr. Fallow. As the saying goes, Ex nihilo nihil fit. There's not a great range of activities in these classes, and so it's hard to compare performances. These boys and girls – sometimes their minds are in the classroom, and sometimes they are not."

"What about Henry Lamb?"

"He's a nice fellow. He's polite, he pays attention, he doesn't give me any trouble. He tries to learn."

"Well, he must have some abilities. His mother told me he was considering going to college."

"That may well be. She's probably talking about C.C.N.Y. That's the City College of New York."

"I believe Mrs. Lamb did mention that."

"City College has an open admissions policy. If you live in New York City and you're a high-school graduate and you want to go to City College, you can go."

"Will Henry Lamb graduate, or would he have?"

"As far as I know. As I say, he has a very good attendance record."

"Well, Mr. Rifkind, can you tell me anything at all about Henry Lamb's performance or aptitude, anything at all?"
"You have to understand that they give me about sixty-five students in each class when the year starts, because they know it'll be down to forty by mid-year and thirty by the end of the year. It's not exactly what you'd call a tutorial system. Henry Lamb's a nice young man who applies himself and wants an education. What more can I tell you?"
"How does he do on his written work?"
Mr. Rifkind let out a whoop. "Written work? There hasn't been any written work at Ruppert High for fifteen years! Maybe twenty! They take multiple-choice tests, reading comprehension. That's all the Board of Education cares about."
"How was Henry Lamb's comprehension?"
"I'd have to look it up. Not bad, if I had to guess."
"Better than most? Or about average? Or what would you say?"
"Well … I know it must be difficult for you to understand, Mr. Fallow, being from England. Am I right? You're British?"
"Yes, I am."
"Naturally – or I guess it's natural – you're used to levels of excellence and so on. But these kids haven't reached the level where it's worth emphasizing the kind of comparisons you're talking about. We're just trying to get them up to a certain level and then keep them from falling back. You are thinking about 'honor students' and 'higher achievers' and all that. But at Colonel Jacob Ruppert High School, an honor student is somebody who attends class, isn't disruptive, tries to learn, and does all right at reading and arithmetic."
"Well, let's use that standard. By that standard, is Henry Lamb an honor student?"
"By that standard, yes."
"Thank you very much, Mr. Rifkind."
"That's okay. I'm sorry to hear about all this. Seems like a nice boy. We're not supposed to call them boys, but that's what they are, poor sad confused boys with a whole lotta problems. Don't quote me, or I'll have a whole lotta problems."

(Adapted from *The Bonfire of the Vanities*)

1 Comprehension

1. What kind of communication problem do the two men have? What does it tell us about Mr. Rifkin?
2. What does Mr. Rifkin tell Peter Fallow about Henry Lamb? Make a list.
3. "Henry Lamb. Doesn't ring a bell. What's he done?" What do these sentences tell you about Mr. Rifkin's attitude towards his students?
4. What makes Henry Lamb an 'honor student' according to standards at Ruppert High?
5. Where's the difference between a ghetto school like Ruppert High and other high schools?
6. At the end Mr. Rifkin calls the students at Ruppert High "poor sad confused boys with a whole lotta problems". What problems may they have? Think of the families they come from and what you've heard about conditions in the ghettos.

§ 12 2 Out of the ghetto

§ 13 The lucky few who make it out of the ghetto often manage to do it through sport. In an interview, Travis Washington, a successful boxer, talks about his youth in the ghetto.
Put in the correct forms of 'dare' and 'need'.

Yeah, I'm one of the lucky ones, I suppose. I remember when I was a kid we all knew deep down that you … a diploma for a good job, … to read and write well just to get along in the world. But with the gang I grew up with, sometimes we were afraid. We felt we didn't … show we were interested. All you … was a gun, a knife, the right gang and once you were with one gang, you didn't … leave or show interest in school stuff. So I got good at the only thing I … to get good at: fighting, using my fists. I was quick and desperate, you … that to be a good fighter. These days I wish I had … to try at school, too. But I guess I didn't have the nerve back then. You might say you … worry, you've got enough money to do whatever you want. But somehow I just wish I were better at school stuff.

A Montgomery, Alabama – then and now

a) Though Montgomery is the capital of the State of Alabama, like many other U.S. state capitals, it is not its largest city. In fact, for most of its history Montgomery has been a quiet place. Only twice can something important be said to have happened here. The first was in 1861, when the leaders of the Southern States met here and decided to break away from the Union. For this reason, Montgomery was said to be the 'Cradle of the Confederacy'. It was also supposed to be its capital, though this was changed a few months later.
The second was on December 1, 1955, when a lady named Rosa Parks sat near the front of a city bus – where she wasn't supposed to sit. When she refused to give up her seat to a man, the bus driver called the police – and she was arrested.
Ms. Parks was black, the man was white, and at that time in many Southern cities, notices on the city buses clearly said that blacks were to sit at the back of the bus. But Rosa wasn't alone in thinking it was time to have the law changed. And in the end, they did get it changed. A preacher at a local Baptist church called for a boycott of the city buses. His name was Martin Luther King, and he was to become famous as the leader of the Civil Rights movement.

b)

Montgomery 40 years later

Checking in at the Montgomery Holiday Inn, I'm weary from a late-night flight. But the black and white women clerks working side by side at the desk are smiling and friendly. Next day at the local Wal-Mart, I'm standing in line behind a rather large black man as he jokes with the thin blonde cashier before carrying his gallon of Diet Coke and bags of low-fat potato chips out to his rusty old Chevrolet.
Later on, I share a bright orange city bus with workers heading out to their homes in the suburbs. Some may be tired and in a bad mood after a hard day at the office. But nobody cares whether the people pushing against them on the not too comfortable seats are black or white! It's clear that Montgomery, Alabama, has changed a lot since 1955, when it took a 381-day bus boycott to integrate the city buses – and change American society forever. Now black men and women are succeeding in business and politics. About half of all government officials in Montgomery are black.
I was too young to have played any part in the movement that changed things so much.
But in December 1995, I was one of many who joined the survivors of the bus boycott in making a symbolic journey back to the city where it all began. The week of celebrations ended with a big meeting in the now famous Baptist Church. Many of the speakers warned that a lot of work remained to be done.
City Councilman Joe L. Reed, for example, tried to put present problems in a historical perspective. He had worked with Martin Luther King during the bus boycott, and became the first black to be elected to Montgomery City Council in 1975.
Now, he said, the segregation they had fought against was dead. "But Mr. Segregation had a son, and his name was Mr. Discrimination. And he doesn't dress like his daddy did, with a sheet over his overalls. Mr. Discrimination wears a suit over his sheet!"
Many people in Montgomery fear that 'Mr. Discrimination' may be even harder to defeat than his daddy was.

(Article by *Mary Riordan*)

1 Segregation

a) *Comprehension*

1. What are you told about the situation for blacks before 1955?
2. There is a clue in part a) about the history that created the problem. What is it? Say what you have already learned about it.
3. In the article (part b), look again at what Councilman Joe L. Reed says about 'Mr. Segregation' and 'Mr. Discrimination'. Why is he talking about people dressing in sheets? (The historical picture on the right will help you to understand what he means.)

Members of the Ku Klux Klan marching in Houston, Texas. Formed after slavery was abolished, its aim was to frighten blacks and keep them 'in their place'.

b) *Complete the word pairs below. Then make sentences with each of these words to make sure you know the differences in meaning.*

…	segregation
to integrate	…
…	discrimination

2 Changes

1. What was Rosa Parks arrested for back in 1955?
2. Could it happen today? How do you know?
3. How did people get the law changed?
4. Have all of the city's race problems been solved?
5. What facts given in the article show that Montgomery is a very different place today?
6. Look at all the details given in the first paragraph of the article. What is their function?

§ 15 3 The Civil Rights movement

to be to   to be said to   to be supposed to

Find out how the above phrases are used in part a). Then decide which of them are needed to complete the following information on the Civil Rights movement. Put in the correct verb form.

Up to the 1950s, segregation was accepted as normal in most parts of the U.S.A., and especially in the Southern states. Blacks and whites … go to separate schools, eat at different rooms in restaurants, etc. Such segregation … be worst in the states of Alabama, Georgia and Arkansas. Although the Supreme Court had ruled in 1954 that all public schools … be open to blacks and whites equally, many districts in these states still refused to integrate their schools.
Up to 1955, any improvements had been won by a small number of people working through the courts. But all this … change with the Montgomery bus boycott. The plan was that no city buses … be used by blacks (and they made up 75% of the passengers) until the city agreed to end segregation. They walked, they shared cars – and in the end they succeeded. Because of what followed, Montgomery … be the 'Cradle of the Civil Rights movement'. The successful bus boycott … be followed by many others all over the South. They also held sit-ins at segregated restaurants and lunch-counters, campaigns to register black voters, etc. Sometimes they have broken the law as part of their campaigns. In 1968, King … make a speech at a poor people's march; but just as he got up to speak, he was shot by a white man.

4 I have a dream

In August 1963, more than 200,000 people, black and white, demonstrated in Washington, D.C.

a) *Look at the picture, and especially at the posters many of the people are carrying. What did these people want?*

b) You can hear part of the famous speech made by Dr. Martin Luther King on that day on the cassette. *Listen to it. Don't try to understand too much at first – just get the atmosphere.*

c) *Now try to describe the atmosphere. And can you remember two or three key words that King repeated over and over again? Write them down.*

d) *The next time you listen, have a pencil ready, and the piece of paper with your key words written on it. Listen for sentences and phrases with these key words in them and write them down.*

§ 16
5 Voices

a) *Read what these people have to say, and take note of all the changes they mention. Then discuss how much of Martin Luther King's 'dream' has come true – and what problems still remain.*

JACK: All the jobs that were closed to us when I was a boy are now open.

CAROL: Montgomery is still the most racist city in America.

KIM: It's an integrated America only when we have to come into contact with each other at work. After five o'clock in the evening, whites and blacks go back to their own separate worlds.

LEROY: Unemployment is still far higher for African-Americans than for whites. That's not equality!

MARLENE: Middle-class blacks just don't care about the brothers and sisters who are still stuck in the slums.

HOWARD: Sure, there are plenty of African-Americans in government now. And many cities have black mayors. But nobody can yet imagine a black President.

JULIA: Affirmative action has helped us a lot. I would never have got my present job without it. Sure, I had a better college degree than any of the other applicants, but without the new rules I know the job would have gone to a white person.

PETE: I think we're beginning to expect too much from the government. I succeeded in business by my own efforts! Hand-outs and special treatment only make people lazy.

b) The same people whose opinions you have just heard also have ideas about what should be done to further improve the situation of African-Americans.
Use these phrases to complete their suggestions:

to have s.th. done – to have s.o. do s.th.

"We've got to ..."
"African-Americans must ..."
"Black people should ..."
"We ought to ..."

affirmative action – stop

affirmative action – introduce in all businesses

all rich blacks – take an interest in social problems

black businesses – create more jobs

one of our best politicians – run for President

racism – make a thing of the past

more white people – visit us in our homes

c) *Now try to guess who said what – and why you think it was that person.*

Example: I think Leroy said ... because he seems to be worried about ...

d) *Have you any suggestions to make? Maybe you know the name of a black person who could run for President, or have an idea how to fight racism ... Make your suggestions using the same phrases or their synonyms:*

to have s.th. done / to get s.th. done – to have s.o. do s.th. / to get s.o. to do s.th.

6 A poem: Harlem

What happens to a dream
deferred[1]?

Does it dry up
Like a raisin[2] in the sun?
Or fester[3] like a sore –
And then run[4]?
Does it stink like rotten[5] meat?
Or crust[6] and sugar over –
Like a syrupy[7] sweet?

Maybe it just sags[8]
Like a heavy load.

Or does it explode?

(By *Langston Hughes,* 1951)

a) *Understanding the poem*

1. What does it mean, to 'defer a dream'?
2. The poet mentions some things that *might* happen. Make sure you understand all the words.
   (You may have to guess some from the context or from the sound, or from words you already know. What about *to dry, a sore, to stink, to sugar, a sweet, to explode*?)
3. Talk about what these 'pictures' really stand for. What might happen to someone whose dream never comes true? What point is the poet making?
4. Harlem is the black 'ghetto' of New York City. Why do you think the poet gave his poem this title?

b) *The poet and his time*

1. Think about what it was like for blacks in America in 1951. Does this make the message of the poem easier to understand?
2. If Hughes were still alive, could he write a poem like this today?

You can read a story by Langston Hughes on pages 51/52.

[1] [dɪ'fɜː] *verschieben;* [2] *Rosine;* [3] *eitern;* [4] *wegfließen;* [5] *schlecht, verfault;* [6] *verkrustet;* [7] ['sɪrəpɪ] *sirupartig, süßlich;* [8] *absacken, durchhängen*

Langston Hughes (1902–1967)

B Thank you, Ma'am

Before you read this story, try to think of all the possible ways of influencing or changing a person's behavior. How can you make someone who is behaving badly do what you think is right? You can't always force them to do as you wish – or can you? Should you even try?

She was a large woman with a large purse that had everything in it but a hammer and nails. It had a long strap[1], and she carried it slung[2] across her shoulder. It was about eleven o'clock at night, and she was walking alone, when a boy ran up behind her and tried to snatch[3] her purse. The strap broke with the tug[4] the boy gave it from behind. The boy fell on his back on the sidewalk, and his legs flew up. The large woman simply turned around and kicked him right square[5] in his blue-jeaned sitter[6]. Then she reached down and picked the boy up by his shirt. She shook him until his teeth rattled.

After that the woman said, "Pick up my pocketbook[7], boy, and give it here."

She still held him tightly. But she bent down enough to let him pick up her purse. Then she said, "Now ain't[8] you ashamed[9] of yourself?"

Firmly[10] gripped by his shirt front, the boy said, "Yes'm."

The woman said, "What did you want to do it for?"

The boy said, "I didn't aim to."

She said, "You lie!"

By that time two or three people passed, turned to look, and some stood watching.

"If I turn you loose, will you run?" asked the woman.

"Yes'm," said the boy.

"Then I won't turn you loose," said the woman. She did not release[11] him.

"Lady, I'm sorry," whispered the boy.

"Um-hum! Your face is dirty. I got a great mind[12] to wash your face for you. Ain't you got nobody home to tell you to wash your face?"

"No'm," said the boy.

"Then it will get washed this evening," said the large woman, starting up the street, dragging the frightened boy behind her. He looked as if he were fourteen or fifteen, thin and wild, in tennis shoes and blue jeans.

The woman said, "You ought to be my son. I would teach you right from wrong. Least[13] I can do right now is to wash your face. Are you hungry?"

"No'm," said the boy. "I just want you to turn me loose."

"Was I bothering[14] you when I turned that corner?" asked the woman.

"No'm."

"But you put yourself in contact with me," said the woman. "If you think that contact is not going to last a while, you got another thought coming. When I get through with you, sir, you are going to remember Mrs. Luella Bates[15] Washington Jones."

Sweat[16] popped out[17] on the boy's face, and he began to struggle. Mrs. Jones continued to drag him up the street. When she got to her door, she dragged the boy inside, down a hall, and into a large room at the rear of the house. She switched on the light and left the door open. The boy could hear other roomers laughing and talking. Some of their doors were open, too; so he knew he and the woman were not alone. The woman still had him by the neck in the middle of her room.

She said, "What is your name?"

"Roger," answered the boy.

"Then, Roger, you go to that sink[18] and wash your face," said the woman. She turned him loose – at last. Roger looked at the door – and went to the sink.

"Let the water run until it gets warm," she said. "Here's a clean towel[19]."

"You gonna take me to jail?" asked the boy, bending over the sink.

"Not with that face. I would not take you nowhere," said the woman. "Here I am trying to get home to cook me a bite to eat, and you snatch my pocketbook! Maybe you ain't been to your supper, either, late as it be. Have you?"

"There's nobody home at my house," said the boy.

"Then we'll eat," said the woman. "I believe you're hungry – or been hungry – to try to snatch my pocketbook!"

---

[1][stræp] *Riemen;* [2][slʌŋ] *überhängen;* [3][snætʃ] *wegreißen;* [4][tʌg] *Zug;* [5]['skweə] *geradewegs;* [6]*Hintern;* [7]*Handtasche (AE);* [8](sl/dialect) aren't; [9][ə'ʃeɪmd] *sich schämen;* [10]*fest;* [11][rɪ'li:s] *loslassen;* [12]*große Lust haben;* [13]*das Wenigste;* [14]['bɒðə] *belästigen;* [15][lu:'elə 'beɪts]; [16][swet] *Schweiß;* [17]*hervorquellen;* [18]*Waschbecken;* [19]['taʊəl] *Handtuch*

"I wanted a pair of suede[20] shoes," said the boy.

"Well, you didn't have to snatch *my* pocketbook to get some suede shoes," said Mrs. Luella Bates Washington Jones. "You could've asked me."

"Ma'am?" The water dripping[21] from his face, the boy looked at her. There was a long pause. A very long pause. After drying his face and not knowing what else to do, the boy dried it again. Then he turned around. The door was open. He could run, run, run, *run*!

The woman was sitting on the day-bed. "I were young once and I wanted things I could not get."

There was another long pause. The boy's mouth opened. Then he frowned[22].

The woman said, "Um-hum! You thought I was going to say, *but I didn't snatch people's pocketbooks.* Well, I wasn't going to say that."

Pause. Silence. "I have done things, too, which I would not tell you, son – neither tell God, if He didn't already know. So you sit down while I fix us something to eat. You might run that comb through your hair so you will look presentable[23]." In another corner of the room behind a screen[24] was a gas plate and an icebox. Mrs. Jones got up and went behind the screen. The woman did not watch the boy to see if he was going to run now. She didn't watch her purse, which she left behind her on the day-bed. But the boy took care to sit on the far side of the room, away from the purse. He did not trust the woman *not* to trust him. And he did not want to be mistrusted now.

"Do you need somebody to go to the store," asked the boy, "to get some milk or something?"

"Don't believe I do," said the woman, "unless you want sweet milk yourself. I was going to make cocoa[25] out of this canned milk I got here."

"That will be fine," said the boy.

She heated some lima beans[26] and ham[27], made the cocoa, and set the table. The woman did not ask the boy anything about where he lived, or his folks, or anything else that would embarrass him. Instead, as they ate, she told him about her job in a hotel beauty shop, what the work was like, and how all kinds of women came in and out. Then she cut him half of her ten-cent cake.

"Eat some more, son," she said.

When they finished eating, she got up and said, "Now here, take this ten dollars and buy yourself some blue suede shoes. And, next time, do not make the mistake of latching[28] onto my pocketbook nor nobody else's – because shoes got by devilish ways will burn your feet. I got to get my rest[29] now. But from here on in, son, I wish you would behave yourself."

She led him down the hall to the front door and opened it. "Good night! Behave yourself, boy!" she said as he went down the steps. The boy wanted to say something more than "Thank you, ma'am," to Mrs. Luella Bates Washington Jones but he couldn't do so as he turned at the foot of the stairs and looked back at the large woman in the door. He barely managed to say "Thank you," before she shut the door.

By *Langston Hughes,* 1958 (slightly abridged)

1 Understanding and discussing the story

1. As the story develops, the characters' behavior to each other changes. Divide a page in your exercise book down the middle into two parts, one for Mrs. Jones, and one for Roger. Write in each part how they behave towards each other in the different parts of the story. *Start like this:*
   At the beginning (ll. 1–…) Mrs. Jones is angry. She kicks … and says … Then …
   At the beginning (ll. 1–…) Roger is aggressive. He tries to … He doesn't care … Then …
2. Now look at your two lists of changes, and try to work out what they have to do with each other. *Make 'cause and effect' sentences:* Mrs. Jones gets angry because Roger …
3. From what (or from whose) point of view is the story told?
4. Collect all the information given in the story about the woman, the kind of person she is, the kind of life she leads. Can you guess any more than you are actually told?
5. What do you learn about the boy and the kind of life he leads? What can you guess?
6. What do you think of the way the woman treats the boy? Does it make sense?

---

[20][sweɪd] *Wildleder;* [21]*tropfen;* [22][fraʊn] *die Stirn runzeln;* [23][prɪ'zentəbl] *vorzeigbar, ordentlich;* [24]*Wandschirm, Trennwand;* [25]['kəʊkəʊ] *Kakao;* [26]['laɪmə'bi:nz] *große weiße Bohnen;* [27][hæm] *Schinken;* [28][lætʃ] *sich an etw. klammern;* [29]*Rast, Ruhepause*

2 Words and meanings WORD POWER

Some of the 'new' words in this story have not been explained because it is easy to guess what they mean. a) *Explain how you knew the meaning of the words on the right.*

blue-jeaned (l. 11)	comb (l. 108)
to rattle (l. 13)	icebox (l. 110)
to grip (l. 19)	to mistrust (l. 118)
to struggle (l . 58)	canned (l. 123)
roomers (l. 63)	to heat (l. 125)
bite (l. 79)	to embarrass (l. 128)
pause (l. 93)	devilish (l. 139)

b) You have already learned the following words. But they are used in this story in rather different ways. *Say what they must mean here – and how you were able to guess:*

purse (l. 1)	but (l. 2)	to reach (l. 12)
to aim (l. 23)	to turn (l. 27)	to last (l. 53)
to fix (l. 107)	to run (l. 107)	(gas) plate (l. 110)

c) *Pick out all the words and phrases that have to do with:*
- wanting something to happen,
- influencing what happens. *Make lists.*

16 3 Poverty and crime – some opinions

a) *Complete these statements with a suitable verb or auxiliary. Decide if it is positive or negative.*
1. "We worked hard to earn our money, so we … give it to some lazy good-for-nothings who … work at all if they could avoid it."
2. "People who have made it out of the slums … be reminded of all that."
3. "I … help the poor, but it's hard to know the best way to do it." – "If you …, I can put you in contact with a good organization."
4. "We … buy a used car, since public transportation is so bad. But we just can't manage to save enough. I asked my sister in Chicago to help, but she …"

b) *Put in 'let' or 'make'.*
1. "Unemployment is extremely high for young black men. That's what … so many of them turn to crime."
2. "A lot of those boys are members of gangs. Parents shouldn't … them stay out so late at night. They should … them go to evening classes or something."
3. "Sure, a lot of criminals are black – but so are most of their victims! We African-Americans *know* we can't … things go on like this. We've got to … the city wake up and do something."
4. "Most of the white police are racists. Yesterday a bank was robbed downtown, and me and my friend, we were walking just a block away. Two cops … us stand up against a wall to be searched – just because we're black! They had to … us go in the end of course, but they weren't very friendly about it."

c) *Use a different verb to explain what 'let' and 'make' mean in the above sentences.*

d) *Compare the opinions of blacks and whites as shown in the opinion poll on the right. Were you surprised by some of these facts? Why? What would you have expected?*

Do middle-class blacks do as much as they should to help improve conditions for poorer blacks?

	WHITES	BLACKS
As much as they should	22%	22%
Not as much	33%	54%
Not need	15%	11%

Why do you think poor blacks have not been able to rise out of poverty?

	WHITES	BLACKS
Fault of blacks	29%	30%
Fault of society	42%	44%

Is the federal government doing enough to help American blacks?

	WHITES	BLACKS
Too much	18%	5%
Too little	29%	71%
About right	36%	13%

How often do whites attack blacks in your city or town?

	WHITES	BLACKS
Very often	4%	13%
Sometimes	41%	56%
Never	49%	28%

How often do blacks attack whites in your city or town?

	WHITES	BLACKS
Very often	8%	13%
Occasionally	44%	58%
Never	44%	24%

Compared to white people charged with crimes, are black people charged with crimes treated differently in the U.S. justice system?

	WHITES	BLACKS
Worse	34%	66%
Better	5%	3%
Same	50%	23%

4 Why so aggressive?

Rap and hip-hop are styles of black music that were created in the urban ghettos. But some of it has been criticized for being too aggressive. Here is what the hip-hop musician LL Cool J had to say in an interview with the magazine 'Black Beat':

"On my albums, any time that I have an aggressive record that sounds like I'm going after someone, it's the microphone and us in a verbal battle, verbal combat. You don't hear anything on there where I'm talking about killing somebody for their money, or something on that level. I think hip-hop is just a sounding board for a problem that already exists. I don't think hip-hop is really doing it, or not doing it. It's just glamorizing it – the same thing Hollywood does. School frustrates the average African-American male. By the time he's 15 years-old, he can't stand it. The teachers don't care, and by the time he leaves school, he's off and running. And those jobs that are available for somebody without a high school diploma or a college degree don't pay anything. So it's almost like a set-up[1], so many fall into the trap. Families have to stay together. If we could get the relationships between African-American men and women to be stronger, if we could have a better understanding of each other, it would be a great start. If African-American women could understand the differences between being a black man and a black woman.
If they could understand that aspect of it. I think that we could get a lot further. I mean, we all have hardships.
I don't think men should get so frustrated that we should let our children be raised alone."

[1]*set-up* = a trick to make s.o. do the wrong thing

a) *Try to understand as much as you can of LL Cool J's opinions. Remember: first guess, then check any meanings you still aren't sure about in your dictionary.*

b) *Discuss his opinions*

1. Do you agree with his view of rap and hip-hop music?
2. What does LL Cool J tell you about certain problems in the black community? Can you find any explanations for them – or say what ought to be done about them?

§ 15 **5 The Million Man March, October 1995**

§ 16 The phrases that are missing in the following can mean either *'sollen', 'wollen',* or *'lassen'* in German – the letter *S*, *W* or *L* tell
§ 17 you which (*'n'* means negative). *Choose suitable English verbs, auxiliaries or phrases for the context. Be careful of the tenses.*

From the start, the March was controversial. The man who organized it, Louis Farrakhan, … *(S)* be a black racist who hated all whites and especially Jews. Many black men decided they … *(nW)* take part for that reason. And it … *(S)* be sexist: the women … *(S)* stay at home, take care of the kids, and … *(L)* their men (…) go off to Washington for the day. They … *(L)* bring their boys with them if they … *(W)*! For this reason, many women's organization that had been asked to support the March said they … *(nW)*.

It seemed a strange way to express the idea that African-American men … *(S)* support their families and respect their women more than they had in the past. Because that's what the March … *(S)* be all about. But in spite of everything, the March … *(S)* be a great success. Most black women … *(L)* their men (…) take part because they badly … *(W)* an improvement in their family life. The number of black men taking part … *(S)* to be less than a million – according to police reports – but nobody cared. The atmosphere was good, and hopes were high that the March … *(L)* everybody (…) sit up and listen.

C A white man singing your song

The following story is set in a time that was very important for the development of American popular music. Use your dictionary to find out the meaning of the words you don't know.

One thing can be said for sure about living with Auntie Mae – it was never boring. There were always people coming and going, dropping in at all hours to our house – or apartment, or wherever we were living at a given time. You see, we did a lot of moving about ourselves.

Anyway, at the time I'm talking about we were back in Memphis, where we'd lived for a few years just after my Mom died. The new house was a good bit better than the old shack. And better than the crummy apartment in South Chicago, or that trailer park in Kansas City. And if you're wondering how we came to be living in a nice house with a trim garden and white picket fence, well, Anna Mae Hawkins had finally hit the big time, with three hit records in a row on the rhythm'n'blues charts. "Now, these bucks ain't gonna last for ever," Mae would say, "so don't go spending 'em all on clothes and comic books!" (Or, if she was talking to Uncle Carl, "What d'you think you doin', spending all my money down at Murphy's Bar? I been workin' my butt off every night, so you get offa your lazy ass ..." etc., etc.) Of course she was right. It didn't last. But for a time, anyway, I was able to watch TV from a very comfortable plush sofa.

Carl had fallen asleep on the other sofa, so I was flicking idly round the other channels. I was looking for something more interesting than baseball to watch. (I was also thinking how long more Auntie Mae was going to put up with Carl.) I stayed for a while with a country music program coming from Nashville, not because of the music, but because I thought one of the singers looked sort of familiar. I knew he couldn't be any of the people that came to our house. The only white men I'd ever seen here were record company bosses, and they were old and bald. This one was at most nineteen, real good-looking for a white boy, with thick, black curly hair hanging over his forehead. And he didn't sound half bad, either. Then I remembered. It was when I was on tour with Auntie Mae.

Not that I often got taken along when Mae went on tour. That only happened once, when she couldn't find anyone to look after me. I think she felt a bit bad about it. At other times she was always reminding me of her promise to my Mom to keep me at school and give me a chance to go to college. "Gotta pay the rent, Honey! Money don't grow on trees!" was what she said that time, with that loud laugh of hers. Besides, she'd be on the road from late July to mid-September, so I'd only be missing three weeks of school. Who cares about college, I thought.

The tour was fun. Mae didn't always succeed in keeping me out of the places she was performing in. Maybe she didn't try very hard. Anyway it was easy enough to find an excuse to get in for rehearsals and sound checks. Sometimes even in the evening, since she'd given me the job of looking after her fancy clothes. "Gotta keep you busy, Hon! I hope you realize I been giving you all this work just to keep you outa harm's way." I think she finally realized her tactics were failing the day she caught me in her dressing-room trying on her high-heeled shoes and the red satin dress with all the sequins down the front.

I was standing in front of the scratchy mirror, swaying my hips like I'd seen her do on stage, and trying to copy her low growl as she belted out a blues. I jumped when I heard her come in behind me. "Lord in heaven! Honey chile, what your poor Mom say if she saw you like this?" I couldn't answer that since I hardly remembered my Mom any more.

But the show had to go on. The following night saw me standing at the back of another smoky club as Mae in her red satin made another audience sigh and moan. I can't remember how I got in; it must have been something Mae forgot. Anyway, it was there that this white boy with dark curly hair asked me what a little girl like me was doing there. I told him it was none of his business, but I happened to be the niece of the star of the show.

"Ain't no harm in it, then, I suppose," he said.

"You're real lucky to have an aunt like Anna Mae." And he told me he had heard all the great black rhythm'n'blues singers, and Anna Mae Hawkins was one of the best. He must have meant it, because he was there the following night as well, and the night after that, and I saw him on two more occasions in different cities. White faces really stuck out like sore thumbs in those clubs.

I never caught his name back then, but he was definitely the same guy as this Rodney Patterson who was singing country music on TV. And it was country music, though it had a better beat than you usually get. And that voice: I just closed my eyes, and sure enough, you could imagine it was a black man! But the next song made me open them again.

"Auntie Mae, switch on the TV in your bedroom!" I screamed. She was taking a nap before another late-night gig. "Channel 7 – there's a white man singing one of your songs!"

When she came out of the bedroom, she said, "Take it easy, hon. Anyone can sing that song. It sure is a good song, but whoever's getting the song-writing royalties, it sure won't be me!"

"But it's yours - you been singing it since ..."

"Sure, honey chile, but I never got to writing down none of the words. Besides, I keep changin' 'em. It was Jimmy Wills who wrote down what I was singing one day. Remember Uncle Jimmy?"

Sure, I remembered Uncle Jimmy. "Jimmy was a no-good b..." She stopped herself, no doubt thinking again of my Mom. "But he sure could play a mean guitar!"

"So it's Uncle Jimmy is getting the royalties when someone else records it or sings it on TV?"

"Don't know, honey. Let me check what it say on my own record ... No, it's them white mens from New York helped Jimmy produce the record. Serve him right, the no-good ... ." She smiled wickedly. "Not that that song gonna make anyone all that much dough."

She was wrong. A week later, Rodney was on TV again, singing the same song. And this time the audience was going wild. All those white girls with ponytails just screaming their heads off. And it was on the radio almost every hour of the day. It was a smash hit on the pop charts – and that meant money – real money.

"Word goin' round that Jimmy Wills is hoppin' mad. He taking them New York boys to court to get back the rights to that goddam song," said Uncle Carl at the dinner table one day.

"Let Jimmy make a fool of hisself," answered Mae. "Them New Yorkers will sure have better lawyers." She was right, as it turned out.

But that wasn't quite the end of the story. There was a phone-call about a week later from a guy saying he was Rodney Patterson's manager. He asked me to give Mae a message. It seems they had now bought the copyright to the song that was such a smash hit, but Rodney felt bad about Mae not getting her share of the royalties. He knew it was really her song. He wanted to pay her something in compensation, and could they call on her at home that evening? I said O.K.

And sure enough, at eight o'clock, up the street comes a big chauffeur-driven limousine, parks in front of our house and out jumps Rodney from one side, and a tall, middle-aged, military-type guy from the other.

Rodney smiles when he sees me. He introduces his manager as 'the Major', and then starts telling Mae what he told me back in that blues club, wherever it was. The Major interrupts and says to cut a long story short, they are offering her a generous lump sum of $500 for her 'undeniable contribution' to Rodney's success ...

"Now would you please sign here?" And he whips out a kind of receipt. Mae shrugs her shoulders and signs. Carl offers them a drink to seal the deal. They accept, and then, in a flash, they are gone.

Only then do I get a look at what Mae has signed. "Hey, look here," I say. "It says you selling them the master-tape of your old recording of the song. ... And since they now have the copyright you won't be able to sing it in public again without payin' 'em!"

"Aw, what the hell!" says Mae. "We can sure use them 500 bucks. And there's plenty more songs where that one came from!"

I made up my mind that day. I'm not going to be a singer, musician or anything like it. To hell with the red satin and sequins! I'm going to go to college. And then I'll be a manager. Or a lawyer.

1 Understanding the story

After your first reading ...

a) *... check your basic comprehension of the story by talking about these points:*

1. Who is the narrator? What do you learn about her family background, her home life, etc.?
2. Who is the most important person in the story? Explain why you think so.
3. What other people are mentioned? Say how they relate to the main character, and to the narrator.

b) *... check how well you understood the story by trying to answer these questions:*

1. What kind of person is Anna Mae Hawkins? Describe her appearance, her character, her behavior, her attitudes to other people, etc.
2. What is the significance of the song mentioned in the title? Try to explain why the narrator and Anna Mae feel differently about it.

2 Using your dictionary WORD POWER

> **roy•al•ty**/'rɔɪəltɪ/, **royalties**. 1 The members of a royal family are sometimes referred to as royalty. EG ... *an official visit by royalty ... ... generations of English royalty.* **2 Royalties** are payments made to authors and musicians which are linked to the sales of their books or records, or to performance of their works. EG ... *all the royalties from my next play ... There should be a substantial income from royalties.*

Very often, your dictionary gives more than one meaning for the word you look up. And it might be a big mistake to think that the first meaning given is the one you are looking for.

a) *You probably needed to look up the word on the right: check all its meanings before deciding which one fits the context best.*

b) *Do the same with these other new words:*

belt (l. 74) mean (l. 92) whip (l. 172)

c) *And what do these words mean in the story:* channel (l. 29), to catch (l. 100), ponytail (l. 138)?

3 Understanding dialect

There is a lot of dialect in the dialogue (Southern English, Black English, or a mixture). But it is not hard to guess what the characters mean. a) *Collect non-standard forms from the text, and put them in three lists, as follows. Then change them to the correct standard forms.*

Different pronunciation:	*Words left out:*	*Different grammatical forms:*
l. 24: offa	l. 21: you ... doin'	l. 18: ain't gonna
l. 19: 'em	l. 23: I ... been workin'	...
... ...		

b) *Go through the story 'Thank you, Ma'am' (Step B) to find more examples of Black English.*

c) If you were able to fill in missing verbs (or parts of verbs), this is because you know the rules for the tenses. *Look again at each verb form in your lists, and say how you knew the standard form.*

§ 18 4 Stative or dynamic?

a) *Look up in the Grammar Pages (§ 18, p. 89) what makes a verb stative or dynamic. Then say which of the verbs in the first two paragraphs (ll. 1-12) are stative, and which dynamic.*

b) *In the fourth paragraph (ll. 28-44) two verbs are used in two different ways: with both stative and dynamic meanings. Find them, and say how the meanings are different.*

c) *Put in the correct verb form - in the progressive if possible:*

1. "This ... great – you really are a talented painter!" – "You ... at the wrong painting!" *(look)*
2. I ... she's crazy – she ... of sailing around the world on her own! *(think)*
3. Mum ... the soup when we came into the kitchen. She thought it ... a bit too salty. *(taste)*
4. "I ... it's an early blues by W.C. Handy." – "Are you sure?" – "Not really, I ..." *(guess)*
5. They really ... strange meal-times! They ... dinner when I called last night, at 10 o'clock! *(have)*

§ 19 5 A short history of black music

§ 20 a) *Put in the verbs in the correct tenses – active or passive, simple or*
progressive forms. Remember you only need a progressive form (for
§ 21 *action that is in progress for a certain time) if the verb is dynamic.*

Music … (always/be) a part of the African-American experience. We … (not know) what kind of music the earliest slaves … (make), but their **work songs** … (be) probably the first new kind of music that … (create) in America. Then … (come) the **spirituals.** Most black slaves … (convert) to Christianity by the 19th century, and in these religious songs they … (use) stories and ideas from the Bible to express their hope that they … (be) free one day. In churches they … (begin) to sing these songs in the African style that … (keep) alive in the work songs – with a strong rhythm, and a dialogue between the lead singer and the group. This … (become) known as **gospel music.**

At the same time another kind of music … (play) privately, usually by one singer with a banjo (an African instrument) or later a guitar. Each 12-bar verse … (have) three lines, the first two being the same. One common line … (be) 'Every day I got the blues' – meaning 'I'm feeling sad'. This … (give) the name to this form of music: **the blues.**

After slavery … (abolish), many blacks … (get) work making music in bars, and they … (develop) a new style of banjo and piano music called **ragtime.** In New Orleans at the turn of the century, when black musicians … (play) in marching bands, they … (like) to improvise on their instruments. This … (be) the beginning of **jazz.** Great jazz musicians like Louis Armstrong and King Oliver … (play) their instruments as if they … (sing) in the blues style, and in fact they … (often, play) together with blues singers like Bessie Smith.

Other styles of jazz … (develop) in Chicago and New York: the **swing** that … (play) by Duke Ellington's big band, and also by white musicians such as Benny Goodman; or the **bebop** that … (develop) by Charlie Parker. **Modern jazz** and **free jazz** … (come) later.

At the same time something else … (happen) in Chicago: the blues … (play) faster and with a stronger rhythm, creating **rhythm'n'blues.** But even in the 1950s, when people like Muddy Waters and B.B. King … (have) hit after hit in the 'race' charts, this music … (remain) unknown among whites – until a country singer called Elvis Presley … (begin) to sing in this style. Since by then **rock'n'roll** … (become) mainly a white style of popular music, blacks … (prefer) to listen to **soul** music in the 60s – although many religious blacks … (shock) that soul singers like Ray Charles and Aretha Franklin … (use) a 'gospel' style to sing about non-religious subjects. **Disco** dance music … (base) on soul.

In the 80s and 90s **rap** and **hip-hop,** which … (originally/create) in the urban ghettos, … (become) the most popular styles of black music. This improvised street poetry … (be) often rather primitive. But today jazz musicians … (begin) to take it seriously, and … (use) rap and hip-hop ideas in their own music. There … (be) no knowing what the future … (bring) in the way of new developments in popular music – except that African-Americans … (always/be) at the center of it.

b) Fact and fiction. *Having read the 'short history', can you say at what time the story 'A white man singing my song' is set? Try to guess who the character 'Rodney' might have been based on.*

⟨6 **A rhythm'n'blues song: Hound Dog** (sung by Big Mama Thornton)⟩

And use your dictionary!

You ain't nothin' but a hound dog, fresh[1] snoopin' round my door,
You ain't nothin' but a hound dog, fresh snoopin' round my door,
You can wag your tail, but I ain't gonna feed you no more!

You told me you were high-class, but I can see through the glass,
You told me you were high-class, but I can see through the glass,
And Daddy, I know you ain't no real polecat[2]!

You made me feel so blue, you made me weep and moan,
You made me feel so blue, you made me weep and moan,
You ain't lookin' for a woman, all you're lookin' for is a home!

[1]*hier: frech*
[2]*Skunk, Stinktier (hier positiv: Teufelskerl)*

Listening comprehension:

1. In what order are the verses sung? Is any verse repeated?
2. What extra words can you make out? (Blues singers hardly ever sing exactly the same words every time.)

⟨7 **Gospel and rap: Do not pass me by** (M.C. Hammer, with Trina Johnson and The Voices)⟩

Listening comprehension: Both the rap singer and the gospel choir repeat many of the words in different ways. *Try to work out who sings what when. You could make a copy of the song to write on.*

I just don't want Him to pass me by!

Pass me not, O gentle savior,
Hear my humble cry,
While the others thou[1] are calling
Do not pass me by!

Yeah!

When you're callin'!

Savior! Please!

Reachin' out!

Help me! I need Him!

Can you feel it?

I can feel it!

Deep down in my soul …

It's something special about the way that you hold me,
Make me, shape me, you take me and you mold[2] me,
And in my heart and in my soul and in my spirit,
The love of God every day I gotta be near it!
They took me to the water, I went down in your name,
I repented of all my sins and I haven't been the same,
My feet started to shakin', my legs had to run,
His love touched my heart and his spirit lifted my tongue,
I'm lovin' my Lord until the day that I die,
So please, please, oh please don't pass me by – Sing!

I got the feelin' and the feelin' is not the same,
I did a little hip-hop, the Hammer[3] and the James[4],
But a touch, a touch from up above.
And I get the feelin', the feelin' of Your love!
Reachin' out and callin' for your people
To keep us all safe from a world that's full of evil,
Trying, Lord, sometimes I'm crying,
The Son gave His life and the people are still denying[5].
When I think of His goodness and what He's done for me,
My soul cries Hallelujah, thanks for saving me – Sing!

When I'm down and I'm out and I can't see my way,
I need the Lord to help me every day,
I need him every hour, I need him every minute,
Whatever I'm doing, I need the Lord in it.
At school I need Him, at work I need Him,
At home I need Him, sick and hurt, I need him!
Do you need him? I know you need him – Sing!

Use your dictionary to check the other words!

[1][ðaʊ] *(alt)* = you; [2][məʊld] (= *BE* mould) *formen;* [3]*gemeint:* his own style of rap music; [4]*wahrscheinlich:* Etta James (b. 1938), famous rhythm'n'blues singer; [5][dɪˈnaɪ] *hier: ablehnen*

The infinitive

1 The first 'western plantings'

Sir Walter Raleigh and his son

For more than a century the English had been happy to sail, to fish, and to rob in the New World, but had not wanted to settle. Why? There are many reasons that explain why at that time the English showed little interest in founding colonies there. One of these reasons was simply the fact that England had not yet developed the idea of such settlements. The word 'colony' did not even enter the English language until about 1550.

It was not until the 1580s that Richard Hakluyt[1] proposed to found a colony, or in his words, 'a planting' in the New World. Such a colony would have many advantages, Hakluyt said. It would offer a market for English exports and might at the same time serve as a source of important materials for England. It would plant the Protestant religion in the New World and could keep the Spanish from "flowing over all the face … of America". The English would have liked to break the power of the Spanish in North America. And, finally, criminals could be sent to the colony.

Some years later Sir Walter Raleigh took up these ideas. Thus he became the first Englishman to found a colony across the seas. England's first colony was Roanoke Island (1585). Though Roanoke was the first English colony to be founded in North America, it was not the model to be followed in the future. It lasted only a year. When the Native Americans stopped giving the settlers food, the colonists ran short of everything and if a ship had not been sent to help them, all of them would have died. As the survivors were too frightened to continue their experiment, they were all happy to get a passage home on the ship.

Raleigh had no better luck with his second colony at Roanoke in 1587. As ships could not return the next year because of England's war with Spain, the colony was left to itself. When an expedition arrived in 1589, it found the settlement empty. What had happened to the settlers? The only hint that they might have been killed was the word 'CROATOAN' (the name of a nearby Native American tribe) written on a piece of wood.

[1]['hæklu:t]

2 Forms of the infinitive

a) If you look at the text, you will find four different forms of the infinitive. Two of these forms refer to the present or future, two to the past. *Use your exercise book and write down one example of each.*

	active	passive
present forms	…	…
past forms	…	…

b) *Explain how the different infinitives are formed.*

3 Infinitives with transitive and intransitive verbs

Only verbs that can take an object – transitive verbs – have all the infinitive forms. Intransitive verbs, i.e. verbs like 'to go', 'to arrive' that can't take an object, don't have any infinitives in the passive voice. *Form all the infinitives of the following verbs:*

to walk	to lose	to arrive	to write	to leave	to sing
to see	to win	to fall	to shoot	to run	to eat
to know	to come	to drive	to break	to love	to be

4 Infinitives and auxiliaries: the infinitive without 'to'

a) An auxiliary can come before all the forms of the infinitive. *Use your exercise book and put the forms you find in the text in the following list. Remember that there is no 'to' with auxiliaries (the only exception is 'ought to').*

	active voice		passive voice	
auxiliaries +	present infinitive	past infinitive	present infinitive	past infinitive
	Such a colony would have many advantages, …	…	…	…

b) *Translate the sentences with these infinitive forms into German.*

5 What happened to the colonists?

Put in the correct infinitive forms.

Nobody knows for sure what happened to the early colonists who settled Roanoke Island in 1587. They were probably killed by the Croatoans, but other possibilities may … (mention), too. They could … (die) of hunger or … (leave) the settlement to look for gold and silver. They might also … (try) to get help from French or Spanish colonists when the ship with food didn't show up. They may also … (kill) themselves when they saw that they would … (fall) into the hands of the Croatoans. In their need they may even … (try) to build a ship to sail back home; then their ship might … (sink) in a storm or it might … (attack) by pirates.

6 Guessing

When the first English colonists arrived, the Native Americans were friendly at first. Then their attitudes changed. For some reason they stopped giving the settlers food. What may have been the reasons that led to a change in their attitude? What could or should the settlers have done to avoid such a change? *Make at least five guesses. Use the auxiliaries 'can, may, might, could, should, ought to'.*

Example: The settlers should have been friendlier to the Croatoans.

7 The infinitive with 'to'

	The infinitive with 'to' is used
The English had been **happy to sail, to fish** and **to rob** in the New World.	after many adjectives,
They thought it was **too dangerous to settle** there. Others believed that it was **not profitable enough to go** there.	after 'too' plus adjective and adjective plus 'enough',
It was not **difficult for Sir Walter Raleigh to get** the money together. A much bigger **problem for him was to find** people who wanted to settle in the New World.	after 'for' plus noun/pronoun if 'for' follows an adjective or a noun,
At the end of the 16th century the English **decided to found** colonies, too. They **would have liked to break** the power of the Spanish in North America.	after verbs like 'to decide, to hope, to agree, to promise', etc. and after the conditionals of 'to like, to love, to hate, to prefer',
Such colonies would **allow them to export** their products. They **wanted their products to be sold** to the new colonists.	after verbs expressing an order, a request, a wish, a permission like 'to tell, to want, to allow', etc. if these verbs are followed by an object,
In 1585, the first English colonists landed on the American coast **to found** (= in order to found) a colony there.	after 'to' or 'in order to' to express an intention or purpose,
As things were different on the new continent, they didn't **know what crops to grow.**	in indirect questions with a question word and an auxiliary after verbs like 'to show, to teach, to learn, to know',
Though Roanoke was **the first** English colony **to be founded** in North America, it was not **the model to be followed** (= that was to be followed) in the future.	for a relative clause after 'the first, the last, the only one/ones' and for relative clauses with an auxiliary.

Look at the text on page 60 (exercise 1) and note what kind of infinitive constructions you find there.

8 Success at Jamestown

Rewrite this text using (shorter) infinitive constructions wherever possible. You can also use the verbs 'to want, to manage, to expect'.

The next colony *which was founded* was Jamestown. In 1607, the Virginia Company sent a group of men *who were to build* an outpost in the region of Chesapeake Bay, Virginia. The story of that outpost is one of the best-known stories of American history. The men the company had sent out on this adventure *were not keen on building* houses or *growing* food, but *on searching* for gold. They *depended on being fed* by the neighboring Powhattan Indians and this plan worked out because John Smith, the first governor of the colony, *succeeded in building* good relations with the Native Americans. But when Smith left the colony and more settlers arrived, relations with the Native Americans became worse. In the winter of 1609 the Native Americans stopped bringing them food, and the settlers were *so afraid that they didn't go outside* their settlement. *As they wanted* to get through the winter, they had to eat anything they could find. Nevertheless, only 60 of the 838 settlers managed to survive.

REVIEW 2

The gerund

1 Mexicans in the United States

For most immigrants, going to the U.S.A. means crossing the sea and leaving their home far behind. This is not true, of course, for Mexican immigrants, the largest group of the 23 million Hispanics who live in the U.S. Many of them entered America illegally, simply by crossing the border at night. Some even tried to reach the U.S.A. by swimming across the Rio Grande, which forms the border between Mexico and Texas. This is, by the way, the explanation for illegal immigrants sometimes being called 'wetbacks'. Why do they come to the U.S.A.? Well, many of them don't see any chance of getting a job at home, and they are afraid of remaining poor all their lives. Many of them, particularly illegal immigrants, remain poor, however, in spite of having got a job. The reason is that jobs for illegals are mostly poorly paid as employers know that they won't complain about getting less money for fear of being sent back to Mexico.

Many Mexicans, both legal and illegal immigrants, only mean to stay in the U.S.A. until they have made enough money to start a small business back home. So many just want to live and work in the U.S.A. without giving up their own culture. Many don't like their children becoming too American in their ways. Yet once they have got used to being in America and to having regular jobs, they often decide to stay. In the end most immigrants don't regret having been forced to leave their home country because of poverty. They think it has been worth crossing the border for a new life.

2 Forms of the gerund

Look at the forms of the gerund. Remember the gerund can have active and passive forms and it can have perfect forms, both in the active and passive voice (these are not often used, however).
Use your exercise book and write down one example of each.

	active	passive
present forms	…	…
perfect forms	…	…

3 Hopes and fears

Immigrants coming into the U.S.A. are often full of hopes and fears, and frequently faced with unexpected problems and surprises, particularly if they don't know the language. *Describe their situation. Work with a partner or in groups. Use gerunds. Here are some phrases to help you.*

to have difficulty in …	to start …	to be in danger of …	to dream of …
to be uncertain about …	to like …	to be afraid of …	to succeed in …
to look forward to …	to hate …	to be successful in …	to worry about …
to be disappointed …	to enjoy …	to be surprised at …	to think of …
(not) to be used to …	to regret …	to be proud of …	to complain of …

4 How to use the gerund

Do you remember how to use the gerund?

Leaving your home country is a big step.	A gerund can be the subject of a sentence.
But Teresa and Juan Mendoza like **living** in San Antonio, Texas.	After verbs the gerund can also be the object of a sentence.
They think that it was **worth crossing** the border.	A gerund must be used as a complement after expressions like 'it's worth, it's (no) good, it's no use, how/what about'.
The Mendozas have just **succeeded in buying** their own restaurant. They are both **good at cooking.** So they should have **no difficulty in running** it.	Gerunds are often used after prepositions following a noun, a verb or an adjective.
On coming home from school, their children help them in many ways. They have to work **instead of visiting** their friends.	A preposition followed by a gerund can replace a subordinate clause. This is particularly true for the following prepositions: on *(als)*, after, before, for *(dafür, dass)*, by *(indem)*, instead of, in spite of, apart from *(abgesehen von)*.
The Mendozas have already **started to paint/ painting** the kitchen. They **mean to open** their restaurant in three weeks' time. This will **mean working** very hard. But in spite of this, they don't **regret having taken** this step.	Some verbs can be followed by a gerund or by an infinitive with 'to'. With some of these verbs the meaning changes. With verbs like 'to forget, to remember, to regret' the gerund is used when the action refers to the past.

Look at the text on page 63 (exercise 1) and find the sentences that match the examples in the above table.

5 An interview with Hispanic immigrants

This is what some Hispanic immigrants told a Miami newspaper about their experiences in the U.S.A. *Put in the gerund or the infinitive of the following verbs:*

to make | to send | to build | to find | to have | to live (2x) | to play | to go | to hope | to look | to learn

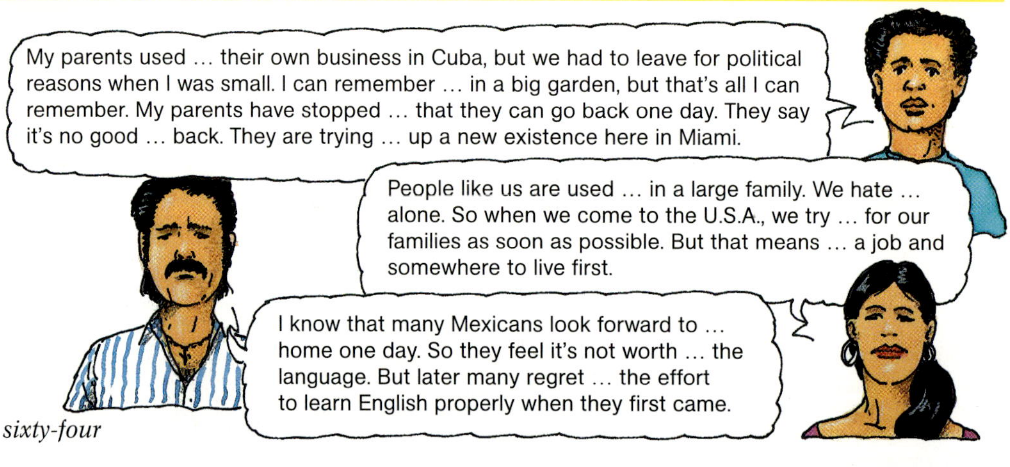

6 Why they came

Rewrite the following statements using gerunds. Add the missing prepositions: by, instead of, without, after, for, on, in spite of, before, apart from.

Example: I wanted to work for myself. I didn't want to work for other people.
I wanted to work for myself *instead of working* for other people.

1. My father was in prison as he belonged to the wrong political party.
2. You couldn't own land in my own country unless you married someone whose father already owned land.
3. We couldn't make enough money to live on even though we worked 14 hours a day.
4. In America you can get anything you want if you work hard.
5. Before we came to America, we never had enough to eat.
6. When he found gold in California, my great-great-grandfather sent enough money home for his family's tickets to America.
7. My children can go to good schools here. They don't have to go to schools which don't have enough teachers.
8. We made the decision to emigrate after we heard that our church had been burned down.
9. We had no jobs. Besides, we were not free in our country.
10. You were not allowed to criticize anything. If you opened your mouth, you were put in prison just because you had told the truth.

7 Translating gerunds

As the gerund can be a verb form or a noun, translations of the gerund vary. *The following examples will help you to translate gerunds into German.*

Losing a job is usually the beginning of problems for an immigrant.	Eine Stelle zu verlieren … *Oder:* Der Verlust eines Arbeitsplatzes kann …	Use a noun or an infinitive with *zu* to translate similar sentences.
Juanita was **afraid of** losing her job. She saw no **chance of** getting another one.	…, ihre Stelle zu verlieren. …, eine andere Stelle zu bekommen.	Use *zu* plus infinitive to translate a verb/a noun/ an adjective followed by a preposition.
Her husband was afraid of **Juanita losing** her job, too. He didn't like **her being** so depressed.	… befürchtete, dass auch Juanita ihre Stelle verlieren könnte. Er mochte es nicht, dass/wenn sie …	Use a *dass*-clause if the noun following the preposition or the verb is different from the subject. Sometimes *wenn* is possible, too.
In the evening she often went to bed **without saying** a word. He tried to help her **by talking** to her boss.	…, ohne ein Wort zu sagen. …, indem er mit ihrem Chef redete.	Use *zu* plus infinitive after a preposition followed by a gerund or use a subordinate clause.

Now have a look at exercise 1 (page 63) again and translate the text.

Participles

1 Forms of the participle

Like the gerund and the infinitive, the participle has different forms, too. These forms are:

	active voice	passive voice
present participle	**calling**	**(being) called**
perfect form	**having called**	**(having been) called**
past participle	——	**called**

Remember that intransitive verbs, i.e. verbs like 'to go', 'to arrive' cannot form a participle in the passive voice. The negative form of 'calling', 'having called', etc. is formed using 'not'.

2 Participles as adjectives

Present and past participles are often used as adjectives. As an adjective, the present participle has an active meaning. Past participles used as adjectives can have a passive meaning or describe a state.

a **falling** tree – a **fallen** tree a **dividing** line – a **divided** country

a) *Complete the sentences with the correct participles from the following verbs:*

to disappoint to isolate to care to divide to promise to hide to segregate

1. Though much progress has been made, relations between the races remain ...
2. Contacts have increased, but often end at the office doors with both African-Americans and whites ... in their own worlds.
3. Society seems to have become less ..., too.
4. Nevertheless, it has not become the deeply ... society a government commission thought it might in the 60s.
5. But it hasn't become King's ... land of racial brotherhood either.
6. ... discrimination still exists, and many whites still consider African-Americans as second-class citizens.
7. There are still ... schools and neighborhoods in many American cities.

b) Some present participles used as adjectives can have a slightly different meaning from the one you might expect. *Use your dictionary to check and explain the meaning of these participles:*

1. The skyline of Manhattan is an *arresting* sight.
2. There are many visitors who ask *searching* questions.
3. What's wrong with you? Nothing *catching,* I hope.
4. There are people who are very *calculating.*
5. There was a *moving* documentary on Martin Luther King on TV last night.
6. It made some *telling* points about the treatment of the African-Americans in the 50s.

3 Participles after certain verb groups

The present and past participle are used to form the progressive forms, the passive voice and the perfect tenses of the active voice. Apart from this, participles can be found after certain verb groups.

One day when I was filling in a form in my bank, I **felt** someone **holding** my arm. When I turned round, I **saw** a man **standing** behind me.	The present and past participles can be used after **verbs of perception** if the action is not over, repeated or very short.
He **stood** there **looking** at me. "Don't move. **Remain seated,**" he told me.	The present and past participle can be used after **verbs expressing rest.**
Then he **put** his right hand in his pocket, **showing** me something that looked like a gun.	The present participle can be used after **verbs expressing a movement.**

4 Participles used for relative and adverbial clauses

a) **Participles used for relative clauses**

The man trying to **rob** (= **who tried** to rob) the bank was not very old. He fled in a car **stolen** (= **which had been** stolen) some days ago. All persons able (= **who are** able) to offer information are asked to contact the police.	Participles can be used for relative clauses if the relative pronoun is the subject of the clause. The relative pronoun must be left out. The verb 'to be' is often left out.

b) **Participles used for adverbial clauses**

As I was afraid, I did what I was told.	**Being afraid,** I did what I was told.
After he had been given the money, the robber left the bank.	**Having been given the money,** the robber left the bank.

Participles can be used for all kinds of adverbial clauses if the subject of the main clause and the subject of the adverbial clause are the same. For problems with the use of conjunctions see 'Grammar', § 7, pp. 80/81.

c) **Participle constructions for adverbial clauses with a different subject**

As the police were well-informed, the robber was soon arrested.	**The police being well-informed,** the robber was soon arrested.

Participle constructions can also be used if the subject of the main and adverbial clause are different. Such participle constructions mostly stand for adverbial clauses of reason. They are very formal in style. These constructions can also begin with 'with'. Then they are less formal and more commonly used. The German translation is mostly *da* or *wenn*.

With the police doing a good job, the robber was soon arrested.	How can I listen to the news **with you making** such a noise?

d) **Participle constructions connecting two main clauses**

The next day a crowd gathered in front of the bank again, **hoping** that something would happen.

Occasionally participles can be used to connect two main clauses.

5 Test your memory

Robberies are quite common in bigger cities. *Imagine you are standing outside a shop opposite a bank. Someone is going to rob the bank, but at the time you don't know that. Later the police interview you and ask you what you saw in the street. How much did you notice?*

Look at this picture for about two minutes, then close your book and say what you might have seen/heard. Use verbs like 'to hear, to watch, to notice, to run, to come', etc.

6 Negroes, blacks or African-Americans?

Read through the following text. Use participle constructions for the phrases in italics.

It seems very likely that the word 'African-Americans' will soon come to replace the expression 'black Americans' or 'blacks', *which up till now has been commonly used* for those Americans whose ancestors came from Africa. *As this term has been used* by black leaders, it has become increasingly popular during recent years. Many black leaders say they prefer 'African-Americans' *when they refer to their black fellow citizens.*

Why this change? *As people have become more and more interested in their 'origins',* those whose families came from Ireland or Holland, for example, no longer call themselves 'European' – they prefer to call themselves 'Irish-Americans' or 'Dutch-Americans'. So the idea of calling people whose ancestors came from Africa 'African-Americans' hardly comes as a surprise.

This, however, is not the first change that has taken place in the history of the black population of the U.S. Originally, slaves were called 'colored' people. Later they were called 'negroes'. Then in the 1960s, the word 'black' was officially introduced, and before long the word 'negro', *although it was still understood,* became old-fashioned.

There will be immediate effects if 'African-American' should become generally used. Books, reports, articles, in fact everything from videos to dictionaries – *if they contain the word 'black'* – will at once become dated. But there is another side to the problem: What will happen to the term 'white' when 'black' disappears from the language? *As white and black do not describe* a person's origin, they should perhaps both be changed.

Translation practice

German ⟶ English

1 The German point of view — Unit 1

Du hast Freunde aus England zu Besuch, die sich für die politische Geschichte eurer beiden Länder interessieren. In der Bücherei stoßt ihr auf ein Buch aus dem Jahre 1925. Es heißt ‚Der englische Volkscharakter' und ist von Karl Wildhagen. *Übersetze den Textauszug, der die deutsche Haltung gegenüber den Briten um die Jahrhundertwende beschreibt, für deine Freunde.*

… Deshalb betrachten die Briten ihre Institutionen als ein Modell für den Rest der Welt und sehen sich selbst als das auserwählte Volk: Gott hat das britische Volk auserwählt, die Welt zu beherrschen, weil diese Herrschaft für die Völker des Empire, vielleicht für die ganze Welt, Fortschritt und Zivilisation bedeutet. Politiker, Philosophen und Dichter wie Disraeli, Carlyle und Kipling singen seit der Mitte des 19. Jahrhunderts das Lob der britischen Expansion. Diese Propaganda war äußerst erfolgreich. Sie erreichte ihren Höhepunkt, als man in Südafrika Gold fand und die Briten sich daran machten, riesige Gebiete Afrikas zu Teilen ihres Empires zu machen. Auf diese Weise erweiterten sie in nur 30 Jahren ihr Territorium um ein Gebiet von der Größe Europas. Joseph Chamberlain, der (Staats-)Sekretär für die Kolonien, band die Kolonien außerdem eng an das Mutterland. Er machte es den neuen, aufstrebenden Mächten USA und Deutschland fast unmöglich, mit britischen Kolonien Handel zu treiben, indem er eine Mauer von Zöllen[1] errichtete. Der Weltkrieg bereitete dem schließlich ein Ende. …

[1]tariff

2 Native Americans of the plains — Unit 2

Du verbringst ein Jahr an einer amerikanischen Schule und hast die Aufgabe erhalten, Informationen zur frühen Besiedelung Amerikas zu sammeln. In einem deutschen Lehrbuch findest du den folgenden Text. *Übersetze ihn für deine amerikanischen Klassenkameraden.*

Da niemand wirklich genau weiß, wie und wann zum ersten Mal Menschen die nordamerikanische Prärie besiedelten, wird allgemein angenommen, dass es asiatische Nomaden[1] waren, die über die Beringstraße nach Alaska gelangten, um sich von dort über ganz Amerika auszubreiten. Schließlich machten mehr als 30 Stämme die Prärie zu ihrer neuen Heimat.

Obwohl jeder dieser Stämme seine eigene Lebensform entwickelte, waren den meisten von ihnen gewisse Lebensweisen gemeinsam. So lebten viele Stämme dieses Gebiets als Nomaden und Jäger, womit sie von den Büffeln der Prärie abhängig waren. Und obwohl einige Stämme die Landwirtschaft vorzogen und in dauerhafteren Siedlungen wohnten, benötigten auch sie in vielen Fällen die Büffel für ihr tägliches Leben.

Es mag überraschend sein zu hören, dass Pferde erst im 16. Jahrhundert durch die Spanier eingeführt wurden. Nachdem sie aber die Möglichkeiten erkannt hatten, die ihnen die Verwendung dieser Tiere bot, integrierten die Indianer sie in ihr tägliches Leben. Reichtum und Prestige konnten bald an der Anzahl der Pferde gemessen werden, die jemand besaß, und in manchen Fällen wurden Pferde auch als Zahlungsmittel für Waren eingesetzt.

Zwischen den verschiedenen Stämmen gab es viele Kontakte. Auch wenn sie nicht alle die gleiche Sprache sprachen, war Kommunikation überhaupt kein Problem. Die Indianer der Prärie entwickelten eine Zeichensprache unter Verwendung der Arme und Hände. Diese Art der Kommunikation, die unter Indianern, die jenseits der Prärie lebten, nicht zu finden war, ist das Merkmal, das die verschiedenen Stämme dieses Gebiets miteinander verband.

[1]nomad

3 Ellis Island

Unit 3

Nina ist als Austauschschülerin in einer Kleinstadt in der Nähe von New York. Sie schreibt ihrer Klasse einen Brief. Nick, ihr Austauschpartner in Amberg, bittet die Schüler darum, den Brief für ihn ins Englische zu übersetzen. *Wie könnte die Übersetzung lauten?*

Hi, friends!

Ich nehme an, ihr seid glücklich, dass ihr wieder etwas von mir hört. Hoffentlich geht es euch auch so gut wie mir. Ich genieße Amerika und vor allem die Schule hier. Ich kann mir die meisten Fächer selbst aussuchen und es gibt ‚leider' keine Hausaufgaben, so dass ich viel Freizeit habe. Letztes Wochenende war ich mit meinen Gasteltern in New York City. Die Stadt ist einfach ein Traum. Ich werde sicher noch einmal hinfahren. Wir haben auch Ellis Island besucht. Ihr wisst doch hoffentlich, welche Rolle Ellis Island in der Geschichte Amerikas spielte, oder? Ellis Island war von 1892 an das Einwanderungszentrum für die Vereinigten Staaten. Millionen Einwanderer – darunter auch die Großeltern meiner Gastfamilie, die vermutlich aus Bayern (!) kamen – betraten dort zum ersten Mal amerikanischen Boden. Ellis Island ist seit 1990 ein Museum. Es war interessant zu hören, wie es den Einwanderern, die hier ankamen, ging. Sie wurden eine große Treppe hinaufgeschickt und dabei von Ärzten beobachtet. Wer hustete oder sonst irgendwelche Schwierigkeiten hatte, wurde untersucht. Stellten die Ärzte eine Krankheit fest, wurden die Einwanderer zurückgeschickt. Denen, die bleiben durften, wurden viele Fragen gestellt: Wie heißt du? Wo bist du geboren? Hast du hier einen Arbeitsplatz? Warst du schon einmal im Gefängnis? Kannst du lesen und schreiben? Die meisten Einwanderer sprachen kaum ein Wort Englisch. Manchmal verstanden die Beamten noch nicht einmal ihre Namen. Es gibt die Geschichte eines Juden, der rief ‚shoyn fargessen' – schon vergessen, als er nach seinem Namen gefragt wurde. Ohne zu zögern schrieb der Beamte ‚Sean Ferguson' in seinen Pass. Vielleicht ging es ja den Vorfahren meiner Gastfamilie ähnlich, sie heißen nämlich 'Taylor' und das ist sicherlich kein bayerischer Name.

Das war's für heute. Mehr im nächsten Brief.

Bye!

Nina

4 In a German music magazine Unit 4

Deine amerikanische Freundin entdeckt diese CD-Besprechungen in einer deutschen Musikzeitschrift. Sie kann ungefähr verstehen, worum es geht, möchte aber gerne genau wissen, was hier über ihre Lieblingsmusiker gesagt wird. *Übersetze die Texte für sie.*

Howlin' Wolf (and others)
The London Sessions (Roots Records)
Howlin' Wolf soll angeblich der Bluessänger mit dem größten Einfluss auf eine ganze Generation britischer Rockmusiker sein. Und diese CD lässt euch sehen (oder vielmehr hören), wie es dazu kam. Es spielen Gitarre und singen im Hintergrund unter anderen Bill Wyman und Charlie Watts von den *Rolling Stones,* Steve Winwood von *Traffic* und Eric Clapton (er sollte kurz danach seine Gruppe *Derek and the Dominoes* gründen). Wolf selbst, schon ein alter Mann als seine Plattenfirma ihn nach London kommen ließ um diese Aufnahme zu machen, kümmert sich überhaupt nicht darum, wer sie sind. Er klingt genau so, wie er in den 40er Jahren in Mississippi geklungen hat. Es war eine großartige Idee, diese alten Bänder für eine neue Generation auf CDs aufzeichnen zu lassen.

Whitney Houston (and others)
Waiting to Exhale (Arista Records)
Aufnahmen für Filmmusik sollen angeblich langweilig sein – aber diese ist anders. Whitney – eine der Hauptdarstellerinnen in dem großen 1996er Film über die Probleme der schwarzen Frauen heute – hat drei Songs auf dieser CD. Außerdem haben die Filmemacher es geschafft, eine ganze Menge anderer großer schwarzer Sängerinnen dazu zu veranlassen, Songs für den Film aufzunehmen: Patti LaBelle, Chaka Khan, Mary J. Blige, und sogar die ‚Königin des Souls' Aretha Franklin!

Stevie Wonder
Natural Wonder (Motown Records)
Es war eine gute Idee, die besten Liveauftritte von Stevie sammeln zu lassen und auf diese Doppel-CD aufzunehmen. Sie enthält fast jeden Hit, den seine Fans noch einmal hören möchten, aber in anderer Form. Tatsächlich hat er es geschafft, einige altvertraute Songs frisch und neu klingen zu lassen. Kein echter Fan sollte diese CD verpassen!

The Jackson Five
Soulsation (Motown Records)
Wenn ihr denkt, die Boy Groups der 90er Jahre sind was Neues, dann wird diese CD euch noch mal zum Nachdenken veranlassen! Es sind die bekanntesten Jungs von allen – mit ihren größten Hits von Anfang bis Mitte der 70er Jahre. Einer der *Five* sollte in den 80ern ein noch größerer Star werden – jetzt solltet ihr bereits wissen, wen ich meine! Wenn ihr nur seine jüngeren Hits (von *Thriller* bis *HIStory*) kennt, wird diese große Sammlung euch herausfinden lassen, wo er herkommt. Und da er die Einleitung von seiner Schwester Janet hat schreiben lassen, ist auch für ihre Fans etwas dabei.

Guru (and others)
Jazzmatazz (Chrysalis Records)
Guru ist allen Hip-hop-Fans gut bekannt – aber nicht, jedenfalls bisher, in Jazzkreisen. Außerdem soll Hip-hop angeblich primitive Straßenmusik sein. Wie hat es dann aber Guru geschafft, so angesehene Jazzmusiker wie Branford Marsalis, Courtney Pine, Carleen Anderson, Donald Byrd und andere dazu zu veranlassen, bei diesem Projekt mitzumachen? Weil sie wissen, dass Hip-hop die wahren Gefühle der Schwarzen in den Städten ausdrückt und sie zurückgehen wollen zu den Wurzeln ihrer eigenen Musik. Ein interessantes Experiment!

English ⟶ German

Some tips for translating English texts into German

When you translate, don't make the mistake of trying to translate each word separately. Two languages, even if they are as closely related to each other as English and German, rarely express the same meaning in exactly the same way. *Look at the following examples:*

Sometimes one language uses more words than the other. →	large areas of land *große Landflächen*
Often the word order is different and you have to avoid old-fashioned and politically incorrect terms. →	At first the Native Americans were friendly towards the whites. *Zuerst waren die Indianer den Weißen gegenüber freundlich.*
Sometimes something is expressed in a totally different way in each of the languages. →	They didn't like leaving their land. *Sie haben ihr Land nur ungern verlassen.*
Occasionally one word has two (or more) meanings for which there are different words in the other language. →	The first settlers felt *(meinten)* that Jamestown was the best place to start a colony. They soon felt *(fühlten sich)* at home.
Sometimes there are different ways of translating something which are all equally correct. →	The first settlers felt that …

When you meet a new word, you can sometimes 'infer' what it means. Perhaps it is related to a word you already know, or you can guess from the context, or it is similar to a German word – but be careful – it might be a 'false friend'! Have you 'inferred' what 'infer' means?

Some (but not all) of the places where you have to be particularly careful have been marked for you.

1 New Englishes and new nations

Unit 1

Translate the following text into German, using your dictionary only where necessary.

A relative clause is often used to translate a participle construction.

Same tense or would a different tense sound more natural in German?

The spread of English to so many parts of the world and the increase in the number of those learning it and using it has been the most striking example of 'language expansion' this century if not in all recorded history. It has far exceeded that other famous case, the spread of Latin during the Roman Empire.

You can't say it like that in German, can you?

You need a different verb and a different preposition in German.

From being the language of a very small nation, England, the English language spread over the rest of the British Isles and from the early days of colonization in the Americas the pace increased. Some of this movement of English to other parts of the world has been by the migration of English-speaking people – to North America and later to Australia, New Zealand and South Africa. Speakers of English settled in new lands and continued to use English.

Which word does this refer to in German?

Word order!

It was also used in those colonies which were under British administration but where only a few British people settled permanently: places like India and Ceylon, West Africa, Malaya and islands in the Pacific, and in the West Indian colonies like Jamaica where small communities of English speakers dominated the West Africans who were brought there as slaves.

You'll have to express this in a different way in German

This has two meanings in German.

The end of the colonial era, however, has not seen a reversal of the spread of English. Many of the new nations which were once British colonies have realized the importance of English not only as a language of commerce, science and technology but also as an international language of communication.

If you don't know this word, think of primary and secondary schools.

You can't use 'ist' here.

In some of these nations, most of the education in schools and tertiary institutions is through the medium of English. Although other nations have decided to use an indigenous language as the medium of instruction in schools, English is nevertheless the main second language.

(From *The New Englishes*, London 1984)

2 Washington

Unit 2

Your neighbour has to go to Washington, in England, on business. He asks you to translate this leaflet for him, so that she'll know something about the town. *Use your dictionary only where necessary.*

How are you going to translate 'you'?

Think which part of the verb this is!

If you hear the name 'Washington', you might think at first of America. In actual fact there are at least fifty places in the world called Washington, but the original Washington is in North-East England, just south of Newcastle.

= the first of his … who …

The ancestors of George Washington, America's first president, came from this village. William de Hertburn, his first ancestor to live there, moved to the village of Washington in 1183. Taking on the name of his new home, he became William de Washington. Imagine – if William hadn't moved to Washington, America's first president and the city of Washington in America might have been called Hertburn instead!

Washington Old Hall

not 'das ist'!

But Washington (near Newcastle) is famous for another reason – it is a 'new town', that is, a town planned and built in the countryside around the old village of Washington. There are nine industrial estates for new industries, and eighteen housing estates. Designed as villages each with a different character, the housing estates are separated from each other by trees and fields, and each has its own shops, primary school and community hall.

You know the noun, so you can infer what the verb means.

You know one meaning of this word, but it has another meaning! Is it a noun or a verb here? Now look it up!

You have had this word in 'Advanced Level'. Try to infer what it means here.

One word in English, two words in German.

There is a special road system linking the industrial estates to each other and to the motorway, thus keeping the residential areas free of industrial traffic. On the one hand the most advanced car plant in the world (built by a Japanese firm) and on the other hand the beautifully restored buildings of the old village are both typical of Washington – the best of what is old and the best of what is new.

3 Pupils' Parliament

Unit 3

Here is part of an article that a 16-year-old girl has written about the Pupils' Parliament in her school. *Translate it into German, using a dictionary only where necessary.*

Stop! You can't say it like that in German, can you?

Think why 'his or her' is in the text – then think how to translate 'pupil'.

This word has more than one meaning. Check the context to find which meaning is suitable.

We have a Pupils' Parliament in our school, which makes it possible for pupils to influence the way in which the school is run. What happens is this:

- Any pupil wanting to suggest a way of improving the school writes his or her idea on a list pinned on the notice-board in each classroom. The class then discusses which suggestions to keep and which to throw out.

You'll have to say this differently in German. The way you say it may affect your translation of the relative clause.

Simple past or past participle?

You know 'Assembly' and 'hall'. There is a special word in German for an Assembly Hall in a school.

- Then a representative chosen by the class presents the suggestions in the Pupils' Parliament. Having discussed the proposals of the various classes, the Pupils' Parliament makes a list of the most sensible ones. The classes are given the list, which they again discuss.
- The decisions made by each class are noted by the representative, who then puts forward the class's opinions at the second meeting of the Pupils' Parliament. Having made a final list, the Pupils' Parliament gives this to the teachers.
- Then the whole school meets in the Assembly Hall, and the head teacher explains which proposals can be put into practice. The next time we have a session, I'm going to ask if we can have more computers in school. I've been suggesting this for years, but they always say they haven't got enough money.

A new word. Try to infer from the context what it means. (Remember – one language may use two words where another language has only one.) Check in your dictionary.

You'll have to add a little word here.

What tense in German?

4 A wild dream

Unit 4

Mario Puzo is a very well-known American writer. His greatest success so far has been 'The Godfather', a novel about the Mafia, which also became a very successful film. The text below is an excerpt from one of his essays. *Translate it into German. Use your dictionary only where necessary.*

What does 'its' refer to?

Different word order in German!

You can't use 'entscheiden' here.

You have to use a clause in German.

My direct ancestors for a thousand years have most probably been illiterate. Italy, the golden land, so loving to vacationing Englishmen, so majestic in its language and cultural treasures (they call it, I think, the cradle of civilization), has never cared for its poor people.
My father and mother were both illiterates. Both grew up on rocky, hilly farms in the countryside adjoining Naples[1]. My mother remembers never being able to taste the ham from the pig they slaughtered every year. It brought too high a price in the marketplace and cash was needed. My mother was also told the family could not afford the traditional gift of linens when she married, and it was this that decided her to emigrate to America to marry her first husband, a man she barely knew. When he died in a tragic work accident on the docks, she married my father. He was a mystery, a Southern Italian with blue eyes. He cursed Italy even more than my mother did. Then again, he wasn't too pleased with America either. My mother never heard of Michelangelo; the great deeds of the Caesars[2] had not yet reached her ears. She never heard the great music of her native land. She could not sign her name. And so it was hard for my mother to believe that her son could become an artist. After all, her one dream in coming to America had been to earn her daily bread, a wild dream in itself. And looking back she was dead right. Her son an artist? To this day she shakes her head. I shake mine with her.

The gerund refers to the past here.

Personal passive – you can't say it like this in German.

'not … either' is the negative of 'also'

used as an adverb to stress the adjective 'right'

[1]*Neapel;* [2]*Kaiser*

Grammar

Unit 1

§ 1 Conjunctions and adverbs used to link sentences
Satzverknüpfende Konjunktionen und Adverbien

Step A

Spain **and** France were among the first countries to found colonies in the New World. **But** towards the end of the 16th century England tried to found colonies there, too, **for** people believed that the New World was full of silver and gold.

- Die Konjunktionen *and, or, but* und *for* (denn) verbinden Sätze oder Satzteile.

Yet most people who went there didn't find any. **So** many people were disappointed. **After all,** they had left everything behind. **Besides,** they had often spent their last penny on the passage to the New World. **Moreover,** many had signed a contract before leaving; **therefore** they were not allowed to go back. **Thus** many people were not happy about their situation. **On the one hand** their hopes had not come true; **on the other hand** they couldn't simply leave and sail back to England.

- Die gleiche Funktion haben die Adverbien bzw. adverbialen Ausdrücke *yet* (doch), *so, thus* (so, auf diese Weise), *however* (jedoch), *though* (jedoch), *therefore* (deshalb), *after all* (schließlich, immerhin), *nevertheless* (nichtsdestoweniger), *on the one hand, on the other hand* (einerseits/andererseits), *besides* (ferner, außerdem), *moreover* (überdies), *furthermore* (ferner, außerdem), *consequently* (folglich).

As most of the settlers were not able to leave, they could **either** give up hope **or** make the best of their situation. In this situation, **neither** the Company **nor** other institutions were of any help. **Both** the Company **and** the administration of the colony left them to help themselves.

- Außerdem gibt es noch:
  either ... *or* (entweder ... oder),
  neither ... *nor* (weder ... noch),
  both ... *and* (sowohl ... als auch).

⚠ *However* und *though* können beide ‚jedoch' bedeuten. In dieser Bedeutung steht *though* am Satzende, *however* dagegen meist nach dem Subjekt oder Verb. Beide Adverbien werden durch Kommas abgetrennt.

The English were newcomers on the colonial scene. They managed, **however,** to build up the greatest colonial empire the world had ever seen. Today it has disappeared, **though,** with the exception of small areas like Gibraltar.

Well, what do you think? We can **either** swim, **or** we can try the bridge.

§ 2 Subordinating conjunctions — Step A
Unterordnende Konjunktionen

Während *and, but, or* usw. gleichwertige Sätze oder Satzteile verbinden und daher beiordnende Konjunktionen *(co-ordinating conjunctions)* sind, ordnen Konjunktionen wie *when, after* einen Nebensatz dem Hauptsatz unter *(subordinating conjunctions)*. Vergleiche:

Nebensätze	Beispielsätze	Konjunktionen
des Grundes (adverbial clauses of reason)	**As** it was raining, you couldn't see what the troops were doing, **because** it was too misty.	*as, because, since* (da ja); *as* wird zumeist gebraucht, wenn der Nebensatz dem Hauptsatz vorausgeht.
der Zeit (adverbial clauses of time)	**When** the rain stopped, they saw that the troops were spreading out into a line. It grew **until** it was three-quarters of a mile long.	*after, before, since* (seit), *while, when, till/until, as, as soon as* (sobald) u.a.
der Einräumung und des Gegensatzes (adverbial clauses of concession and contrast)	**Although/Though** it was only a parade, this steady movement had a frightening effect on most of the spectators. **Whereas** the Viceroy remained unmoved by this spectacle, the Amir showed signs of growing excitement.	*although/though, even though* (obwohl) *whereas* (während)
des Vergleichs (adverbial clauses of comparison)	For a minute it seemed **as if/as though** he might draw his sword.	*as/as if/as though* (als ob)
der Folge (adverbial clauses of result)	One of the chiefs who had come down with the Amir was **so** impressed **that** he began to ask how it was done.	*so that/so ... that*

- Einige der aufgeführten Konjunktionen haben je nach Kontext verschiedene Bedeutungen (*as* – da, wenn, als; *since* – seit, da ja).
- Steht der adverbiale Nebensatz vor dem Hauptsatz, wird er meist durch ein Komma vom Hauptsatz abgetrennt.
- Die Wortstellung im Nebensatz ist genau wie im Hauptsatz **(SVP)**.

§ 3 Adverbial clauses and adverbial phrases — Step A
Adverbiale Nebensätze und adverbiale Bestimmungen

Nebensätze der Zeit, des Grundes usw. werden oft adverbiale Nebensätze genannt, weil sie adverbiale Bestimmungen oder Adverbien ersetzen. Vergleiche:

adverbiale Bestimmung	**After lunch**	we went home.
adverbialer Nebensatz	**After we had had lunch,**	we went home.

Beide Möglichkeiten können in der Regel nebeneinander verwendet werden, sie unterscheiden sich nur stilistisch.

§ 4 The subjunctive in subordinate clauses **Step B**
Der Konjunktiv in Nebensätzen

Im Gegensatz zum Indikativ drückt der Konjunktiv keine tatsächlichen, sondern nur mögliche oder gewünschte Sachverhalte aus. Anders als im Deutschen wird der Konjunktiv im Englischen nur noch selten verwendet.

1. The present subjunctive

The British – and other European nations – were convinced that it was their mission to civilize the world. Therefore they **demanded** that people all over the world, **be** they yellow, brown or black, **become** Christians and **give** up their religion. They insisted that everybody **be christianized** and that every nation **follow** the path of European civilization.

- Der *present subjunctive* hat in allen Personen die gleiche Form wie der Infinitiv *(tell – be told)*. Daher steht in der 3. Pers. Sg. kein *-s;* der Konjunktiv Präsens von *to be* heißt immer *be.*
- Den *present subjunctive* findet man vor allem in *that*-Sätzen nach Verben, die eine Forderung oder einen Entschluss ausdrücken. Gelegentlich wird er auch in Nebensätzen der Einräumung verwendet, die nicht mit Konjunktionen eingeleitet werden.
- Der *present subjunctive* ist im britischen Englisch vor allem im Amtsstil anzutreffen. Im amerikanischen Englisch begegnet man ihm teilweise in den Medien (Zeitungen, Nachrichten usw.).
- In einem weniger förmlichen Sprachstil wird er meist durch einen *that*-Satz mit *should* ersetzt.

2. The past subjunctive

This is what the Amir thought when he watched the parade: ***If** only my men **were** so well trained, too. They behave **as if** they **were** not men but animals. **I wish I were** as powerful as the King of England. **If I were** in his place, I'd have an army like that, too.*

- Im *past subjunctive* hat nur das Verb *to be* spezielle Konjunktivformen (*were* in allen Personen). Alle anderen Verben behalten die *past*-Formen. In der Umgangssprache wird zunehmend *was* für *were* verwendet.
- Der *past subjunctive* steht vor allem in irrealen Bedingungssätzen, in adverbialen Nebensätzen, die mit *as if* (als ob) eingeleitet werden und einen Vergleich ausdrücken, sowie in irrealen Wunschsätzen nach *if only* und *I wish* (ich wünschte). Bezieht sich die Aussage auf die Vergangenheit, steht das *past perfect:*

I wish I **had known** that before.	If only I **had been told** before.

§ 5 Conditional clauses with and without conjunctions — Step C
Bedingungssätze mit und ohne Konjunktionen

a) Revision — Wiederholung

- Wie bereits bekannt (siehe GL 2, § 36 und GL 4, §§ 5, 6, 8), bestehen Bedingungssätze aus einem Haupt- und einem Nebensatz, der in der Regel mit *if* eingeleitet wird. Weitere mögliche Konjunktionen sind *unless* (= falls nicht) und *even if* (= selbst wenn).
- Je nach Art der Bedingung oder Annahme, die der Nebensatz enthält, lassen sich Bedingungsätze in drei Haupttypen einteilen:

		if-clause	*main clause*
Typ I	enthält eine erfüllbare Annahme, die sich auf die Zukunft bezieht.	*if + simple present*	*will-future*
		If I **have** time tomorrow,	I **will talk** to you.
Typ II	enthält eine kaum oder nur theoretisch erfüllbare Annahme, die sich auf die Gegenwart oder die Zukunft bezieht.	*if + simple past*	*conditional*
		If I **had** time now, **If** I **were** you,	I **would talk** to you. I **wouldn't look** so angry.
Typ III	enthält eine völlig irreale Annahme, die sich auf die Vergangenheit bezieht.	*if + past perfect*	*conditional perfect*
		If I **had had** time yesterday,	I **would have phoned** you.

- Bei realen Bedingungssätzen (Typ I) steht im Hauptsatz normalerweise das *will-future*. Je nach Sprechabsicht sind auch ein Imperativ oder das Präsens der Hilfsverben im Hauptsatz möglich. Im Nebensatz darf kein *will-future* stehen.
- Bei irrealen Bedingungsätzen des Typs II und III sind das *conditional* und das *conditional perfect* nur im Hauptsatz möglich. Je nach Sprechabsicht können statt *would* hier auch die *conditionals* der anderen Hilfsverben *(could, might, should, ought to)* stehen.
- Beim Typ II ist *were* im Nebensatz zum Ausdruck einer irrealen Annahme in allen Formen möglich. Allerdings wird dieses *were* in der heutigen Umgangssprache zunehmend durch *was* ersetzt.

b) *Should* in conditional clauses

If you **should** meet the butler again, **don't kick** him.
If you **should** kick him again, **you'll have to leave** the club.
If he **should** need a good kicking, we **might kick** him but not you.

- Ebenso wie das deutsche ‚sollte' drückt *should* eine denkbare Möglichkeit aus. Im zugehörigen Hauptsatz kann je nach Sprechabsicht der Imperativ, das *will-future* oder das *conditional* stehen.

c) Inversion in conditional clauses

Should you come to the club again, don't kick our servants. (**If** you **should** come to the club again, …)

Had Britain **not given** independence to her colonies, there would have been wars. (**If** Britain **had not given** independence to her colonies, …)
Had the colonies **not been given** their freedom, they would have fought for it. (**If** the colonies **had not been given** their freedom, …)

- Wie im Deutschen kann bei *should* im Nebensatz *if* entfallen.
- In förmlichem Englisch kann in Bedingungssätzen des Typs III *if* auch weggelassen werden.
- In beiden Fällen tritt wie im Deutschen Inversion ein.

Unit 2

§ 6 Gerunds for adverbial clauses — Step A
Gerundien für adverbiale Nebensätze

Wie bereits bekannt (siehe GL 4, § 11 und GL 5, § 20), können adverbiale Nebensätze zum Teil durch eine Präposition plus *gerund* ersetzt werden. Vergleiche:

After hearing *of the new opportunities,* many people thought of leaving their homes.	*Nachdem sie von den neuen Möglichkeiten gehört hatten,* dachten viele Leute daran, ...
Before arriving *in America,* many pioneers had suffered hardship and persecution in their home countries.	*Bevor sie in Amerika ankamen,* hatten viele Pioniere ...
On arriving *in America,* they wanted to lead a different life.	*Als sie in Amerika ankamen,* wünschten sie ...
Some hoped to become rich ***by finding*** *gold,* others ***by working*** *hard.*	Einige hofften, reich zu werden, *indem sie* ...
Many realized, however, that ***instead of becoming*** *rich,* they would suffer more hardships than before.	Viele stellten fest, daß sie, *anstatt reich zu werden,* ...
In spite of working very *hard,* many of the early settlers remained poor.	*Obwohl sie sehr hart arbeiteten,* blieben viele ...
At first, the companies treated them almost as slaves ***for having paid*** *their passage.*	Anfänglich behandelten die Gesellschaften sie beinahe als Sklaven *dafür, dass sie ihre Überfahrt bezahlt hatten.*

⚠ *For + gerund* kann auch einen Zweck ausdrücken, wenn er allgemein und knapp angegeben wird. Ansonsten steht zur Angabe eines Zweckes immer der Infinitiv mit *to*.

This land is made **for farming.**	This machine was designed **for milking cows.**

Zu weiteren Funktionen des Gerunds siehe **Review 2,** Seite 63–65.

§ 7 Participle constructions for adverbial and relative clauses — Step B
Partizipialkonstruktionen für Adverbien und adverbiale Nebensätze

1. Participle constructions for adverbial clauses with the same subject

Wie bereits bekannt (siehe GL 5, §§ 9 und 10), können adverbiale Nebensätze auch durch Partizipialkonstruktionen ersetzt werden. Dies gilt für alle adverbialen Nebensätze, egal ob sie einen Zeitpunkt, einen Grund o.ä. angeben. Besonders zu beachten sind dabei die Konjunktionen:

Fearing *conflicts with the Native American tribes,* the English government had declared the land beyond the Appalachians as Native American territory, ***forbidding*** *all settlers* to cross the mountains to settle there.

- Beim Ersatz adverbialer Nebensätzen des Grundes und der Art und Weise (Nebensätze, die im Deutschen mit *indem* oder *wobei* eingeleitet werden) werden alle Konjunktionen ausgelassen.

***Having won** the territories west of the Appalachians from the British,* the U.S.A. began to reach out for the west.
***(While) cultivating** the new land,* people were completely independent of any form of government.
In the 19th century many settlers believed that they were following God's will ***when taking** the Native Americans' land.*
Most Native American tribes didn't stop fighting ***until being forced*** to do so.

- Bei adverbialen Nebensätzen der Zeit entfällt *after*, dafür muss das Partizip der Vergangenheit stehen.
- Steht der Nebensatz vor dem Hauptsatz, können *while* und *when* entfallen.
- Steht der Nebensatz nach dem Hauptsatz, so werden *when* und *while* meist beibehalten, um Missverständnisse zu vermeiden.
- Alle anderen temporalen Konjunktionen *(before, until/till, since)* müssen beibehalten werden, um Missverständnisse auszuschließen.

2. Participle constructions for adverbial clauses with a different subject

Adverbiale Nebensätze können auch dann durch Partizipialkonstruktionen ersetzt werden, wenn die Subjekte von Nebensatz und Hauptsatz verschieden sind. Solche Partizipialkonstruktionen stehen meist für adverbiale Nebensätze des Grundes. Sie wirken sehr förmlich und werden nur in der Schriftsprache verwendet. Werden diese sogenannten absoluten Partizipialkonstruktionen durch *with* eingeleitet, wirkt die Konstruktion weniger förmlich und findet sich auch in der gehobenen Umgangssprache:

With more and more people ***coming*** to the new territories, *a period of suffering* began for the Native Americans.
(= As *more and more people* came …, *a period of suffering* began …)

- Bei absoluten Partizipialkonstruktionen müssen die verschiedenen Subjekte beibehalten werden.

⚠ Die Präposition *with* darf im Deutschen nicht als ‚mit' wiedergegeben werden. Für *with* steht im Deutschen meist ein Nebensatz mit ‚da', ‚wenn', ‚wobei' oder ‚indem'.

3. Participle constructions for relative clauses

A large part of the territory ***forming*** *the U.S.A.* today was won by peaceful means.	A large part of the territory ***which forms*** *the U.S.A. today* was won by peaceful means.
In 1803, all the territory ***stretching*** *from the Mississippi to the Rocky Mountains* was bought from France.	In 1803, all the territory ***that stretches*** *from the Mississippi to the Rocky Mountains* was bought from France.

- Partizipialkonstruktionen können für Relativsätze stehen, wenn das Relativpronomen Subjekt des Relativsatzes ist. Das Relativpronomen wird dabei ausgelassen.
- Wie beim Ersatz adverbialer Nebensätze werden bei den aktiven Zeiten die aktiven Formen, beim Passiv die passiven Formen des Partizips gebraucht.
- Ist *to be* das Verb des Relativsatzes, so wird es oft ausgelassen:

A lot of people **(who were)** *willing to face all kinds of hardship were needed.*

Zu weiteren Funktionen der Partizipien siehe **Review 3**, Seite 66–68.

§ 8 Infinitives for relative clauses and indirect questions — Step C
Infinitive für Relativsätze und indirekte Fragesätze

1. Der Infinitiv mit *to* für einen Relativsatz

In 1619, the **first** Africans **to be shipped** (= who were shipped) from Africa to North America arrived in Virginia. They were not **the only ones to be taken** (= who were taken) to the new colony.

- Wie bekannt (siehe GL 4, § 17), kann nach *the first, the last, the only one/ones* ein Infinitiv mit *to* einen Relativsatz ersetzen.

'Roots' is one of the books **to read** (= which you can/should/must read) if you want to inform yourself about slavery.

- Für einen Relativsatz mit modalem Hilfsverb kann ebenfalls ein Infinitiv mit *to* verwendet werden.

2. Der Infinitiv mit *to* für indirekte Fragesätze

When the slaves arrived in North America, they didn't know **what to think of** (= what they should think of) their situation. But they soon learned **how to express** their feelings.

- Der Infinitiv mit *to* kann auch für einen indirekten Fragesatz mit einem modalen Hilfsverb nach Verben wie *to show, to teach, to learn, to tell, to ask, to know* stehen (siehe GL 4, § 14). Das Subjekt des Hauptsatzes und des indirekten Fragesatzes muss allerdings gleich sein.

Beide Konstruktionen werden im Englischen häufig gebraucht. Sie sind kürzer und klingen besser als die Varianten ohne den Infinitiv.

Could you tell me **where to park** the car?

§ 9 The infinitive with *to* for adverbial clauses of purpose and result — Step C
Der Infinitiv mit *to* für adverbiale Nebensätze des Zwecks und der Folge

More and more slaves were taken to North America **to (= in order to) work** the land.

Though slavery was **too** cruel a business **to last** for ever, there were people who were stupid **enough to believe** that it wouldn't be ended.

- Der Infinitiv mit *to* drückt oft einen Zweck oder eine Absicht aus. In dieser Funktion kann er durch *in order to* (um … zu) verstärkt werden (siehe GL 4, § 14).
- Nach *too* und *enough* steht der Infinitiv mit *to* für einen Nebensatz der Folge (siehe GL 4, § 16).

⚠ Ein adverbialer Nebensatz der Folge kann auch durch *so/such … that* eingeleitet werden:

Many slaves were **so** unhappy **that** they tried to kill themselves.
Many had **such** a hard life **that** they preferred to die.

Zu weiteren Funktionen des Infinitivs siehe **Review 1**, Seite 60–62.

10 The passive voice — Revision — Step C
Das Passiv — Wiederholung

1. The formation of the passive voice

The letter **was written** yesterday. It **will be signed** by the President.
It **was being typed** yesterday at 9 o'clock.
It **must be shown** to the President tomorrow. He **should have been informed** about the matter yesterday.

- Wie bekannt (siehe GL 3, §§ 17ff.), werden die *simple forms* des Passivs mit einer Form von *to be* und dem *past participle* gebildet.
- Die Verlaufsformen, die es nur im *present* und *past* gibt, werden mit *to be* und der Passivform des *present participle* gebildet *(being called/ being written)*.
- Bei Hilfsverben steht einer der beiden Infinitive der *passive voice* direkt nach dem Hilfsverb.

⚠ Da das Passiv im Englischen mit einer Form von *to be* gebildet wird, findet man nie eine Form von *to do*. Die Verneinung wird mit *not* gebildet, Fragen durch Inversion. Zu den Formen und zur Verwendung der Zeiten siehe §§ 19 und 21.

2. The 'personal passive'

Wie im Deutschen können alle Verben ein Passiv bilden, denen ein direktes Objekt folgt. Darüber hinaus ist bei Verben mit doppeltem Objekt im Englischen ein sogenanntes ‚persönliches' Passiv möglich (siehe GL 3, § 32):

active voice	passive voice
They showed **<u>him</u>** the letter. They told **<u>him</u>** to read it.	**<u>He</u>** was shown the letter. **<u>He</u>** was told to read it.
indirect object	subject

- Beim ‚persönlichen' Passiv ist das indirekte Objekt (meist eine Person) Subjekt des Passivsatzes.

⚠ Im Deutschen ist diese Konstruktion nicht möglich. Sie wird am besten mit ‚man' oder ‚jemand' wiedergegeben.

3. The use of the passive voice

Passivsätze stellen eine Handlung aus anderer Sicht als Aktivsätze dar. Im Unterschied zu einem Aktivsatz ‚tut' das Subjekt des Passivsatzes nichts, sondern es geschieht etwas mit ihm. Vergleiche:

active voice	passive voice
<u>J.W. Booth</u> killed **<u>Abraham Lincoln.</u>**	**<u>Abraham Lincoln</u>** was killed <u>by **J.W. Booth.**</u>
subject ——► object	subject ◄—— by-agent

- Der eigentliche Handlungsträger im Passivsatz ist der *by-agent*. Er wird häufig ausgelassen, vor allem wenn man ihn nicht kennt, nicht nennen will oder er unwichtig ist.
- Im Unterschied zum Deutschen wird das Passiv im Englischen häufiger verwendet. Passivsätze findet man u.a. in Zeitungsberichten, historischen Darstellungen und technischen Beschreibungen.

Unit 3

§ 11 Verbs or verbal expressions for German adverbs — Step B

Verben oder verbale Ausdrücke für deutsche Adverbien

Im Englischen werden oft Verben oder verbale Ausdrücke für deutsche Adverbien gebraucht. Je nach Art des Verbs oder des verbalen Ausdrucks folgt als Ergänzung das *gerund*, ein *that*-Satz oder ein Infinitiv. Die wichtigsten dieser Ausdrücke sind:

English verb/verbal expression	German adverb
To many people in the U.S.A. immigration **seems/appears to** be	anscheinend
a big problem, **I'm afraid.**	leider
Immigration, it is true, hasn't stopped yet. People **keep on/go on**	weiter
coming in large numbers. They **continue to** cross the U.S. border.	weiter
Most immigrants, however, **don't like/enjoy** leaving their home countries.	ungern
They **hate to** be forced to live in another country.	ungern
They would **prefer to** stay in their home towns or villages.	lieber
Many would **love/like to** go back as soon as they can.	gern
Not all, however, **are likely to** return.	wahrscheinlich
I **suppose** you know that.	vermutlich
Do you **happen to** know any immigrants?	zufällig
I'm sure/certain there are some immigrant children in your class.	sicherlich
I **hope** they have made some friends here.	hoffentlich

⚠ Nach *to hope, to suppose, to seem, to appear, be sure/certain* muss ein *that*-Satz stehen, wenn Haupt- und Nebensatz verschiedene Subjekte haben:

I hope **to visit** her.	**I** hope **(that) you can visit** her.

We **seem to** have lost our way!

12 *Need* as an auxiliary and as a full verb
Need als Hilfsverb und als Vollverb

Step C

1. *need* as an auxiliary

"**Need** I take all these courses?"
"No, you **needn't.** You **needn't** take French this year, and you **needn't have taken** it last year."
"**Did I have to** do Spanish?"
"No, you **needn't have done** Spanish either."

- Hier ist *need* (müssen) und *needn't* (nicht müssen, nicht brauchen) ein Hilfsverb. Es hat nur Formen für das Präsens und das *conditional perfect,* das mit *needn't* und dem Infinitiv der Vergangenheit *(have taken/have been taken)* gebildet wird. In allen anderen Zeiten wird *need/needn't* durch *(not) to have to* ersetzt.
- Im Präsens kommt *need/needn't* nur in der Frage und in der Verneinung vor.

2. *need* as a full verb

Guidance counselors tell pupils what courses they **need to** take and what they **don't need to** do during their school life. John, for example, **needs to** take a lot of maths and science courses if he wants to become an engineer, but he **doesn't need to** take any French.
As the American school system offers a lot of choice, there are always students who **will need** good advice. So guidance counselors **are not** only **needed** now, they **will be needed** in the future, too.

- *Need* kann auch ein Vollverb sein. Es wird dann in allen Zeiten verwendet und wie ein Vollverb behandelt (*-s* in der 3. Pers. Sg. im Präsens, Verneinung und Frage mit *to do* im *simple present/past*). Ein nachfolgendes Verb wird mit *to* angeschlossen.

13 *Dare* as an auxiliary and as a full verb
Dare als Hilfsverb und als Vollverb

Step D

1. *dare* as an auxiliary

"I'm sure you **daren't** go there."
"Who? Me? **How dare** you say that!
How dare you tell me that I'm scared!"

- Als Hilfsverb kommt *dare* (wagen) nur in verneinten Sätzen und in Ausrufen mit *how* vor. Außer dem *simple past* von *dare (dared)* – einer Form, die nur selten verwendet wird – können keine weiteren Zeiten gebildet werden.

2. *dare* as a full verb

There are kids who **don't dare to** go to school because they are afraid of being robbed or treated badly. Why **don't they dare to** complain? Well, they often **don't** because they are afraid of further violence. But if they **dared to** complain, teachers might be able to help them.

- Als Vollverb kommt *to dare* in allen Zeiten vor. Es wird vor allem in Fragen und verneinten Aussagen gebraucht. Ein nachfolgendes Verb wird mit *to* angeschlossen.

§ 14 Revision of modal auxiliaries
Wiederholung der modalen Hilfsverben

- *Need/needn't* und *dare/daren't* gehören, wenn sie nicht als Vollverben gebraucht werden, zu den modalen Hilfsverben. Im Unterschied zu den Hilfsverben *be* und *have*, die zur Bildung der Zeiten gebraucht werden, bringen modale Hilfsverben eine persönliche Haltung zum Ausdruck, z. B: etwas erlauben/verbieten, etwas raten usw.
- Modale Hilfsverben können im Englischen nie alleine stehen. Ihnen folgt immer ein Infinitiv (Ausnahme: *short answers*).
- Der Infinitiv wird ohne *to* an die modalen Hilfsverben angeschlossen (Ausnahme: *ought to*). Siehe hierzu **Review 1**, Seite 60–62
- Die 3. Person Singular der modalen Hilfsverben hat kein *-s*.
- Die modalen Hilfsverben haben oft nur eine Zeitform. Die fehlenden Zeitformen werden von *substitutes* (Ersatzverben) übernommen.
- Modale Hilfsverben haben keinen Infinitiv. Es wird der Infinitiv der *substitutes* verwendet.

Modale Hilfsverben können

• eine Fähigkeit ausdrücken (etwas tun können),	can/can't/cannot	I **can** swim. **Can** you swim, too? No, I **can't.**
• eine Möglichkeit ausdrücken (kann/könnte/vielleicht/dürfte),	can/could/may/might	He **could** come. This **can/could/ may/might** be true.
• eine Schlussfolgerung ziehen (muss/kann nicht),	must/can't	This **must** be John. He **can't** be right.
• ein Verbot ausdrücken (nicht dürfen),	may not/mustn't	You **mustn't/may not** smoke here.
• eine Erlaubnis ausdrücken (können/dürfen),	can/may	**Can** I help you? **May** I kiss you?
• eine Notwendigkeit ausdrücken (müssen),	must/need	I **must** go now. **Need** you go, too?
• ausdrücken, dass etwas nicht nötig ist (nicht müssen, nicht brauchen),	needn't	You **needn't** help me if you don't want to.
• einen Rat geben (sollte/sollte eigentlich),	should/ought to	You **should** go now. You **ought to** do your homework before you go out.
• ein Angebot machen oder sich nach den Wünschen einer anderen Person erkundigen (soll ich/sollen wir).	shall I/we	**Shall** I help you? **Shall** we have a picnic?

Unit 4

15 English equivalents for German *sollen* — Step A

Englische Entsprechungen für *sollen*

Zum Ausdruck des deutschen ‚sollen' gibt es mehrere Entsprechungen im Englischen. Der Grund ist, dass ‚sollen' im Deutschen mehrdeutig ist.

"**Shall I** give you a lift? **Shall we** take your car or shall we take mine?" This was a question often heard during the Montgomery bus boycott.

- Mit *shall I/we* kann man einen Wunsch erfragen oder Vorschläge machen (siehe GL 3, § 11).

"You **shouldn't** take the bus. In this situation we **ought to** help each other."

- *Should* (sollte) und *ought to* (sollte eigentlich) drücken häufig einen Rat oder eine Ermahnung aus (siehe GL 3, § 7).

"You know that African-Americans **are** often **said to be** unable to make decisions. We **are** not **supposed to** be able to complete a plan of action. So let's show them."
In the eyes of most whites the bus boycott was considered illegal; African-Americans **were not supposed to** do anything that could lead to changes. They **were supposed to** know their place in society and to do as they were told.

- *To be said to* und *to be supposed to* können ebenfalls ‚sollen' bedeuten. Sie drücken aus, was man über jemanden oder etwas gehört hat oder denkt (angeblich sollen). Daneben drückt *to be supposed* oft auch eine Erwartung oder Verpflichtung aus.

Thus notices in the city buses told them that they **were to** sit at the back of the bus. If the bus was full, they **were to** stand up and give up their seats to whites.

Among the African-Americans who thought it was time to change this was Martin Luther King, a local Baptist preacher, who **was to** become the famous leader of the Civil Rights movement.

- Mit *to be to* wird eine Anordnung ausgedrückt. Wie bei *to be supposed to* kommt diese Anordnung von außen.
- *To be to* kann auch ausdrücken, dass etwas später geschehen wird. Bei dieser Verwendung handelt es sich um einen erzählerischen Vorgriff auf Zukünftiges.

⚠ Für eine Anordnung kann *shall* nicht verwendet werden.
Es muss *to be to* oder der Imperativ stehen:

You are not **to** sit here.
Stand up!

§ 16 English equivalents for German *lassen* — Step A

Englische Entsprechungen für *lassen*

Das deutsche ‚lassen' ist ebenfalls mehrdeutig. Es kann ‚etwas veranlassen' oder ‚etwas zulassen' bedeuten. Dieser Bedeutungsunterschied wird im Englischen berücksichtigt.

etwas veranlassen	etwas zulassen
The weight of the bag **made him lose** his balance. The woman reached down, grabbed his shirt, and **made him stand** up.	She continued to hold him tight and didn't **let him go.** She only **let him go** when they arrived at her home.

- *To make* drückt aus, dass man jemanden veranlasst, etwas zu tun. *To let* bedeutet dagegen, dass man jemandem erlaubt, etwas zu tun.
- Nach *to make/to let* steht ein indirektes Objekt. Der nachfolgende Infinitiv wird ohne *to* angeschlossen.

⚠ Im Passiv muss bei *to make* ein *to* vor dem Infinitiv stehen:

He **was made to** wash his face.

- Das deutsche ‚lassen' im Sinne von ‚etwas veranlassen' kann im Englischen auch durch *to have s.th. done* ausgedrückt werden. In dieser Konstruktion ist *to have* ein Vollverb, das in allen Zeiten verwendet werden kann.

I don't need I	**to have** **won't have**	**my food** **it**	**brought.** **fetched**	by you.
	have	direct object	past participle	

⚠ Verwechsle *to have s.th. done* nicht mit dem *present* oder *past perfect:*

present perfect past perfect	She has cooked the food. She had cooked the food.	She has the food cooked. She had the food cooked.
	(= She does/did it herself.)	(= She tells/told s.b. else to cook it.)

She usually **has** her hair **cut.**

Today **she's cut** it herself.

- Für ‚lassen' im Sinne von ‚zurücklassen', ‚überlassen' wird meist *to leave* gebraucht:

Leave that to me. Don't **leave** it here.	überlassen zurücklassen

17 English equivalents for German *wollen* — Step B
Englische Entsprechungen für *wollen*

Auch für das deutsche ‚wollen' gibt es im Englischen mehrere Entsprechungen:

"What did you **want** to steal my bag for?" she said to the boy. "I **wish** you hadn't tried."	• Im Englischen verwendet man meist *to want,* um einen Wunsch auszudrücken. *To wish* gehört einer formaleren Sprachebene an und ist umgangssprachlich meist nur in der Form *I wish* (ich wünschte) anzutreffen.
She knew that he wanted her to let him go, but she **wouldn't.** She knew he would run away. "If I turn you loose, will you run?" "Yes'm," he said. "Then **I won't let** you go."	• *Won't* und *wouldn't* drücken eine Weigerung aus. *Wouldn't* entspricht dabei dem deutschen *wollte nicht,* während *won't* die Entprechung zu *ich werde nicht/ich will nicht* ist.

18 Dynamic and stative verbs — Step C
Dynamische und statische Verben

1. Dynamic verbs

Verben, die eine *progressive form* bilden können, nennt man im Englischen auch *dynamic verbs.* Dazu gehören:

What **were** they **doing** in this neighborhood? I **hadn't** actually **been watching** them because I **had been** sort of **daydreaming.**	• Verben, die wie *to do, to watch* usw. eine Tätigkeit ausdrücken. Die meisten englischen Verben gehören zu dieser Gruppe.
It **was getting** dark. It **was growing** cold.	• Verben, die wie *to get, to become, to grow* eine Veränderung ausdrücken.

2. Stative verbs

Unter *stative verbs* versteht man Verben, die normalerweise keine *progressive form* haben. Dazu gehören:

I **saw** them coming up the walk and I **heard** them ring the bell.	• Verben der Sinneswahrnehmung *(verbs of perception),* wie *to notice, to see, to hear, to feel, to taste, to smell.*
I didn't **know** what to think of it. I didn't **understand** what they were doing in this neighborhood.	• Verben, die wie *to believe, to think, to know, to suppose, to understand, to remember, to realize* usw. ein Wissen, eine Vermutung oder eine Meinung ausdrücken.
They had come because of our songs. The older man said that he just **loved** one of our songs and that they **wanted** to buy it and all the records as well.	• Verben, die wie *to love, to like, to hate, to prefer, to want, to wish* usw. eine gefühlsmäßige Einstellung oder einen Wunsch ausdrücken.
As this song **had** never **been** a big success, I **was** glad to sell it.	• Verben, die wie *to be, to have, to belong, to possess, to consist of* einen Besitz oder eine Beziehung ausdrücken.

3. Verbs with stative and dynamic meanings

Einige zum Teil häufig gebrauchte Verben haben teils statische, teils dynamische Bedeutungen. Je nach Kontext und Bedeutung werden sie mit der *simple* oder der *progressive form* gebraucht.

verbs	with a stative meaning	with a dynamic meaning
to think	Why not accept their offer, I **thought.** (denken)	I didn't accept immediately, though, because I was still **thinking.** (überlegen)
to guess	I **guess** you can understand the situation I was in. (annehmen, vermuten)	I **was** just **guessing.** (raten)
to look	The younger man was about five foot nine. He **looked** kind of womanish to me. (aussehen)	He **was looking at** me. (ansehen)
to see	When I **saw** that they wanted to leave, I showed them the way out. (sehen)	You needn't **see** us to the car, they told me. (begleiten)
to taste	When they had left, I opened a good bottle of wine. It **tasted** really good. (schmecken)	Come and **taste** it, it's really good stuff, I said to J.T. (versuchen, kosten, probieren).
to have	I **had** a lot of money now and was quite happy about it. (haben)	The wine we **were having** tasted good, too. (trinken)

§ 19 The progressive forms – Die Verlaufsformen | Revision – Wiederholung | Step C

1. Progressive forms – active and passive voice

tenses	active voice	passive voice
present	I *am calling*	I *am being called*
past	she *was calling*	she *was being called*
future	he *will be calling*	
conditional/future in the past	he *would be calling*	
present perfect	they *have been calling*	
past perfect	we *had been calling*	
future perfect	you *will have been calling*	
conditional perfect	he *would have been calling*	

- Die *progressive forms* werden immer mit *to be* gebildet. Im Aktiv folgt der Form von *to be* das *present participle,* im Passiv *being* + *past participle* (die Passivform des *present participle*). Im Passiv sind nur die *present*- und *past*-Formen üblich.

2. The use of progressive forms

Look, Kevin **is talking** to his friend.	Im Wesentlichen stellen Verlaufsformen Handlungen dar, • die zu einem bestimmten Zeitpunkt der Gegenwart, der Vergangenheit oder der Zukunft im Ablauf begriffen sind,
He **has been talking** for half an hour now.	• die daher noch nicht abgeschlossen sind,
When we came home last night, he **was talking** to his girlfriend.	• die nur als vorübergehend angesehen werden.

⚠ *Progressive forms* sind bei Handlungen, die sehr kurz sind und daher keinen Verlauf beinhalten, nicht möglich. Das Gleiche gilt für Handlungen, die nicht als vorübergehend empfunden werden. Hier muss man – wie bei den *stative verbs* – die einfachen Formen verwenden.

He **lived** in London.	kein vorübergehender Zustand
Yesterday he **had** an accident.	eine Handlung, die keine Dauer aufweist
He **crashed** into a tree.	sehr kurze Handlung

Mr Brown **works** as a reporter for the 'Gazette'.

Mr Brown **is working** on an article about comprehensive schools.

§ 20 The simple forms — Die einfachen Formen | Revision — Wiederholung | Step C

1. The active voice – simple forms

tenses	positive statements	negative statements/ questions
present	*I call* *she calls/he dresses*	*I don't dress* *he doesn't call* *does he call?*
past	*I called/she wrote*	*she didn't call* *did she write?*

- Das *simple present* und das *simple past* bilden die bejahten Formen mit Endungen (Nullendungen im Präsens bzw. *-s/-es* in der 3. Pers. Sg.; *-ed* im *simple past* oder eine unregelmäßige Verbform). Ferner werden – bis auf die Frage nach dem Subjekt – in diesen beiden Zeiten Fragen und verneinte Aussagen mit einer Form von *to do* gebildet. Danach steht immer der Infinitiv.

tenses	positive statements	negative statements/ questions
future	*I'll (will) call*	*she won't (will not) call* *will you call?*
conditional/ future in the past	*I'd (would) call*	*she wouldn't (would not) call* *would they call?*
present perfect	*I've (have) called* *she's (has) written*	*you haven't called* *have they written?* *Has she written?*
past perfect	*I'd (had) called* *she had written*	*you hadn't called* *had they called?* *had she written?*
future perfect	*I'll (will) have called* *she'll have written*	*she won't have called* *will she have written?*
conditional perfect	*I'd (would) have called* *they'd (would) have written*	*he wouldn't have called* *would she have written?*

- Alle übrigen Zeiten werden mit einem Hilfsverb gebildet. Fragen werden durch Inversion, verneinte Aussagen mit *not* gebildet. *To do* darf hier nicht gebraucht werden. Dem Hilfsverb folgt je nach Zeit eine bestimmte Verbform. Nach *will/would* steht der Infinitiv, nach *have* das *past participle*.

2. The passive voice – simple forms

tenses	forms
present	*I am called/it is written*
past	*I was called/it was written*
future	*I will be called/it will be written*
conditional/ future in the past	*I would be called/ it would be written*
present perfect	*I have been called/it has been written*
past perfect	*I had been called/it had been written*
future perfect	*I will have been called/ it will have been written*
conditional perfect	*I would have been called/ it would have been written*

- Das Passiv wird im Englischen mit einer Form von *to be* und dem *past participle (infinitive + ed* oder eine unregelmäßige Verbform) gebildet. Die Verneinung erfolgt immer mit *not;* Fragen werden durch Inversion gebildet.

⚠ Das Passiv ist nur bei Verben möglich, nach denen ein Objekt stehen kann (transitive Verben). Intransitive Verben, d. h. Verben, denen kein Objekt folgen kann (z. B. *to go, to come, to arrive*), bilden wie im Deutschen kein Passiv.

21 The use of the simple forms — Revision — Step C
Der Gebrauch der einfachen Formen — Wiederholung

Während die *progressive forms* betonen, dass eine Handlung noch nicht abgeschlossen und als vorübergehend betrachtet wird, heben die *simple forms* – im Aktiv und Passiv – die folgenden Aspekte einer Handlung hervor:

Das *simple present* steht	Most people **like** music. I **live** in a small town in the south.	• bei allgemeinen Aussagen (auch Naturgesetzen), • bei Handlungen, die nicht als vorübergehend angesehen werden,
	I **sing** a little and **write** songs. When I **get up** in the morning, I first **turn** the radio on. I often **listen** to music in the evenings, too.	• bei beruflichen und anderen Fähigkeiten, • bei gewohnheitsmäßigen und wiederholten Handlungen,
	One morning, a car **passes** my house. It **slows** down, then it **stops.**	• bei aufeinander folgenden Handlungen, z. B. in Erzählungen im Präsens,
	The story 'A white man singing my song' **tells** the story of a black song that **gets** into the 'wrong' hands.	• bei Inhaltsangaben, Buchbesprechungen, Interpretationen u. ä.
Das *simple past* steht	J. T often **watched** TV in the evenings.	• wie das *simple present* bei wiederholten und gewohnheitsmäßigen Handlungen,
	All this **happened** some time ago.	• bei abgeschlossenen Handlungen,
	I **saw** them get out of their car, and come up the walk. Then they **rang** the bell.	• bei neuen und aufeinander folgenden Handlungen. Das *simple past* ist die Erzählzeit im Englischen.
Das *will-future* steht	"**Will** they **come** back?" J.T. asked. "I hope they **won't**," I answered.	• vor allem bei zukünftigen Ereignissen, die vom Willen des Sprechers unabhängig sind,
	"What are you going to do with the money?" – "I'm going to buy some new clothes." – "Oh, **I'll buy** a new shirt then, too."	• zum Ausdruck eines spontanen Entschlusses.
Das *conditional* steht	**Would** they **sell** the song or keep it?	• vor allem zum Ausdruck einer Möglichkeit.
Das ebenfalls mit *would* + *infinitive* gebildete *future in the past* steht	I had no idea what they **would do** with it.	• für Ereignisse, die aus der Vergangenheit betrachtet, später stattfinden.

Das *present perfect* steht	I **have** never **seen** such a great success in my life. "You**'ve made** a mistake," I said to myself.	• für Ereignisse, die in der Vergangenheit begonnen haben und noch nicht zu Ende sind, • für Handlungen, die vorüber sind, deren Ergebnis aber für die Gegenwart von Bedeutung ist.
Das *past perfect* steht	I realized that I **had been** wrong to sell it.	• für Handlungen oder Ereignisse, die vor anderen Handlungen der Vergangenheit stattfanden.
Das *conditional perfect* steht	If I had known, I **would have acted** differently. I **wouldn't have sold** them my song.	• für eine auf die Vergangenheit bezogene Annahme, die rein hypothetisch ist.
Das *future perfect* steht	I **will have lost** some weight by August.	• für eine Handlung, die bis zu einem bestimmten zukünftigen Zeitpunkt abgeschlossen ist.

Register des Grammatikanhangs

Useful grammatical terms

adjective [ˈædʒɪktɪv] — Adjektiv
adverb [ˈædvɜːb] — Adverb
adverb of manner [ˈædvɜːb‿əvˈmænə] — Adverb der Art und Weise
adverbial phrase [ədˈvɜːbjəl ˈfreɪz] — adverbiale Bestimmung
auxiliary [ɔːɡˈzɪljərɪ] — Hilfsverb
defective auxiliary [dɪˈfektɪv‿ɔːɡˈzɪljərɪ] — unvollständiges Hilfsverb
modal auxiliary [ˈməʊdl ɔːɡˈzɪljərɪ] — modales Hilfsverb

article [ˈɑːtɪkl] — Artikel
definite article [ˈdefɪnɪt ˈɑːtɪkl] — bestimmter Artikel
indefinite article [ˌɪnˈdefɪnɪt ˈɑːtɪkl] — unbestimmter Artikel
by-agent [ˈbaɪˌeɪdʒənt] — Verursacher einer Handlung im Passivsatz
clause [klɔːz] — Nebensatz
adverbial clause [ədˈvɜːbjəl ˈklɔːz] — adverbialer Nebensatz

adverbial clause of comparison [əd'vɜ:bjəl 'klɔ:z‿əv‿kəm'pærɪsn]	adverbialer Nebensatz des Vergleichs
adverbial clause of purpose and result [əd'vɜ:bjəl 'klɔ:z‿əv 'pɜ:pəs‿ənd rɪ'zʌlt]	adverbialer Nebensatz des Zwecks und der Folge
conditional clause/ if-clause [kən'dɪʃənl 'klɔ:z/'ɪf'klɔ:z]	Bedingungssatz/ *if*-Satz
relative clause ['relətɪv 'klɔ:z]	Relativsatz
defining relative clause [dɪ'faɪnɪŋ 'relətɪv 'klɔ:z]	notwendiger Relativsatz
non-defining relative clause [ˌnɒn‿dɪ'faɪnɪŋ 'relətɪv 'klɔ:z]	nicht-notwendiger Relativsatz
main clause ['meɪn 'klɔ:z]	Hauptsatz
subordinate clause [sə'bɔ:dnət 'klɔ:z]	Nebensatz
comparison [kəm'pærɪsn]	Steigerung, Vergleich
concord ['kɒŋkɔ:d]	Kongruenz, Übereinstimmung
concord of gender ['kɒŋkɔ:d‿əv 'dʒendə]	Genuskongruenz
concord of nouns ['kɒŋkɔ:d‿əv 'naʊnz]	Numeruskongruenz
conjunction [kən'dʒʌŋkʃn]	Konjunktion
coordinating conjunction [kəʊ'ɔ:dɪneɪtɪŋ kən'dʒʌŋkʃn]	beiordnende Konjunktion
subordinating conjunction [sə'bɔ:dɪneɪtɪŋ kən'dʒʌŋkʃn]	unterordnende Konjunktion
determiner [dɪ'tɜ:mɪnə]	Begleiter
indefinite determiner [ɪn'defɪnɪt dɪ'tɜ:mɪnə]	unbestimmter Begleiter
possessive determiner [pə'zesɪv dɪ'tɜ:mɪnə]	Possessivbegleiter
genitive ['dʒenɪtɪv]	Genitiv
s-genitive ['es 'dʒenɪtɪv]	*s*-Genitiv
of-genitive (of-phrase) ['ɒv'dʒenɪtɪv/'ɒv'freɪz]	*of*-Genitiv
noun [naʊn]	Substantiv
countable ['kaʊntəbl]	zählbares Substantiv
uncountable [ˌʌn'kaʊntəbl]	nicht-zählbares Substantiv
object ['ɒbdʒɪkt]	Objekt
direct object ['daɪrekt ˌɒbdʒɪkt]	direktes Objekt
indirect object [ˌɪndaɪ'rekt ˌɒbdʒɪkt]	indirektes Objekt
participle ['pɑ:tɪsɪpl]	Partizip
participle construction ['pɑ:tɪsɪpl kən'strʌkʃn]	Partizipialkonstruktion
phrase [freɪz]	kurzer Satz, Wendung
position [pə'zɪʃn]	Stellung (eines Satzteils)
preposition [ˌprepə'zɪʃn]	Präposition
progressive form [prə'gresɪv 'fɔ:m]	Verlaufsform
pronoun ['prəʊnaʊn]	Pronomen
indefinite pronoun [ɪn'defɪnɪt 'prəʊnaʊn]	unbestimmtes Pronomen
personal pronoun ['pɜ:snl 'prəʊnaʊn]	Personalpronomen
possessive pronoun [pə'zesɪv 'prəʊnaʊn]	Possessivpronomen
reciprocal pronoun [rɪ'sɪprəkl 'prəʊnaʊn]	reziprokes (rückbezügliches) Pronomen
reflexive pronoun [rɪ'fleksɪv 'prəʊnaʊn]	Reflexivpronomen
relative pronoun ['relətɪv 'prəʊnaʊn]	Relativpronomen
pro-form ['prəʊfɔ:m]	Pro-Form
prop word ['prɒpwɜ:d]	Stützwort
question ['kwestʃən]	Frage
indirect question [ˌɪndɪ'rekt 'kwestʃən]	indirekte Frage
question tag ['kwestʃən tæg]	Bestätigungsfrage
question word ['kwestʃən wɜ:d]	Fragewort
sentence ['sentəns]	Satz
cleft sentence ['kleft 'sentəns]	Spaltsatz
conditional sentence [kən'dɪʃənl 'sentəns]	Bedingungssatz
speech [spi:tʃ]	Rede
direct speech ['daɪrekt 'spi:tʃ]	direkte Rede
indirect speech [ˌɪndaɪ'rekt 'spi:tʃ]	indirekte Rede
subject ['sʌbdʒɪkt]	Subjekt
subjunctive [səb'dʒʌŋktɪv]	Konjunktiv
substitute ['sʌbstɪtju:t]	Ersatzverb
tense [tens]	Zeit
simple present [ˌsɪmpl 'preznt]	Präsens
simple past [ˌsɪmpl 'pɑ:st]	Imperfekt
will-future ['wɪlˌfju:tʃə]	*will*-Futur
going-to-future ['gəʊɪŋ‿tu: ˌfju:tʃə]	*going-to*-Futur
present perfect [ˌpreznt 'pɜ:fɪkt]	Perfekt
past perfect [ˌpɑ:st 'pɜ:fɪkt]	Plusquamperfekt
future in the past ['fju:tʃə‿ɪn‿ðə 'pɑ:st]	Futur der Vergangenheit
conditional [kən'dɪʃənl]	Konditional
conditional perfect [kən'dɪʃənl 'pɜ:fɪkt]	Konditional der Vergangenheit

verb [vɜ:b]	Vollverb
dynamic/stative verb [daɪ'næmɪk/'steɪtɪv 'vɜ:b]	dynamisches/ statisches Verb
introductory verb [ˌɪntrə'dʌktərɪ 'vɜ:b]	einführendes Verb (in der indirekten Rede)
transitive/intransitive verb ['trænsətɪv/ ɪn'trænsətɪv 'vɜ:b]	transitives/ intransitives Verb
verb of perception ['vɜ:b‿əv pə'sepʃn]	Verb der Wahrnehmung
verb of movement ['vɜ:b‿əv 'mu:vmənt]	Verb der Bewegung
verb of rest ['vɜ:b‿əv 'rest]	Verb der Ruhe
verb form ['vɜ:b ˌfɔ:m]	Verbform
infinitive [ɪn'fɪnətɪv]	Infinitiv
gerund ['dʒerənd]	Gerund
non-finite verb form [ˌnɒn'faɪnaɪt 'vɜ:b ˌfɔ:m]	infinite Verbform (Gerund, Infinitiv, Partizip)
present participle ['preznt 'pɑ:tɪsɪpl]	Partizip Präsens
past participle ['pɑ:st 'pɑ:tɪsɪpl]	Partizip der Vergangenheit
progressive form [prə'gresɪv 'fɔ:m]	Verlaufsform
simple form ['sɪmpl 'fɔ:m]	einfache Form
voice [vɔɪs]	
active voice ['æktɪv 'vɔɪs]	Aktiv
passive voice ['pæsɪv 'vɔɪs]	Passiv
word formation ['wɜ:d fɔ:'meɪʃn]	Wortbildung
prefix ['pri:fɪks]	Präfix (Vorsilbe)
suffix ['sʌfɪks]	Suffix (Nachsilbe)

Vocabulary

Lautzeichen (Phonetic symbols)

Vokale (Vowels)

[ɑ:]	father
[ʌ]	brush
[e]	pen
[ə]	away
[ɜ:]	turn
[æ]	bank
[ɪ]	this
[i:]	piece
[ɒ]	shop
[ɔ:]	door
[ʊ]	pullover
[u:]	blue

Doppellaute (Diphthongs)

[aɪ]	right
[aʊ]	house
[eə]	their
[eɪ]	late
[ɪə]	idea
[ɔɪ]	boy
[əʊ]	road
[ʊə]	moor

Konsonanten (Consonants)

[j]	your
[l]	listen
[ŋ]	sing
[ŋg]	England
[r]	red
[t]	sister
[z]	has
[ʒ]	garage
[dʒ]	German
[ʃ]	she
[tʃ]	child
[st/sp]	story, special
[ð]	them
[θ]	thanks
[v]	leave
[w]	week

'	= Hauptbetonung	ˌ	= Nebenbetonung	
‿	= besonders enge Bindung zweier Wörter aneinander			
~	Dieses Zeichen in der mittleren Spalte ersetzt das neue Wort.			
⟨ ⟩	= fakultativ	*(AE)*	= American English	
s.th.	= something	*(BE)*	= British English	
s.o.	= someone	*(coll)*	= colloquial *(Umgangssprache)*	
s.b.	= somebody	*(sl)*	= slang *(saloppe Umgangssprache)*	

Unit 1

A Britannia rules the waves

Britannia [brɪ'tænjə]	(Roman) name for Great Britain	Britannien
empire ['empaɪə]	The end of the British ~ began in 1919.	(Welt-)Reich
upon [ə'pɒn]	on	auf, an
to **include** [ɪn'klu:d]	to bring in as part of the whole	einschließen
Falkland Islands ['fɔ:klənd 'aɪləndz]	a group of islands southeast of South America	Falklandinseln
1 **product** ['prɒdʌkt]	The company exported all their ~s.	Erzeugnis, Produkt
wool [wʊl]	hair of animals, especially sheep	Wolle
beef [bi:f]	~ is the meat of cows and bulls.	Rindfleisch
settlement ['setlmənt]	The settlers built new ~s.	Siedlung
the **Commonwealth** ['kɒmənwelθ]	The British ~ changed in 1931 to the ~ of Nations.	Staatenbund, Commonwealth
Jamestown ['dʒeɪmztaʊn]	The first European settlement was in ~.	*erste Siedlung der europäischen Einwanderer in Nordamerika*
dominion [də'mɪnjən]	a self-governing country of the British Commonwealth	*sich selbst regierendes Land des britischen Staatenbundes*
St. Kitts [snt'kɪts]	name of two islands	*zwei Inseln der Kleinen Antillen in der Ostkaribik*
Barbados [bɑ:'beɪdɒs]	name of an island	*östlichste Insel der Kleinen Antillen*

Victoria [vɪkˈtɔːrɪə]	a British queen	*britische Königin (1819–1901)*
empress [ˈemprɪs]	a woman ruler of an empire	Kaiserin
split [splɪt]	The problem led to a ~ in the party.	Spaltung, Teilung
Pakistan [ˌpɑːkɪˈstɑːn]	a state in eastern Asia	Pakistan
Cape of Good Hope [ˈkeɪp‿əv‿ˈgʊd‿ ˈhəʊp]	a piece of land in the far southwest of South Africa	Kap der guten Hoffnung
Ghana [ˈgɑːnə]	a state in western Africa	Ghana
Kenya [ˈkenjə]	a state in eastern Africa	Kenia
Nigeria [naɪˈdʒɪərɪə]	a state in western Africa	Nigeria
Roanoke Island [ˈrəʊəˌnəʊk ˈaɪlənd]	The first colony of European settlers was on ~ ~ in North Carolina.	*Insel vor North Carolina*
moreover [mɔːˈrəʊvə]	~, the colony was wiped out.	außerdem, ferner
trading post [ˈtreɪdɪŋ ˈpəʊst]	They opened ~ ~s all over Europe.	Handelsniederlassung
master [ˈmɑːstə]	The colonial ~s left the country.	Herr, Meister
nevertheless [ˌnevəðəˈles]	There was no news, ~ she went on hoping.	nichtsdestoweniger, dessen ungeachtet
to **retain** [rɪˈteɪn]	She ~s a clear memory of her schooldays.	behalten, erhalten
furthermore [ˌfɜːðəˈmɔː]	moreover	außerdem, weiterhin
both ... and [bəʊθ ... ænd]	~ Britain ~ the USA ...	sowohl ... als auch
thus [ðʌs]	in this way	so, folglich
colonialism [kələʊnjəˈlɪzəm]	having colonies	Kolonialismus
consequently [ˈkɒnsɪkwəntlɪ]	~, we will make these changes.	infolgedessen, folglich
all the same [ˌɔːl‿ðə‿ˈseɪm]	I enjoyed the party ~.	trotzdem
2 **independence** [ˌɪndɪˈpendəns]	~ Day is a holiday in the USA.	Unabhängigkeit
3 to **connect** [kəˈnekt]	The two towns are ~ed by a railway.	verbinden
to **consist (of)** [kənˈsɪst]	Her job ~s mainly of writing letters.	bestehen (aus)
direction [dɪˈrekʃn]	Are you sure that this is the right ~?	Richtung
4 **Tasmania** [tæzˈmeɪnjə]	an island and state in Australia	*Insel und Bundesstaat in Australien*
Sandwich Islands [ˈsænwɪdʒ ˈaɪləndz]	historical name for the Hawaiian Islands	*historischer Name für die hawaiischen Inseln*
scurvy *pl* [ˈskɜːvɪ]	Sailors used to suffer ~ because they ate too much meat and not enough vegetables and fruit.	Skorbut

B The white man's burden?

burden [ˈbɜːdn]	He was always a ~ to his parents.	Last, Belastung
Oriental [ˌɔːrɪˈentl]	The people who live in the East are ~s.	orientalisch; Orientale/ Orientalin
duty [ˈdjuːtɪ]	What are the ~ies of this police officer?	Pflicht, Aufgabe
cultural [ˈkʌltʃərəl]	to do with the theatre, music, art, etc.	kulturell, Kultur-
barbarian [bɑːˈbeərɪən]	uncivilized	barbarisch, unzivilisiert
manifest [ˈmænɪfest]	clear and obvious	offenkundig, deutlich
destiny [ˈdestɪnɪ]	It was her ~ to die far away from home.	Schicksal
mission [ˈmɪʃn]	sending out a number of people to do a special job	Mission, Auftrag
to **christianize** [ˈkrɪstjənaɪz]	to make s.o. a Christian	christianisieren, zum Christentum bekehren
to **propose** [prəˈpəʊz]	I ~ to start early tomorrow morning.	vorschlagen, vorhaben
Lord Palmerston [ˈlɔːd ˈpɑːməstən]	two times British Prime Minister (1855–58, 1859–65)	*britischer Premierminister (1784–1865)*

	to **enslave** [ɪn'sleɪv]	to make a slave of	zum Sklaven machen, versklaven
	boast [bəʊst]	It is his ~ that he is the fastest runner at the school.	Stolz
	moral ['mɒrəl]	to do with what is right and wrong	moralisch
	task [tɑ:sk]	a piece of work to be done	Aufgabe
	to **direct** [dɪ'rekt]	to tell or show s.o.how to get somewhere	lenken, dirigieren, den Weg weisen
	march [mɑ:tʃ]	They left for a day's ~.	Marsch
1	**military** ['mɪlɪtərɪ]	of the army	militärisch
	claim [kleɪm]	His ~ to own the house was not very strong.	Anspruch; Behauptung
	questionable ['kwestʃənəbl]	It is ~ whether his decision was right.	fraglich, fragwürdig
	gift [gɪft]	I need a birthday ~ for my sister.	Geschenk, Gabe
	individual [ˌɪndɪ'vɪdʒʊəl]	A teacher cannot give ~ attention to the pupils if the class is too large.	eigen, individuell
	item ['aɪtəm]	single unit, thing or article	Gegenstand, Punkt, Artikel
	harmful ['hɑ:mfʊl]	causing damage	schädlich, nachteilig
2	to **request** [rɪ'kwest]	Visitors are ~ed not to touch the paintings.	bitten um, ersuchen um
	Nelson Mandela ['nelsn mæn'delə]	the first black president of South Africa	*Präsident von Südafrika (seit 1994)*
	Aeneas [i:'ni:æs]	the most famous poem of the Roman poet Virgil	Äneis
	Virgil ['vɜ:dʒɪl]	a Roman poet	*römischer Dichter (70–19 v. Chr.)*
	to **address** [ə'dres]	to make a speech to s.o.	jmd anreden, adressieren
	Rudyard Kipling ['rʌdjəd 'kɪplɪŋ]	a British writer	*britischer Schriftsteller (1865–1936)*
	quotation [kwəʊ'teɪʃn]	If you use a ~ in your article, you must name the author.	Zitat
	excerpt ['eksɜ:pt]	a passage taken from a book or an article	Auszug, Exzerpt
	jungle ['dʒʌngl]	You have to cut a path through the ~.	Dschungel
3	**artillery** [ɑ:'tɪlərɪ]	(soldiers who fight with) big guns on wheels	Artillerie
	cavalry ['kævlrɪ]	soldiers who fight on horseback	Kavallerie
	sergeant ['sɑ:dʒənt]	an army officer	Feldwebel
	precision [prɪ'sɪʒn]	It has the ~ of a clock.	Genauigkeit, Präzision
	command [kə'mɑ:nd]	an order	Befehl
	troops *pl* [tru:p]	a group of soldiers	Truppe/n
	Amir [ə'mɪə]	title used by some Muslim rulers	Emir
	bodyguard ['bɒdɪgɑ:d]	The President has a strong ~.	Leibwächter/in
	locomotive ['ləʊkəˌməʊtɪv]	engine for use on railways	Lokomotive
4a)	**Afghan** ['æfgæn]	The people who live in Afghanistan are ~.	afghanisch; Afghane/ Afghanin
	wish [wɪʃ]	She didn't respect the ~es of her parents.	Wunsch
	Afghanistan [æf'gænɪstæn]	a country in southern Asia	Afghanistan
b)	**Bismarck** ['bɪzmɑ:k]	first chancellor of the German Reich	*erster deutscher Reichskanzler (1815–1898)*
	William Ewart Gladstone ['wɪljəm 'ju:ət 'glædstən]	four times British Prime Minister (1868–1874, 1880–85, 1886, 1892–94)	*britischer Premierminister (1809–1898)*
	leadership ['li:dəʃɪp]	Who has the ~ in the commission?	Führung, Leitung
	academic [ˌækə'demɪk]	of teaching and studying	akademisch
	fairness ['feənɪs]	The first thing you have to learn in sports is ~.	Fairness
	commission [kə'mɪʃn]	The university ~ had a meeting last night.	Ausschuss, Kommission
	Walter Wingfield ['wɔ:ltə 'wɪŋfi:ld]	the man who introduced tennis in the way it is still played today	*Personenname (männlich)*
	formulation [ˌfɔ:mjʊ'leɪʃn]	the way of saying or writing s.th.	Formulierung, Fassung

	Marquess of Queensberry ['mɑ:kwɪs‿əv‿'kwi:nzbərɪ]	The rules of modern boxing take the name of the ~.	Marquis von Queensberry *(englischer Adelstitel zwischen Duke und Earl)*
	William Webb Ellis ['wɪljəm 'web 'elɪs]	the boy who first played rugby	*Personenname (männlich)*

C The black man's burden

	butler ['bʌtlə]	a male servant	Diener, Butler
	outpost ['aʊtpəʊst]	a post at a distance from the main body of troops	(militärischer) Vorposten
	Burmese [ˌbɜ:'mi:z]	of Burma	birmanisch; Birmane/Birmanin
	Verrall ['verɔ:l]		*Vorname (männlich)*
1	to **anger** ['æŋgə]	to make s.o. angry	ärgern, wütend machen
	to **suspect** [sə'spekt]	to have an idea or a feeling	vermuten, den Verdacht haben
	to **disapprove** [ˌdɪsə'pru:v]	She wanted to become an actress but her parents ~d of her plans.	missbilligen, ablehnen
2	**comedy** ['kɒmədɪ]	a drama with funny events	Lustspiel, Komödie
	racist ['reɪsɪst]	a person who doesn't accept people of other races	Rassist/in
	swear-word ['sweəwɜ:d]	Stop using ~s in my house!	Fluch
3	to **tend to** [tend]	He ~s to come early.	zu etw neigen, tendieren zu
	to **corrupt** [kə'rʌpt]	Racism ~s people and society.	verderben, korrumpieren
4	**status** ['steɪtəs]	a person's social position in relation to others	Status, (Rechts-)Stellung
	polite [pə'laɪt]	Children should be ~ to older people!	höflich
	royal ['rɔɪəl]	Have you heard the latest news about the ~ family?	königlich
	self-determination ['selfdɪˌtɜ:mɪ'neɪʃn]	deciding for yourself as a nation	Selbstbestimmung
	Versailles [veə'saɪ]	a city near Paris in France	*Stadt in Frankreich*
	Mahatma Gandhi [mə'hɑ:tmə 'gændi:]	leader of the Indian movement against British rule	*Führer der indischen Bewegung gegen die britische Kolonialherrschaft (1869–1948)*
	disobedience [ˌdɪsə'bi:djəns]	not obeying an order	Ungehorsam
	Sudan [su:'dɑ:n]	a country in eastern Africa	Sudan
	Malaya [mə'leɪə]	the western part of Malaysia, a country in southeastern Asia	Westmalaysia
	Rhodesia [rəʊ'di:zjə]	a country in eastern Africa	Rhodesien *(seit 1980 Simbabwe)*
	EEC (European Economic Community) ['i:i:'si:]	The ~ was founded in 1957.	Europäische Wirtschaftsgemeinschaft
	Gibraltar [dʒɪ'brɔ:ltə]	a port in the south of Spain	*Hafenstadt an der Südspitze Spaniens*
	Hong Kong [ˌhɒŋ'kɒŋ]	a British colony in the south of China (until 1997)	*Britische Kronkolonie an der Südküste Chinas*
5	**George V** [dʒɔ:dʒ]	king of Great Britain from 1910–1936	*britischer König (1865–1936)*
	multicultural [ˌmʌltɪ'kʌltʃərəl]	of several cultures	multikulturell

6	**Quebec** [kwɪ'bek]	a city in eastern Canada	*Provinz und Stadt im Osten Kanadas*
	apartheid [ə'pɑ:theɪd]	The blacks in South Africa fought for years against ~.	Apartheid *(Politik der Rassentrennung in Südafrika)*

D The Commonwealth and multicultural Britain

	legacy ['legəsɪ]	You should take care of your grandparents' ~.	Erbe
1	**infrastructure** ['ɪnfrəˌstrʌktʃə]	The railways are an important part of the ~ of a country.	Verkehrsnetz, Infrastruktur
	to **influence** ['ɪnflʊəns]	Don't be ~d by bad examples.	beeinflussen
2	**prestige** [pre'sti:ʒ]	Abraham Lincoln was a politician with great ~.	Ansehen, Prestige
	insult ['ɪnsʌlt]	a remark or an action which hurts another person	Beleidigung
3	**image** ['ɪmɪdʒ]	How can we improve our ~?	Ansehen; Bild
	to **thrash** [θræʃ]	to beat	schlagen, verdreschen
4	**appropriate** [ə'prəʊprɪət]	Sports clothes are not ~ for a wedding.	angemessen, geeignet
	selectors [sɪ'lektəz]	the people who choose players for a (national) team	Auswahlgremium
	Nigerian [naɪ'dʒɪərɪən]	of Nigeria	nigerianisch; Nigerianer/in
	Biafra [bɪ'æfrə]	a region in eastern Nigeria	Biafra
⟨5⟩	forum ['fɔ:rəm]	any place for public discussions	(öffentliche) Diskussionsveranstaltung, Forum
	multiculturalism [ˌmʌltɪ'kʌltʃərəlɪzəm]	~ should be seen as a chance for a country, not as a problem.	*das Zusammentreffen verschiedener Kulturen*
	statement ['steɪtmənt]	Her ~ was useful for the discussion.	Aussage, Behauptung
	non-Brits ['nɒnˌbrɪts]	anyone who is not British	Nicht-Briten
	employment [ɪm'plɔɪmənt]	He was looking for ~.	Arbeit, Beschäftigung
	heyday ['heɪdeɪ]	The 19th centrury was the ~ of steam railways.	Höhepunkt
	career [kə'rɪə]	Her ~ took up all her time.	Karriere
	Ravi ['rævɪ]		*indischer Vorname (männlich)*

Word formation: abstract nouns

-(a)tion	to admire	– **admiration**
	to connect	– **connection**
	to examine	– **examination**
	to imagine	– **imagination**
	to educate	– **education**
	to inform	– **information**
	to introduce	– **introduction**
	to complete	– **completion**
-ness	happy	– **happiness**
	lonely	– **loneliness**
	dark	– **darkness**
-ity	real	– **reality**
	popular	– **popularity**
	similar	– **similarity**
	possible	– **possibility**
	equal	– **equality**
	able	– **ability**
-ment	to employ	– **employment**
	to develop	– **development**
	to arrange	– **arrangement**
	to enjoy	– **enjoyment**
	to agree	– **agreement**
-ing	to understand	– **understanding**
	to begin	– **beginning**
	to record	– **recording**
	to cross	– **crossing**
-al	to arrive	– **arrival**
	to survive	– **survival**
-ship	friend	– **friendship**
	hard	– **hardship**
	scholar	– **scholarship**
-ence	silent	– **silence**
	independent	– **independence**

These verbs/adjectives and nouns belong to the same family!

to **believe** / **belief**	glauben / Glaube	to **hate** / **hatred**	hassen / Hass	to **satisfy** / **satisfaction**	befriedigen, zufrieden stellen / Befriedigung
to **contain** / **content**	enthalten / Inhalt, Gehalt	to **live** / **life**	leben / Leben	to **see** / **sight**	sehen / Sehenswürdigkeit
to **die** / **death**	sterben / Tod	to **perform** / **performance**	aufführen, auftreten / Leistung, Vorstellung	to **succeed** / **success**	Erfolg haben / Erfolg
to **enter** / **entrance**	eintreten / Eingang	to **pray** / **prayer**	beten / Gebet		
high / **height**	hoch / Höhe	**important** / **importance**	wichtig / Wichtigkeit	**poor** / **poverty**	arm / Armut
hot / **heat**	heiß / Hitze	**long** / **length**	lang / Länge	**proud** / **pride**	stolz / Stolz

Unit 2

A With God on its side

	Bob Dylan ['bɒb 'dɪlən]	a famous musician of the sixties	*Musikidol der 60er Jahre*
	economic [ˌi:kə'nɒmɪk]	of economics	wirtschaftlich, ökonomisch
	relocation [ˌri:ləʊ'keɪʃn]	moving, or being moved, to a new place or area	Umsiedlung, Verlegung
	to **emigrate** ['emɪgreɪt]	to leave home to settle in another country	auswandern, emigieren
	hardship ['hɑ:dʃɪp]	The ~ began in the first days of the war.	Not, Elend
	skin [skɪn]	We all got wet to the ~.	Haut
	cattle ['kætl]	They have 50 head of ~ on this farm.	Vieh
	ownership ['əʊnəʃɪp]	I know nothing about the ~ of this land.	Eigentum, Besitz
	Horace M. Greeley ['hɒrɪs 'em 'gri:lɪ]	an American newspaper editor	*amerikanischer Zeitungsredakteur (1811–1872)*
	Jacob ['dʒeɪkəb]		*Vorname (männlich)*
	Jack Schaefer ['dʒæk 'ʃæfə]	an American writer	*amerikanischer Schriftsteller*
	Montana [ˌmɒn'tænə]	a state in the northwest of the USA	*amerikanischer Bundesstaat*
	Nez Percé ['nez 'pɜ:s]	a Native American people	*Name eines Indianerstammes*
2a)	**grateful** ['greɪtfʊl]	I am so ~ to you for your help.	dankbar
3	the **plains** [pleɪnz]	the grassland in the middle of the USA	die (großen) Ebenen im Zentrum der USA
	the **Prairie Belt** ['preərɪ 'belt]	The plains in America are called the ~ ~.	Präriegürtel
	human ['hju:mən]	In this story animals act like ~s.	Menschen
	Bering Strait ['berɪŋ 'streɪt]	water in the northern Pacific Ocean between the continents of Asia and North America	Beringstraße
	common ['kɒmən]	English is a ~ language to the pupils at that school.	gemeinsam, gemeinschaftlich
	to **communicate** [kə'mju:nɪkeɪt]	We can ~ with people in most parts of the world by fax.	sich verständigen, kommunizieren
4	the **Heartland** ['hɑ:tlənd]	The states Illinois, Indiana, Iowa, Missouri are called the American ~.	das amerikanische Kernland
5	**humor** *(AE)* ['hju:mə]	My father has a good sense of ~.	Humor
	to **doubt** [daʊt]	I ~ the truth of this information.	(be)zweifeln
	salmon ['sæmən]	a large fish	Lachs
	to **satisfy** ['sætɪsfaɪ]	Nothing ~ies him, he's always complaining.	zufrieden stellen, befriedigen

B Opening up the West

eastward ['i:stwəd]	towards the east	nach Osten, in östlicher Richtung
westward ['westwəd]	towards the west	nach Westen, in westlicher Richtung
Henry David Thoreau ['henrɪ 'deɪvɪd θɔ:'rəʊ]	an American poet and philosopher	*amerikanischer Dichter und Philosoph (1817–1862)*
to **declare** [dɪ'kleə]	I ~ this meeting closed.	erklären
the **Frontier** ['frʌntjə]	where civilization met the wilderness	*Grenze zwischen der Zivilisation und der Wildnis*
experience [ɪk'spɪərɪəns]	He hasn't had enough ~ for this job.	Erfahrung
spirit ['spɪrɪt]	The ~ of their forefathers is still felt.	Geist
to **cultivate** ['kʌltɪveɪt]	They ~d the land for farming.	bebauen, kultivieren
to **prompt to** [prɒmpt]	What ~ed him to spend all his pocket money on sweets?	zu etw bewegen, zu etw veranlassen
Louisiana [lu:ˌi:zɪ'ænə]	a state in the south of the USA	*amerikanischer Bundesstaat*
Napoleon Bonaparte [nə'pəʊljən 'bəʊnəpɑ:t]	a French ruler	*französischer Kaiser (1769–1821)*
transcontinental ['trænzˌkɒntɪ'nentl]	crossing a continent	einen Erdteil durchquerend, transkontinental
track [træk]	a set of rails for trains	Gleis, Schienenstrang
transportation [ˌtrænspɔ:'teɪʃn]	transporting or being transported	Beförderung, Transportsystem
railroad *(AE)* ['reɪlrəʊd]	railway *(BE)*	Eisenbahn
Central Pacific ['sentrəl pə'sɪfɪk]	name of a railroad company	*Name einer amerikanischen Eisenbahngesellschaft*
Union Pacific ['ju:njən pə'sɪfɪk]	name of a railroad company	*Name einer amerikanischen Eisenbahngesellschaft*
Nebraska [nɪ'bræskə]	a state in the west of the USA	*amerikanischer Bundesstaat*
Promontory ['prɒməntrɪ]	a town in Utah	*Stadt im Bundesstaat Utah*
to **owe** [əʊ]	I ~ it to you that I am still alive.	jmd etw schuldig sein, jmd etw verdanken
growth [grəʊθ]	At what age does an elephant reach full ~?	Wachstum, Größe
2 **region** ['ri:dʒən]	area	Region, Gebiet
Yankee ['jæŋkɪ]	native of the Northern States	Nordstaatler/in
3 **statement** ['steɪtmənt]	Her ~ was useful for the discussion.	Aussage, Behauptung
trapper ['træpə]	a person who hunts animals, especially bears	Pelztierjäger, Trapper
Meredith ['merədɪθ]		*Vorname (männlich und weiblich)*
Zachary ['zækərɪ]		*Vorname (männlich)*

C Slavery

revolutionary [ˌrevə'lu:ʃnərɪ]	The great philosophers often had ~ ideas.	revolutionär, Revolutions-
plantation [plæn'teɪʃn]	a large area of land planted with tea, cotton, etc.	Plantage, Pflanzung
to **abolish** [ə'bɒlɪʃ]	to put an end to s.th.	abschaffen
root [ru:t]	You should pull up the plant by its ~s.	Wurzel
Alex Haley ['ælɪks 'heɪlɪ]	an American writer	*amerikanischer Schriftsteller*
Kunta Kinte ['kʊntə 'kɪntə]	an African name	*afrikanischer Name*

1a)	to **sum up** [ˈsʌm‿ˌʌp]	She ~med up the main points of the discussion.	zusammenfassen
2b)	**Northerner** [ˈnɔːðənə]	Yankee	Nordstaatler/in
	respect [rɪˈspekt]	Children should show ~ for their parents.	Respekt
3	**Henning** [ˈhenɪŋ]	a town in Tennessee	*Stadt im Bundesstaat Tennessee*
	Tennessee [ˌtenəˈsiː]	southeastern state of the USA	*amerikanischer Bundesstaat*
	draft [drɑːft]	She has written the ~ for the President's speech.	Entwurf
	Murray Fisher [ˈmʌrɪ ˈfɪʃə]		*Personenname (männlich)*

D Abraham Lincoln

a	**honest** [ˈɒnɪst]	Please let me know your ~ opinion.	aufrichtig, offen, ehrlich
	destruction [dɪˈstrʌkʃn]	The ~ of the town was caused by an earthquake.	Zerstörung
	*to **bind up** [ˈbaɪnd ˌʌp]	Can you ~ ~ my finger, please?	verbinden
	wound [wuːnd]	She has a knife wound in her arm.	Wunde
	John Wilkes Booth [ˈdʒɒn ˈwɪlks ˈbuːð]	the man who killed Abraham Lincoln	*Mörder Abraham Lincolns*
b	**Gettysburg** [ˈgetɪzbɜːg]	a city in Pennsylvania	*Stadt in Pennsylvania*
	to **dedicate** [ˈdedɪkeɪt]	He ~d his life to the service of his country.	widmen
	battlefield [ˈbætlfiːld]	a place where a battle was fought	Schlachtfeld
	cemetery [ˈsemɪtrɪ]	an area of land used to bury people	Friedhof
1	**dull** [dʌl]	The film we saw was so ~ that I fell asleep.	langweilig
	to **produce** [prəˈdjuːs]	More and more companies ~ software in Asian countries.	herstellen, produzieren
	remark [rɪˈmɑːk]	The most important ~ was made at the end of the meeting.	Bemerkung, Äußerung
	annals *pl* [ˈænlz]	a report of historical events	historischer Bericht, Annalen
2	**amendment** [əˈmendmənt]	This was the second ~ to the Constitution.	Ergänzung, Nachtrag
	reconstruction [ˌriːkənˈstrʌkʃn]	The ~ of the ruined abbey was very expensive.	Wiederherstellung, Wiederaufbau
3	**citizen** [ˈsɪtɪzn]	a person who has full rights in a country	Bürger/in
	means *pl* [miːnz]	All possible ~ have been tried out.	Methoden, Hilfsmittel
	violence [ˈvaɪələns]	~ at school has increased in the last few years.	Gewalt
	ex-Confederate [ˌeks‿kənˈfedərət]	After the Civil War a Confederate was called an ~.	*ehemaliges Mitglied der Konföderierten*
	Ku Klux Klan [ˈkuːklʌksˈklæn]	a secret organization, mainly in the southern states of the USA, which was formed after the Civil War	*Geheimorganisation, die nach dem Bürgerkrieg gegründet wurde, mit dem Ziel, die Vorrechte der Weißen in Amerika zu erhalten*

Any problems?

- The postman **brought** us a letter. — (her)bringen
  I **took** a letter to the post office. — (hin)bringen
- "Can I **borrow** your book about computers, please?" – — borgen, ausleihen
  "Sorry, I've **lent** it to Pauline." — verleihen
- Two burglars **stole** a famous painting last night. — stehlen, rauben
  Thieves **robbed** a bank in the city centre. — aus-, berauben
- "Did you **listen** to the news last night?" — an-, zuhören
  "Can you **speak** louder, please. I can't **hear** you." — hören, *(akustisch)* verstehen
  "Can you **say** that more clearly, please. I don't **understand** you." — verstehen, begreifen
- "I **think** Australia is a wonderful country." — denken, meinen
  "What does soap opera **mean** in German?" — bedeuten

Word building: -ing and -ed

to **care** (for)	sich um jdn/etw sorgen	to **experience**	etw erfahren
caring	mitmenschlich, fürsorglich	**experienced**	erfahren

to **disappoint**	enttäuschen			to **embarrass**	in Verlegenheit bringen
disappointing	enttäuschend			**embarrassing**	peinlich
disappointed	enttäuscht			**embarrassed**	verlegen
to **surprise s.o.**	jdn überraschen	to **tire**	ermüden	to **worry**	beunruhigen
surprising	überraschend	**tiring**	ermüdend	**worrying**	beunruhigend
surprised	überrascht	**tired**	müde	**worried**	beunruhigt

British and American English

Different words:

AE:	BE:		AE:	BE:	
elevator	**lift**	Aufzug	**gas**	**petrol**	Benzin
porch	**veranda**	(überdachte) Veranda	**Mom**	**Mum**	Mama
apartment	**flat**	Wohnung	**cookie**	**biscuit**	Keks
store	**shop**	Geschäft	**freeway**	**motorway**	Autobahn
sidewalk	**pavement**	Bürgersteig	**I guess**	**I suppose**	ich denke
subway	**underground**	U-Bahn			
downtown	**city centre**	Stadtzentrum			
student	**pupil**	Schüler/in			
allowance	**pocket money**	Taschengeld			
janitor	**caretaker**	Hausmeister/in			
principal	**headmaster** **headmistress**	Schulleiter/in			
candy	**sweet**	Süßigkeiten			
backpack	**rucksack**	Rucksack			
vacation	**holidays**	Ferien			
movie	**film**	Film			
pants	**trousers**	Hose			
fall	**autumn**	Herbst			
mailman	**postman**	Briefträger			

Different spelling:

	AE		BE	
	gray		**grey**	grau
	traveler		**traveller**	Reisende/r
	tire		**tyre**	Reifen
	check		**cheque**	Scheck
	math		**maths**	Mathematik
-o	**behavior**	-ou	**behaviour**	Verhalten
-o	**honor**	-ou	**honour**	Ehre
-o	**labor**	-ou	**labour**	Arbeit
-o	**harbor**	-ou	**harbour**	Hafen
-o	**neighbor**	-ou	**neighbour**	Nachbar
er	**center**	re	**centre**	Zentrum
er	**kilometer**	re	**kilometre**	Kilometer
-m	**program**	-mme	**programme**	Programm
-c	to **practice**	-s	to **practise**	üben

Unit 3

A A nation of immigrants

a	**ancestor** ['ænsestə]	My ~s came from Russia.	Vorfahr, Ahne
	to **immigrate** ['ɪmɪgreɪt]	to come to a country as a settler	einwandern
	racial ['reɪʃl]	~ conflicts often end in a civil war.	rassisch, Rassen-
	mix [mɪks]	a mixture	Mischung
	Census Bureau ['sensəs 'bjʊərəʊ]	an office where the population is counted	Büro zur Volkszählung
	origin ['ɒrɪdʒɪn]	Are these words of Latin or Greek ~?	Ursprung
	Cuban ['kju:bən]	The people who live in Cuba are ~s.	kubanisch; Kubaner/in
b	**illegal** [ɪ'li:gl]	If you immigrate into another country without any papers, you come ~ly.	ungesetzlich, illegal
	Asian ['eɪʃn]	The people who live in Asia are ~s.	asiatisch; Asiat/in
	trend [trend]	The ~ is towards higher prices.	Tendenz, Trend
	entire [ɪn'taɪə]	whole, complete	ganz, komplett
	Havana [hə'vænə]	capital of Cuba	*Hauptstadt von Kuba*

	Saigon [saɪˈgɒn]	city and port in South Vietnam, new name: Ho Chi Minh City	*Hafenstadt in Südvietnam*
	elementary (school) [ˌelɪˈmentərɪ]	My daughter is seven, she goes to ~ ~.	Grundschule
c	**income** [ˈɪnkʌm]	You have to pay tax on your ~.	Einkommen
	unemployment [ˌʌnɪmˈplɔɪmənt]	There are many reasons for ~.	Arbeitslosigkeit
2a)	**peak** [pi:k]	the highest point	Spitze, Gipfel
3b)	**famine** [ˈfæmɪn]	Parts of India have often suffered from ~.	Hungersnot
	to **fail** [feɪl]	In the history of Europa many revolutions have ~ed.	versagen, keinen Erfolg haben
	pogrom [ˈpɒgrəm]	violence against a group of people, especially the Jews	*Ausschreitungen gegen religiöse oder ethnische Gruppen*
	Holocaust [ˈhɒləkɔ:st]	The ~ in Germany ended in 1945.	*Massenvernichtung der europäischen Juden durch die Nationalsozialisten*
	discrimination [dɪˌskrɪmɪˈneɪʃn]	Is there racial ~ in your country?	Benachteiligung, Diskriminierung
	Hungary [ˈhʌŋgərɪ]	a country in eastern Europe	Ungarn
	Jewish [ˈdʒu:ɪʃ]	of the Jews	jüdisch
4	**multiracial** [ˌmʌltɪˈreɪʃl]	A country where people of different races live is called a ~ country.	Vielvölker-
5	**promise** [ˈprɒmɪs]	He made a ~ to help.	Versprechen
	dream [dri:m]	She didn't sleep well because of a bad dream.	Traum
6	**ability** [əˈbɪlətɪ]	I do not doubt your ~ to do that work.	Fähigkeit, Können
	tradition [trəˈdɪʃn]	The stories of Robin Hood are based mainly on ~.	(überliefertes) Brauchtum, Tradition
	honey [ˈhʌnɪ]	Do you prefer ~ or jam for breakfast?	Honig
7	to **pave** [peɪv]	This path should be ~d.	pflastern, den Boden belegen

B Prejudices

	prejudice [ˈpredʒʊdɪs]	There is racial ~ all over the world.	Vorurteil
a	to be **likely to** [ˈlaɪklɪ]	The weather is ~ to stay fine.	wahrscheinlich
	to be **sure to** [ʃɔ:]	They are ~ to win the match on Saturday.	sicherlich
	I **hope** [həʊp]	I ~ you will have a great time.	hoffentlich
	I **suppose** [səˈpəʊz]	I ~ I'll be back late.	vermutlich
	Cuba [ˈkju:bə]	an island southeast of the U.S.A.	Kuba
	Vietnam [ˌvjetˈnæm]	a country in southeastern Asia	Vietnam
	to **happen to** [ˈhæpən]	I ~ed to meet some friends of mine at the seaside.	zufällig
b	**opinion poll** [əˈpɪnjən ˈpəʊl]	The latest ~ ~ dealt with social questions.	Meinungsumfrage
	to **confirm** [kənˈfɜ:m]	Please ~ this telephone message by fax.	bestätigen
2	**definition** [ˌdefɪˈnɪʃn]	To give a ~ of a word is more difficult than to show how to use it.	Definition
	identity [aɪˈdentətɪ]	Take your passport with you, you may have to prove your ~.	Identität
3	**attitude** [ˈætɪtju:d]	What is your ~ towards immigrants?	Haltung, Einstellung
	fear [fɪə]	A sudden ~ came over him.	Angst, Furcht
	to **justify** [ˈdʒʌstɪfaɪ]	The Prime Minister ~ied the action of the Government.	rechtfertigen
	Korean [kəˈrɪən]	The people who live in Korea are called ~s.	koreanisch; Koreaner/in
4	**Chanrithy Oak** [tʃænˈrɪθɪ ˈəʊk]		*Personenname (männlich)*
	Battant [ˈbætənt]	a city in Cambodia	*Stadt in Kambodscha*

Cambodia [kæm'bəʊdjə]	a country in southeastern Asia	Kambodscha
to **seem to** [si:m]	Summer ~s to have come at last.	anscheinend, scheinbar
Khmer Rouge ['kmeə 'ru:ʒ]	The ~ ~ won the war against the Cambodian government.	Rote Khmer
Cambodian [kæm'bəʊdjən]	The people who live in Cambodia are called ~s.	kambodschanisch; Kambodschaner/in
refugee [ˌrefjʊ'dʒi:]	a person who is forced to leave his country because of war or political persecution	Flüchtling
Thailand ['taɪlænd]	a country in southeastern Asia	Thailand
obvious ['ɒbvɪəs]	clear	offensichtlich, nahe liegend
Red Cross ['red 'krɒs]	an international organization for helping the sick	Rotes Kreuz
to **adapt** [ə'dæpt]	When you go to a new country, you must ~.	sich anpassen, angleichen
a) to **appear to** [ə'pɪə]	He ~s to have visitors.	anscheinend
to **be certain to** ['sɜ:tn]	I think we're ~ to win the match.	sicherlich, bestimmt

C School systems

level ['levl]	The language practice courses are on a very high ~.	Stufe, Niveau
course [kɔ:s]	Students can choose between many different ~s.	Kurs, Unterrichtsfach
keyboarding ['ki:bɔ:dɪŋ]	It's easier to work with your computer if you have learned ~.	Maschinenschreiben (mit Computertastatur)
compulsory [kəm'pʌlsərɪ]	Is military service ~ in your country?	vorgeschrieben, obligatorisch
geography [dʒɪ'ɒgrəfɪ]	~ was my favourite subject at school because I dreamed of travelling around the world.	Erdkunde, Geografie
civics *pl* ['sɪvɪks]	the study of government, the rights and duties of citizens	Staatsbürgerkunde
physical education ['fɪzɪkl ˌedʒʊ'keɪʃn]	sports at school	Sportunterricht, Leibeserziehung
to **depend on** [dɪ'pend‿ɒn]	Children ~ ~ their parents for food.	abhängen von, abhängig sein von
college ['kɒlɪdʒ]	Students can go to ~ after high school	*Teil einer Universität, höhere Lehranstalt*
credit ['kredɪt]	I need only two more ~s to finish my studies.	*Anrechnungspunkt für den Erwerb eines akademischen Grades an der Hochschule*
to **graduate** ['grædjʊəɪt]	My sister ~d from high school two years ago.	absolvieren, die Abschlussprüfung machen
emphasis ['emfəsɪs]	The ~ is at the beginning of the word.	Betonung, Nachdruck
to **attend** [ə'tend]	Are your parents ~ing your concert?	beiwohnen, anwesend sein
primary school ['praɪmərɪ 'sku:l]	My son is seven, he goes to ~ ~.	Grundschule
comprehensive school [ˌkɒmprɪ'hensɪv 'sku:l]	After primary school we want him to go to ~ ~ .	*weiterführende Schule, entspricht etwa der Gesamtschule*
secondary school ['sekəndərɪ 'sku:l]	where pupils go after primary school in Great Britain	*weiterführende Schule in Großbritannien*
boarding school ['bɔ:dɪŋ 'sku:l]	a school where the students live	Internat
Winchester ['wɪntʃɪstə]	a famous boarding school in Britain	*bekanntes Internat in Großbritannien*

	Harrow ['hærəʊ]	a famous boarding school in Britain	*bekanntes Internat in Großbritannien*
	fee-paying ['fi:peɪɪŋ]	She is a ~ student.	Schulgeld zahlend (…, der/die Schulgeld zahlt)
	critical ['krɪtɪkl]	It was a ~ moment.	kritisch
	Dole [dəʊl]		*Familienname*
3	**literacy** ['lɪtərəsɪ]	the ability to read and write	Fähigkeit zu lesen und zu schreiben
	to **industrialize** [ɪn'dʌstrɪəlaɪz]	Germany is an ~d country.	industrialisieren
	embarrassment [ɪm'bærəsmənt]	the state of being embarrassed	Verlegenheit
	counter-argument ['kaʊntə,ɑ:gjʊmənt]	an argument in opposition to another argument	Gegenargument
4	**graduate** ['grædʒʊət]	He is a ~ of Harrow.	(Hochschul-) Absolvent/in
	bachelor ['bætʃələ]	first university degree	*erster akademischer Grad*
5	**taste** [teɪst]	You have good ~ in clothes.	Geschmack, Vorgeschmack
⟨6⟩	James Thurber ['dʒeɪmz 'θɜ:bə]	an American writer	*amerikanischer Schriftsteller (1894–1961)*
	wolf, wolves *(pl)* [wʊlf, wʊlvz]	There are not many ~es in western Europe.	Wolf
	fable ['feɪbl]	a story in which animals act like humans	(Tier-)Fabel
	cliché ['kli:ʃeɪ]	This article is full of ~s.	Klischee
	to summarize ['sʌməraɪz]	to say or write something in a shorter way	zusammenfassen
	moral ['mɒrəl]	What is the ~ of the story?	Moral, sittliche Lehre

D In a ghetto school

	ghetto ['getəʊ]	All the poor people lived in the ~.	Elendsviertel, Getto
	bonfire ['bɒn,faɪə]	We sang around the ~.	Freudenfeuer
	vanity ['vænətɪ]	Her ~ did not allow her to wear glasses.	(persönliche) Eitelkeit
	Fallow ['fæləʊ]		*Familienname*
1	**communication** [kə,mju:nɪ'keɪʃn]	exchanging information with other people	Verständigung, Kommunikation
	Rifkin ['rɪfkɪn]		*Familienname*
	Lamb [læm]		*Familienname*
	honor student *(AE)* ['ɒnə]	a person who wants to finish his studies with high standard	*Person, die einen besonders guten akademischen Abschluss anstrebt*
	Ruppert High ['rʌppət 'haɪ]	name of an American high school	*Name einer amerikanischen High School*
2	**Travis** ['treɪvɪs]		*Vorname (männlich)*
	to **dare** [deə]	She ~d to ask unpopular questions.	es wagen, sich (ge)trauen
	diploma [dɪ'pləʊmə]	There will be a party after the diplomas are handed out.	Diplom, (akademische) Urkunde
	fist [fɪst]	He held his money in his ~.	Faust

What you do at school

to **call on s.o.**	jdn aufrufen	to **attend a school**	eine Schule besuchen	to **get a report**	ein Zeugnis bekommen
to **do one's homework**	seine Hausaufgaben machen	to **pass an exam(ination)**	eine Prüfung bestehen	to **join a club**	einem(r) Klub (AG) beitreten
to **prepare** for	sich vorbereiten auf	to **have a lesson/ a break**	eine Stunde/ Pause haben	to **take part in an activity**	an einer AG/Aktivität teilnehmen
to **cheat**	mogeln	to **leave school**	die Schule verlassen	to **start training for a job**	eine Berufsausbildung anfangen
to **be good/ bad/ brilliant/ hopeless at**	in etw gut/ schlecht/ hervorragend/ hoffnungslos sein	to **choose a course**	einen Kurs wählen		
to **read s.th. out**	etw vorlesen				

Schools and exams

primary school	Grundschule	**technical college**	technische Fachschule	**GCSE (General Certificate of Secondary Education)**	*etwa:* Haupt-/ Realschulabschluss
secondary school	weiterführende Schule in GB	**YTS (Youth Training School)**	berufliches Ausbildungsprogramm in GB	**A-level (Advanced Level)**	*etwa:* Abitur
grammar school	*etwa:* Gymnasium	**university**	Universität		
comprehensive school	*etwa:* Gesamtschule	**state school**	staatliche Schule	**boarding school**	Internat
secondary modern school	*etwa:* Realschule	**independent school**	freie Schule	**public school**	*BE:* Privatschule *AE:* staatliche Schule, Gymnasium
Sixth Form College	*etwa:* Oberstufe				

Adjectives for describing people

Appearance — Aussehen

tall	groß	**good-looking**	gut aussehend	**ugly**	hässlich
small, short	klein	**pretty**	hübsch	**blond(e)**	blond
fat	dick	**beautiful**	schön	**fair-haired**	hellhaarig
slim	schlank	**well-dressed**	gut angezogen	**dark-haired**	dunkelhaarig

State of mind — Gemütslage

happy	glücklich	**surprised**	überrascht	**bored**	gelangweilt
glad	froh	**excited**	aufgeregt	**unhappy**	unglücklich
pleased	zufrieden	**worried**	besorgt	**sad**	traurig

Character and qualities — Charakter und Eigenschaften

honest	ehrlich	**quiet**	ruhig	**proud**	stolz
friendly	freundlich	**clever**	klug	**boring**	langweilig
sensible	vernünftig	**smart**	intelligent	**shy**	schüchtern
pleasant	angenehm	**hard-working**	fleißig	**bad-tempered**	schlecht gelaunt
helpful	behilflich	**dishonest**	unehrlich	**lazy**	faul
brave	mutig	**unfriendly**	unfreundlich	**stupid**	dumm
modest	bescheiden	**careless**	nachlässig	**cruel**	grausam
interesting	interessant	**greedy**	gierig	**ambitious**	ehrgeizig
thoughtful	nachdenklich	**selfish**	selbstsüchtig	**patient**	geduldig

Unit 4

A Montgomery, Alabama – then and now

a	**Montgomery** [mənt'gʌmərɪ]	capital of Alabama	*Hauptstadt des Bundesstaates Alabama*
	Alabama [ˌælə'bæmə]	a state in the southeast of the USA	*amerikanischer Bundesstaat*
	the **Confederacy** [kən'fedərəsɪ]	the eleven southern states that left the Union in 1860–61	Staatenbund, Konföderation *(der Südstaaten im Sezessionskrieg)*
	to **be said to** [sed]	Cricket is ~ to be very difficult to understand	(angeblich, vermutlich) sollen
	to **be supposed to** [sə'pəʊzd]	Jogging is ~ to be good for your health, but I prefer swimming.	(angeblich, vermutlich) sollen
	Rosa Parks ['rəʊzə 'pɑ:ks]		*amerikanische Bürgerrechtlerin*
	to **have* s.o. do s.th.** [hæv]	I wouldn't have her clean the car.	jmd zu etw veranlassen, jmd etw machen lassen
	preacher ['pri:tʃə]	the speaker in Protestant churches	Prediger
	Baptist ['bæptɪst]	The ~s believe that baptism should be chosen freely when a person is old enough to understand the ceremony.	baptistisch, Baptisten-
	boycott ['bɔɪkɒt]	to join with others and refuse to have anything to do with s.o. or s.th.	Boykott
	Martin Luther King ['mɑ:tɪn 'lu:θə 'kɪŋ]	black Baptist minister who led the American Civil Rights movement in the mid-50s	*berühmter amerikanischer Bürgerrechtler (1929–1968)*
	to **be to** ['bi:‿tʊ]	He was to become famous.	sollen
	Civil Rights movement ['sɪvlˌraɪts 'mu:vmənt]	The American ~ of the 50s became famous all over the world.	Bürgerrechtsbewegung
b	**weary** ['wɪərɪ]	tired in body and mind	müde, erschöpft
	clerk [klɜ:k]	I don't like this bank. The ~s are so unfriendly!	Angestellte/r
	cashier [kæ'ʃɪə]	a person who receives and gives out money in a bank, a supermarket, etc.	Kassierer/in
	gallon ['gælən]	We need two more ~s of juice for the party.	Gallone *(3,79 l in USA, 4,55 l in GB)*
	Wal-Mart ['wɔ:lˌmɑ:t]	name of an American supermarket chain	*amerikanische Supermarktkette*
	rusty ['rʌstɪ]	I have a very old car but it's still not ~.	rostig
	bright [braɪt]	The sun is ~ today.	leuchtend, strahlend
	to **head (out)** [hed]	to move in a certain direction	gehen, fahren
	to **integrate** ['ɪntɪgreɪt]	The Civil Rights movement helped ~ the schools.	eingliedern, integrieren
	forever [fə'revə]	always	auf immer, für alle Zeiten
	official [ə'fɪʃl]	a person who works for the government	Beamte/r
	symbolic [sɪm'bɒlɪk]	used as a symbol	sinnbildlich, symbolisch
	Reed [ri:d]		*Familienname*
	historical [hɪ'stɒrɪkl]	A ~ novel deals with real events in history.	geschichtlich, historisch
	perspective [pə'spektɪv]	You must get the story in its right ~.	Blickwinkel, Perspektive
	segregation [ˌsegrɪ'geɪʃn]	The Civil Rights movement fought against ~.	(Rassen-)Trennung
	to **dress** [dres]	to put on clothes	bekleiden, (sich) anziehen
	sheet [ʃi:t]	Put clean ~s on the bed!	Bettlaken, Betttuch
	overall ['əʊvərɔ:l]	Small children are often dressed in ~s.	(einteiliger) Anzug, Overall
	suit [su:t]	She always wears a ~ to the office.	Anzug, Kostüm

1a)	to **march** [mɑ:tʃ]	The soldiers have ~ed thirty miles today.	marschieren
	to **form** [fɔ:m]	They ~ed a beginners' class of Russian.	bilden, schaffen, einrichten
	to **solve** [sɒlv]	My parents often help me to ~ my problems.	lösen, beseitigen
3	**separate** ['seprət]	The children sleep in ~ beds.	getrennt, separat
	racism ['reɪsɪzəm]	~ is found in many forms.	Rassismus
	strict [strɪkt]	The parents keep a ~ hand over their children.	streng, genau
	Georgia ['dʒɔ:dʒjə]	a state in the southeast of the USA	*amerikanischer Bundesstaat*
	Arkansas ['ɑ:kənsɔ:]	a state in the south of the USA	*amerikanischer Bundesstaat*
	equal ['i:kwəl]	They want ~ pay for the same work.	gleich, gleichermaßen
	improvement [ɪm'pru:vmənt]	I have noticed a great number of ~s in this school since I have been working here.	Verbesserung
	sit-in ['sɪtˌɪn]	Sometimes students use a ~ to demonstrate for their interests.	Sitzstreik, Sit-in
	to **segregate** ['segrɪˌgeɪt]	to keep apart (from the rest)	*(nach Rassen, Geschlechtern etc.)* trennen, absondern
	to **register** ['redʒɪstə]	Where can I ~ for the Italian course?	*(in die Liste)* eintragen, einschreiben
4c)	to **repeat** [rɪ'pi:t]	to say or do s.th. again	wiederholen
5a)	**equality** [ɪ'kwɒlətɪ]	the state of being equal	Gleichberechtigung
	middle-class ['mɪdlˌklɑ:s]	people between the upper and lower classes.	zur Mittelschicht gehörend
	mayor [meə]	head of a city or town	Bürgermeister
	affirmative action [ə'fɜ:mətɪv]	an American programme to fight discrimination against minorities	*amerikanisches Programm, das die Diskriminierung von Minderheiten bekämpft*
	hand-out ['hændaʊt]	a sheet of paper with special information	Handzettel, Werbezettel
	treatment ['tri:tmənt]	Is the ~ of prisoners fair in your country?	Behandlung
	Leroy ['li:rɔɪ]		*Vorname (männlich)*
	Kim [kɪm]		*Vorname (weiblich und männlich)*
d)	**synonym** ['sɪnənɪm]	a word with the same meaning as another in the same language	bedeutungsgleiches oder -ähnliches Wort, Synonym
6	**Harlem** ['hɑ:ləm]	an area of New York City	*Bezirk in New York*
	Langston Hughes ['læŋstən 'hju:z]	a famous African- American poet and writer	*amerikanischer Schriftsteller (1902–1967)*

B Thank you, Ma'am

	behavior *(AE)* [bɪ'heɪvjə]	behaviour *(BE)*	Verhalten, Benehmen
	to **make* s.o. do s.th.** [meɪk]	His boss ~s him finish his studies.	jmd veranlassen, etw zu tun
	to **force s.o. to do s.th.** [fɔ:s]	Her parents ~d her to leave school.	jmd zwingen, etw zu tun
	to **behave** [bɪ'heɪv]	Can't you make your children ~?	sich benehmen; sich verhalten
1	**cause** [kɔ:z]	You have no ~ to complain.	Ursache
3a)	**good-for-nothing** ['gʊdfəˌnʌθɪŋ]	a person who does nothing	Taugenichts, Nichtsnutz
	to **remind** [rɪ'maɪnd]	Please ~ me to answer that letter.	jmd erinnern (an)
	the **poor** [pɔ:]	The ~ live in very bad conditions.	die Armen
b)	**criminal** ['krɪmɪnl]	Thieves and murderers are ~s.	Verbrecher

	to **search** [sɜ:tʃ]	He ~ed through all his pockets to find some money.	durchsuchen
d)	**occasional** [ə'keɪʒənl]	happening from time to time, not regularly	gelegentlich
4	**rap** [ræp]	Many young people like ~.	*Musikrichtung*
	hip-hop ['hɪphɒp]	They only play ~ at that disco.	*Musikrichtung*
	LL Cool J ['el‿'el‿'ku:l‿'dzeɪ]	an American musician	*amerikanischer Rapmusiker*
	beat [bi:t]	In the 60s ~ was very popular with young people.	*Musikrichtung*
5	**controversial** [ˌkɒntrə'vɜ:ʃl]	The environmental group had a very ~ discussion yesterday.	umstritten, kontrovers
	Louis Farrakhan ['lu:ɪ 'færəkən]		*amerikanischer Bürgerrechtler*
	sexist ['seksɪst]	discriminating against others because of their being men or women	sexistisch, andere auf grund des Geschlechts benachteiligend

C A white man singing your song

1b)	**Anna Mae Hawkins** ['ænə 'meɪ 'hɔ:kɪnz]		*Personenname (weiblich)*
	appearance [ə'pɪərəns]	~ is important in the business world.	(äußere) Erscheinung, Auftreten
2a)	to **fit** [fɪt]	This key doesn't ~ the lock.	passen, geeignet sein
4	**stative** ['steɪtɪv]	These verbs are called ~.	statisch
	dynamic [daɪ'næmɪk]	the opposite of stative	dynamisch
c)	**salty** ['sɔ:ltɪ]	If you use a lot of salt, your food is ~.	salzig
	W.C. Handy ['hændɪ]	an American blues musician	*amerikanischer Bluesmusiker*
5a)	**certain** ['sɜ:tn]	I am certain that two and two make four.	bestimmt, sicher
	spiritual ['spɪrɪtʃʊəl]	They often sing ~s in church.	*Musikrichtung*
	to **convert** [kən'vɜ:t]	to change from one religion to another	(zu einer anderen Religion) überwechseln, konvertieren
	Christianity [ˌkrɪstɪ'ænətɪ]	one of the main religions	Christentum
	lead singer ['li:dˌsɪŋə]	a person with a special role in a group of singers	Vorsänger(in)
	bar [bɑ:]	The lines in this music are divided into ~s.	Takt
	gospel ['gɒspl]	I really like ~ songs.	*evangelische Musikrichtung*
	ragtime ['rægtaɪm]	My favourite music is ~.	*Musikrichtung*
	swing [swɪŋ]	It's easy to dance to ~.	*Musikrichtung*
	bebop ['bi:bɒp]	Don't you enjoy listening to ~?	*Musikrichtung*
	soul [səʊl]	Many famous ~ singers are blacks.	*Musikrichtung*
	primitive ['prɪmɪtɪv]	simple, basic	einfach, primitiv
	respectable [rɪ'spektəbl]	No ~ person would do that.	ehrbar, anständig
⟨6⟩	rhythm'n'blues ['rɪðəm‿n‿'blu:z]	I like to listen to ~ music.	*Musikrichtung*
	hound (dog) ['haʊnd ('dɒg)]	a dog used for hunting	Jagdhund
	Big Mama Thornton ['bɪg 'mæmə 'θɔ:ntən]	an African-American blues singer	*amerikanische Bluessängerin*
	verse [vɜ:s]	A poem is always written in ~s.	Vers, Strophe
⟨7⟩	M.C. Hammer ['hæmə]	an African-American rap musician	*amerikanischer Rapmusiker*
	Trina Johnson ['tri:nə 'dʒɒnsən]	an African-American gospel singer	*amerikanische Gospelsängerin*

Note the following word pairs!

slavery Sklaverei	≠ **freedom** Freiheit		**segregation** Trennung	≠ **integration** Eingliederung		**life** Leben	≠ **death** Tod
question Frage	≠ **answer** Antwort		**war** Krieg	≠ **peace** Frieden		**opponent** Gegner/in	≠ **supporter** Anhänger/in
to **separate** trennen	≠ to **unite** vereinigen		to **import** importieren	≠ to **export** exportieren		to **permit** zulassen	≠ to **forbid** verbieten
to **join** beitreten	≠ to **leave** verlassen		to **introduce** einführen	≠ to **abolish** abschaffen		to **open** öffnen	≠ to **close** schließen

Examples of colloquial English

I'm gonna	=	I'm going to
you gotta	=	you have to got to
there ain't	=	there isn't, there aren't
you wanna	=	you want to

No dice! / No way! / You're kidding!
Hi, you guys! / Howdy, folks!
Gee! / Gosh! / Wow! / Yeah! / Sure! / You bet!
dear, baby, honey, love (BE), son, dad, etc. *(als Anrede)*

Be careful with these words!

New Orleans is one of the most important **ports** in the U.S.	Hafen(stadt)
Our hotel had a nice view of the **harbor**.	(natürlicher) Hafen
Evanston is **between** Chicago and Milwaukee.	zwischen (zwei Personen oder Sachen)
Mansfield is a nice village **among** the hills.	zwischen (mehrere Personen oder Sachen)
Peter won first **prize** in the chess competition.	Preis (den man gewinnt)
The **price** of corn has fallen in the past few years.	Preis (den man bezahlt)
The Mendozas have lived in San Antonio **since** 1985.	seit (einem Zeitpunkt)
Carlos Alvarez has worked here **for** 25 years.	seit (einem Zeitraum)

Alphabetical word list

In dieser alphabetischen Wortliste ist das gesamte Vokabular von **Green Line 1–6, Ausgabe Bayern** enthalten.
- Die Zahlen verweisen auf das erstmalige Vorkommen der Wörter. Kommt ein Wort in zwei verschiedenen Bedeutungen vor, sind beide Belegstellen ausgewiesen:
  wish VI 1B 10,4a Wunsch
  VI = Band 6, **1B** = *Unit* 1, *Step* B; 10,4a = Seite 10, Übung 4a
  Neben den Angaben *Unit* und *Step*, gibt es noch folgende Abkürzungen:
  FS = *First Scenes* (Band 1), **FF** = *Festivals* (Band 3), **AB** = *History/Politics* (Bände 4 und 5).
- Das Zeichen * nach einem Verb weist darauf hin, dass dieses Verb unregelmäßig ist.
  Die Formen des *simple past* und *past participle* sind in der **List of irregular verbs** auf Seite 147 zu finden.
- Die Zeichen ⟨ ⟩ bei einer Angabe weisen darauf hin, dass das Wort fakultativ ist.
  (AE) = American English, (BE) = British English

A

a [ə; eɪ] **I FS4** 12 ein/e
abbey ['æbɪ] **IV 3C** 41 Kloster, Abteikirche
abbot ['æbət] **IV 3AB** 46 Abt
abbreviation [əˌbri:vɪ'eɪʃn] **IV 4D** 61,4 Abkürzung
ability [ə'bɪlətɪ] **VI 3A** 36,6 Fähigkeit, Können
to be **able to** ['eɪbl] **II 7B** 94 können, fähig sein
to **abolish** [ə'bɒlɪʃ] **VI 2C** 28 abschaffen
about [ə'baʊt] **II 2B** 24,6 circa; von, über
How about ...? [ˌhaʊ ə'baʊt] **III 3A** 34 Wie wäre es mit ...?
What about ...? **I FS7** 18 Wie steht's mit ...?
above [ə'bʌv] **III 6A** 71 über; oben, darüber
abroad [ə'brɔ:d] **III 2A** 21,1 im/ins Ausland
absolutely ['æbsəlu:tlɪ] **IV 6B** 79 völlig, absolut
abstract ['æbstrækt] **III 3B** 37 abstrakt
academic [ˌækə'demɪk] **VI 1B** 11 akademisch
accent ['æksənt] **II 6A** 78,2 Akzent
to **accept** [ək'sept] **IV 3AB** 48 annehmen, akzeptieren
accident ['æksɪdənt] **I 7C** 110 Unfall
⟨accidently⟩ [ˌæksɪ'dentlɪ] **I FS10** 28,3 versehentlich
according to [ə'kɔ:dɪŋ] **V 2C** 25,1 laut, gemäß
accurate ['ækjʊrət] **III 6AB** 82 genau
to **accuse** [ə'kju:z] **IV 3AB** 48 beschuldigen, anklagen
across [ə'krɒs] **I 7B** 108,6 über
to **act** [ækt] **I 7A** 104,5 (vor-)spielen
action ['ækʃn] **IV 5D** 74,2 Handlungsablauf
activity [æk'tɪvɪtɪ] **III 4B** 49 Unternehmung, Veranstaltung
actor ['æktə] **II 7A** 91 Schauspieler
actress ['æktrɪs] **V 4A** 50,4 Schauspielerin
actual ['æktʃʊəl] **IV 5D** 77,10 wirklich, tatsächlich
actually ['æktʃʊəlɪ] **II 7B** 94 eigentlich
⟨ad⟩ [æd] **III 7FE** 104 Anzeige
AD ['eɪ'di:] **IV 1A** 8,5 Anno Domini, nach Christi Geburt
to **adapt** [ə'dæpt] **VI 3B** 39,4 sich anpassen, angleichen
to **add** [æd] **I 4A** 67,2 dazutun, addieren
additional [ə'dɪʃənl] **V 2B** 23,2 zusätzlich, ergänzend
address [ə'dres] **I 2B** 46 Adresse
to **address** [ə'dres] **VI 1B** 9 jmd anreden, adressieren
adjective ['ædʒɪktɪv] **I 7A** 104,6 Adjektiv
to **adjust** [ə'dʒʌst] **II 4B** 50,2 einstellen
administration [ədˌmɪnɪ'streɪʃn] **V 5AB** 76 Verwaltung, Administration
admiration [ˌædmə'reɪʃn] **IV 6D** 87,3 Bewunderung
to **admire** [əd'maɪə] **IV 6D** 85 bewundern
to **admit** [əd'mɪt] **IV 4AB** 64 zugeben, zulassen
adult ['ædʌlt] **II 5C** 71,8 Erwachsene/r
advantage [əd'va:ntɪdʒ] **V 5AB** 78 Vorteil
adventure [əd'ventʃə] **II 2C** 27,2 Abenteuer
ad(*vertisement*) [æd, (əd'vɜ:tɪsmənt)] **III 6A** 72,4 Werbung, Reklame, Anzeige
advice [əd'vaɪs] **III 2A** 21,2 Rat (-schlag)
to **advise** [əd'vaɪz] **III 5B** 61,5 raten, beraten
aeroplane (*BE*) ['eərəpleɪn] **IV 5D** 76,8 Flugzeug
affirmative action [ə'fɜ:mətɪv] **VI 4A** 49,5 *amerikanisches Programm, das die Diskriminierung von Minderheiten bekämpft*
Afghan ['æfgæn] **VI 1B** 10,4 afghanisch; Afghane/Afghanin
to be **afraid** [ə'freɪd] **I 2C** 50,6 Angst haben
I'm **afraid** **I 4C** 72,6 leider
African ['æfrɪkən] **IV 1B** 11,6 afrikanisch; Afrikaner/in
after ['a:ftə] **I 3C** 59 nach
after all **I 2C** 49,3 überhaupt, schließlich
to look after **I 4A** 66,3 auf jdn aufpassen
to rush after **I 3B** 57 hinter jdm hereilen
afternoon [ˌa:ftə'nu:n] **I FS7** 18 Nachmittag
again [ə'gen] **I 3A** 54,1 wieder
against [ə'genst] **II 5C** 67 gegen
age [eɪdʒ] **II 7A** 91 Alter
agency ['eɪdʒənsɪ] **IV 4B** 54 (Handels-)Vertretung, Agentur
travel **agent** ['trævl ˌeɪdʒənt] **I 7A** 104,5 Reisebürokaufmann/-frau
travel **agent's** **I 7A** 104,5 Reisebüro
aggressive [ə'gresɪv] **V 3B** 33 aggressiv, angriffslustig
ago [ə'gəʊ] **I 8B** 118 vor
to **agree** [ə'gri:] **II 3C** 35 einverstanden sein
agriculture ['ægrɪkʌltʃə] **IV 4A** 53,4 Landwirtschaft
ahead (*of*) [ə'hed] **II 8C** 108 vor, voran
go **ahead** [ˌgəʊ‿ə'hed] **I 7A** 104,5 Nur zu!
first **aid** [ˌfɜ:st 'eɪd] **III 4A** 46 erste Hilfe
Aids [eɪdz] **V 1A** 9,7 *tödliche Immunschwächekrankheit*
to **aim** [eɪm] **III 7C** 90 zielen; anstreben
air [eə] **I 3B** 57 Luft
air-conditioning ['eəkənˌdɪʃənɪŋ] **III 6A** 70 Klimaanlage
airplane (*AE*) ['eəpleɪn] **IV 5D** 76,8 Flugzeug
airport ['eəpɔ:t] **I 7A** 104,6 Flughafen
alarm [ə'la:m] **IV 5D** 73 Alarmanlage
alarm clock [ə'la:mklɒk] **IV 2B** 26,2 Wecker
to **alarm** [ə'la:m] **V 5AB** 75 alarmieren, beunruhigen
alcohol ['ælkəhɒl] **V 1C** 15,2 Alkohol
alive [ə'laɪv] **IV 2A** 22 lebend, am Leben
all [ɔ:l] **I FS10** 28,1 all/es
all over [ˌɔ:l'əʊvə] **II 6B** 80 überall in ...
after all **I 2C** 49,3 überhaupt, schließlich
all about **II 4B** 49 alles über
all right [ˌɔ:l 'raɪt] **III 3A** 35 in Ordnung
all round him **I 6D** 97 um ihn herum
all the same [ˌɔ:l‿ðə‿'seɪm] **VI 1A** 6 einerlei, ganz gleich
all the time **II 6B** 80 die ganze Zeit
Let's all push. **I 1C** 40,6 Lasst uns alle schieben.
not ... at all **I 5C** 85 (ganz und) gar nicht

alligator ['ælɪgeɪtə] **III 7C** 92,6 Alligator
to **allow** [ə'laʊ] **IV 2A** 22 erlauben, gestatten
to be **allowed to*** [ə'laʊd] **II 5A** 60 dürfen, erlaubt sein
almost ['ɔ:lməʊst] **II 4C** 53 fast, beinahe
alone [ə'ləʊn] **I 4A** 66,2 allein
along [ə'lɒŋ] **IV 1AB** 19 entlang
alphabet ['ælfəbet] **I 1C** 43 Alphabet
already [ɔ:l'redɪ] **II 2C** 25 schon
also ['ɔ:lsəʊ] **II 8B** 105 auch
although [ɔ:l'ðəʊ] **III 6D** 79 obwohl, obgleich
⟨altogether⟩ [ˌɔ:ltə'geðə] **III 7FE** 99 ganz und gar
always ['ɔ:lweɪz] **I 1C** 39,4 immer
am* [æm] **I FS2** 9 bin
a.m. [ˌeɪ 'em] **III 2D** 27 vormittags, morgens
to **amaze** [ə'meɪz] **V 4D** 59,4 verblüffen, erstaunen
ambulance ['æmbjʊləns] **III 4A** 46 Krankenwagen
amendment [ə'mendmənt] **VI 2D** 32,2 Ergänzung, Nachtrag
American [ə'merɪkən] **I 7B** 108,6 amerikanisch, Amerikaner/in
Amir [ə'mɪə] **VI 1B** 10,3 Emir
ammonite ['æmənaɪt] **IV 3C** 43,2 Ammonit, Ammonshorn
among [ə'mʌŋ] **IV 3C** 42 inmitten (von)
⟨among⟩ [ə'mʌŋ] **III 3C** 44,9 unter, in
amount [ə'maʊnt] **IV 4AB** 64 Betrag, Summe
ancestor ['ænsestə] **VI 3A** 33,a) Vorfahr, Ahne
⟨to anchor⟩ ['æŋkə] **III 7FE** 105 ankern
and [ænd; ənd] **I FS9** 9,3 und
to **anger** ['æŋgə] **VI 1C** 12,1 ärgern, wütend machen
Anglican ['æŋglɪkən] **V 5AB** 74 anglikanisch
Anglo-Saxon [ˌæŋgləʊ'sæksən] **IV 1AB** 19 angelsächsisch
angry ['æŋgrɪ] **I 1C** 40,7 böse, verärgert
animal ['ænɪml] **II 1C** 11,1 Tier
ankle ['æŋkl] **V 5C** 65 Fußknöchel
annals *pl* ['ænlz] **VI 2D** 32,1 historischer Bericht, Annalen
announcer [ə'naʊnsə] **II 6C** 82 Ansager/in
to **annoy** [ə'nɔɪ] **IV 4D** 60,2 ärgern
annual ['ænjʊəl] **II 7A** 91 Jahrbuch
anorak ['ænəræk] **I 4C** 71,1 Anorak
another [ə'nʌðə] **I 2B** 46 noch ein; ein anderes
answer ['ɑ:nsə] **I FS3** 11,1 Antwort
to **answer** **I FS5** 14 antworten
  to answer the telephone **I 2B** 6,4 ans Telefon gehen
anti-foreign ['æntɪˌfɒrən] **V 2C** 25,2 fremdenfeindlich, ausländerfeindlich
⟨anvil⟩ ['ænvɪl] **I 7** 102 Amboss
any ['enɪ] **I 6B** 92,3 (irgend-)ein/e/es
any more [ˌenɪ 'mɔ:] **II 4B** 49 sonst noch
anybody, anyone ['enɪbɒdɪ, 'enɪwʌn] **II 2C** 26 (irgend-)jemand
anything ['enɪθɪŋ] **I 6C** 94,2 irgendetwas
anyway ['enɪweɪ] **I 7B** 105 sowieso
anyway ['enɪweɪ] **III 1C** 14 jedenfalls, wie dem auch sei
⟨apart⟩ [ə'pɑ:t] **III 7FE** 104 getrennt
apart from [ə'pɑ:t frɒm] **IV 6D** 86 getrennt von
apartheid [ə'pɑ:theɪd] **VI 1C** 14,6 Apartheid *(Politik der Rassentrennung in Südafrika)*
apartment (*AE*) [ə'pɑ:tmənt] **V 4C** 55 Wohnung, Apartment
  apartment building [ə'pɑ:tmənt ˌbɪldɪŋ] **IV 5B** 66 Wohnhaus
to **apologize** [ə'pɒlədʒaɪz] **IV 6B** 79 sich entschuldigen
to **appear** [ə'pɪə] **IV 3B** 38 erscheinen, auftreten
  to appear to [ə'pɪə] **VI 3B** 39,4 anscheinend
appearance [ə'pɪərəns] **VI 4C** 57,1 (äußere) Erscheinung, Auftreten
appendix [ə'pendɪks] **III 4B** 49 Blinddarm
appetite ['æpɪtaɪt] **II 6A** 76 Appetit
apple ['æpl] **I 4C** 71,2 Apfel
applicant ['æplɪkənt] **IV 4B** 55,2 Bewerber/in
application [ˌæplɪ'keɪʃn] **IV 4B** 54 Bewerbung
to **apply for** [ə'plaɪ] **IV 4B** 54 sich bewerben um
to **appoint** [ə'pɔɪnt] **V 5AB** 76 ernennen, berufen
appointment [ə'pɔɪntmənt] **II 3A** 30 Termin, Verabredung
  to make an appointment **II 3A** 30 einen Termin vereinbaren
appropriate [ə'prəʊprɪət] **VI 1D** 18,4 angemessen, geeignet
apron ['eɪprən] **IV 5C** 71,3 Schürze
aquarium [ə'kweərɪəm] **III 5D** 69,9 Aquarium
Arab ['ærəb] **V 2C** 24 arabisch; Araber/in
archbishop [ˌɑ:tʃ'bɪʃəp] **V 3AB** 43 Erzbischof
architect ['ɑ:kɪtekt] **V 5B** 63 Architekt/in
architecture ['ɑ:kɪtektʃə] **V 3A** 31,3 Architektur
are* [ɑ:; ə] **I FS3** 10 sind
area ['eərɪə] **III 2A** 22 Gebiet, Bereich, Zone
aren't* [ɑ:nt] **I FS5** 14 sind nicht
to **argue** ['ɑ:gju:] **IV 6B** 81,5 streiten, sich auseinander setzen
argument ['ɑ:gjʊmənt] **IV 2C** 30,5 Wortwechsel, Auseinandersetzung, Streit
aristocracy [ˌærɪ'stɒkrəsɪ] **V 3AB** 45 Adel, Aristokratie
arm [ɑ:m] **I FS6** 16 Arm
army ['ɑ:mɪ] **V 4A** 51,6 Armee
around [ə'raʊnd] **I 7B** 106,2 herum
to **arrange** [ə'reɪndʒ] **IV 2C** 31,8 planen, arrangieren
arrangement [ə'reɪndʒmənt] **IV 3C** 41 Vorbereitung
to **arrest** [ə'rest] **II 2B** 21 gefangen nehmen
arrival [ə'raɪvl] **IV 3A** 34 Ankunft
  arrival hall [ə'raɪvl ˌhɔ:l] **II 6B** 80 Ankunftshalle
to **arrive** (*at*) [ə'raɪv‿ət] **I 4B** 69,1 ankommen (in, bei)
arrow ['ærəʊ] **II 2C** 25 Pfeil
art [ɑ:t] **III 3A** 34 Kunst
article ['ɑ:tɪkl] **III 4A** 48 Artikel; Ware
artillery [ɑ:'tɪlərɪ] **VI 1B** 10,3 Artillerie
artist ['ɑ:tɪst] **II 7C** 97 Künstler/in
as [æz; əz] **III 2C** 24 als
  as ... as [æz] **II 2A** 19 so ... wie
  as soon as [əz 'su:n ˌəz] **III 4B** 49 sobald (wie)
ash [æʃ] **V 4D** 59,4 Asche
  ash-tray ['æʃtreɪ] **II 4A** 47 Aschenbecher
Asian ['eɪʃn] **VI 3A** 33,b) asiatisch; Asiat(in)
to **ask** [ɑ:sk] **I FS4** 12,1 fragen
  to ask for [ɑ:sk] **II 6A** 78,4 bitten um
to be **asleep** [ə'sli:p] **III 7C** 89 eingeschlafen, schlafend
assistant [ə'sɪstənt] **IV 4B** 55,2 Assistent/in, Mitarbeiter/in
astern [ə'stɜ:n] **III 2D** 26 achtern, achteraus
astronaut ['æstrənɔ:t] **II 6D** 87,5 Astronaut/in
astronomy [ə'strɒnəmɪ] **IV 3A** 36,4 Astronomie, Sternenkunde
at [æt; ət] bei
  at Alison's [ət‿'ælɪsnz] **IV 2C** 28 bei Alison
  at Barbara's house **I 2C** 49,1 bei Barbara zu Hause
  at half past seven **I 3A** 54,1 um halb acht
  at home **I FS7** 18 zu Hause
  at last **I 2C** 49,2 zuletzt
  at least [li:st] **II 4C** 53 mindestens
  at night **I FS7** 18 nachts
  at once **I 3C** 59 sofort
  at school **I FS7** 20,5 in der Schule
  at the bottom **II 1D** 13 unten
  at the bus stop **I 5C** 99 an der Haltestelle
  at the moment **I 6D** 99,6 im Augenblick
  at the window ['wɪndəʊ] **I FS8** 23 am Fenster
  at weekends ['wi:kendz] **II 3D** 38 am Wochenende
  not ... at all **I 5C** 85 (ganz und) gar nicht
⟨Atishoo!⟩ [ə'tɪʃu:] **III 4C** 53 Hatschi!
atmosphere ['ætməˌsfɪə] **IV 3B** 38 Atmosphäre
to **attack** [ə'tæk] **III 2AB** 32 angreifen
to **attend** [ə'tend] **VI 3C** 40 beiwohnen, anwesend sein
attention [ə'tenʃn] **V 1B** 11 Aufmerksamkeit
attic ['ætɪk] **I 1C** 39,4 Dachboden
⟨attitude⟩ ['ætɪtju:d] **IV 6D** 88,5 Haltung
  attitude ['ætɪtju:d] **VI 3B** 38,3 Haltung, Einstellung
to **attract** [ə'trækt] **V 1B** 11 anziehen, anlocken
attraction [ə'trækʃn] **IV 5C** 70 Attraktion
attractive [ə'træktɪv] **V 3A** 30 attraktiv, anziehend
to **attribute** (*to*) [ə'trɪbju:t] **V 4A** 48 zuschreiben, beimessen
audience ['ɔ:djəns] **IV 1C** 13 Publikum, Zuhörer
aunt [ɑ:nt] **I 7A** 102 Tante
Austrian ['ɒstrɪən] **IV 1B** 11,6 österreichisch; Österreicher/in

⟨authentic⟩ [ɔːˈθentɪk] **I 2** 47 echt, authentisch
author [ˈɔːθə] **V 3AB** 46 Autor/in
to **authorize** [ˈɔːθəraɪz] **V 4B** 52 ermächtigen, bevollmächtigen
⟨autograph⟩ [ˈɔːtəgrɑːf] **I 7C** 113,5 Autogramm
autumn [ˈɔːtəm] **II 6C** 83,3 Herbst
available [əˈveɪləbl] **IV 4AB** 64 verfügbar, vorhanden
avenue [ˈævənjuː] **IV 5B** 68,4 (breite) Straße, Allee
average [ˈævərɪdʒ] **IV 5A** 65 Durchschnitt
⟨average⟩ [ˈævərɪdʒ] **III 7FE** 103 Durchschnitts-
to **avoid** [əˈvɔɪd] **IV 4C** 57 vermeiden, umgehen
away [əˈweɪ] weg (von)
to ride away **I 3C** 59 wegreiten
to run away **I 3B** 57 wegrennen
to throw away **I 5B** 82,2 wegwerfen
awful [ˈɔːfʊl] **IV 2B** 26,4 scheußlich, schrecklich

B

baby [ˈbeɪbɪ] **I FS7** 18 Baby
baby brother **I FS7** 18 kleiner Bruder
babysitter [ˈbeɪbɪˌsɪtə] **IV 2A** 24,6 Babysitter
babysitting [ˈbeɪbɪˌsɪtɪŋ] **IV 2B** 25 auf ein Baby aufpassen
bachelor [ˈbætʃələ] **VI 3C** 42,4 *erster akademischer Grad*
back [bæk] **II 3C** 35 Rücken
back door **I 5B** 81 Hintertür
like the back of my hand **III 1B** 11 wie meine Westentasche
back [bæk] **I 3B** 57 zurück
in the back of … [bæk] **II 6B** 80 hinten in
background [ˈbækgraʊnd] **II 1A** 7 Hintergrund
backpacking (*AE*) [ˈbækpækɪŋ] **IV 6C** 83,4 (mit dem Rucksack) Verreisen, Wandern
backyard (*AE*) [ˌbækˈjɑːd] **II 7B** 94 Hinterhof, Garten
⟨bacon⟩ [ˈbeɪkn] **I 3** 53 Speck
bad [bæd] **I 2C** 49,3 schlecht, schlimm
bad luck [ˈbædˌlʌk] **I 5B** 81 Pech
badge [bædʒ] **II 5C** 67 Abzeichen, Button, Anstecker
badly [ˈbædlɪ] **II 3D** 39 sehr, heftig, schlecht
bag [bæg] **I 4A** 67,2 Tasche, Tüte
⟨carrier bag⟩ [ˈkærɪə bæg] **III 1C** 19,10 Tragetasche, -tüte
to **bake** [beɪk] **III 5C** 63,3 backen
baked beans [ˌbeɪkt ˈbiːnz] **II 1C** 10 weiße Bohnen in Tomatensoße
balance [ˈbæləns] **V 3AB** 47 Gleichgewicht, Balance
ball [bɔːl] **I 1C** 42,6 Ball
banana [bəˈnɑːnə] **I 4C** 71,2 Banane
band [bænd] **II 8B** 105 Musikband
to **bandage** [ˈbændɪdʒ] **III 4A** 48 verbinden, bandagieren
to **bang** [bæŋ] **II 1D** 13 (zu-)schlagen
bang [bæŋ] **I 1C** 40,8 Peng! Bums!
banjo [ˈbændʒəʊ] **II 7A** 91 Banjo
bank [bæŋk] **III 1A** 8 Bank, Geldinstitut
bank [bæŋk] **V 3C** 35 (Fluss-)Ufer
baptism [ˈbæptɪzəm] **IV 5C** 71,2 Taufe
Baptist [ˈbæptɪst] **VI 4A** 47,a) baptistisch, Baptisten-
bar [bɑː] **I 4C** 71,2 Tafel
bar [bɑː] **VI 4C** 58,5 Takt
barbarian [bɑːˈbeərɪən] **VI 1B** 8 barbarisch, unzivilisiert
barbecue [ˈbɑːbɪkjuː] **II 6A** 78,2 Grillparty
bare [beə] **V 5B** 63 kahl, leer
to **bark** [bɑːk] **I 3C** 59 bellen
barn [bɑːn] **IV 5C** 70 Scheune, Schuppen
barn dance [ˈbɑːnˌdɑːns] **IV 3A** 34 *ländlicher Tanz*
baron [ˈbærən] **V 3AB** 43 Baron *(niedrigster Titel des britischen Hochadels)*
⟨base⟩ [beɪs] **III 6D** 81 Mal, Base
to **base** (*on*) [beɪs] **V 2A** 19,1 basieren, beruhen (auf)
baseball [ˈbeɪsbɔːl] **I 7A** 103,3 Baseball
basic [ˈbeɪsɪk] **V 3AB** 42 Grund-, Basis-
basket [ˈbɑːskɪt] **II 2C** 26,3 Korb
basketball [ˈbɑːskɪtbɔːl] **I 7A** 103,4 Basketball
⟨bat⟩ [bæt] **III 6D** 80 Schlagholz, Keule
⟨to bat⟩ [bæt] **III 6D** 81 schlagen
bath [bɑːθ] **I 5B** 81 Bad
to have a bath **I 5B** 81 baden
bathroom [ˈbɑːθrʊm] **I FS11** 30 Badezimmer
battle [ˈbætl] **III 2AB** 32 Schlacht, Kampf
battle-axe [ˈbætlæks] **IV 1AB** 20 Streitaxt
battlefield [ˈbætlfiːld] **VI 2D** 31,b) Schlachtfeld
Bavarian [bəˈveərɪən] **III 3C** 42,4 bayerisch, Bayer/in
⟨bay⟩ [beɪ] **I 4** 65 Bucht
BC [ˈbiː ˈsiː] **IV 1AB** 18 vor Christus
to **be*** [biː] **I 2B** 46 sein
⟨there'd be⟩ **I FS10** 28,3 es würde/n sein
to be able to do s.th. [ˈeɪbl] **II 7B** 94 etw. tun können, in der Lage sein etw. zu tun
to be asleep [əˈsliːp] **III 7C** 89 eingeschlafen sein, schlafen
to be aware [əˈweə] **IV 5D** 75,4 sich bewusst sein
to be born [ˌbiː ˈbɔːn] **III 2AB** 32 geboren sein
to be called [kɔːld] **II 5A** 60 heißen
to be certain to [ˈsɜːtn] **VI 3B** 39,4 sicherlich, bestimmt
to be fond of [fɒnd] **IV 6B** 80,3 gerne haben, mögen
to be helpless [ˈhelplɪs] **III 4C** 51 hilflos sein
to be in a hurry [ˈhʌrɪ] **IV 3B** 38 in Eile (sein)
to be in for (*a surprise*) **II 6D** 84 jdm bevorstehen
to be in trouble [ˈtrʌbl] **III 5C** 64,6 Ärger, Schwierigkeiten bekommen/haben
to be involved (*in*) [ɪnˈvɒlvd] **V 4D** 58,1 verwickelt, beteiligt sein
to be keen on [kiːn] **II 7A** 92,4 scharf sein auf
to be likely to [ˈlaɪklɪ] **VI 3B** 37,a) wahrscheinlich
to be loose [luːs] **III 3C** 39 frei herumlaufen
to be on **II 1D** 16,9 eingeschaltet sein
to be on a diet [ˈdaɪət] **IV 2B** 25 eine Diät machen, abnehmen
to be out of the question **II 7C** 97 nicht in Frage kommen
to be out shopping **I 8B** 118 einkaufen sein
to be proud of [praʊd] **III 2D** 26 stolz sein auf
to be quiet **I 2C** 50,5 ruhig sein
to be said to [sed] **VI 4A** 47,a) (angeblich, vermutlich) sollen
to be sick [sɪk] **III 2C** 24 sich übergeben, brechen
to be supposed to [səˈpəʊzd] **VI 4A** 47,a) (angeblich, vermutlich) sollen
to be sure to [ʃɔː] **VI 3B** 37,a) sicherlich
to be up to s.th. **II 6D** 84 etw. vorhaben, aushecken
⟨to be responsible (*for*)⟩ [rɪˈspɒnsəbl] **V 3D** 40,5 verantwortlich sein (für)
beach [biːtʃ] **I 4A** 66,2 Strand
bear [beə] **III 6AB** 82 Bär
beard [bɪəd] **IV 5C** 70 Bart
beat [biːt] **VI 4B** 54,4 *Musikrichtung*
to **beat*** [biːt] **III 2AB** 32 schlagen
to beat up [ˈbiːt‿ˌʌp] **IV 2C** 30,5 zusammenschlagen, krankenhausreif schlagen
beautiful [ˈbjuːtɪfʊl] **I 7C** 110 schön
beauty [ˈbjuːtɪ] **III 5A** 58 Schönheit
bebop [ˈbiːbɒp] **VI 4C** 58,5 *Musikrichtung*
because [bɪˈkɒz] **I 1A** 35,3 weil
because of [bɪˈkɒz‿əv] **III 1B** 12,3 wegen
to **become*** [bɪˈkʌm] **II 2B** 24,6 werden
bed [bed] **I 2B** 46 Bett
to go to bed **I 2B** 46 ins Bett gehen
to take to bed **I 3C** 60 zu Bett bringen
bedroom [ˈbedrʊm] **I 1B** 37,1 Schlafzimmer
beef [biːf] **VI 1A** 5,1 Rindfleisch
beer [bɪə] **V 1C** 13 Bier
before [bɪˈfɔː] **I 8B** 119,3 vor, vorher
to **begin*** [bɪˈgɪn] **II 2B** 24,6 anfangen, beginnen
beginner [bɪˈgɪnə] **II 7A** 91 Anfänger/in
beginning [bɪˈgɪnɪŋ] **V 2C** 27,7 Anfang, Beginn
to **behave** [bɪˈheɪv] **VI 4B** 51 sich benehmen; sich verhalten
behavior (*AE*) [bɪˈheɪvjə] **VI 4B** 51 Verhalten, Benehmen
behaviour [bɪˈheɪvjə] **V 1C** 15,2 Verhalten, Benehmen
behind [bɪˈhaɪnd] **I FS6** 17 hinter
to **believe** (*in*) [bɪˈliːv] **II 1B** 8 glauben (an)
bell [bel] **I 2C** 49,4 Klingel, Glocke
to **belong to** [bɪˈlɒŋ] **I 7B** 106,2 gehören
below [bɪˈləʊ] **III 2B** 22 unter; unten
to **bend*** [bend] **III 6D** 78 (sich) biegen, beugen, krümmen
⟨to be bent on⟩ [bent] **III 7FE** 105 unbedingt wollen

⟨berth⟩ [bɜ:θ] **III 2AB** 31 Liegeplatz eines Schiffes

beside [bɪ'saɪd] **IV 6D** 86 neben

best [best] **I 3C** 60 der, die, das beste; am besten

bet [bet] **II 6D** 84 Wette

to **bet*** [bet] **I 7B** 105 wetten

you **bet** [bet] **I 8B** 118 und ob

better ['betə] **II 1D** 13 besser

between [bɪ'twi:n] **II 1C** 10 zwischen

Bible ['baɪbl] **IV 3AB** 49 Bibel, Heilige Schrift

bicycle ['baɪsɪkl] **II 2A** 20,2 Fahrrad

big [bɪg] **I FS8** 23 groß

bike [baɪk] **I 3C** 59 Fahrrad

bill (*AE*) [bɪl] **IV 4C** 57 Geldschein, Banknote

bill (*BE*) [bɪl] **IV 5D** 76,8 Rechnung

bill [bɪl] **V 3AB** 45 (Gesetzes-)-Vorlage, Gesetzentwurf

to **bind up** ['baɪnd ˌʌp] **VI 2D** 31 verbinden

binoculars (*pl*) [bɪ'nɒkjʊləz] **V 4B** 53,1 Fernglas

biologist [baɪ'ɒlədʒɪst] **V 3A** 32,6 Biologe/Biologin

biology [baɪ'ɒlədʒɪ] **II 7A** 91 Biologie

bird [bɜ:d] **I 7C** 110 Vogel

bird-bath ['bɜ:dbɑ:θ] **II 3B** 33 Vogelbad

bird seed ['bɜ:d ˌsi:d] **II 3B** 33 Vogelfutter

biro ['baɪrəʊ] **I FS9** 26 Kugelschreiber

birth [bɜ:θ] **V 2D** 29,3 Geburt

birthday ['bɜ:θdeɪ] **I 6A** 91,1 Geburtstag

birthplace ['bɜ:θpleɪs] **IV 4B** 54 Geburtsort

biscuit ['bɪskɪt] **I 3B** 57 Hundekuchen, Keks

bishop ['bɪʃəp] **V 5AB** 74 Bischof

a **bit** [bɪt] **I 4C** 74,6 ein bisschen

a bit of [bɪt] **I 6D** 96 ein bisschen von

bit by bit ['bɪt‿baɪ‿'bɪt] **IV 1AB** 20 allmählich

to **bite*** [baɪt] **III 7B** 86 beißen

black [blæk] **I 1A** 35,1 schwarz

blazer ['bleɪzə] **I 1A** 35,1 Blazer

to **bleed*** [bli:d] **III 4B** 49,4 bluten

block [blɒk] **V 3C** 35 (Häuser-)Block

to **block** [blɒk] **V 5AB** 76 verhindern, blockieren

blond [blɒnd] **III 5D** 66 blond

blood [blʌd] **IV 6D** 85 Blut

blood pressure ['blʌdˌpreʃə] **II 3A** 30 Blutdruck

blouse [blaʊz] **I 1A** 35,1 Bluse

to **blow*** [bləʊ] **II 5C** 68 blasen

to blow up [ˌbləʊ‿'ʌp] **IV 5D** 75,5 sprengen, zur Explosion bringen

⟨to blow up⟩ [bləʊ] **III 7FE** 99 in die Luft jagen

blue [blu:] **I 1A** 35,1 blau

blues [blu:z] **V 5B** 63 Blues *(Musikrichtung)*

board [bɔ:d] **II 7A** 92,4 Tafel

notice board ['nəʊtɪs bɔ:d] **III 4B** 49 Schwarzes Brett, Anschlagbrett

to **board** [bɔ:d] **II 6A** 77 an Bord gehen

to board (*up*) [ˌbɔ:d 'ʌp] **V 3C** 35 vernageln, mit Bretter zunageln

on **board** [bɔ:d] **I 8C** 122 an Bord

boarder ['bɔ:də] **IV 3C** 41 Internatsschüler/in

boarding pass ['bɔ:dɪŋ ˌpɑ:s] **II 6A** 78,4 Bordpass

boarding school ['bɔ:dɪŋ 'sku:l] **VI 3C** 41 Internat

boast [bəʊst] **VI 1B** 8 Stolz

boat [bəʊt] **I 8B** 118 Boot

body ['bɒdɪ] **III 4C** 51 Körper

bodyguard ['bɒdɪgɑ:d] **VI 1B** 10,3 Leibwächter/in

bone [bəʊn] **I 7B** 105 Knochen

⟨bonfire⟩ ['bɒnfaɪə] **III 7FE** 99 Freudenfeuer

bonfire ['bɒnˌfaɪə] **VI 3D** 45 Freudenfeuer

⟨Bonnie⟩ ['bɒnɪ] **I FS11** 32,4 Geliebte/r, Schatz

⟨bonny⟩ ['bɒnɪ] **III 3C** 44,9 hübsch, schön

to **boo** [bu:] **II 5C** 68 (aus-)buhen

Booh! [bu:] **II 5C** 68 Buh!

book [bʊk] **I FS9** 26 Buch

exercise book ['eksəsaɪz ˌbʊk] **I 1B** 37,2 Heft

boot (*BE*) [bu:t] **IV 5D** 76,8 Kofferraum

boot [bu:t] **II 2B** 23,5 Stiefel

border ['bɔ:də] **IV 1AB** 19 Grenze

boredom ['bɔ:dəm] **V 2D** 28,1 Langeweile

boring [bɔ:rɪŋ] **I 8A** 116,3 langweilig

to be **born*** [ˌbi: 'bɔ:n] **III 2AB** 32 geboren sein

to **borrow** ['bɒrəʊ] **III 3A** 35,2 borgen, sich leihen, ausleihen

boss [bɒs] **II 6A** 77 Chef/in, Vorgesetzte/r

both [bəʊθ] **II 2B** 21 beide

both ... and [bəʊθ ... ænd] **VI 1A** 6 sowohl ... als auch

⟨bottle⟩ ['bɒtl] **I FS10** 28,3 Flasche

bottom ['bɒtəm] **V 4A** 51,5 Boden, Fuß (eines Berges)

to **bounce off** [baʊns] **II 8A** 103 abprallen (an)

bow [bəʊ] **II 2B** 23,5 Bogen

to **bow** (*to*) [baʊ] **II 8C** 108 sich neigen, sich verbeugen (vor)

bowler (*hat*) [ˌbəʊlə 'hæt] **III 1A** 10,2 Melone

bowls [bəʊlz] **IV 3C** 44,4 *englisches Kugelspiel*

box [bɒks] **I FS6** 16 Karton, Kiste, Schachtel

to **box** [bɒks] **IV 3B** 38 (leicht) boxen, puffen

boy [bɔɪ] **I FS1** 8 Junge

boycott ['bɔɪkɒt] **VI 4A** 47,a) Boykott

boyfriend ['bɔɪfrend] **I 8C** 122 Freund

brace ['breɪs] **IV 6D** 85 Zahnspange

brain [breɪn] **II 6D** 84 Gehirn

to have s.th. on the brain **II 6D** 84 von etw. besessen sein

brake [breɪk] **II 4B** 49 Bremse

branch [brɑ:ntʃ] **IV 3AB** 46 Ast

brave [breɪv] **III 4C** 51 mutig, tapfer

bread [bred] **II 3D** 38 Brot

break [breɪk] **II 1B** 8 Pause

to **break*** **I 4C** 71,3 zerbrechen, kaputtgehen

to break down **II 6A** 77 eine Panne haben

to **breakdance** ['breɪkdɑ:ns] **II 7A** 91 *nach Modetänzen mit abgehackten Bewegungen und akrobatischen Einlagen tanzen*

breakdancer ['breɪkˌdɑ:nsə] **I 8A** 117,6 Breakdance-Tänzer/in

⟨breakfast⟩ ['brekfəst] **I 3** 53 Frühstück

for breakfast **I 4B** 70,4 zum Frühstück

to have breakfast **I 3C** 59 frühstücken

out of **breath** [ˌaʊt‿əv 'breθ] **III 3C** 40 außer Atem

to **breathe** [bri:ð] **V 2B** 23,3 atmen

⟨bride⟩ [braɪd] **III 7FE** 106 Braut

bridge [brɪdʒ] **I 2A** 44,2 Brücke

bright [braɪt] **VI 4A** 47,b) leuchtend, strahlend

⟨bright⟩ [braɪt] **III 7FE** 101 hell

brilliant ['brɪljənt] **II 1B** 8 strahlend, großartig

to **bring*** [brɪŋ] **I 3C** 59 bringen

⟨to bring back⟩ **I FS11** 32,4 zurückbringen

British ['brɪtɪʃ] **III 2A** 22 britisch

broad dialect [brɔ:d 'daɪəlekt] **IV 3A** 35 breiter Dialekt, ausgeprägte Mundart

brochure ['brəʊʃə] **IV 4A** 52,2 Prospekt, Broschüre

broken ['brəʊkən] **II 3B** 33 gebrochen

brother ['brʌðə] **I FS7** 18 Bruder

brown [braʊn] **I FS11** 32,3 braun

to be **bruised** [bru:zd] **II 5A** 61 blaue Flecken haben

brush [brʌʃ] **I FS6** 16 Besen, Bürste, Schrubber

to **brush** [brʌʃ] **II 3D** 38 bürsten

bucket ['bʌkɪt] **I FS6** 16 Eimer

budget ['bʌdʒɪt] **V 5AB** 74 Budget, staatlicher Haushaltsplan

budgie ['bʌdʒɪ] **II 3B** 33 Wellensittich

buffalo, *pl.* buffalo or buffaloes ['bʌfələʊ] **V 4A** 48 Büffel

buggy ['bʌgɪ] **IV 5C** 70 *leichter einspänniger Wagen*

to **build*** [bɪld] **II 6A** 77 bauen

building ['bɪldɪŋ] **I 7C** 110 Gebäude

bunk [bʌŋk] **III 7C** 89 Koje

burden ['bɜ:dn] **VI 1B** 8 Last, Belastung

burger ['bɜ:gə] **II 6B** 80 Hamburger

burglar ['bɜ:glə] **I 2C** 50,5 Einbrecher/in

Burmese [ˌbɜ:'mi:z] **VI 1C** 12 birmanisch; Birmane/Birmanin

to **burn*** [bɜ:n] **III 2AB** 32 brennen

burst [bɜ:st] **V 3D** 39 Zerbersten, Explosion

to **bury** ['berɪ] **III 4C** 52 begraben, beerdigen

bus [bʌs] **I 3A** 54 Bus

bus station **I 4C** 71,1 Busbahnhof

bus stop **I 5C** 84 Bushaltestelle

business ['bɪznɪs] **III 5B** 59 Geschäft, Betrieb

on business ['bɪznɪs] **III 2A** 21,1 geschäftlich

businessman ['bɪznɪsmæn] **V 3D** 39,2 Geschäftsmann

busy ['bɪzɪ] **II 1C** 10 belebt, verkehrsreich, beschäftigt

but [bʌt] **I FS6** 16 aber, sondern

⟨butcher⟩ ['bʊtʃə] **I 6** 90 Fleischer, Metzger

butcher's ['bʊtʃəz] **I 6C** 94,1 Fleischerei, Metzgerei

butler ['bʌtlə] **VI 1C** 12 Diener, Butler

butter ['bʌtə] **II 4C** 58,10 Butter

⟨butterfly⟩ ['bʌtəflaɪ] **III 7FE** 104 Schmetterling

button [ˈbʌtn] **IV 5C** 71,2 Knopf
to **buy*** [baɪ] **I 1A** 35,2 kaufen
to **buzz** [bʌz] **V 5C** 66 schwirren, summen
⟨by⟩ [baɪ] **III 3C** 39 neben, bei, an
by nine o'clock **I 2B** 46 bis (spätestens) neun Uhr
by train **I 4A** 66 mit dem Zug
by the way [ˌbaɪ‿ðə‿ˈweɪ] **IV 5B** 67,2 übrigens, nebenbei (bemerkt)
bye-bye [ˌbaɪˈbaɪ] **I 6C** 94,3 Wiedersehen!

C

cab(*in*) [ˈkæbɪn] **III 7C** 89 Führerhaus; Kabine, Passagierraum
cabinet [ˈkæbɪnɪt] **V 5AB** 73 Kabinett, Kreis der regierenden Minister
café [ˈkæfeɪ] **III 7B** 86 Café, Restaurant
cafeteria [ˌkæfɪˈtɪərɪə] **II 5B** 63 Cafeteria
cage [keɪdʒ] **II 3B** 33 Käfig
cake [keɪk] **II 4A** 48,3 Kuchen
calculation [ˌkælkjʊˈleɪʃn] **IV 6D** 87,3 Berechnung, Kalkulation
calculator [ˈkælkjʊˌleɪtə] **III 5C** 63,5 Rechner
calendar [ˈkælɪndə] **IV 1C** 13 Kalender
(phone) **call** [ˈfəʊn ˌkɔːl] **III 4A** 46 Anruf
to **call** [kɔːl] **I 3C** 59 rufen; nennen; anrufen
to call out [ˌkɔːl‿ˈaʊt] **II 8C** 109 ausrufen
caller [ˈkɔːlə] **IV 3B** 38 Ansager (für Tanzschritte)
thanks for **calling** **I 8B** 118 danke für den Anruf
Cambodian [kæmˈbəʊdjən] **VI 3B** 39,4 kambodschanisch; Kambodschaner/in
camcorder [ˈkæmkɔːdə] **II 2B** 21 Videokamera
camera [ˈkæmərə] **I 7B** 105 Fotoapparat
camp [kæmp] **IV 6D** 85 (Zelt-)Lager
campaign [kæmˈpeɪn] **V 5AB** 75 Kampagne, Feldzug
campaign [kæmˈpeɪn] **V 3C** 36 Kampagne, Aktion
campfire [ˈkæmpˌfaɪə] **II 8B** 105 Lagerfeuer
camping-site [ˈkæmpɪŋˌsaɪt] **II 1A** 7 Campingplatz
can [kæn] **III 3C** 42,5 Dose; Büchse; Kanne
can* [kæn; kən] **I FS8** 24 können
Canadian [kəˈneɪdjən] **IV 1B** 11,6 kanadisch, Kanadier/in
canal [kəˈnæl] **V 2A** 19 Kanal
candidate [ˈkændɪdət] **III 6B** 73 Kandidat/in
candle [ˈkændl] **III 7FE** 98 Kerze
cannot* [ˈkænɒt‚‿nɒt] **I 1B** 37,2 nicht können
canoe [kəˈnuː] **III 6AB** 82 Kanu
can't* [kɑːnt] **I FS8** 24,2 nicht können
canyon [ˈkænjən] **V 4A** 48 (Fels-)Schlucht
cap [kæp] **I 8C** 122 Kappe, Mütze
capital [ˈkæpɪtl] **I 8C** 124,2 Hauptstadt
capital letter [ˈkæpɪtl ˈletə] **V 4D** 58,1 Großbuchstabe
captain [ˈkæptn] **I 8C** 122 Kapitän
caption [ˈkæpʃn] **II 4B** 51,5 Überschrift, Titel
car [kɑː] **I FS8** 23 Auto
police car **I 5A** 80,4 Polizeiwagen
toy car **I 5A** 78 Spielzeugauto
caravan [ˈkærəˌvæn] **II 1B** 8 Wohnwagen
card [kɑːd] **I FS11** 30 Karte
cardigan [ˈkɑːdɪgən] **I 1A** 35,1 Strickjacke
to **care** [keə] **IV 6C** 82 sich etw. aus einer Sache machen
⟨career⟩ [kəˈrɪə] **VI 1D** 18,5 Karriere
⟨careerist⟩ [kəˈrɪərɪst] **V 3D** 40,5 Karrierist/in
careful [ˈkeəfʊl] **I 4C** 71,2 vorsichtig
careless [ˈkeəlɪs] **III 7C** 93,7 nachlässig, unvorsichtig
caretaker [ˈkeəˌteɪkə] **II 5C** 69,2 Hausmeister/in
⟨carrier bag⟩ [ˈkærɪə bæg] **III 1C** 19,10 Tragetasche, -tüte
carrot [ˈkærət] **II 3D** 40,2 Mohrrübe
to **carry** [ˈkærɪ] **I FS11** 30 tragen *(Gegenstände)*
cart [kɑːt] **V 2A** 20 Karren
cartoon [kɑːˈtuːn] **IV 1A** 8,5 Karikatur, Witzzeichnung
⟨cartoon⟩ [kɑːˈtuːn] **III 7B** 88,5 Karikatur, lustige Zeichnung
case [keɪs] **III 7C** 91,3 Koffer; Fall
cashier [kæˈʃɪə] **VI 4A** 47,b) Kassierer/in
cassette [kəˈset] **I 6B** 92,2 Kassette
cassette-recorder [kəˈset rɪˌkɔːdə] **I 6B** 92,2 Kassettenrekorder
castle [ˈkɑːsl] **I 5C** 84 Schloss, Burg
casualty department [ˈkæʒʊəltɪ dɪˌpɑːtmənt] **III 4A** 46 Unfallstation, Notaufnahme
cat [kæt] **I FS7** 19,1 Katze
⟨catalogue⟩ [ˈkætəlɒg] **III 7FE** 101 Katalog
to **catch*** [kætʃ] **II 2C** 25 fangen
to catch fire [ˌkætʃ ˈfaɪə] **II 8C** 108 Feuer fangen
to catch s.o.'s eye **III 5D** 66 jdn auf sich aufmerksam machen
cathedral [kəˈθiːdrəl] **IV 3A** 34 Dom
Catholic [ˈkæθəlɪk] **IV 3AB** 48 katholisch
cattle [ˈkætl] **VI 2A** 19 Vieh
cause [kɔːz] **VI 4B** 52,1 Ursache
to **cause** [kɔːz] **III 6A** 70 machen, verursachen
cavalry [ˈkævlrɪ] **VI 1B** 10,3 Kavallerie
CB (= **Citizens' Band**) [ˌsɪ ˈbɪ, ˈsɪtɪznz ˈbænd] **III 7C** 89 CB-Funk
CD (*compact disc*) [ˈsiːˈdiː] **V 5B** 64,3 CD
ceiling [ˈsiːlɪŋ] **IV 5C** 71,3 Decke
to **celebrate** [ˈselɪbreɪt] **IV 4A** 52 feiern, festlich begehen
⟨to celebrate⟩ [ˈselɪbreɪt] **III 7FE** 105 feiern
cellar [ˈselə] **III 7C** 93,7 Keller
Celt [kelt] **III 7FE** 98 Kelte, Keltin
Celtic [ˈkeltɪk] **IV 1A** 6 keltisch
cemetery [ˈsemɪtrɪ] **VI 2D** 31,b) Friedhof
center (*AE*) [ˈsentə] **IV 6D** 85 Zentrum
central [ˈsentrəl] **II 6C** 82 Zentral-
centre [ˈsentə] **II 2A** 18 Zentrum
century [ˈsentʃərɪ] **III 1A** 8 Jahrhundert
certain [ˈsɜːtn] **VI 4C** 54,5 bestimmt, sicher
certainly [ˈsɜːtnlɪ] **II 2A** 19 sicherlich, bestimmt
chain [tʃeɪn] **II 4B** 49 Kette
chainsaw [ˈtʃeɪnˌsɔː] **V 2C** 27,7 Motorsäge
chair [tʃeə] **I FS6** 16 Stuhl
chairman [ˈtʃeəmən] **V 2C** 24 Vorsitzende/r
chairperson [ˈtʃeəpɜːsn] **V 4B** 53,2 Vorsitzende/r
chalk [tʃɔːk] **II 7C** 97 Kreide
challenge [ˈtʃælɪndʒ] **III 6B** 73 Herausforderung, Anforderung
chamber [ˈtʃeɪmbə] **V 3AB** 46 Kammer, gesetzgebende Körperschaft
chance [tʃɑːns] **III 1B** 13,6 Chance, Aussicht, Möglichkeit
chancellor [ˈtʃɑːnsələ] **V 5AB** 77 Kanzler
change [tʃeɪndʒ] **III 1A** 9 Veränderung, Wechsel; Wechselgeld, Kleingeld
to **change** [tʃeɪndʒ] **II 5B** 63 ändern, (aus-)wechseln, umsteigen, sich (ver-)ändern
⟨to change your mind⟩ [maɪnd] **III 1C** 19,10 deine Meinung ändern
chap (*coll, BE*) [tʃæp] **IV 5D** 76,8 Kerl, Bursche
chapter [ˈtʃæptə] **II 7C** 96 Kapitel
character [ˈkærəktə] **II 7C** 96 Person, Figur
characteristic [ˌkærəktəˈrɪstɪk] **III 5B** 61,5 Merkmal
to **characterize** [ˈkærəktəraɪz] **V 4D** 58,2 charakterisieren, beschreiben
to **charge** (*with*) [tʃɑːdʒ] **V 1B** 11 beschuldigen, anklagen
charter [ˈtʃɑːtə] **V 3AB** 43 Charta, (Verfassungs-)Urkunde
the **charts** [tʃɑːts] **IV 2A** 24,5 Hitliste
chase [tʃeɪs] **II 8C** 109 Jagd
to **chat** [tʃæt] **IV 3B** 38 plaudern, schwatzen
cheap [tʃiːp] **II 4C** 57,8 billig
check (*AE*) [tʃek] **IV 5D** 76,8 Rechnung
check-in counter [ˈtʃek‿ɪn ˈkaʊntə] **I 7C** 111 Abfertigungsschalter
check list [ˈtʃekˌlɪst] **II 4A** 47 Kontrolliste
check-up [ˈtʃekʌp] **II 3A** 30 Untersuchung, Kontrolle
to **check** [tʃek] **IV 2C** 33,12 überprüfen, kontrollieren
to **cheer** [ˈtʃɪə] **V 3D** 38 jubeln, Beifall spenden
cheerful [ˈtʃɪəfʊl] **II 3A** 30 fröhlich, vergnügt
cheese [tʃiːz] **II 5B** 63 Käse
⟨cheeseburger⟩ [ˈtʃiːzˌbɜːgə] **III 7B** 88,6 *Hamburger mit Käse*
cheetah [ˈtʃiːtə] **II 1C** 11,1 Gepard
chemical [ˈkemɪkl] **III 3C** 41,2 Chemikalie
chemistry [ˈkemɪstrɪ] **III 5B** 60,3 Chemie
cheque [tʃek] **II 6B** 80 Scheck

chest [tʃest] **II 3A** 30 Brust
chewing gum ['tʃu:ɪŋgʌm] **II 7C** 97 Kaugummi
Chicagoan [ʃɪ'kɑ:gəʊən] **V 5B** 63 Chicagoer/in
chicken ['tʃɪkɪn] **II 5B** 63 Hühnchen, Hähnchen
chief [tʃi:f] **V 4A** 48 Häuptling, Anführer
child [tʃaɪld] **I 2A** 44,7 Kind
childhood ['tʃaɪldhʊd] **V 5C** 65 Kindheit
children (*pl*) ['tʃɪldrən] **I 1C** 40,7 Kinder
⟨chimney⟩ ['tʃɪmnɪ] **III 7FE** 100 Kamin, Schornstein
chimp [tʃɪmp] **II 3C** 36,2a Schimpanse
china ['tʃaɪnə] **V 2A** 19,2 Porzellan
Chinese [ˌtʃaɪ'ni:z] **III 1A** 9 chinesisch, Chinese/Chinesin
chip shop ['tʃɪp ʃɒp] **I 6C** 94,1 Imbissstube
chips [tʃɪps] **I 6C** 94,1 Pommes frites
to **chirp** [tʃɜ:p] **II 3C** 35 zwitschern
chocolate ['tʃɒklət] **I 4C** 71,2 Schokolade
choice [tʃɔɪs] **IV 4AB** 62 Wahl
choir ['kwaɪə] **IV 1A** 6 Chor
to **choke** (*s.o.*) [tʃəʊk] **III 7C** 90 ersticken; (er-)würgen
⟨cholera⟩ ['kɒlərə] **III 6C** 76,6 Cholera
Chomp! [tʃɒmp] **III 7FE** 99 Mampf!
to **choose*** [tʃu:z] **III 1C** 17,7 (aus-)wählen, sich aussuchen
chord [kɔ:d] **III 7B** 86 Akkord, Saite
⟨chorus⟩ ['kɔ:rəs] **IV 6D** 88,5 Chor
Christian ['krɪstjən] **III 7FE** 98 Christ/in, christlich
Christianity [ˌkrɪstɪ'ænətɪ] **VI 4C** 58,5 Christentum
to **christianize** ['krɪstjənaɪz] **VI 1B** 8 christianisieren, zum Christentum bekehren
Christmas ['krɪsməs] **IV 2C** 29,3 Weihnachten
church [tʃɜ:tʃ] **III 4C** 51 Kirche
(*church*) service ['sɜ:vɪs] **III 4C** 52 Gottesdienst
cigarette [ˌsɪgə'ret] **V 1C** 15,4 Zigarette
cinema ['sɪnəmə] **III 3A** 36,7 Kino
circle ['sɜ:kl] **II 8C** 108 Kreis
circus ['sɜ:kəs] **IV 2A** 22 Zirkus
citizen ['sɪtɪzn] **VI 2D** 32,3 Bürger/in
city ['sɪtɪ] **I 7B** 108,6 Stadt, Großstadt
civics (*pl*) ['sɪvɪks] **VI 3C** 40 Staatsbürgerkunde
civil war ['sɪvl 'wɔ:] **IV 4AB** 62 Bürgerkrieg
Civil Rights movement ['sɪvlˌraɪts 'mu:vmənt] **VI 4A** 47,a) Bürgerrechtsbewegung
civilization [ˌsɪvɪlaɪ'zeɪʃn] **V 3AB** 45 Zivilisation
to **civilize** ['sɪvɪlaɪz] **IV 4D** 59 zivilisieren
claim [kleɪm] **VI 1B** 8,1 Anspruch; Behauptung
clan [klæn] **IV 1A** 8,4 Clan, Stamm, Sippe
to **clap** [klæp] **II 5C** 68 klatschen
class [klɑ:s] **I FS3** 10 Klasse
classmate ['klɑ:smeɪt] **IV 5C** 72,5 Mitschüler/in, Klassenkamerad/in
classroom ['klɑ:srʊm] **II 5B** 66,7 Klassenzimmer
to **clean** [kli:n] **I FS11** 30 putzen, sauber machen
clean [kli:n] **I FS6** 16 sauber
to **clear** [klɪə] **V 3A** 30 (weg-) räumen
clearly ['klɪəlɪ] **II 4B** 51,4 natürlich, klar
clerk [klɜ:k] **VI 4A** 47,b) Angestellte/r
clever ['klevə] **I 3B** 57 klug
⟨cliché⟩ ['kli:ʃeɪ] **VI 3C** 43,6 Klischee
click [klɪk] **I 8C** 123 Klick
cliff [klɪf] **III 2A** 20 Felsen, Klippe, Kliff
climate ['klaɪmɪt] **III 6A** 70 Klima
climax ['klaɪmæks] **III 5B** 61,5 Höhepunkt
to **climb** [klaɪm] **I 1C** 39,4 klettern, steigen
climber ['klaɪmə] **IV 1B** 9 Bergsteiger, Kletterer
cloak [kləʊk] **II 2B** 21 Umhang, Cape
clock [klɒk] **I 4B** 69 Uhr
to **close** [kləʊz] **I 6D** 97 schließen
close (*closer*) [kləʊs] **I 8C** 123 nahe, näher
closely ['kləʊslɪ] **II 3C** 35 genau
closet ['klɒzɪt] **IV 5D** 77,10 (begehbarer Wand-)Schrank
cloth [klɒθ] **II 3D** 39 Stoff, Tuch
piece of cloth **II 3D** 39 Lappen
clothes [kləʊðz] **I 2C** 49,2 Kleider, Kleidung
cloud [klaʊd] **II 6C** 83,3 Wolke
cloudy ['klaʊdɪ] **II 6C** 82 wolkig
clown [klaʊn] **III 4B** 49 Clown
club [klʌb] **II 2A** 18 Club, Verein
clue [klu:] **III 6C** 75,1 Hinweis, Tipp, Anhaltspunkt
coach [kəʊtʃ] **III 2A** 21,2 Reisebus; Kutsche; Wagon
coach park ['kəʊtʃ ˌpɑ:k] **III 3B** 37 Busparkplatz
to **coach** [kəʊtʃ] **IV 5D** 74 trainieren
coal [kəʊl] **IV 1B** 9 Kohle
coal-mine ['kəʊlmaɪn] **IV 1B** 9 Kohlenbergwerk, Kohlenmine
coalition [ˌkəʊə'lɪʃn] **V 5AB** 78 Bündnis, Koalition
coast [kəʊst] **III 2A** 20 Küste
coat [kəʊt] **I 2C** 49,3 Mantel
coat (*of paint*) [kəʊt] **II 7C** 96 Anstrich
⟨cock⟩ [kɒk] **III 7FE** 105 Hahn
Cockney ['kɒknɪ] **III 1B** 12,2 (Ost-)Londoner Dialekt
cocktail stick ['kɒkteɪl ˌstɪk] **II 1C** 10 Cocktailspieß
coffee ['kɒfɪ] **III 3A** 35,3 Kaffee
coke [kəʊk] **V 2C** 26,6 Koks
cold [kəʊld] **I 4C** 72,5 Kälte
to have a cold **I 4C** 71,1 eine Erkältung/einen Schnupfen haben
cold [kəʊld] **I 4C** 75,9 kalt
to get cold **I 6D** 97 kalt werden
to **collapse** [kə'læps] **III 4B** 49 zusammenbrechen
colleague ['kɒli:g] **IV 5D** 75,4 Kollege/Kollegin
to **collect** [kə'lekt] **I 2B** 46 abholen, sammeln
college ['kɒlɪdʒ] **VI 3C** 40 *Teil einer Universität, höhere Lehranstalt*
colliery ['kɒljərɪ] **V 3A** 30 (Kohlen-)Grube, Zeche
colonial [kə'ləʊnjəl] **IV 6C** 84,5 Siedlungs-, Kolonial-
colonialism [kələʊnjə'lɪzəm] **VI 1A** 6 Kolonialismus
colonist ['kɒlənɪst] **IV 4A** 51 Siedler/in, Kolonist/in
colony ['kɒlənɪ] **IV 4A** 52 Siedlungsgebiet, Kolonie
color (*AE*) ['kʌlə] **IV 5B** 66 Farbe
colour ['kʌlə] **I 1A** 35,1 Farbe
school colours **I 1A** 35 Farben von Schuluniformen, -abzeichen usw.
What colour is/are **I 1A** 36,2 Welche Farbe hat/haben …?
colourful ['kʌləfʊl] **III 1C** 17 farbenfroh, bunt
to **comb** [kəʊm] **V 2A** 20 kämmen
to **combine** [kəm'baɪn] **V 2A** 20 verbinden, verknüpfen
Come on! **I FS6** 17 Los! Gehen wir! Komm schon!
to **come*** [kʌm] kommen
to come along **II 7B** 94 mitkommen
to come down **I 1C** 40,5 herunterkommen
to come in **I 2B** 46 sich melden *(Funksprache)*
to come out **I 4C** 72,5 herauskommen
to come over [ˌkʌm‿'əʊvə] **II 3D** 38 herüberkommen
to come running **II 5C** 67 angelaufen kommen
⟨to come true⟩ **I 7C** 113,5 Wirklichkeit werden
to come upstairs **I FS11** 30 nach oben kommen
comedy ['kɒmədɪ] **VI 1C** 13,2 Lustspiel, Komödie
comfortably (*adv*) ['kʌmftəblɪ] **II 4B** 49 bequem
comic ['kɒmɪk] **I FS10** 29,4 Comicheft
comic strip ['kɒmɪkˌstrɪp] **IV 1AB** 20 lustige Bilderfolge mit Texten
command [kə'mɑ:nd] **VI 1B** 10,3 Befehl
commission [kə'mɪʃn] **VI 1B** 11 Ausschuss, Kommission
common ['kɒmən] **VI 2A** 22,3 gemeinsam, gemeinschaftlich
commoner ['kɒmənə] **V 3AB** 45 Bürger
to **communicate** [kə'mju:nɪkeɪt] **VI 2A** 22,3 sich verständigen, kommunizieren
communication [kəˌmju:nɪ'keɪʃn] **VI 3D** 45,1 Verständigung, Kommunikation
community [kə'mju:nətɪ] **IV 5C** 72,6 Gemeinschaft
company ['kʌmpənɪ] **II 6A** 76 Gesellschaft, Firma
to **compare** [kəm'peə] **II 1D** 16,7 vergleichen
comparison [kəm'pærɪsn] **V 2B** 22,1 Vergleich
compartment [kəm'pɑ:tmənt] **III 2D** 26 Abteil, Schotte *(naut.)*
competition [ˌkɒmpɪ'tɪʃn] **II 5A** 61 Wettbewerb
competitive [kəm'petətɪv] **V 2C** 24 konkurrenzfähig, wettbewerbfähig
to **complain** [kəm'pleɪn] **IV 2C** 28 sich beklagen, sich beschweren

to **complete** [kəm'pliːt] **II 1B** 9,2 vervollständigen
completely [kəm'pliːtlɪ] **III 4C** 52 völlig, vollständig
comprehension [ˌkɒmprɪ'henʃn] **I 1A** 36,1 (Fragen zum) Textverständnis
comprehensive school [ˌkɒmprɪ'hensɪv 'skuːl] **VI 3C** 41 *weiterführende Schule, entspricht etwa der Gesamtschule*
⟨comprehensive school⟩ [ˌkɒmprɪ'hensɪv] **I 1** 34 Gesamtschule
compromise ['kɒmprəmaɪz] **IV 5C** 72,6 Zugeständnis, Kompromiss
compulsory [kəm'pʌlsərɪ] **VI 3C** 40 vorgeschrieben, obligatorisch
computer [kəm'pjuːtə] **I 8A** 116,3 Computer
to **concentrate** ['kɒnsəntreɪt] **IV 2C** 27 konzentrieren, aufmerksam sein
to **concern** [kən'sɜːn] **V 3A** 30 betreffen, angehen
concert ['kɒnsət] **I 8A** 117,6 Konzert
conclusion [kən'kluːʒn] **V 4A** 50,3 Schluss(folgerung), Fazit
condition [kən'dɪʃn] **V 2A** 20 Bedingung, Voraussetzung
the **Confederacy** [kən'fedərəsɪ] **VI 4A** 47,a) Staatenbund, Konföderation *(der Südstaaten im Sezessionskrieg)*
to **confirm** [kən'fɜːm] **VI 3B** 38,b) bestätigen
conflict ['kɒnflɪkt] **IV 4AB** 62 Auseinandersetzung, Konflikt
Congratulations! [kənˌgrætjʊ'leɪʃnz] **III 3B** 37 Herzlichen Glückwunsch!
Congress ['kɒŋgres] **V 3AB** 46 Kongress, gesetzgebende Versammlung *(der amerikanischen Regierung)*
to **connect** [kə'nekt] **VI 1A** 7,3 verbinden
connection [kə'nekʃn] **III 5B** 58 Verbindung; Zusammenhang; Anschluss
to **conquer** ['kɒŋkə] **II 2B** 24,6 erobern
consent [kən'sent] **V 3AB** 47 Zustimmung, Einverständnis
consequently ['kɒnsɪkwəntlɪ] **VI 1A** 6 infolgedessen, folglich
conservationist [ˌkɒnsə'veɪʃnɪst] **V 4A** 48 Umweltschützer/in
conservative [kən'sɜːvətɪv] **IV 5C** 70 konservativ
to **consist** (*of*) [kən'sɪst] **VI 1A** 7,3 bestehen (aus)
constitution [ˌkɒnstɪ'tjuːʃn] **IV 4AB** 64 Verfassung
constitutional [ˌkɒnstɪ'tjuːʃənl] **V 3AB** 42 Verfassungs-, verfassungsmäßig, konstitutionell
contact ['kɒntækt] **V 5AB** 78 Kontakt
contact clause ['kɒntækt ˌklɔːz] **II 6A** 78,3 Relativsatz ohne Relativpronomen
to **contain** [kən'teɪn] **IV 4D** 61,4 beinhalten, enthalten
context ['kɒntekst] **VI 1B** 11 Zusammenhang
continent ['kɒntɪnənt] **III 2B** 22 Kontinent
to **continue** [kən'tɪnjuː] **V 5B** 63 fortsetzen, weitermachen
continued on page … [kən'tɪnjuːd] **I 4A** 66 Fortsetzung auf Seite …
contrast ['kɒntrɑːst] **IV 1B** 9 Kontrast, Unterschied
control [kən'trəʊl] **V 1A** 6 Kontrolle, Herrschaft
control room [kən'trəʊl ˌruːm] **II 7B** 94 Kontrollraum
controversial [ˌkɒntrə'vɜːʃl] **VI 4B** 54,5 umstritten, kontrovers
convention [kən'venʃn] **V 3AB** 46 Versammlung, Kongress
conversation [ˌkɒnvə'seɪʃn] **V 1C** 13 Gespräch, Unterhaltung
⟨conversation⟩ [ˌkɒnvə'seɪʃn] **IV 2C** 30,6 Gespräch, Unterhaltung
to **convert** [kən'vɜːt] **VI 4C** 58,5 (zu einer anderen Religion) überwechseln, konvertieren
convertible [kən'vɜːtəbl] **IV 5C** 70 Kabriolett *(Fahrzeug mit Faltdach)*
to **convict** [kən'vɪkt] **V 1C** 15,4 überführen, für schuldig erklären
to **convince** [kən'vɪns] **V 1C** 16,6 überzeugen
to **cook** [kʊk] **II 5A** 60 kochen
cookery ['kʊkərɪ] **II 5A** 61 Koch-, Kochen
cooking ['kʊkɪŋ] **V 5C** 66 Küche, Art zu kochen
cool [kuːl] **II 6C** 82 kühl
cop (*sl*) [kɒp] **IV 5D** 73 Polizist, Bulle
to **copy** ['kɒpɪ] **V 5C** 65 nachmachen, kopieren
corn [kɔːn] **IV 4A** 51 Getreide; *(AE)* Mais
corner ['kɔːnə] **II 3B** 33 Ecke
⟨cornflakes⟩ ['kɔːnfleɪks] **I 3** 53 Cornflakes
to **correct** [kə'rekt] **I 7A** 102,1 korrigieren
correct [kə'rekt] **II 4B** 52,7 richtig
to **corrupt** [kə'rʌpt] **VI 1C** 13,2 verderben, korrumpieren
to **cost*** [kɒst] **I 5A** 78 kosten
costume ['kɒstjuːm] **II 2B** 21 Kostüm
cottage ['kɒtɪdʒ] **V 3A** 30 (kleines) Landhaus
cotton ['kɒtn] **V 2A** 19 Baumwolle
could* [kʊd] **I 8C** 123 konnte
could you …? ['kʊd juː] **II 2C** 25 Könnten Sie …? Könntest du …?
couldn't ['kʊdnt] **II 2B** 24,6 konnte nicht
council ['kaʊnsl] **V 3AB** 45 Rat, beratende Versammlung
guidance **counselor** (*AE*)**/counsellor** (*BE*) ['gaɪdns ˌkaʊnsələ] **III 5B** 59 Verbindungslehrer
to **count** [kaʊnt] **II 7C** 97 zählen
counter ['kaʊntə] **II 6B** 80 Spielmarke; Theke
check-in counter ['tʃek‿ɪn 'kaʊntə] **I 7C** 111 Abfertigungsschalter
counter-argument ['kaʊntəˌɑːgjʊmənt] **VI 3C** 42,3 Gegenargument
country ['kʌntrɪ] **III 1A** 9 Land
country music [ˌkʌntrɪ 'mjuːzɪk] **II 6A** 78,2 Country Musik *(Musikrichtung)*
countryside ['kʌntrɪsaɪd] **V 3C** 36 Landschaft; ländliche Gegend
a **couple** (*of*) ['kʌpl] **II 3C** 35 ein paar, einige; ein Paar
courage ['kʌrɪdʒ] **II 8C** 109 Mut
course [kɔːs] **II 5B** 63 Gang *(beim Essen)*
course [kɔːs] **VI 3C** 40 Kurs, Unterrichtsfach
of **course** [ɒv 'kɔːs] **I FS8** 24 natürlich, sicher
court [kɔːt] **V 1C** 15,4 Gerichtshof, Gericht
⟨to court⟩ [kɔːt] **III 3C** 44,9 umwerben, werben um
cousin ['kʌzn] **II 1B** 8 Cousin/e
cover ['kʌvə] **V 5A** 60 Decke, Abdeckung
to **cover** ['kʌvə] **III 2C** 24 bespritzen, bedecken
cow [kaʊ] **II 6B** 80 Kuh
cowboy ['kaʊbɔɪ] **II 6A** 79,5 Cowboy
cradle ['kreɪdl] **V 5AB** 74 Wiege, Ursprung
cradle-robbing ['kreɪdlˌrɒbɪŋ] **V 1C** 14 *hier:* eine/n wesentlich jüngere/n Freund/in haben
crane [kreɪn] **V 3D** 39,2 Kran
crash [kræʃ] **III 4B** 49 Krach; Schlag; Zusammenstoß
to **crash** [kræʃ] **III 2C** 24 krachen, knallen; zusammenstoßen
crazy ['kreɪzɪ] **I 8A** 114 verrückt
(*to be*) crazy about ['kreɪzɪ] **II 7A** 92,4 verrückt nach etwas (sein)
to **create** [kriː'eɪt] **V 3AB** 44 erschaffen, erzeugen
creative writing [kriː'eɪtɪv 'raɪtɪŋ] **III 5B** 60,3 dichterisches Schreiben
credit ['kredɪt] **VI 3C** 40 *Anrechnungspunkt für den Erwerb eines akademischen Grades an der Hochschule*
creepy ['kriːpɪ] **II 1D** 12 gruselig, unheimlich
crew [kruː] **III 2D** 26 Besatzung, Mannschaft, Crew
cricket ['krɪkɪt] **IV 3C** 45,6 Kricket
crime [kraɪm] **IV 4C** 57 Straftat, Verbrechen
criminal ['krɪmɪnl] **V 1B** 11 kriminell
criminal ['krɪmɪnl] **VI 4B** 53,3 verbrecherisch, kriminell
crisps [krɪsps] **I 6C** 94,1 Chips
critical ['krɪtɪkl] **VI 3C** 42 kritisch
to **criticize** ['krɪtɪsaɪz] **IV 3AB** 48 kritisieren
crocodile ['krɒkədaɪl] **II 3C** 36,2a Krokodil
crook [krʊk] **III 6C** 75 Gauner/in
crop [krɒp] **IV 4A** 52 (Feld-)Frucht, Getreide
⟨cross⟩ [krɒs] **III 7FE** 105 Kreuz, Kreuzung
to **cross** **I 8A** 114 überqueren
crossing ['krɒsɪŋ] **III 2A** 20 Überfahrt, Überquerung
⟨to crow⟩ [krəʊ] **III 7FE** 105 krähen
crowd [kraʊd] **II 2C** 26 (Menschen-)Menge
crowded ['kraʊdɪd] **III 1A** 8 voll, überfüllt
crown [kraʊn] **III 1A** 8 Krone
to **crown** [kraʊn] **IV 1AB** 20 krönen
cruel ['krʊəl] **II 2A** 18 grausam
cry [kraɪ] **III 3C** 39 Schrei, Ruf
to **cry** [kraɪ] **I 4A** 66,3 weinen, schreien
Cuban ['kjuːbən] **VI 3A** 33,a) kubanisch; Kubaner/in
to **cultivate** ['kʌltɪveɪt] **VI 2B** 24 bebauen, kultivieren
cultural ['kʌltʃərəl] **VI 1B** 8 kulturell, Kultur-
culture ['kʌltʃə] **IV 1A** 6 Kultur

cup [kʌp] **II 5C** 72,11 Tasse
cupboard ['kʌbəd] **I FS6** 16 Schrank
⟨curiosity⟩ [ˌkjʊəri'ɒsəti] **III 3C** 41,3 Neugier, Wißbegierde
curry ['kʌri] **III 1C** 16,5 *indisches Gericht, Gewürz*
to **curse** [kɜ:s] **V 1C** 14 fluchen, Flüche ausstoßen
curve [kɜ:v] **V 5B** 63 Kurve
custom ['kʌstəm] **IV 4A** 51 Brauch, Sitte
(the) **customs** ['kʌstəmz] **III 2B** 23 Zoll
short **cut** ['ʃɔ:t ˌkʌt] **III 1B** 12,2 Abkürzung, Schnellverfahren
to **cut*** [kʌt] **I 4A** 67,2 schneiden
Cut! [kʌt] **II 2B** 21 Schnitt!
cycle ['saɪkl] **II 2A** 18 Fahrrad
to **cycle** ['saɪkl] **II 3D** 38 Rad fahren
to go **cycling** ['saɪklɪŋ] **II 1B** 8 Fahrrad fahren

D

dad [dæd] **I FS7** 18 Vati
daily ['deɪli] **III 4B** 49 täglich
dairy cow ['deəriˌkaʊ] **II 7B** 94 Milchkuh
dairy farm ['deəri] **II 7B** 94 Milchwirtschaftshof
damage ['dæmɪdʒ] **III 7C** 93,7 Schaden
to **damage** ['dæmɪdʒ] **III 4A** 48 (be-)schädigen, schaden
to **dance** [dɑ:ns] **I 2A** 44,9 tanzen
dancer ['dɑ:nsə] **II 8C** 108 Tänzer/in
danger ['deɪndʒə] **III 2D** 26 Gefahr
dangerous ['deɪndʒərəs] **II 2A** 18 gefährlich
Danish ['deɪnɪʃ] **I FS8** 24,2 dänisch; Dänisch
dare [deə] **VI 3D** 46,2 es wagen, sich (ge)trauen
dark [dɑ:k] **IV 3AB** 46 Dunkelheit, Dunkel
dark [dɑ:k] **I 1C** 40,5 dunkel
date [deɪt] **I 6A** 91 Datum
daughter ['dɔ:tə] **II 1D** 15,6 Tochter
day [deɪ] **I 3A** 54,2 Tag
to **day-dream** ['deɪdri:m] **IV 2A** 24,6 tagträumen
day-to-day ['deɪ‿tə‿'deɪ] **IV 2A** 23,1 Tag für Tag, alltäglich
the day before yesterday **II 1D** 14,4 vorgestern
dead [ded] **II 7C** 96 tot
deadlock ['dedlɒk] **V 5C** 66 völliger Stillstand, Sackgasse
to **deal*** (*in*) [di:l] **V 1B** 11 handeln (mit), Handel treiben
dear [dɪə] **I FS6** 17 Schatz
Oh **dear!** O je! Ach du meine Güte!
⟨dearly⟩ ['dɪəli] **III 3C** 44,9 von ganzem Herzen
death [deθ] **IV 2B** 26,2 Tod
debate [dɪ'beɪt] **V 5AB** 74 Debatte, parlamentarische Diskussion
to **decay** [dɪ'keɪ] **V 3C** 35 verfallen, zerfallen
to **decide** [dɪ'saɪd] **II 5B** 65,5 (sich) entscheiden
decision [dɪ'sɪʒn] **III 4C** 51 Entscheidung, Entschluss
deck [dek] **I 8C** 122 Deck
to **declare** [dɪ'kleə] **VI 2B** 24 erklären
decline [dɪ'klaɪn] **V 2C** 24 Rückgang, Verfall
⟨decorations⟩ [ˌdekə'reɪʃnz] **III 7FE** 100 Dekorationen
to **dedicate** ['dedɪkeɪt] **VI 2D** 31,b) widmen
deep [di:p] **II 8C** 108 tief
deer (*sing. and pl.*) [dɪə] **II 2A** 19 Hirsch, Reh, Rotwild
to **defeat** [dɪ'fi:t] **IV 3AB** 49 besiegen
defense attorney (*AE*) [dɪ'fens ə'tɜ:ni] **V 1B** 12,2 Rechtsanwalt/-anwältin, Verteidiger/in
definition [ˌdefɪ'nɪʃn] **VI 3B** 38,2 Definition
degree [dɪ'gri:] **II 6C** 82 Grad
to **delay** [dɪ'leɪ] **IV 1C** 12 verschieben, aufschieben
delicious [dɪ'lɪʃəs] **II 5B** 63 köstlich
demand [dɪ'mɑ:nd] **IV 1B** 9 Nachfrage
to **demand** [dɪ'mɑ:nd] **IV 4AB** 64 verlangen, erfordern
democracy [dɪ'mɒkrəsi] **IV 4AB** 64 Demokratie
democratic [ˌdemə'krætɪk] **V 3AB** 43 demokratisch
to **demonstrate** ['demənstreɪt] **IV 6D** 87,3 vorführen, demonstrieren
department store [dɪ'pɑ:tmənt stɔ:] **III 1A** 8 Kaufhaus
casualty department ['kæʒuəlti dɪˌpɑ:tmənt] **III 4A** 46 Unfallstation, Notaufnahme
departure [dɪ'pɑ:tʃə] **IV 3A** 34 Abfahrt, Abreise
to **depend on** [dɪ'pend‿ɒn] **VI 3C** 40 abhängen von, abhängig sein von
deposit [dɪ'pɒzɪt] **V 3A** 30 Ablagerung
depot ['depəʊ] **III 7C** 89 Depot
depressed [dɪ'prest] **V 5C** 65 deprimiert, niedergeschlagen
⟨to descend⟩ [dɪ'send] **III 4C** 54 hinuntergehen
to **describe** [dɪ'skraɪb] **III 3C** 41,1 beschreiben, schildern
description [dɪ'skrɪpʃn] **IV 4D** 59 Beschreibung
desert ['dezət] **III 6A** 70 Wüste
to **deserve** [dɪ'zɜ:v] **IV 4D** 59 verdienen, Anspruch haben auf
to **design** [dɪ'zaɪn] **IV 3C** 44,5 gestalten, entwerfen
desk [desk] **V 5C** 69,9 Schreibtisch
desperate ['despərət] **V 5C** 66 verzweifelt
despotism ['despətɪzəm] **V 3AB** 44 Tyrannei, Despotismus
dessert [dɪ'zɜ:t] **II 5B** 63 Nachspeise
destiny ['destɪni] **VI 1B** 8 Schicksal
to **destroy** [dɪ'strɔɪ] **III 1A** 8 zerstören, vernichten
destruction [dɪ'strʌkʃn] **VI 2D** 31,a) Zerstörung
⟨detached house⟩ [dɪ'tætʃt] **I 5** 77 Einzelhaus
detail ['di:teɪl] **III 6A** 71,1 Einzelheit; Detail, Ausschnitt
detective [dɪ'tektɪv] **II 7A** 91 Detektiv
to **develop** [dɪ'veləp] **IV 4AB** 63 (sich) entwickeln
development [dɪ'veləpmənt] **V 2A** 19 Entwicklung
devil ['devl] **IV 3AB** 47 Teufel
⟨dialect⟩ ['daɪəlekt] **III 1C** 19,10 Dialekt
dialect ['daɪəlekt] **IV 4AB** 63 Dialekt, Mundart
dialogue ['daɪəlɒg] **I FS1** 8,1 Dialog
diary ['daɪəri] **II 2B** 21 Tagebuch
dice [daɪs] **I 5B** 81 Würfel
dictionary ['dɪkʃənri] **IV 4D** 61,4 Wörterbuch
to **die** [daɪ] **III 1A** 8 sterben
to die down [ˌdaɪ 'daʊn] **III 4C** 51 schwächer, leiser werden
difference ['dɪfrəns] **IV 5B** 67,3 Unterschied, Differenz
different ['dɪfrənt] **I 4A** 66,2 verschieden, unterschiedlich
difficult ['dɪfɪkəlt] **I 1B** 37,3 schwierig, schwer
to **dig***, dug [dɪg, dʌg] **V 2A** 20 (aus-)graben
dining-room ['daɪnɪŋ rʊm] **I 5B** 81 Esszimmer
dinner ['dɪnə] **IV 2A** 22 Abendessen
diploma [dɪ'pləʊmə] **VI 3D** 46,2 Diplom, (akademische) Urkunde
to **direct** [dɪ'rekt] **VI 1B** 8 lenken, dirigieren, den Weg weisen
direction [dɪ'rekʃn] **VI 1A** 7,3 Richtung
directly [dɪ'rektli] **III 7C** 93,7 direkt, unmittelbar; sofort
⟨dirt⟩ [dɜ:t] **III 1C** 19,10 Schmutz
dirty ['dɜ:ti] **I FS6** 16 schmutzig
disabled [dɪs'eɪbld] **V 3C** 36 benachteiligt, behindert
disadvantage [ˌdɪsəd'vɑ:ntɪdʒ] **V 5AB** 78 Nachteil
to **disagree** [ˌdɪsə'gri:] **V 4B** 53,2 ablehnen, nicht einverstanden sein
to **disappear** [ˌdɪsə'pɪə] **III 3C** 39 verschwinden
disappointed [ˌdɪsə'pɔɪntɪd] **III 5D** 67 enttäuscht
disappointment [ˌdɪsə'pɔɪntmənt] **IV 6C** 82 Enttäuschung
to **disapprove** [ˌdɪsə'pru:v] **VI 1C** 12,1 missbilligen, ablehnen
disaster [dɪ'zɑ:stə] **III 1A** 8 Unglück, Katastrophe
to **discover** [dɪs'kʌvə] **III 2D** 26 entdecken, erfinden
to **discriminate** (*against s.o.*) [dɪ'skrɪmɪnət] **V 3AB** 42 jdn benachteiligen, diskriminieren
discrimination [dɪˌskrɪmɪ'neɪʃn] **VI 3A** 35,3 Benachteiligung, Diskriminierung
to **discuss** [dɪ'skʌs] **IV 3A** 37,5 besprechen, diskutieren
discussion [dɪ'skʌʃn] **V 1C** 16,6 Diskussion, Gespräch
disease [dɪ'zi:z] **III 4C** 51 Krankheit
disgusting [dɪs'gʌstɪŋ] **IV 6D** 85 widerlich, ekelhaft
dish [dɪʃ] **II 5B** 63 Gericht, Schüssel
dishonest [dɪs'ɒnɪst] **III 5D** 67,2 unehrlich
disobedience [ˌdɪsə'bi:djəns] **VI 1C** 14 Ungehorsam
dissolution [ˌdɪsə'lu:ʃn] **IV 3AB** 48 Auflösung, Zerstörung
to **dissolve** [dɪ'zɒlv] **V 5AB** 76 auflösen
distance ['dɪstəns] **IV 3C** 41 Entfernung
district ['dɪstrɪkt] **V 5A** 61,3 Bezirk, Kreis

to **disturb** [dɪ'stɜ:b] **V 1B** 12,3 beunruhigen, stören
to **dive** [daɪv] **III 3C** 40 tauchen, springen
to **divide** [dɪ'vaɪd] **IV 4AB** 63 teilen
divorce [dɪ'vɔ:s] **IV 3AB** 47 Scheidung
to **divorce** [dɪ'vɔ:s] **IV 3AB** 47 sich scheiden lassen
dizzy ['dɪzɪ] **II 3A** 30 schwindlig
do-it-yourself [ˌdu:ɪtjɔ:'self] **V 1A** 10,8 Heimwerken
to **do*** [du:] **I FS11** 30 machen, tun
to do my homework **I 1B** 37,1 meine Hausaufgaben machen
to do the washing up [ˌwɒʃɪŋ'ʌp] **III 3A** 36,6 abspülen
⟨do fit⟩ (*coll*) [fɪt] **III 7C** 95,12 passt
dock [dɒk] **III 1A** 9 Dock, (Pl. Hafen)
doctor ['dɒktə] **II 3A** 30 Ärztin, Arzt
Dr = Doctor **II 3A** 30 Doktor
document ['dɒkjʊmənt] **IV 4A** 52 Urkunde, Dokument
dog [dɒg] **I FS7** 20,6 Hund
doggy ['dɒgɪ] **II 7C** 97,3 Hündchen
dollar ['dɒlə] **II 6B** 80 Dollar *(amerikanische Währung)*
dolphin ['dɒlfɪn] **III 5D** 69,9 Delfin
to **dominate** (*over*) ['dɒmɪneɪt] **V 5AB** 78 beherrschen, dominieren
dominion [də'mɪnjən] **VI 1A** 6 *sich selbst regierendes Land des britischen Staatenbundes*
⟨done brought⟩ (*coll*) [brɔ:t] **III 7C** 95,12 hat gebracht
door [dɔ:] **I FS6** 16 Tür
front door [ˌfrʌnt 'dɔ:] **I 2C** 49,4 Haustür
doorstep ['dɔ:step] **I 5C** 85 Stufe vor der Tür
double ['dʌbl] **I FS10** 28,2 doppelt, Doppel-
double oh ['dʌbl ˌəʊ] **I FS10** 28,2 null null
to **doubt** [daʊt] **VI 2A** 23,5 (be)zweifeln
doughnut ['dəʊnʌt] **II 7C** 97 Krapfen, Berliner *(Fettgebäck)*
down [daʊn] **I FS3** 10 her-, hinunter
down (*the road*) **I 7B** 108,6 entlang
to come down **I 1C** 40,5 herunterkommen
to die down [ˌdaɪ 'daʊn] **III 4C** 51 schwächer, leiser werden
to fall down **I 3B** 57 herunterfallen, hinfallen
to knock down **III 4A** 48,5 anfahren, umwerfen
to put down **III 5B** 59,1 auflegen; wegtun; zuklappen
to sit down **I FS3** 10 sich hinsetzen, Platz nehmen
to slow down **III 4A** 46 langsamer fahren
downstairs [ˌdaʊn'steəz] **I FS11** 30 (nach) unten
downtown (*AE*) ['daʊnˌtaʊn] **IV 5B** 66 Innenstadt, Geschäftsviertel
draft [drɑ:ft] **VI 2C** 30,3 Entwurf
to **drag** [dræg] **IV 6D** 86 zerren, ziehen
drama ['drɑ:mə] **IV 3A** 36,4 Schauspiel, Drama
draw [drɔ:] **II 5C** 69 unentschieden
to **draw*** [drɔ:] **IV 3B** 40,5 zeichnen
dream [dri:m] **I 6C** 96 Traum
to **dream*** [dri:m] **I 6D** 97 träumen
dress [dres] **I 2C** 49,3 Kleid
to **dress** [dres] **VI 4A** 47,b) bekleiden, (sich) anziehen
to **drift** [drɪft] **V 5C** 65 sich treiben lassen, ziellos umhergehen
drink [drɪŋk] **I 8C** 123 Getränk
to **drink*** [drɪŋk] **I 5C** 86,3 trinken
drive [draɪv] **III 7C** 89 Autofahrt; Einfahrt
to **drive*** **I FS11** 30 fahren
to drive out [ˌdraɪv‿'aʊt] **IV 1AB** 19 vertreiben, verjagen
to drive s. o. mad [mæd] **IV 2C** 31,7 jmd. verrückt machen
driver ['draɪvə] **V 1C** 14 Fahrer/in
driver's license (*AE*) ['draɪvəz ˌlaɪsəns] **IV 5C** 70 Führerschein
driving licence (*BE*) ['draɪvɪŋ ˌlaɪsəns] **IV 5D** 76,8 Führerschein
to **drop** [drɒp] **II 2C** 26 fallen lassen
to drop s.o. from [drɒp] **IV 5D** 74 jmd hinauswerfen
to **drown** [draʊn] **V 5C** 66 ertrinken
drug [drʌg] **V 1A** 9,7 Droge, Rauschgift
drug dealer ['drʌg ˌdi:lə] **IV 5D** 75,4 Drogenhändler/in
dry [draɪ] **II 6C** 82 trocken
duck [dʌk] **I 2A** 44,6 Ente
to **duck** [dʌk] **III 7C** 90 sich ducken
dude (*AE*) [du:d] **II 8B** 105 feiner Stadtpinkel
dude ranch ['du:d 'ræntʃ] **II 7A** 91 Ferienranch, Touristenranch
dugout ['dʌgaʊt] **IV 4A** 51 Einbaumkanu
dull [dʌl] **VI 2D** 32,1 langweilig
dump [dʌmp] **V 3A** 30 Müllabladeplatz, Müllhalde
dune [dju:n] **III 3C** 39 Düne
during ['djʊərɪŋ] **III 5C** 64,6 während
dust [dʌst] **V 5C** 66 Staub
Dutch [dʌtʃ] **IV 1B** 11,6 niederländisch, (die) Niederländer
Dutchman ['dʌtʃmən] **IV 5A** 65 Holländer
duty ['dju:tɪ] **VI 1B** 8 Pflicht, Aufgabe
dynamic [daɪ'næmɪk] **VI 4C** 57,4 dynamisch

E

each [i:tʃ] **III 6B** 73 jede/r/s
each other [ˌi:tʃ 'ʌðə] **III 5C** 62 sich, einander
eagle ['i:gl] **I 7A** 102 Adler
ear [ɪə] **I 8B** 120,4 Ohr
early ['ɜ:lɪ] **I 3A** 54,1 früh
to **earn** [ɜ:n] **IV 2A** 24,6 verdienen
earphones ['ɪəfəʊnz] **IV 1C** 13 Kopfhörer
earring ['ɪərɪŋ] **IV 3B** 38 Ohrring
earth [ɜ:θ] **II 8C** 108 Erde
earthquake ['ɜ:θkweɪk] **III 6A** 71 Erdbeben
east [i:st] **I 8B** 121,8 östlich
Easter ['i:stə] **IV 3A** 35 Ostern
eastern ['i:stən] **V 2C** 24 östlich
eastward ['i:stwəd] **VI 2B** 24 nach Osten, in östlicher Richtung
easy ['i:zɪ] **I 1B** 37,3 leicht
to **eat*** [i:t] **I 3C** 59 essen
eater ['i:tə] **II 1C** 10 Esser/in
economic [ˌi:kə'nɒmɪk] **VI 2A** 19 wirtschaftlich, ökonomisch
economics (*pl*) [ˌi:kə'nɒmɪks] **V 4B** 53,1 Wirtschaft, Ökonomie
economy [ɪ'kɒnəmɪ] **V 2A** 19,1 Wirtschaft, Ökonomie
edge [edʒ] **III 3C** 40 Rand, Ufer
editor ['edɪtə] **III 6A** 72,4 Redakteur/in
editor-in-chief [ˌedɪtər‿ɪn 'tʃi:f] **III 6A** 72,4 Herausgeber/in, Chefredakteur/in
editorial [ˌedɪ'tɔ:rɪəl] **V 2C** 24 Leitartikel (einer Zeitung)
education [ˌedʒʊ'keɪʃn] **IV 5C** 71,2 Erziehung
effect [ɪ'fekt] **IV 6D** 86,1 Wirkung, Einfluss
effort ['efət] **V 3C** 36 Anstrengung, Mühe
⟨egg⟩ [eg] **I 3** 53 Ei
Egyptian [ɪ'dʒɪpʃn] **V 2C** 26,6 ägyptisch; Ägypter/in
⟨either⟩ ['aɪðə] **III 7FE** 104 entweder
either ... **or** ['aɪðə ɔ:] **III 6D** 79 entweder ... oder
to **elect** [ɪ'lekt] **V 5AB** 74 wählen
election [ɪ'lekʃn] **V 1C** 15,4 Wahl
elective [ɪ'lektɪv] **III 5B** 60,3 Wahlfach *(AE)*; Wahl-
electric [ɪ'lektrɪk] **III 7C** 91,3 elektrisch
electrician [ˌɪlek'trɪʃn] **III 7B** 86 Elektriker/in
electricity [ˌɪlek'trɪsətɪ] **IV 5C** 70 Strom, Elektrizität
electronics [ˌɪlek'trɒnɪks] **IV 1B** 9 Elektronik
elementary (school) [ˌelɪ'mentərɪ ('sku:l)] **VI 3A** 34,b) Grundschule
elephant ['elɪfənt] **II 3C** 36,2a Elefant
Elizabethan [ɪˌlɪzə'bi:θn] **IV 3C** 44,5 elisabethanisch
else [els] **I 6C** 94,2 sonst noch
anything **else?** **I 6C** 94,2 sonst noch etwas?
embarrassed [ɪm'bærəst] **IV 6D** 86 verlegen
embarrassing [ɪm'bærəsɪŋ] **IV 6B** 79 peinlich
embarrassment [ɪm'bærəsmənt] **VI 3C** 42,3 Verlegenheit
emergency [ɪ'mɜ:dʒənsɪ] **III 2B** 22 Notfall; Not-
emigrant ['emɪgrənt] **III 2D** 27 Auswanderer/in, Emigrant/in
to **emigrate** ['emɪgreɪt] **VI 2A** 19 auswandern, emigieren
emphasis ['emfəsɪs] **VI 3C** 40 Betonung, Nachdruck
empire ['empaɪə] **VI 1A** 5 (Welt-)Reich
to **employ** [ɪm'plɔɪ] **V 2B** 23,2 beschäftigen, einstellen
⟨employment⟩ [ɪm'plɔɪmənt] **VI 1D** 18,5 Arbeit, Beschäftigung
empress ['emprɪs] **VI 1A** 6 Kaiserin
to **empty** ['emptɪ] **II 4A** 47 (aus-)leeren
empty ['emptɪ] **I FS7** 18 leer
to **enclose** [ɪn'kləʊz] **V 3A** 30 beifügen, beilegen
to **encourage** [ɪn'kʌrɪdʒ] **III 5B** 59 ermutigen, anregen, fördern
encyclopedia [ɪnˌsaɪkləʊ'pi:djə] **IV 4D** 61,4 Lexikon, Nachschlagewerk
end [end] **I 8C** 122 Ende

to **end** [end] **I 5B** 81 enden
to end up [ˌend_ˈʌp] **V 5C** 65 schließlich landen, enden
ending [ˈendɪŋ] **II 8B** 105 Ende (einer Geschichte)
enemy [ˈenəmɪ] **II 2A** 18 Feind/in
energy [ˈenədʒɪ] **V 4C** 55 Energie
engaged [ɪnˈgeɪdʒd] **IV 5D** 77,10 beschäftigt, gebunden
engine [ˈendʒɪn] **II 4A** 47 Motor, Maschine
engineer [ˌendʒɪˈnɪə] **III 2B** 22 Ingenieur/in
English [ˈɪŋglɪʃ] **I FS3** 10 englisch; Englisch
to **enjoy** [ɪnˈdʒɔɪ] **III 3C** 39 gern machen, genießen
he enjoyed it **III 3C** 40 es machte ihm Spaß
to enjoy *(oneself)* [ɪnˈdʒɔɪ] **III 5C** 62 sich amüsieren, Spaß haben
enormous [ɪˈnɔːməs] **II 5C** 67 riesig
enough [ɪˈnʌf] **I 8B** 118 genug
to **enrol** [ɪnˈrəʊl] **IV 4C** 57 einschreiben, immatrikulieren
to **enslave** [ɪnˈsleɪv] **VI 1B** 8 zum Sklaven machen, versklaven
to **entertain** [ˌentəˈteɪn] **II 8A** 103 unterhalten
entertainer [ˌentəˈteɪnə] **V 3D** 38 Unterhaltungskünstler/in, Entertainer/in
entire [ɪnˈtaɪə] **VI 3A** 34,b) ganz, komplett
entrance [ˈentrəns] **II 1D** 12 Eingang
entryphone [ˈentrɪˌfəʊn] **V 3C** 36 Gegensprechanlage
environment [ɪnˈvaɪərənmənt] **V 2A** 21,4 Umwelt
environmental [ɪnˌvaɪərənˈmentl] **V 1A** 7 Umwelt-
to **envy** [ˈenvɪ] **IV 2A** 22 beneiden
epidemic [ˌepɪˈdemɪk] **IV 4A** 52 Seuche, Epidemie
equal [ˈiːkwəl] **IV 4AB** 63 Gleichberechtigte/r
equal [ˈiːkwəl] **VI 4A** 48,3 gleich, gleichermaßen
equality [ɪˈkwɒlətɪ] **VI 4A** 49,5 Gleichberechtigung
equipment [ɪˈkwɪpmənt] **V 5B** 62 Ausrüstung
eruption [ɪˈrʌpʃn] **V 4D** 59,4 Ausbruch
to **escape** [ɪˈskeɪp] **IV 4A** 52,2 fliehen
especially [ɪˈspəʃlɪ] **II 4B** 49 besonders
⟨essay⟩ [ˈeseɪ] **III 5D** 68,7 Aufsatz
estate [ɪˈsteɪt] **IV 6A** 78 Grundbesitz, Gut
etc. (*etcetera*) [ɪtˈsetərə] **III 2B** 22 usw.
ethnic [ˈeθnɪk] **IV 5B** 67,1 ethnisch
European [ˌjʊərəˈpiːən] **II 1C** 10 europäisch; Europäer/in
even [ˈiːvn] **II 3D** 38 sogar, auch
evening [ˈiːvnɪŋ] **I FS7** 18 Abend
event [ɪˈvent] **IV 4A** 52 Ereignis
eventually [ɪˈventʃʊəlɪ] **IV 5D** 76,9 schließlich, endlich
ever [ˈevə] **II 8C** 108 je zuvor
every [ˈevrɪ] **I 3A** 54,1 jeder, jede, jedes
everybody [ˈevrɪˌbɒdɪ] **I 3C** 59 jede/r
everyday [ˈevrɪdeɪ] **IV 5D** 74,2 alltäglich, Alltags-
everyone [ˈevrɪwʌn] **I 5B** 81 jede/r, alle
everything [ˈevrɪθɪŋ] **I 6C** 94,2 alles
everywhere [ˈevrɪweə] **I 8C** 122 überall
evil spirit [ˌiːvl ˈspɪrɪt] **III 7FE** 98 böser Geist
ex-Confederate [ˌeks_kənˈfedərət] **VI 2D** 32,3 *ehemaliges Mitglied der Konföderierten*
exact [ɪgˈzækt] **I 4B** 69 genau
⟨to exaggerate⟩ [ɪgˈzædʒəreɪt] **V 2C** 26,5 übertreiben
exam [ɪgˈzæm] **IV 2C** 27 Examen, Prüfung
to **examine** [ɪgˈzæmɪn] **II 3A** 30 untersuchen
example [ɪgˈzɑːmpl] **I FS4** 12,2 Beispiel
for example **I 3C** 59 zum Beispiel
except [ɪkˈsept] **II 8C** 109 außer
exception [ɪkˈsepʃn] **IV 4AB** 64 Ausnahme
excerpt [ˈeksɜːpt] **VI 1B** 9 Auszug, Exzerpt
exchange [ɪksˈtʃeɪndʒ] **IV 2C** 32,9 Austausch
to **exchange** [ɪksˈtʃeɪndʒ] **IV 1C** 12 austauschen
excited [ɪkˈsaɪtɪd] **II 5C** 68 aufgeregt
excitement [ɪkˈsaɪtmənt] **V 5B** 63 Aufregung, Erregung
exciting [ɪkˈsaɪtɪŋ] **I 1C** 39,3 aufregend
excursion [ɪkˈskɜːʃn] **IV 2A** 23,3 Ausflug, Exkursion
excuse [ɪkˈskjuːs] **V 1C** 14 Entschuldigung
Excuse me [ɪkˈskjʊz ˌmiː] **I 7B** 108,6 Entschuldigung
to **execute** [ˈeksɪkjuːt] **IV 3AB** 46 hinrichten, töten
execution [ˌeksɪˈkjuːʃən] **II 1D** 12 Hinrichtung, Exekution
executive [ɪgˈzekjʊtɪv] **V 3AB** 47 ausübend, vollziehend, executiv
exercise [ˈeksəsaɪz] **I 1B** 37,2 Übung
exercise book **I 1B** 37,2 (Schul-) Heft
exhibit [ˌɪgˈzɪbɪt] **III 3A** 34 Ausstellungsstück
exhibition [ˌeksɪˈbɪʃn] **III 3A** 34 Ausstellung
to **expect** [ɪkˈspekt] **III 1A** 8 erwarten; rechnen mit
expedition [ˌekspɪˈdɪʃn] **III 6AB** 82 Expedition, Forschungsreise
expensive [ɪkˈspensɪv] **I 7A** 102 teuer
experience [ɪkˈspɪərɪəns] **VI 2B** 24 Erfahrung
expert [ˈekspɜːt] **IV 4A** 51 Fachmann (-frau), Experte/Expertin
to **explain** [ɪkˈspleɪn] **III 5D** 68,3 erklären, erläutern
explanation [ˌekspləˈneɪʃn] **IV 6D** 87,3 Erklärung, Erläuterung
to **explore** [ɪkˈsplɔː] **IV 4A** 50 erforschen, erkunden
explorer [ɪkˈsplɔːrə] **III 2AB** 32 Forschungsreisende/r
explosion [ɪkˈspləʊʒn] **V 2A** 20 Explosion
export [ˈekspɔːt] **V 3D** 39,2 Export, Ausfuhr
to **export** [ɪkˈspɔːt] **V 3C** 37,3 ausführen, exportieren
to **express** [ɪksˈpres] **V 2C** 25,2 ausdrücken
expression [ɪkˈspreʃn] **V 5C** 66 Ausdruck, Äußerung
extra [ˈekstrə] **I 5B** 81 zusätzlich
extracurricular [ˌekstrəkəˈrɪkjələ] **III 5B** 60,3 außerhalb des Stundenplans
extraordinary [ɪkˈstrɔːdnrɪ] **IV 5C** 70 außergewöhnlich
extreme [ɪkˈstriːm] **IV 4AB** 62 äußerste/r, extrem
eye [aɪ] **I 6D** 97 Auge
to catch s.o.'s eye **III 5D** 66 jdn auf sich aufmerksam machen

F

⟨fable⟩ [ˈfeɪbl] **VI 3C** 43,6 (Tier-) Fabel
face [feɪs] **I 3C** 59 Gesicht
to pull a **face** [feɪs] **II 5C** 67 ein Gesicht ziehen
fact [fækt] **IV 4D** 60,2 Tatsache
in **fact** [ɪn ˈfækt] **III 1B** 11 in der Tat, tatsächlich
factor [ˈfæktə] **IV 4AB** 64 Faktor
factory [ˈfæktərɪ] **II 2A** 18 Fabrik
factual [ˈfæktʃʊəl] **V 3C** 37,1 sachlich, auf Tatsachen beruhend
to **fail** [feɪl] **IV 1AB** 19 misslingen, nicht aufgehen
to fail [feɪl] **VI 3A** 35,3 versagen, keinen Erfolg haben
fair [feə] **II 2A** 18 Jahrmarkt, Kirmes
fair [feə] **II 5C** 67 gerecht
fairly [ˈfeəlɪ] **III 4B** 49 ziemlich
fairness [ˈfeənɪs] **VI 1B** 11 Fairness
fall (*AE*) [fɔːl] **IV 4D** 59 Herbst
to **fall*** [fɔːl] fallen
to fall asleep [ˌfɔːl əˈsliːp] **IV 6B** 81,6 einschlafen
to fall down **I 3B** 57 herunterfallen, hinfallen
to fall in love [ˈfɔːl_ɪn_ˈlʌv] **IV 3AB** 47 sich verlieben
to fall off **II 6A** 79,6 abreißen
to fall over **I 4C** 71,3 fallen über
false [fɔːls] **IV 5D** 76,9 falsch
familiar [fəˈmɪljə] **III 5A** 58 gewohnt, vertraut, bekannt
family [ˈfæməlɪ] **I FS8** 24,2 Familie
famine [ˈfæmɪn] **VI 3A** 35,3 Hungersnot
famous [ˈfeɪməs] **I 7C** 110 berühmt
fan [fæn] **II 5B** 66,7 Fan
fanatic [fəˈnætɪk] **IV 4AB** 63 Fanatiker/in
fanatical [fəˈnætɪkl] **IV 4AB** 64 fanatisch
to **fancy** [ˈfænsɪ] **IV 3A** 35 gern tun, mögen
fancy [ˈfænsɪ] **IV 6B** 79 bunt, ausgefallen
fantastic [fænˈtæstɪk] **I 8A** 114 phantastisch
fantasy [ˈfæntəsɪ] **V 1B** 12,2 Phantasie
far [fɑː] **I 5C** 84 weit
farm [fɑːm] **II 3C** 36,3a Bauernhof, Farm
farmer [ˈfɑːmə] **II 2C** 25 Bäuerin/Bauer, Landwirt/in
farmhand [ˈfɑːmhænd] **II 7B** 94 Landarbeiter/in
farming [ˈfɑːmɪŋ] **II 7B** 95,2 Landwirtschaft

to **fascinate** [ˈfæsɪneɪt] **IV 4C** 58,4 beeindrucken, faszinieren
fashion [ˈfæʃn] **III 1A** 8 Mode
fast [fɑːst] **II 1C** 10 schnell
fast (*asleep*) [fɑːst] **III 7C** 89 fest
fat [fæt] **II 3D** 38 dick
father [ˈfɑːðə] **I FS4** 12 Vater
fault [fɔːlt] **III 1C** 14 Schuld; Fehler
favorite (*AE*) [ˈfeɪvərɪt] **II 7A** 91 Lieblings-
favourite (*BE*) [ˈfeɪvərɪt] **II 5B** 65,6 Lieblings-
fax [fæks] **II 8A** 103 Fax
fear [fɪə] **VI 3B** 38,3 Angst, Furcht
to **fear** [fɪə] **V 5B** 64,3 (be-)fürchten
⟨feast⟩ [fiːst] **III 7FE** 100 Festtag, Festessen
feature [ˈfiːtʃə] **IV 2A** 22 Vorstellung
to be **fed up** [ˌfedˈʌp] **I 8C** 123 die Nase voll haben
federal [ˈfedərəl] **V 5AB** 73 Bundes-, föderativ
fee-paying [ˈfiːpeɪɪŋ] **VI 3C** 41 Schulgeld zahlend (…, der/die Schulgeld zahlt)
to **feed*** [fiːd] **II 3B** 33 füttern
feeding machine [ˈfiːdɪŋ məˈʃiːn] **II 7B** 94 Füttermaschine
I **feel dizzy. II 3A** 30 Mir ist schwindlig.
to feel well* [ˌfiːl ˈwel] **I 6D** 97 sich wohl fühlen
feeling [ˈfiːlɪŋ] **V 1C** 17,8 Gefühl
feet [fiːt] **III 6D** 78 Fuß *(Längenmaß = 0.3048 m)*
felt pen [ˌfelt ˈpen] **I FS9** 26 Filzstift
fence [fens] **II 7C** 96 Zaun
ferry [ˈferɪ] **III 2A** 20 Fähre
festival [ˈfestəvl] **III 7FE** 98 Fest, Feiertag
to **fetch** [fetʃ] **I 1C** 39,4 holen
a **few** [fjuː] **I 6D** 96 ein paar
field [fiːld] **II 3C** 36,3 Feld
⟨to field⟩ [fiːld] **III 6D** 81 als Fänger/in spielen
a/one **fifth** [fɪfθ] **III 1A** 8 ein Fünftel
to **fight*** [faɪt] **II 2B** 21 kämpfen, raufen, streiten
fighter [ˈfaɪtə] **IV 1AB** 18 Kämpfer
figure [ˈfɪɡə] **II 1D** 13 Gestalt, Person
figure [ˈfɪɡə] **IV 5D** 77,10 Zahl
to **fill** [fɪl] **II 3D** 39 füllen
to fill in **II 6B** 80 ausfüllen
film [fɪlm] **I 7C** 110 Film
final [ˈfaɪnl] **III 2B** 22 letzte/r/s, endgültig
finally [ˈfaɪnəlɪ] **II 4C** 54 schließlich
to **find*** [faɪnd] **I FS3** 11,2 finden
fine [faɪn] **IV 4D** 60,2 Geldstrafe, Bußgeld
fine [faɪn] **I FS4** 12 schön, prima
finger [ˈfɪŋɡə] **II 5A** 61 Finger
to **finish I 8B** 120,6 beenden
fire [ˈfaɪə] **II 8A** 104,3 Feuer
firearm [ˈfaɪərɑːm] **V 1C** 15,4 Schusswaffe
fireman [ˈfaɪəmən] **III 7FE** 99 Feuerwehrmann
firewood [ˈfaɪəwʊd] **II 8A** 103 Brennholz
fireworks [ˈfaɪəwɜːks] **III 7FE** 107 Feuerwerk
first [fɜːst] **I 1C** 40,8 zuerst, zunächst
first aid [ˌfɜːst ˈeɪd] **III 4A** 46 erste Hilfe
first things first **II 6B** 80 eins nach dem anderen

fish (*sing. and pl.*) [fɪʃ] **II 4C** 58,10 Fisch(e)
(*fish*) bone [bəʊn] **II 5B** 63 (Fisch-)Gräte
to **fish** [fɪʃ] **II 7A** 93,5 angeln
fisherman, (*pl*) fishermen [ˈfɪʃəmən] **III 2A** 22 Fischer
fishing port [ˈfɪʃɪŋˌpɔːt] **III 2A** 21,1 Fischereihafen
fist [fɪst] **VI 3D** 46,2 Faust
to **fit** [fɪt] **VI 4C** 57,2 passen, geeignet sein
to **fix** [fɪks] **II 3B** 33 reparieren
to **fix** [fɪks] **V 3C** 36 befestigen
fixed [fɪkst] **III 2B** 22 fest
flag [flæɡ] **I 7C** 110 Flagge
flame [fleɪm] **III 1C** 14 Flamme
flamingo [fləˈmɪŋɡəʊ] **II 5C** 70,4 Flamingo
⟨flash⟩ [flæʃ] **III 7C** 95,12 Blitz
to **flash by** [flæʃ] **III 7C** 89 vorbeisausen, vorbeifliegen
flat [flæt] **I FS4** 12 Wohnung
flight [flaɪt] **II 6A** 77 Flug
to **float** [fləʊt] **V 5C** 65 schwimmen, treiben
floodlight [ˈflʌdˌlaɪt] **III 6D** 78 Flutlicht
floor [flɔː] **I 7B** 107,5 Stockwerk
floor [flɔː] **I FS6** 16 Fußboden, Boden
⟨to flow⟩ [fləʊ] **III 3C** 44,9 fließen, strömen
to flow [fləʊ] **V 5A** 61,2 fließen
flower [ˈflaʊə] **II 7C** 96 Blume
to **fly*** [flaɪ] **I 3B** 57 fliegen, fliegen lassen
fog [fɒɡ] **II 6C** 83,3 Nebel
foggy [ˈfɒɡɪ] **II 6C** 83,3 neblig
folk hero [ˈfəʊk ˌhɪərəʊ] **II 2A** 18 Volksheld
folk-rock [ˈfəʊkrɒk] **IV 1C** 12 *Musikrichtung*
to **follow** [ˈfɒləʊ] **II 4C** 54 folgen
food [fuːd] **I 6D** 96 Essen
foot [fʊt] **III 6D** 78 Fuß *(Längenmaß = 0.3048 m)*
foot (*feet*) **I 8B** 120,4 Fuß, Füße
football [ˈfʊtbɔːl] **I FS10** 28,1 Fußball
footwear [ˈfʊtweə] **IV 3C** 43,2 Schuhwerk, Fußbekleidung
to wait **for I FS11** 32 warten auf
for [fɔː] **I FS8** 23 für
for a minute **I 1A** 35,2 einen Augenblick/eine Minute lang
for a while [waɪl] **III 4C** 51 (für) eine Weile, eine Zeit lang
for an answer **I 5A** 78 als Antwort
for breakfast **I 4B** 70,4 zum Frühstück
for example **I 3C** 59 zum Beispiel
(*for*) long [lɒŋ] **II 3A** 30 lange
for luck [ˌfɔː ˈlʌk] **II 4C** 54 als Glücksbringer
to look for **I 1C** 40 suchen
for dear life III 6D 78 um ihr/sein Leben
force [fɔːs] **V 3AB** 43 Stärke, Kraft
to **force s.o. to do s.th.** [fɔːs] **VI 4B** 51 jmd zwingen, etw zu tun
forecast [ˈfɔːkɑːst] **III 2D** 28,3 Vorhersage
forefathers [ˈfɔːˌfɑːðəz] **IV 4AB** 64 Vorfahren, Ahnen
foreign [ˈfɒrən] **II 5A** 60 Fremd-, ausländisch

foreigner [ˈfɒrənə] **IV 4B** 55,2 Ausländer/in
forest [ˈfɒrɪst] **II 2A** 18 Wald
forever [fəˈrevə] **VI 4A** 47,b) auf immer, für alle Zeiten
to **forget*** [fəˈɡet] **I 5B** 81 vergessen
to **forgive,** forgave, forgiven* [fəˈɡɪv, fəˈɡeɪv, fəˈɡɪvn] **IV 6D** 86,1 vergeben, verzeihen
fork [fɔːk] **II 5C** 72,11 Gabel
form [fɔːm] **I FS8** 25 Form; Klasse
to **form** [fɔːm] **VI 4A** 48,1 bilden, schaffen, einrichten
form [fɔːm] **V 3A** 30 Formular
formal [ˈfɔːml] **V 3C** 37,1 formal, förmlich
former [ˈfɔːmə] **III 6C** 75 früher, ehemalig
formulation [ˌfɔːmjʊˈleɪʃn] **VI 1B** 11 Formulierung, Fassung
fortune [ˈfɔːtʃuːn] **IV 6A** 78 Vermögen
⟨forum⟩ [ˈfɔːrəm] **VI 1D** 18,5 (öffentliche) Diskussionsveranstaltung, Forum
forward [ˈfɔːwəd] **II 2C** 26 nach vorn, vorwärts
fossil [fɒsl] **IV 3A** 36,2 Versteinerung, Fossil
foul [faʊl] **II 5C** 68 Foul
to **foul** [faʊl] **II 5C** 68 foulen
to **found** [faʊnd] **III 6A** 72,4 gründen
frame [freɪm] **II 4B** 49 Rahmen
free [friː] **I 2B** 46 frei, kostenlos
free kick [ˌfriː ˈkɪk] **II 5C** 68 Freistoß
freedom [ˈfriːdəm] **IV 4A** 52 Freiheit
freeman [ˈfriːmən] **V 3AB** 43 freier Bürger, freier Mann
to **freeze***, froze, frozen [friːz, frəʊz, ˈfrəʊzn] **V 5B** 63 (ge-)frieren, einfrieren
freezing [ˈfriːzɪŋ] **IV 5B** 66 eisig, eiskalt
freight [freɪt] **V 5B** 62 Fracht, Ladung
French [frentʃ] **III 2AB** 32 (die) Franzosen
French [frentʃ] **II 5A** 60 französisch
⟨French fries⟩ (*AE*) [ˌfrentʃ ˈfraɪz] **III 7B** 88,6 Pommes frites
frequent [ˈfriːkwənt] **V 1A** 8,3 häufig
fresh [freʃ] **II 3B** 33 frisch
friend [frend] **I FS4** 12,1 Freund/in
friendly [ˈfrendlɪ] **III 5C** 62 freundlich
friendship [ˈfrendʃɪp] **IV 6B** 80,3 Freundschaft
to **frighten away** [ˈfraɪtn] **II 8B** 105 abschrecken
from [frɒm] **I FS3** 10 von, aus
front [frʌnt] **I 2C** 49,4 Vorderseite, Vorder-
front door [ˌfrʌnt ˈdɔː] **I 2C** 49,4 Haustür
in front of **I FS6** 17 vor
the **Frontier** [ˈfrʌntjə] **VI 2B** 24 *Grenze zwischen der Zivilisation und der Wildnis*
fruit [fruːt] **I 6C** 94,1 Obst
fuel [ˈfjuːəl] **V 2C** 27,7 Brennstoff, Benzin
full [fʊl] **I 1B** 37,2 voll
Have **fun!** [hæv ˈfʌn] **I 8B** 118 Viel Spaß!
to make fun of s.o. **III 5D** 66 sich über jdn lustig machen
function [ˈfʌŋkʃn] **V 3AB** 42 Funktion, Aufgabe

funeral [ˈfjuːnərəl] **V 5C** 65 Beerdigung
funny [ˈfʌnɪ] **I FS7** 18 witzig, komisch
furious [ˈfjʊərɪəs] **IV 6D** 85 wütend, wild
further [ˈfɜːðə] **IV 3AB** 47 weiter/e, näher/e
⟨further⟩ [ˈfɜːðə] **III 2D** 30,10 weiter (weg)
furthermore [ˌfɜːðəˈmɔː] **VI 1A** 6 außerdem, weiterhin
⟨fury⟩ [ˈfjʊərɪ] **III 4C** 54 Wut
fuse-box [ˈfjuːzbɒks] **II 1D** 13 Sicherungskasten
future [ˈfjuːtʃə] **IV 3AB** 48 Zukunft

G

gallon [ˈgælən] **VI 4A** 47,b) Gallone *(3,79 l in USA, 4,55 l in GB)*
gallows [ˈgæləʊz] **II 2C** 25 Galgen
game [geɪm] **I 3C** 60 Spiel
gamekeeper [ˈgeɪmˌkiːpə] **III 4C** 54 Wildhüter/in
gang [gæŋ] **III 6B** 73 Bande
gangster [ˈgæŋstə] **V 5C** 69,9 Gangster, Verbrecher
garage [ˈgærɑːʒ] **II 6A** 77 Garage
garbage (*AE*) [ˈgɑːbɪdʒ] **IV 4D** 59 Unfug; Müll, Abfall
garden [ˈgɑːdn] **I 3C** 59 Garten
gardener [ˈgɑːdnə] **IV 3AB** 46 Gärtner/in
gas (*AE*) [gæs] **III 7A** 84 Benzin
gas [gæs] **IV 5C** 72,6 Gas
gate [geɪt] **II 3C** 36,3a Tor
gear [gɪə] **II 4B** 49 Gang
Gee! (*AE*) [dʒiː] **II 7B** 94 Mensch! *(Ausruf des Erstaunens)*
goose, **geese** [guːs, giːs] **III 3C** 39 Gans
general [ˈdʒenrəl] **II 6D** 87,5 General
generation [ˌdʒenəˈreɪʃn] **IV 5C** 72,6 Generation
generator [ˈdʒenəreɪtə] **V 3D** 39,2 Generator
gentleman, (*pl*) gentlemen [ˈdʒentlmən] **III 1A** 10,2 Gentleman, Herr
geography [dʒɪˈɒgrəfɪ] **VI 3C** 40 Erdkunde, Geografie
geologist [dʒɪˈɒlədʒɪst] **III 5A** 58 Geologe/Geologin
German [ˈdʒɜːmən] **I FS8** 23 deutsch; Deutsch
Germanic [dʒɜːˈmænɪk] **IV 1AB** 19 germanisch
to **get*** [get] **I 3C** 60 bekommen, kriegen
to get back (*into*) **I 6D** 97 zurückgehen (in)
to get bored [bɔːd] **IV 3A** 37,6 sich langweilen
to get cold **I 6D** 97 kalt werden
to get divorced [dɪˈvɔːst] **III 7B** 86 sich scheiden lassen
to get home **I 4C** 74,6 nach Hause kommen
to get homesick [ˈhəʊmˌsɪk] **III 7B** 87,3 Heimweh bekommen
to get in **I 4C** 71,1 einsteigen
to get lost [lɒst] **I 3C** 59 verloren gehen, sich verlaufen
to get married [ˈmærɪd] **III 7B** 86 heiraten
to get off **I 5C** 84 aussteigen *(aus einem Bus/Zug)*
to get on with s.th. **II 2C** 26 weitermachen; vorwärts-, vorankommen
to get out **I 1C** 40,6 herauskommen
to get out of **I 4C** 71,3 aussteigen
to get over [get‿ˈəʊvə] **IV 1C** 13 *hier:* überwinden
to get ready **I 6D** 96 sich bereitmachen
to get to school **I 3A** 54,1 die Schule erreichen, zur Schule kommen
to get up **I 3A** 54,1 aufstehen
ghetto [ˈgetəʊ] **VI 3D** 45 Elendsviertel, Getto
ghost [gəʊst] **I 6B** 92,2 Geist, Gespenst
giant [ˈdʒaɪənt] **II 6A** 71 Riese, Riesen-
giant redwood [ˈdʒaɪənt ˈredwʊd] **III 6A** 71 Mammutbaum
gift [gɪft] **VI 1B** 8,1 Geschenk, Gabe
gigantic [dʒaɪˈgæntɪk] **I 8A** 114 riesig
⟨gimme (*give me*)⟩ [ˈgɪmɪ] **III 7B** 88,6 gib mir
girl [gɜːl] **I FS2** 9 Mädchen
⟨girlfriend⟩ [ˈgɜːlfrend] **I 7C** 113,5 Freundin
girlfriend [ˈgɜːlfrend] **V 1A** 6 (feste) Freundin
to **give*** [gɪv] **I 2B** 46 geben
to give a signal [ˈsɪgnəl] **II 6D** 84 ein Zeichen geben
to give birth [bɜːθ] **IV 3AB** 48 gebären, zur Welt bringen
⟨to give out⟩ **III 6C** 76,6 am Ende der Kräfte sein
to give out **II 2B** 21 verteilen
to give s.o. a lift [lɪft] **IV 3B** 38 jmd (im Auto) mitnehmen
to give up [gɪv‿ˈʌp] **IV 2A** 23,2 *hier:* aufgeben
glad [glæd] **II 5A** 60 froh
glass [glɑːs] **II 3D** 41,5 Glas
glasses [ˈglɑːsɪz] **III 6D** 80,5 Brille
⟨glee⟩ [gliː] **III 7FE** 101 Freude
to **glitter** [ˈglɪtə] **IV 3C** 42 glitzern, funkeln, glänzen
gloomy [ˈgluːmɪ] **IV 6B** 79 düster, trübe
glorious [ˈglɔːrɪəs] **V 3AB** 45 glorreich, ruhmvoll
glove [glʌv] **II 2B** 23,5 Handschuh
⟨to glow⟩ [gləʊ] **III 7FE** 101 glühen
to **go*** [gəʊ] **I FS2** 9 gehen
go ahead [ˌgəʊ‿əˈhed] **I 7A** 104,5 Nur zu!
to go for a walk **I FS11** 30 spazieren gehen
to go home **I FS4** 12 nach Hause gehen
to go in **I FS2** 9 hineingehen
to go mad [ˌgəʊ ˈmæd] **III 1C** 14 durchdrehen
to go off **II 5C** 68 das Spiel verlassen
to go on **I FS7** 19,2 weitermachen, fortfahren
to go on **II 7A** 92,2 vorgehen
to go on strike [straɪk] **IV 1B** 10,3 streiken, die Arbeit niederlegen
to go out **I 2C** 49,1 weggehen
to go past **I 7B** 108,6 vorbeifahren
to go round **II 4C** 53 vorbeikommen, jdn besuchen
to go shopping **I 6C** 94,1 einkaufen gehen
to go skateboarding **I 7A** 103,4 Skateboard fahren
to go swimming **I 7A** 103,4 schwimmen gehen
to go to bed **I 2B** 46 ins Bett gehen
to go to school **I 3C** 59 in die/zur Schule gehen
goal [gəʊl] **II 5C** 68 Tor
goalkeeper [ˈgəʊlkiːpə] **II 5C** 68 Torhüter/in
Oh **God!** [əʊ ˈgɒd] **I 7C** 110 Oh, Gott!
God bless you! [ˌgɒd ˈbles juː] **II 2C** 25 Gott segne Dich!
What's **going on here?*** **I 1C** 40,8 Was geht hier vor?
I'm **going to** … [ˈgəʊɪŋ tʊ] **I 7A** 102 ich werde …
gold [gəʊld] **III 2AB** 32 Gold
golden [ˈgəʊldn] **III 5B** 59 golden, Gold-; einmalig
golf [gɒlf] **II 6A** 77 Golf
gone [gɒn] **I 5A** 78 weg
good-for-nothing [ˈgʊdfəˌnʌθɪŋ] **VI 4B** 53,3 Taugenichts, Nichtsnutz
good [gʊd] **I FS1** 8 gut
good at [ˈgʊd‿æt] **II 7A** 93,6 gut in
goodbye [ˌgʊdˈbaɪ] **I 2C** 49,1 auf Wiedersehen
goods [gʊdz] **III 1A** 9 Güter, Waren
goose, geese [guːs, giːs] **III 3C** 39 Gans
Gosh! [gɒʃ] **I 7B** 105 Mensch!
gospel [ˈgɒspl] **VI 4C** 58,5 *evangelische Musikrichtung*
to **gossip** [ˈgɒsɪp] **I FS8** 24,2 Gerüchte verbreiten
got to* [gɒt] **I 7B** 105 muss
has got **I FS6** 16 hat
hasn't got **I FS6** 16 hat nicht
have (*got*) to **I 7B** 105 müssen
haven't got **I** 19,1 nicht haben
to have got **I FS7** 18 haben
to have (*got*) on **I 2C** 49,3 tragen, anhaben
to **govern** [ˈgʌvn] **V 3AB** 47 regieren
government [ˈgʌvnmənt] **I 8C** 124,2 Regierung
to **grab** [græb] **II 4C** 55,2 schnappen
grace [greɪs] **II 7C** 96 Tischgebet
grade [greɪd] **III 5B** 60,3 Klasse (*AE*); Niveau; Note
to **grade** [greɪd] **III 5C** 64,6 benoten; sortieren
gradually [ˈgrædʒʊəlɪ] **IV 6C** 82 allmählich
graduate [ˈgrædʒʊət] **VI 3C** 42,4 (Hochschul-)Absolvent/in
to **graduate** [ˈgrædjʊeɪt] **VI 3C** 40 absolvieren, die Abschlussprüfung machen
graffiti [grəˈfiːtɪ] **V 3C** 35 Graffiti, Wandmalereien
grain [greɪn] **V 5A** 60 Getreide
grammar school [ˈgræmə ˈskuːl] **V 3B** 34,3 *weiterführende Schule (entspricht etwa dem Gymnasium)*
gran (*coll*) [græn] **IV 2C** 30,5 Oma
grand slam [ˌgrændˈslæm] **II 2A** 18,4 Grand Slam
grandchild [ˈgræntʃaɪld] **II 1D** 15,6 Enkel/in
grandfather [ˈgrænˌfɑːðə] **II 1D** 15,6 Großvater
grandma [ˈgrænmɑː] **II 1D** 15,6 Oma
grandmother [ˈgrænˌmʌðə] **II 1D** 15,6 Großmutter
grandpa [ˈgrænpɑː] **II 1D** 15,6 Opa

grandparents [ˈgræn,peərənts] **II 1D** 15,6 Großeltern
grape [greɪp] **IV 3C** 45,7 (Wein-)Traube
graph [grɑːf] **V 2D** 29,3 graphische Darstellung, Graph
grass [grɑːs] **II 5C** 71,8 Gras
grateful [ˈgreɪtfʊl] **VI 2A** 22,2 dankbar
grave [greɪv] **IV 3C** 41 Grab
great [greɪt] **I FS8** 23 prima, toll, klasse
Greek [griːk] **IV 1B** 11,6 griechisch, Grieche/Griechin
green [griːn] **I 1A** 35 grün
⟨greengrocer's⟩ [ˈgriːn,grəʊsəz] **I 6** 90 (Obst- und) Gemüseladen
grey [greɪ] **I 1A** 35,1 grau
to **grill** [grɪl] **II 8A** 103 grillen
grip [grɪp] **V 5C** 66 Griff
grizzly [ˈgrɪzlɪ] **V 4A** 51,6 Grizzlybär
to **groan** [grəʊn] **III 2C** 24 stöhnen
ground [graʊnd] **II 2B** 21 Boden, Erde
group [gruːp] **II 2B** 21 Gruppe
grouse-shooting [ˈgraʊs] **III 4C** 54 Moorhuhnjagd
to **grow*** [grəʊ] **I 6D** 97 wachsen
to grow s.th. [grəʊ] **II 8B** 105 etw. anbauen
to grow up [grəʊ] **III 7B** 86 aufwachsen
grown-ups [ˈgrəʊnʌps] **IV 6C** 82 Erwachsene
growth [grəʊθ] **VI 2B** 25 Wachstum, Größe
to **guarantee** [,gærənˈtiː] **IV 4AB** 63 versprechen, garantieren
guard [gɑːd] **I 7C** 110 Wache
to **guess** (*AE*) [ges] **IV 5B** 66 vermuten, annehmen
Guess what! [ges] **II 6B** 80 Rate mal!
to guess [ges] **I 5A** 78 raten
guest [gest] **IV 3A** 35 Gast
guidance counselor (*AE*)/**counsellor** (*BE*) [ˈgaɪdns ,kaʊnsələ] **III 5B** 59 Verbindungslehrer
guide [gaɪd] **IV 1B** 11,5 Fremdenführer/in
⟨to guide⟩ [gaɪd] **III 7FE** 101 führen
to guide [gaɪd] **V 4B** 53,2 führen, leiten
guided tour [ˈgaɪdɪd ˈtʊə] **IV 5A** 65 (Rund-)Fahrt mit Fremdenführer/in
guilty (*of*) [ˈgɪltɪ] **V 1B** 11 schuldig
guitar [gɪˈtɑː] **II 5A** 61 Gitarre
gun [gʌn] **III 7FE** 107 Gewehr, Pistole
⟨gunpowder⟩ [ˈgʌn ,paʊdə] **III 7FE** 99 Schießpulver
guy (*AE*) [gaɪ] **II 6B** 80 Typ, Kerl
gym(*nasium*) [dʒɪmˈneɪzjəm] **IV 5D** 77,10 Turn-, Sporthalle

H

⟨haggis⟩ [ˈhægɪs] **III 3C** 44,11 gefüllter Schafsmagen
hair [heə] **II 8C** 108 Haare
half [hɑːf] **I 3A** 54,1 halb
half a million [hɑːf] **III 1A** 8 eine halbe Million
half past seven **I 3A** 54,1 halb acht
two and a half **II 7A** 91 zweieinhalb
hall [hɔːl] **I 5B** 81 Diele, Flur
hall [hɔːl] **IV 1A** 6 *hier:* Halle, großer Saal
hammer [ˈhæmə] **III 3A** 34 Hammer
hamster [ˈhæmstə] **II 3D** 40,2 Hamster
hand [hænd] **I 2C** 50,6 Hand
hand-out [ˈhændaʊt] **VI 4A** 49,5 Handzettel, Werbezettel
like the back of my hand **III 1B** 11 wie meine Westentasche
to **hand** [hænd] **III 6A** 72,4 reichen, geben
handkerchief [ˈhæŋkətʃɪf] **III 4C** 56,12 Taschentuch
handle [ˈhændl] **I 1C** 39,2 Griff, Klinke
to **handle** [ˈhændl] **IV 4D** 59 behandeln
handlebars [ˈhændlbɑːz] **II 4B** 49 Lenkstange
Hands up! **I 5A** 78 Hände hoch!
hang-gliding [ˈhæŋ,glaɪdɪŋ] **V 5C** 65 Drachenfliegen
⟨to hang*⟩ [hæŋ] **I FS10** 28,3 hängen
to hang around [hæŋ əˈraʊnd] **IV 6B** 80,3 herumhängen, herumlungern
to hang up [hæŋ ˈʌp] **III 3A** 34 aufhängen
hangman [ˈhæŋmən] **II 2C** 26 Henker
to **happen** [hæpən] **I 2C** 50,7 geschehen, passieren
to happen to [ˈhæpən] **VI 3B** 37,a) zufällig
happy [ˈhæpɪ] **I 4A** 66,2 glücklich
harbor (*AE*) [ˈhɑːbə] **IV 4A** 50 Hafen
⟨harbour⟩ [ˈhɑːbə] **I 4** 65 Hafen
hard [hɑːd] **III 2C** 24,4 krampfhaft; hart, schwer, schwierig
hardly [ˈhɑːdlɪ] **II 2C** 25,2 kaum, fast nicht
hardship [ˈhɑːdʃɪp] **VI 2A** 19 Not, Elend
harmful [ˈhɑːmfʊl] **VI 1B** 8,1 schädlich, nachteilig
harmony [ˈhɑːmənɪ] **IV 1B** 9 Harmonie, Einklang
harp [hɑːp] **IV 1A** 6 Harfe
harvest [ˈhɑːvɪst] **IV 4A** 52 Ernte
has to* **I 7C** 110 muss
has got **I FS6** 16 hat
hasn't got* **I FS6** 16 hat nicht
hat [hæt] **I 2C** 49,3 Hut
to **hate** [heɪt] **II 2B** 24,6 hassen
Have ... **I 4C** 71,2 Nimm/Nehmt ein Stück Schokolade.
to have* [hæv] haben
Have a good time! **I 5C** 84 Viel Spaß!
have got **I FS7** 18 haben
have got to **I 7B** 105 müssen
haven't got **I FS7** 19,1 nicht haben
to have a bath **I 5B** 81 baden
to have a cold **I 4C** 71,1 eine Erkältung/einen Schnupfen haben
to have a date [deɪt] **IV 2B** 26,3 eine Verabredung haben
to have a go [gəʊ] **II 7C** 97 etw. versuchen, probieren
to have a look at **I 7A** 104,5 ansehen
to have breakfast **I 3C** 59 frühstücken
to have fun **I 8B** 118 Spaß haben
to have (*got*) on **I 2C** 49,3 anhaben, tragen
to have (*got*) to **I 7B** 105 müssen
to have in mind [maɪnd] **IV 6C** 82 im Sinn haben
to have tea **I 4C** 74,6 Abendbrot essen
to have* s.o. do s.th. [hæv] **VI 4A** 47,a) jmd zu etw veranlassen, jmd etw machen lassen
he [hiː] **I FS2** 9 er
head [hed] **I 2C** 50,6 Kopf
to **head (out)** [hed] **VI 4A** 47,b) gehen, fahren
headache [ˈhedeɪk] **II 3A** 30 Kopfschmerzen
heading [ˈhedɪŋ] **II 8C** 109,2 Überschrift
headlight [ˈhedlaɪt] **V 1C** 14 Scheinwerfer
headline [ˈhedlaɪn] **V 5AB** 77 (Zeitungs-)Schlagzeile
headmaster [,hedˈmɑːstə] **IV 3B** 38 Direktor/in, Schulleiter/in
headquarters [,hedˈkwɔːtəz] **II 6A** 76 Hauptstelle, Zentrale
health [helθ] **IV 3B** 40,6 Gesundheit
healthy [ˈhelθɪ] **V 4C** 56,4 gesund
to **hear*** [hɪə] **I 2B** 46 hören
heart [hɑːt] **IV 4AB** 63 Herz
the **Heartland** [ˈhɑːtlənd] **VI 2A** 23,4 das amerikanische Kernland
heat [hiːt] **V 2B** 23,3 Hitze
heavy [ˈhevɪ] **I 2C** 49,2 schwer
height [haɪt] **II 4B** 49 Höhe
helicopter [ˈhelɪkɒptə] **III 3A** 34 Hubschrauber
heliport [ˈhelɪpɔːt] **III 3A** 34 Hubschrauberlandeplatz
heliskiing [ˈhelɪskiːɪŋ] **V 4B** 53,2 *Skilaufen mit Hubschrauber als Lift*
⟨hell⟩ [hel] **III 6C** 77,6 Hölle
hell [hel] **V 2A** 18 Hölle
hello [həˈləʊ] **I FS1** 8 hallo, guten Tag
helmet [ˈhelmɪt] **II 5C** 71,7 Helm
help [help] **II 4C** 54 Hilfe
to **help** **I FS11** 30 helfen
helpful [ˈhelpfʊl] **III 5B** 60,3 hilfreich, hilfsbereit
hen [hen] **I 2A** 44,6 Huhn, Henne
her [hɜː] **I FS2** 9 ihr, sie
her name **I FS2** 9 ihr Name
take her to the station **I 2B** 46 bring sie zum Bahnhof
herd [hɜːd] **V 4A** 48 Herde
here [hɪə] **I FS3** 10 hier
here you are **I 6B** 92,3 bitte schön
heritage [ˈherɪtɪdʒ] **IV 6C** 84,5 Erbe, Vermächtnis
hero [ˈhɪərəʊ] **II 2A** 18 Held
hers [hɜːz] **III 1C** 14 ihre, ihrer, ihres
he's = he is [hiːz] **I FS2** 9 er ist
Hey! [heɪ] **I 1A** 35,3 He!
⟨heyday⟩ [ˈheɪdeɪ] **VI 1D** 18,5 Höhepunkt
hi-tech [,haɪˈtek] **II 7B** 94 Hi-Tech
Hi! [haɪ] **II 1B** 8 Hallo!
to **hide*** [haɪd] **II 2B** 21 (sich) verstecken
high [haɪ] **I 1C** 40,6 hoch
high school (*AE*) [ˈhaɪskuːl] **IV 4D** 59 *Oberschule bis zur Hochschulreife*
high school [ˈhaɪskuːl] **III 7B** 86 weiterführende Schule
highbrow [ˈhaɪbraʊ] **IV 6C** 82 hochgestochen, intellektuell
hiker [ˈhaɪkə] **IV 6B** 80,2 Wanderer/Wanderin

hiking ['haɪkɪŋ] **IV 6A** 78 Wandern
hill [hɪl] **III 4C** 54,6 Hügel
him [hɪm] **I 2B** 46 ihn, ihm
himself [hɪm'self] **II 3B** 33 sich, (sich) selbst *(männlich)*
hint [hɪnt] **III 6D** 80,5 Hinweis, Andeutung
hip-hop ['hɪphɒp] **VI 4B** 54,4 *Musikrichtung*
hippie ['hɪpɪ] **III 7B** 86 *Anhänger/in einer Bewegung in den 60er Jahren*
hippo ['hɪpəʊ] **II 3C** 36,2a Nilpferd
his [hɪz] **I FS2** 9 sein
Hispanic [hɪ'spænɪk] **V 5C** 69,8 Spanier/in; spanisch
historian [hɪ'stɔ:rɪən] **IV 4B** 54 Geschichtswissenschaftler/in, Historiker/in
historic [hɪ'stɒrɪk] **IV 6A** 78 historisch (bedeutsam)
historical [hɪ'stɒrɪkl] **VI 4A** 47,b) geschichtlich, historisch
history ['hɪstərɪ] **II 6D** 86,5 Geschichte
hit-and-run (*accident*) [ˌhɪt‿ən‿'rʌn] **III 4A** 48,6 Unfall mit Fahrerflucht
to **hit*** [hɪt] **II 7C** 97,3 treffen
to **hitchhike** ['hɪtʃhaɪk] **V 1C** 16,6 trampen, per Anhalter fahren
hitlist ['hɪtlɪst] **V 1A** 8,3 *hier:* Liste der Spitzenreiter
hobby ['hɒbɪ] **II 6B** 80 Hobby
hockey ['hɒkɪ] **II 5A** 60 Hockey
hog (*mainly AE*) [hɒg] **V 5B** 63 (Mast-)Schwein
to **hold*** [həʊld] **I 3A** 54,2 halten, abhalten, veranstalten
 Hold your horses! ['həʊld jɔ: 'hɔ:sɪz] **II 7C** 96 Langsam!
 to hold on (*to s.th.*) [ˌhəʊld‿'ɒn] **III 2C** 24 (sich) festhalten (an)
hole [həʊl] **I 3B** 57 Loch
holiday ['hɒlədeɪ] **I 4C** 72,6 Ferien, Urlaub
⟨**holly**⟩ ['hɒlɪ] **III 7FE** 100 Stechpalme
Holocaust ['hɒləkɔ:st] **VI 3A** 35,3 *Massenvernichtung der europäischen Juden durch die Nationalsozialisten*
holy ['həʊlɪ] **V 3AB** 42 heilig
home [həʊm] Haus, Heim
 at home **I FS7** 18 zu Hause
 Home Economics [ˌhəʊm i:kə'nɒmɪks] **II 5A** 60 Hauswirtschaftslehre
 to get home **I 4C** 74,6 nach Hause kommen
 to go home **I FS4** 12 nach Hause gehen
 to take home **I 3A** 54,1 nach Hause bringen
homeless ['həʊmlɪs] **IV 5A** 65 Obdachlose/r
homesick ['həʊmsɪk] **V 4C** 55 Heimweh haben, krank vor Heimweh sein
homework ['həʊmwɜ:k] **I 1B** 37 Hausaufgaben
 to do my homework **I 1B** 37,1 meine Hausaufgaben machen
honest ['ɒnɪst] **VI 2D** 31,a) aufrichtig, offen, ehrlich
honey ['hʌnɪ] **VI 3A** 36,6 Honig
honor student (*AE*) ['ɒnə] **VI 3D** 46,1 *Person, die einen besonders guten akademischen Abschluss anstrebt*
hoof [hu:f] **II 3D** 39 Huf
hooligan ['hu:lɪgən] **II 5C** 68 Fußballrowdy
hooray [hʊ'reɪ] **I 5A** 78 hurra
hooves [hu:vz] **II 3D** 39 Hufe
to **hop** [hɒp] **II 3B** 33 hüpfen
hope [həʊp] **V 3C** 35 Hoffnung
to **hope** [həʊp] **I 4C** 71,3 hoffen
hopeless ['həʊplɪs] **III 5B** 59 hoffnungslos, aussichtslos, unmöglich
hopscotch ['hɒpskɒtʃ] **I FS11** 30 Huckekasten, Himmel und Hölle
horn [hɔ:n] **II 2B** 23,4 Horn
horrified ['hɒrɪfaɪd] **III 6D** 78 entsetzt
horse [hɔ:s] **I 2A** 44,3 Pferd
hose [həʊz] **II 6D** 84 Schlauch
hospital ['hɒspɪtl] **I 8C** 124,2 Krankenhaus
host family ['həʊstˌfæməlɪ] **IV 3A** 34 Gastgeberfamilie
⟨**hot dog**⟩ [ˌhɒt 'dɒg] **III 7B** 88,5 *heißes Würstchen*
hot [hɒt] **II 3D** 40,2 heiß; scharf
hot [hɒt] **III 1C** 16,5 scharf
hotel [həʊ'tel] **I 2B** 46 Hotel
⟨**hound** (*dog*)⟩ ['haʊnd ('dɒg)] **VI 4C** 59,6 Jagdhund
hour ['aʊə] **I 4C** 72,5 Stunde
house [haʊs] **I FS4** 12 Haus
hovercraft ['hɒvəkrɑ:ft] **III 2A** 20 *Luftkissenfahrzeug*
how [haʊ] wie
 How about …? [ˌhaʊ ə'baʊt] **III 3A** 34 Wie wäre es mit …?
 how much **I 6B** 92,3 wie viel
how old **I FS8** 25,3 wie alt
 ⟨How are you?⟩ [ˌhaʊə'ju:] **I FS7** 21,9 Wie geht's dir/euch/Ihnen?
 how many **I FS10** 29,4 wie viele
however [haʊ'evə] **III 5A** 58 jedoch, aber
⟨to **hug**⟩ [hʌg] **III 7FE** 104 umarmen
to hug [hʌg] **V 1C** 13 umarmen
huge [hju:dʒ] **IV 4C** 58 riesengroß, gewaltig, mächtig
human ['hju:mən] **VI 2A** 22,3 Menschen
humor (*AE*) ['hju:mə] **VI 2A** 23,5 Humor
to be **hungry** ['hʌŋgrɪ] **I 4C** 71,2 Hunger haben
to **hunt** [hʌnt] **II 2A** 19 jagen
hunter ['hʌntə] **IV 6A** 78 Jäger/in
hurricane ['hʌrɪkən] **III 7C** 93,7 Orkan, Hurrikan
to **hurry** (*up*) ['hʌrɪ] **II 2C** 26 sich beeilen
to **hurt*** [hɜ:t] **III 4A** 46 verletzen, schaden, wehtun
husband ['hʌzbənd] **II 1D** 15,6 Ehemann
hygiene ['haɪdʒi:n] **V 2D** 29,3 Gesundheitspflege, Hygiene
hymn [hɪm] **III 2D** 27 Hymne

I

I hope [həʊp] **VI 3B** 37,a) hoffentlich
 I won't* [wəʊnt] **II 3A** 30 ich werde nicht
 I suppose [sə'pəʊz] **VI 3B** 37,a) vermutlich
I [aɪ] **I FS1** 8 ich
I'm = I am [aɪm] **I FS1** 8 ich bin
 I can't bear [beə] **IV 3A** 36,2 nicht ertragen können, nicht ausstehen können
 I can't stand … [stænd] **II 7A** 92,4 ich kann … nicht ausstehen
 I'll = I will [wɪl] **II 3A** 30 ich werde
 I'm going to … ['gəʊɪŋ tʊ] **I 7A** 102 ich werde …
ice-cream [ˌaɪs'kri:m] **I 6C** 94,1 Eis (-krem)
 ice skater ['aɪs ˌskeɪtə] **II 2A** 18 Schlittschuhläufer/in
 ice skating ['aɪsˌskeɪtɪŋ] **II 2A** 20,2 Schlittschuhlaufen
iceberg ['aɪsbɜ:g] **III 2D** 26 Eisberg
icy ['aɪsɪ] **II 6C** 83,3 eisig
idea [aɪ'dɪə] **I FS2** 9 Idee, Vorstellung, Ahnung
to **identify** [aɪ'dentɪfaɪ] **V 5C** 65 wiedererkennen, identifizieren
identity [aɪ'dentətɪ] **VI 3B** 38,2 Identität
idiot ['ɪdɪət] **II 5A** 61 Idiot
if [ɪf] **II 3C** 35 wenn, falls, ob
⟨**if**⟩ [ɪf] **I FS10** 28,3 falls
ill [ɪl] **I FS3** 10 krank
illegal [ɪ'li:gl] **VI 3A** 33,b) ungesetzlich, illegal
image ['ɪmɪdʒ] **VI 1D** 18,3 Ansehen; Bild
to **imagine** [ɪ'mædʒɪn] **III 5B** 61,5 sich (etw.) vorstellen
imaginery [ɪ'mædʒɪnərɪ] **V 3AB** 46 nur in der Vorstellung vorhanden, eingebildet, imaginär
immediately [ɪ'mi:djətlɪ] **I 2B** 46 sofort
immigrant ['ɪmɪgrənt] **IV 5A** 65 Einwanderer/Einwanderin
to **immigrate** ['ɪmɪgreɪt] **VI 3A** 33,a) einwandern
importance [ɪm'pɔ:tns] **IV 3B** 38 Bedeutung, Wichtigkeit
important [ɪm'pɔ:tnt] **II 2A** 18 wichtig, bedeutend
impossible [ɪm'pɒsəbl] **II 6D** 84 unmöglich
to **impress** [ɪm'pres] **III 4A** 46 beeindrucken, imponieren
impression [ɪm'preʃn] **IV 5B** 66 Eindruck
to **improve** [ɪm'pru:v] **V 1B** 11 verbessern
improvement [ɪm'pru:vmənt] **VI 4A** 48,3 Verbesserung
to **improvise** ['ɪmprəvaɪz] **IV 1C** 12 improvisieren, ohne Vorbereitung (spielen)
in [ɪn] **I FS4** 12 in
 in brackets [ɪn 'brækɪts] **IV 6C** 83,2 in Klammern
 in charge of ['tʃɑ:dʒ] **IV 2C** 27 verantwortlich für
 in common [ˌɪn‿'kɒmən] **V 3AB** 45 gemeinsam
 ⟨in great terror⟩ ['terə] **III 6C** 76,6 erschrocken
 in horror [ɪn 'hɒrə] **IV 6D** 85 mit Grausen, entsetzt
 in jail [ɪn 'dʒeɪl] **IV 5D** 74 im/ins Gefängnis
 (*in order*) to **III 5D** 66 um … zu
 in pairs [peəz] **IV 2C** 33,12 zu zweit, in Paaren
 ⟨(*in*) spite of⟩ [spaɪt] **III 6C** 76,6 trotz

in spite of [ɪn ˈspaɪt‿əv] **IV 3B** 40,5 trotz, ungeachtet
in three weeks' time [taɪm] **IV 1C** 12 in 3 Wochen
in time [ɪn‿ˈtaɪm] **IV 2A** 24,4 rechtzeitig, pünktlich
Is he in? **I 6D** 99,6 Ist er zu Hause?
to be in pain [peɪn] **II 3D** 39 Schmerzen haben
to come in **I 2B** 46 sich melden *(Funksprache)*
to get in **I 4C** 71,1 einsteigen
to go in **I FS2** 9 hineingehen
to **include** [ɪnˈkluːd] **VI 1A** 5 einschließen
income [ˈɪnkʌm] **VI 3A** 34,c) Einkommen
to **increase** [ɪnˈkriːs] **V 3AB** 45 zunehmen, ansteigen
incredible [ɪnˈkredəbl] **IV 5B** 66 unglaublich
independence [ˌɪndɪˈpendəns] **VI 1A** 7,2 Unabhängigkeit
independent [ˌɪndɪˈpendənt] **III 7FE** 107 unabhängig
Indian [ˈɪndɪən] **II 6B** 80 indisch, Inder/in; indianisch, Indianer/in
indirect [ˌɪndɪˈrekt] **V 5AB** 74 indirekt
individual [ˌɪndɪˈvɪdʒʊəl] **VI 1B** 8,1 eigen, individuell
indoor [ˈɪndɔː] **IV 5A** 65 Hallen-
industrial [ɪnˈdʌstrɪəl] **IV 1B** 9 industriell, Industrie-
to **industrialize** [ɪnˈdʌstrɪəlaɪz] **VI 3C** 42,3 industrialisieren
industry [ˈɪndəstrɪ] **II 2A** 18 Industrie
⟨influence⟩ [ˈɪnflʊəns] **IV 2C** 30,6 Einfluss
to **influence** [ˈɪnflʊəns] **VI 1D** 15,1 beeinflussen
influence [ˈɪnflʊəns] **V 1B** 12,2 Einfluss
to **inform** [ɪnˈfɔːm] **III 4B** 49 benachrichtigen, informieren
information [ˌɪnfəˈmeɪʃn] **I 7A** 103,2 Information
infrastructure [ˈɪnfrəˌstrʌktʃə] **VI 1D** 15,1 Verkehrsnetz, Infrastruktur
injection [ɪnˈdʒekʃn] **II 3D** 39 Spritze, Injektion
to **injure** [ˈɪndʒə] **III 4A** 46 verletzen
injured [ˈɪndʒəd] **V 4A** 51,6 verletzt
injury [ˈɪndʒərɪ] **II 5C** 68 Verletzung
injustice [ɪnˈdʒʌstɪs] **V 3AB** 44 Ungerechtigkeit
inland [ˈɪnlænd] **V 5B** 62 Inland-
inner city [ˌɪnə‿ˈsɪtɪ] **V 3C** 35 Innenstadt, innerstädtisch
the **inside** [ˌɪnˈsaɪd] **II 4A** 47 Innenraum, das Innere
inside [ˌɪnˈsaɪd] **II 1D** 12 innen, drinnen, hinein
to **insist** [ɪnˈsɪst] **IV 3B** 40,4 verlangen, bestehen (auf)
to **inspect** [ɪnˈspekt] **V 3A** 30 überprüfen, untersuchen
inspector [ɪnˈspektə] **III 4A** 48,7 Polizeiinspektor/in; Kontrolleur/in
instead [ɪnˈsted] **III 1B** 12,2 statt dessen
institution [ˌɪnstɪˈtjuːʃn] **V 3AB** 46 Einrichtung, Institution
instruction [ɪnˈstrʌkʃn] **I 4A** 66,1 Anweisung, Anleitung
instrument [ˈɪnstrʊmənt] **III 7C** 93,7 Instrument; Gerät
insult [ˈɪnsʌlt] **VI 1D** 17,2 Beleidigung
to **integrate** [ˈɪntɪgreɪt] **VI 4A** 47,b) eingliedern, integrieren
intelligent [ɪnˈtelɪdʒənt] **III 5D** 66 intelligent, klug
interest [ˈɪntrəst] **IV 3A** 36,2 Interesse
interested in [ˈɪntrɪstɪd] **II 7A** 92,4 interessiert an
interesting [ˈɪntrɪstɪŋ] **I 5C** 84 interessant
international [ˌɪntəˈnæʃənl] **IV 3B** 38 international
interpreter [ɪnˈtɜːprɪtə] **IV 4A** 52,1 Dolmetscher/in
to **interrupt** [ˌɪntəˈrʌpt] **V 3B** 33 unterbrechen
interval [ˈɪntəvl] **IV 3B** 38 Pause, Unterbrechung
interview [ˈɪntəvjuː] **IV 4B** 55,2 Vorstellungsgespräch, Interview
to **interview** [ˈɪntəvjuː] **II 5B** 66,7 interviewen
interviewer [ˈɪntəvjuːə] **IV 4D** 59 Interviewer/in
into [ˈɪntʊ] **I FS11** 30 in (hinein)
to **introduce** [ˌɪntrəˈdjuːs] **IV 4D** 59 einführen, vorstellen
to introduce s.o. [ˌɪntrəˈdjuːs] **III 5C** 65,7 jdn vorstellen
to **invade** [ɪnˈveɪd] **IV 1AB** 19 einmarschieren
invention [ɪnˈvenʃn] **V 2A** 19 Erfindung
inventor [ɪnˈventə] **V 2A** 19,2 Erfinder/in
invitation [ˌɪnvɪˈteɪʃn] **I 6B** 92,1 Einladung
to **invite** [ɪnˈvaɪt] **II 7B** 94 einladen
Irish [ˈaɪərɪʃ] **IV 1A** 6 irisch, (die) Iren
⟨Irish⟩ [ˈaɪərɪʃ] **III 7FE** 105 irisch
iron [ˈaɪən] **V 2A** 19 Eisen
irregular [ɪˈregjʊlə] **II 4B** 50,3 unregelmäßig
is* [ɪz] **I FS1** 8 ist
is/are lying* [ˈlaɪɪŋ] **I 4A** 66,2 liegt, -en
island [ˈaɪlənd] **I 7C** 110 Insel
isn't = is not* [ˈɪznt] **I FS5** 14 ist nicht
it [ɪt] **I FS3** 10 es
Italian [ɪˈtæljən] **II 5B** 65,5 italienisch, Italiener/in
in **italics** [ɪn ɪˈtælɪks] **IV 5D** 75,6 kursiv, schräg geschrieben
item [ˈaɪtəm] **VI 1B** 8,1 Gegenstand, Punkt, Artikel
its [ɪts] **I 3B** 57 sein/e, ihr/e
it's = it is [ɪts] **I FS3** 10 es ist

J

Jack Schaefer [ˈdʒæk ˈʃæfə] **VI 2A** 20 *amerikanischer Schriftsteller*
jack-o'-lantern [ˌdʒækəʊˈlæntən] **III 7FE** 98 Kürbislaterne
jacket [ˈdʒækɪt] **I 2C** 49,3 Jacke, Frack, Jackett
Jamaican [dʒəˈmeɪkən] **I 6B** 92,1 jamaikanisch, Jamaikaner/in
Japanese [ˌdʒæpəˈniːz] **II 2B** 21 japanisch, Japaner/in
jazz [dʒæz] **V 5B** 63 Jazz *(Musikrichtung)*
jeans [dʒiːnz] **I 1A** 35,3 Jeans
jeep [dʒiːp] **V 3D** 38 Jeep, Geländefahrzeug
jetty [ˈdʒetɪ] **II 8B** 105 Landesteg, Mole
Jew [dʒuː] **IV 5A** 65 Jude/Jüdin
jewel [ˈdʒuːəl] **III 1A** 8 Juwel, Edelstein
Jewish [ˈdʒuːɪʃ] **VI 3A** 35,3 jüdisch
job [dʒɒb] **I 3A** 54,1 Arbeit, Job; Aufgabe, Auftrag
to **jog** [dʒɒg] **I 7C** 110 joggen
to **join** [dʒɔɪn] **III 2AB** 32 beitreten, Mitglied werden von; verbinden
to join in [ˈdʒɔɪn‿ˈɪn] **IV 1C** 12 sich beteiligen, mitmachen
joke [dʒəʊk] **IV 6D** 85 Witz, Spaß
to **joke** [dʒəʊk] **III 1C** 18,8 Witze machen, scherzen
⟨joke⟩ [dʒəʊk] **I 7C** 113,5 Streich
⟨joker⟩ [ˈdʒəʊkə] **I 7C** 113,5 Witzbold, Spaßvogel
journalist [ˈdʒɜːnəlɪst] **V 2B** 22 Journalist/in
journey [ˈdʒɜːnɪ] **III 6AB** 82 Reise
Jr *(Junior)* [ˈdʒuːnjə] **II 7A** 91 junior
judge [dʒʌdʒ] **V 3AB** 44 Richter/in
judicial [dʒuːˈdɪʃl] **V 3AB** 47 gerichtlich, richterlich
to **juggle** [ˈdʒʌgl] **V 3B** 33 jonglieren
juggler [ˈdʒʌglə] **V 3D** 38 Jongleur/in
juice [dʒuːs] **IV 3B** 38 Saft
⟨juke box⟩ [ˈdʒuːkbɒks] **III 7C** 95,12 Musikbox
jumble sale [ˈdʒʌmbl ˌseɪl] **I 3A** 54,2 Flohmarkt *(für Wohltätigkeitszwecke)*
jumbo jet [ˈdʒʌmbəʊˌdʒet] **I 7A** 103,3 Jumbojet
jumbo steak [ˈdʒʌmbəʊ ˌsteɪk] **II 6A** 76 Riesensteak
to **jump** *(down)* [dʒʌmp] **II 2B** 21 (herunter-)springen
to jump about [dʒʌmp] **II 6D** 85 herumspringen
jungle [ˈdʒʌŋgl] **VI 1B** 9 Dschungel
junior disco [ˈdʒuːnjə ˈdɪskəʊ] **IV 2C** 27 Jugenddiskothek
jury [ˈdʒʊərɪ] **V 3AB** 43 die Geschworenen, Jury
just [dʒʌst] nur, gerade
just a minute **I 2B** 46 einen Moment
just like [ˌdʒʌstˈlaɪk] **II 4C** 54 genauso wie
Just our luck! **III 1C** 14 Pech (gehabt), wie immer!
just when **I 5A** 78 jetzt, wo
justice [ˈdʒʌstɪs] **V 3AB** 44 Gerechtigkeit
to **justify** [ˈdʒʌstɪfaɪ] **VI 3B** 38,3 rechtfertigen

K

to **keep*** [kiːp] **II 3A** 30 (da) behalten; halten, aufbewahren
to keep on *(doing s.th.)* [kiːp] **III 7A** 84 etw. weitermachen, fortsetzen
keeper [ˈkiːpə] **IV 3C** 44,4 Aufseher, Wärter
⟨kennel⟩ [ˈkenl] **III 7FE** 104 Hundehütte
ketchup [ˈketʃəp] **I 6C** 94,1 Ketschup
kettle [ˈketl] **III 3B** 37 Kochkessel
key [kiː] **I 1C** 39,2 Schlüssel

key word ['ki: ˌwɜ:d] **II 8C** 109,2 Schlüsselwort

keyboarding ['ki:bɔ:dɪŋ] **VI 3C** 40 Maschinenschreiben (mit Computertastatur)

to **kick** [kɪk] **I 1C** 40,7 treten (gegen)

to **kick one's legs up** **II 8C** 108 die Beine hochwerfen

kid brother/sister ['kɪd 'brʌðə] **III 7C** 89 kleiner Bruder/kleine Schwester

to **kidnap** ['kɪdnæp] **IV 4D** 59 entführen, kidnappen

kids [kɪdz] **II 6B** 80 Kinder

to **kill** [kɪl] **II 2C** 26 töten

kilo ['ki:ləʊ] **II 1C** 10 Kilo

kind [kaɪnd] **III 3C** 43 Art, Sorte, Typ

⟨kind⟩ [kaɪnd] **III 3C** 44,9 nett, freundlich

king [kɪŋ] **I 7C** 110 König

kingdom ['kɪŋdəm] **IV 1AB** 19 Königreich

⟨kipper⟩ ['kɪpə] **I 7C** 113,5 Räucherhering

⟨to kiss⟩ [kɪs] **III 7FE** 103 küssen

to kiss [kɪs] **IV 1C** 14,2 küssen

kitchen ['kɪtʃɪn] **I 5B** 81 Küche

kite [kaɪt] **I 3B** 57 Drachen

knife [naɪf] **II 5C** 72,11 Messer

knight [naɪt] **V 3AB** 45 Ritter

knives [naɪvz] **II 5C** 72,11 Messer

to **knock** [nɒk] **IV 5D** 73 schlagen, stoßen

  to knock down [ˌnɒk 'daʊn] **III 4A** 48,5 anfahren, umwerfen

to **know*** [nəʊ] **I 5C** 85 wissen, kennen

  to know one's way about **III 1B** 11 sich auskennen, sich zurechtfinden

knowledge ['nɒlɪdʒ] **IV 5C** 71,2 Kenntnis, Wissen

Korean [kə'rɪən] **VI 3B** 38,3 koreanisch; Koreaner/in

L

labour ['leɪbə] **V 2A** 21,4 Arbeit

lady ['leɪdɪ] **I 2A** 45,1 Dame

lake [leɪk] **I 7C** 110 See

lamb [læm] **III 1C** 16,5 Lamm

lamp [læmp] **II 1D** 13 Lampe

lampshade ['læmpʃeɪd] **III 5B** 59 Lampenschirm

land [lænd] **II 2B** 24,6 Land

to **land** [lænd] **I 7C** 111 landen

landmark ['lændmɑ:k] **III 5A** 58 Wahrzeichen

landrover ['lændˌrəʊvə] **III 3C** 40 *Geländewagen*

landscape ['lænskeɪp] **III 6A** 70 Landschaft(s-)

language ['læŋgwɪdʒ] **II 5A** 60 Sprache

  language lab [læb] **II 5A** 60 Sprachlabor

lap [læp] **IV 5C** 71,3 Schoß

large [lɑ:dʒ] **II 1C** 10 groß

⟨lassie⟩ ['læsɪ] **III 3C** 44,9 Mädchen, Mädel

⟨to last⟩ [lɑ:st] **III 1C** 19,10 dauern, (aus-)reichen

last [lɑ:st] **I 8B** 119,3 letzte, letzter, letztes

at **last** **I 2C** 49,2 endlich

to last [lɑ:st] **V 1A** 6 (aus-)reichen

late [leɪt] **I FS3** 10 spät

to be **late** **I FS3** 10 zu spät kommen

later [leɪtə] **I 4C** 72,5 später

latest ['leɪtɪst] **II 7A** 92,2 neueste, neuester, neuestes

Latin ['lætɪn] **IV 3AB** 49 Latein, lateinisch

to **laugh** [lɑ:f] **I 2C** 49,4 lachen

law [lɔ:] **III 7C** 92,6 Gesetz

lawn [lɔ:n] **II 6D** 84 Rasen

lawyer ['lɔ:jə] **III 6C** 75 (Rechts-)Anwältin/Anwalt

lazy ['leɪzɪ] **I 7B** 107,4 faul

lead [li:d] **III 3C** 39 Leine

  lead singer ['li:dˌsɪŋə] **VI 4C** 58,5 Vorsänger(in)

to **lead*** [li:d] **II 8C** 108 führen

leader ['li:də] **IV 1AB** 18 (An-)Führer/in, Leiter/in

leadership ['li:dəʃɪp] **VI 1B** 11 Führung, Leitung

leaflet ['li:flɪt] **I 7A** 104,5 Prospekt

League [li:g] **II 2A** 18 Liga

to **learn*** [lɜ:n] **II 3C** 35 lernen

to **leave*** [li:v] **I 4B** 70,2 verlassen, abfahren (von), (weg)gehen

left [left] **III 7C** 94,9 übrig, noch

on the **left** **I 1A** 35,3 auf der linken Seite

leg [leg] **I 6D** 97 Bein

legacy ['legəsɪ] **VI 1D** 15 Erbe

leggings ['legɪŋz] **II 2B** 23,5 Überhose, Leggings

legislation [ˌledʒɪs'leɪʃn] **V 5AB** 76 Gesetzgebung

legislative ['ledʒɪslətɪv] **V 3AB** 46 gesetzgebend, legislativ

lemonade [ˌlemə'neɪd] **I 4C** 71,2 Limonade

to **lend*** [lend] **II 3B** 33 (ver-)leihen

less [les] **II 4B** 51,5 weniger

lesson ['lesn] **II 5A** 61 (Unterrichts-)Stunde

let me see **I 1B** 37,3 laß mich mal sehen

  to let s.o. in [let] **II 6D** 84 jdn hereinlassen

let's = let us [lets] **I FS2** 9 laß(t) uns, lassen Sie uns

letter ['letə] **I 3C** 63,6 Brief

⟨letter⟩ ['letə] **IV 6D** 89,6 Buchstabe

level ['levl] **VI 3C** 40 Stufe, Niveau

  sea level ['si: ˌlevəl] **III 6A** 71 Meeresspiegel

liberty ['lɪbətɪ] **V 3AB** 46 Freiheit

library ['laɪbrərɪ] **IV 3C** 41 Bibliothek

lid [lɪd] **I 2C** 49,2 Deckel

to **lie** [laɪ] **IV 2C** 28 lügen, die Unwahrheit sagen

to lie* [laɪ] **I 4A** 66,2 liegen

life [laɪf] **II 2B** 21 Leben

  way of life [ˌweɪ‿əv 'laɪf] **III 1A** 9 Lebensstil, -art

lifebelt ['laɪfbelt] **III 2D** 26 Rettungsgürtel, -ring

lifeboat ['laɪfbəʊt] **III 2D** 26 Rettungsboot, Seenotkreuzer

lifeline ['laɪflaɪn] **IV 6A** 78 *hier:* Lebensader

lift [lɪft] **I 7B** 107,5 Fahrstuhl

to **lift** [lɪft] **V 5B** 64,3 (hoch-)heben

light [laɪt] **II 1D** 12 Licht

light [laɪt] **IV 2C** 27 hell

lighthouse ['laɪthaʊs] **IV 3C** 44,4 Leuchtturm

lightning ['laɪtnɪŋ] **II 6C** 82 Blitz

lightshow ['laɪtʃəʊ] **IV 2A** 22 Lichteffekte

to **like** [laɪk] **I 3C** 60 mögen, gern haben

  we'd like to … [wi:d] **I 7A** 104,5 wir möchten

like [laɪk] wie

  like the back of my hand **III 1B** 11 wie meine Westentasche

  like this **I 3C** 63,6 so, folgendermaßen

I **like collecting** [kə'lektɪŋ] **II 7A** 91 Ich sammle gern

⟨limerick⟩ ['lɪmərɪk] **V 5D** 71,3 Limerick *(fünfzeiliges Gedicht mit ironischem Inhalt)*

limit ['lɪmɪt] **III 7C** 89 Grenze, Begrenzung

limo(*usine*) ['lɪməʊ/'lɪməzi:n] **V 5C** 65 Limousine

line [laɪn] **II 4B** 49 Linie; Zeile

link [lɪŋk] **III 2B** 22 Verbindung; Beziehung

to **link** [lɪŋk] **I 6D** 100 verbinden

list [lɪst] **I 4C** 75,8 Liste

to **listen** ['lɪsn] **I FS2** 9,3 zuhören

listener ['lɪsnə] **V 1A** 7 (Zu-)Hörer/in

literacy ['lɪtərəsɪ] **VI 3C** 42,3 Fähigkeit zu lesen und zu schreiben

litre ['li:tə] **III 3B** 38,2 Liter

little ['lɪtl] **I 3C** 63,6 wenig

a **little** **I 2C** 50,6 ein bisschen, ein wenig

little time **I 3C** 63,6 wenig Zeit

to **live** [lɪv] **I 5A** 80,2 wohnen, leben

lives [laɪvz] **II 2B** 21 *(Pl.)* Leben

living-history ['lɪvɪŋ 'hɪstərɪ] **IV 4A** 50 historisch-lebendig

load [ləʊd] **III 7C** 90 Ladung; Last

to **load** [ləʊd] **V 3D** 39,2 (be-)laden

local ['ləʊkl] **III 7C** 92,6 lokal, Lokal-, örtlich, Orts-

lock [lɒk] **V 3C** 36 (Tür-)Schloss, Riegel

to **lock** [lɒk] **I 7B** 106,3 abschließen

locked [lɒkt] **I 2C** 49,2 ab-, zugeschlossen

locomotive ['ləʊkəˌməʊtɪv] **VI 1B** 10,3 Lokomotive

logical ['lɒdʒɪkl] **V 2C** 27,8 logisch

Londoner ['lʌndənə] **III 1A** 10,4 Londoner/in

⟨lonely⟩ ['ləʊnlɪ] **III 1C** 19,10 einsam

long [lɒŋ] **I FS8** 25 lang

as **long as** **II 4B** 49 so lange (wie)

no **longer** [ˌnəʊ 'lɒŋgə] **III 2B** 22 nicht mehr

to **look** [lʊk] sehen, aussehen

  Look out! [ˌlʊk 'aʊt] **III 3B** 37 Vorsicht! Achtung!

  to have a look at **I 7A** 104,5 ansehen

  to look after s.o. **I 4A** 66,3 auf jdn aufpassen

  to look at **I FS2** 9 anschauen, ansehen

  to look for **I 1C** 40 suchen

  to look forward to **I 6B** 92,1 sich freuen auf

  to look like ['lʊk laɪk] **I 8A** 116,3 aussehen wie

  to look round **I 8C** 123 herumschauen

  to look unhappy **I 5C** 85 unglücklich aussehen

  to look up **I 4A** 66,2 aufblicken

to be **loose*** [lu:s] **III 3C** 39 frei herumlaufen

⟨loosely⟩ ['lu:slɪ] **III 1C** 19,10 lose, locker

lorry [ˈlɒrɪ] **III 2B** 22 Lastwagen, LKW
to **lose*** [lu:z] **II 2B** 24,6 verlieren
to lose one's way **II 5C** 70,5 sich verlaufen
loser [ˈlu:zə] **III 5D** 66 Verlierer, „Flasche“
⟨loser⟩ [ˈlu:zə] **I 7C** 113,5 Verlierer/in
to get **lost*** [lɒst] **I 3C** 59 verloren gehen, sich verlaufen
a **lot of** [ˈlɒt‿əv] **I 1A** 35,1 viel/e
lots of [ˈlɒts‿ɒv] **I 8A** 116,3 viel/e
lottery [ˈlɒtərɪ] **II 6B** 80 Lotterie
loud [laʊd] **III 1C** 14 laut
loudspeaker [ˌlaʊdˈspi:kə] **I 8C** 122 Lautsprecher
⟨louse⟩ [laʊs] **III 4C** 54 Laus
love [lʌv] **I 6C** 94,2 Liebe
to **love I 8A** 116,3 lieben
love (*from*) **I 3C** 63,6 viele liebe Grüße (von)
love affair [ˈlʌvəˌfeə] **IV 3AB** 48 Liebesaffäre
lovely [ˈlʌvlɪ] **I 6C** 94,2 schön, herrlich
low [ləʊ] **II 8C** 108 niedrig
luck [lʌk] **II 4C** 53 Glück
bad luck [ˈbædˌlʌk] **I 5B** 81 Pech
Just our luck! **III 1C** 14 Pech (gehabt), wie immer!
luckily [ˈlʌkɪlɪ] **II 5A** 61 glücklicherweise
lucky [ˈlʌkɪ] **I FS8** 24 glücklich
you're **lucky I FS8** 24 du hast Glück, du hast es gut
luggage [ˈlʌgɪdʒ] **IV 5D** 76,8 Gepäck
lumber [ˈlʌmbə] **V 4A** 48 Bauholz, Nutzholz
lumberjack [ˈlʌmbədʒæk] **V 4A** 48 Holzfäller/in
lunch [lʌntʃ] **I 3C** 59 Mittagessen
lunch hour [ˈlʌnʃˌaʊə] **II 5A** 61 Mittagspause
lunchtime [ˈlʌntʃtaɪm] **IV 5B** 69,4 Mittagszeit

M

machine [məˈʃi:n] **III 5C** 62 Gerät; Maschine, Apparat
to go **mad** [ˌgəʊ ˈmæd] **III 1C** 14 durchdrehen
made of wax [ˈmeɪd‿əv ˈwæks] **I 7C** 110 aus Wachs
magazine [ˌmægəˈzi:n] **I FS9** 26 Zeitschrift, Illustrierte
magic tricks [ˈmædʒɪk] **II 6B** 80 Zauberkunststücke
magician [məˈdʒɪʃn] **III 5D** 67 Magier, Zauberer, Zauberkünstler
magpie [ˈmægpaɪ] **IV 3C** 42 Elster
⟨mailbox⟩ (*AE*) [ˈmeɪlbɒks] **III 7FE** 104 Briefkasten
main [meɪn] **II 2B** 24,6 Haupt-, hauptsächlich
majestic [məˈdʒestɪk] **IV 6A** 78 erhaben, majestätisch
majesty [ˈmædʒəstɪ] **V 5AB** 76 Majestät, königliche Hoheit
⟨major⟩ [ˈmeɪdʒə] **III 6D** 81 Haupt-, bedeutende/r/s
majority [məˈdʒɒrətɪ] **V 5AB** 74 Mehrheit
make-up [ˈmeɪkʌp] **IV 2C** 31,7 Make-up, Schminke

to **make*** [meɪk] **I FS4** 12,2 machen, bilden
to make a mess on s.th. [mes] **III 1C** 14 etw. beschmutzen, auf etwas ‚machen‘
to make fun of s.o. **III 5D** 66 sich über jdn lustig machen
to make jokes about [dʒəʊks] **II 6A** 78,2 über jdn Witze machen
to make up [ˈmeɪk‿ˈʌp] **IV 1A** 8,4 ausdenken, erfinden
to make* s.o. do s.th. [meɪk] **VI 4B** 51 jmd veranlassen, etw zu tun
man [mæn] **I FS5** 14 Mann
to **manage** [ˈmænɪdʒ] **IV 2A** 22 zurechtkommen, es schaffen
manager [ˈmænɪdʒə] **V 3D** 39,2 Manager/in
manifest [ˈmænɪfest] **VI 1B** 8 offenkundig, deutlich
manners [ˈmænəz] **IV 6B** 81,5 Benehmen, Manieren
mansion [ˈmænʃn] **IV 6C** 84,5 Gutsbesitz, Villa
how **many** [ˈmenɪ] **I FS10** 29,4 wie viele
map [mæp] **I FS9** 26 (Land-)Karte
march [mɑ:tʃ] **VI 1B** 8 Marsch
to **march** [mɑ:tʃ] **VI 4A** 48,1 marschieren
mark [mɑ:k] **IV 2C** 28 Note, Zensur
to **mark** [mɑ:k] **II 4B** 49 markieren, kennzeichnen
⟨market⟩ [ˈmɑ:kɪt] **I 6** 90 Markt
market [ˈmɑ:kɪt] **V 2A** 19 Markt
marmalade [ˈmɑ:məleɪd] **II 5C** 72,11 Orangenmarmelade
marram grass [ˈmærəm ˌgrɑ:s] **III 3C** 39 Strandhafer, Dünengras
to get **married** [ˈmærɪd] **III 7B** 86 heiraten
to **marry** [ˈmærɪ] **IV 1AB** 20 heiraten
mask [mɑ:sk] **III 7FE** 98 Maske
mass [mæs] **V 2A** 19 Masse
⟨master⟩ [ˈmɑ:stə] **III 4C** 54 Herr
master [ˈmɑ:stə] **VI 1A** 6 Herr, Meister
masterpiece [ˈmɑ:stəpi:s] **III 3A** 34 Meisterwerk
match (*AE*) [mætʃ] **II 5B** 63 Spiel, Wettkampf
math (*AE*) [mæθ] **III 5B** 60,3 Mathe
maths [mæθs] **III 5B** 60,3 Mathe
to **matter** [ˈmætə] **III 1C** 14 etw. (aus-)machen
What's the **matter?** [ˈmætə] **I 4A** 66,2 Was ist (los)?
may* [meɪ] **III 1B** 11 Es kann sein, dass …
May I…? [ˈmeɪ‿aɪ] **I 7A** 102 Darf ich …?
maybe [ˈmeɪbi:] **II 7B** 94 vielleicht
mayor [meə] **VI 4A** 49,5 Bürgermeister
me [mi:] **I FS9** 26 mir, mich; ich
meal [mi:l] **II 3D** 40,2 Mahlzeit
to **mean*** [mi:n] **I 5B** 81 bedeuten, meinen
meaning [ˈmi:nɪŋ] **IV 5D** 76,9 Bedeutung
means pl [mi:nz] **VI 2D** 32,3 Methoden, Hilfsmittel
meat [mi:t] **V 5B** 63 Fleisch
meat-packing [ˈmi:tˌpækɪŋ] **V 5B** 62 Fleischverarbeitung, -herstellung
media [ˈmi:djə] **V 5AB** 78 (Massen-)Medien

medical [ˈmedɪkl] **V 2D** 29,3 medizinisch, ärztlich
medicine [ˈmedsɪn] **II 3A** 32,5 Arznei; Medizin
to **meet*** [mi:t] **I 7A** 103,3 treffen, begegnen, kennen lernen
meeting [mi:tɪŋ] **III 6A** 72 Besprechung, Treffen
meeting-place [ˈmi:tɪŋpleɪs] **IV 3C** 41 Treffpunkt
melon [ˈmelən] **II 5B** 65,5 Melone
member [ˈməmbə] **IV 4A** 51 Mitglied
membership [ˈmembəʃɪp] **V 5AB** 74 Mitgliedschaft
men [men] **I 2A** 44,8 Männer
to **mention** [ˈmenʃn] **IV 1A** 7,2 erwähnen
menu [ˈmenju:] **IV 5D** 76,9 Speisekarte
merry [ˈmerɪ] **II 4B** 51,5 fröhlich, lustig
to make a **mess on s.th.** [mes] **III 1C** 14 etw. beschmutzen, auf etwas ‚machen‘
to **mess around** [mes] **II 5B** 63 Unfug machen
message [ˈmesɪdʒ] **V 5C** 66 Mitteilung, Benachrichtigung
⟨message⟩ [ˈmesɪdʒ] **IV 6D** 88,5 Botschaft, Mitteilung
metal [ˈmetl] **III 6C** 76,5 Metall
metaphor [ˈmetəfə] **II 8D** 115,7 Metapher
meter (*AE*) [ˈmi:tə] **III 6A** 71 Meter
method [ˈmeθəd] **IV 5C** 70 Verfahren, Methode
metre (*BE*) [ˈmi:tə] **II 1C** 10 Meter
Mexican [ˈmeksɪkən] **III 6A** 71 Mexikaner/in, mexikanisch
mice (*pl*) [maɪs] **II 8C** 108 Mäuse
microchip [ˈmaɪkrəʊtʃɪp] **II 7B** 94 Mikrochip
middle-class [ˈmɪdlˌklɑ:s] **VI 4A** 49,5 zur Mittelschicht gehörend
in the **middle** [ˈmɪdl] **I 1A** 35,3 in der Mitte
⟨midnight⟩ [ˈmɪdnaɪt] **III 7FE** 100 Mitternacht
might* [maɪt] **III 1B** 11 Es könnte sein, dass …
mild [maɪld] **III 6A** 70 mild, leicht, sanft
mile [maɪl] **I 8A** 114 Meile
military [ˈmɪlɪtərɪ] **VI 1B** 8,1 militärisch
milk [mɪlk] **I 3C** 63,6 Milch
to **milk** [mɪlk] **IV 3A** 35 melken
milking parlour [ˈmɪlkɪŋ ˌpɑ:lə] **II 7B** 94 Melkstand
milkman [ˈmɪlkmən] **I 3C** 63,6 Milchmann
milkshake [ˈmɪlkʃeɪk] **II 6B** 80 Milchshake
mill [mɪl] **V 2A** 18 Fabrik; Mühle
million [ˈmɪljən] **II 1C** 10 Million
⟨millionaire⟩ [ˌmɪljəˈneə] **I 7C** 113,5 Millionär/in
⟨peace of mind⟩ [ˌpi:s‿əv ˈmaɪnd] **III 3C** 44,9 innere Ruhe, Seelenfrieden
⟨to change your mind⟩ [maɪnd] **III 1C** 19,10 deine Meinung ändern
to **mind** [maɪnd] etw. dagegen haben
I don't mind **I 5C** 86,2 es ist mir egal
mind your head [ˌmaɪnd jɔ: ˈhed] **II 1D** 16,9 Vorsicht! Niedrige Tür!
never mind **I 2C** 49,2 macht nichts

⟨mine⟩ [maɪn] **III 6D** 80,4 Mine
mine [maɪn] **III 1C** 14 meine, meiner, meines
miner ['maɪnə] **III 6C** 76,5 Bergarbeiter, Bergmann
minestrone *(soup)* [ˌmɪnɪ'strəʊnɪ] **II 5B** 65,5 Minestrone *(italienische Gemüsesuppe)*
mining ['maɪnɪŋ] **V 4A** 48 Bergbau
minister ['mɪnɪstə] **IV 4AB** 63 (protestantischer) Pfarrer
minor ['maɪnə] **IV 3B** 38 Moll (Tonart)
minority [maɪ'nɒrətɪ] **IV 5C** 70 Minderheit
minute ['mɪnɪt] **I FS7** 19,5 Minute
just a **minute** **I 2B** 46 einen Augenblick
minutes ['mɪnɪts] **IV 5D** 77,10 Protokoll
miracle ['mɪrəkl] **III 6D** 78 Wunder
mirror ['mɪrə] **III 3C** 42,4 Spiegel
misfit ['mɪsfɪt] **V 1B** 11 Außenseiter/in
Miss [mɪs] **II 5B** 63 Fräulein *(höfliche Anrede für eine junge Frau/ Lehrerin)*
to **miss** [mɪs] **I 7B** 108,6 verfehlen, verpassen; vermissen
to miss a turn **I 5B** 81 eine Runde aussetzen
missing ['mɪsɪŋ] **I 1A** 36,3 fehlend
mission ['mɪʃn] **VI 1B** 8 Mission, Auftrag
mistake [mɪ'steɪk] **V 3AB** 43 Fehler
to **misunderstand*** [ˌmɪsʌndə'stænd] **IV 5D** 77,10 missverstehen
mix [mɪks] **VI 3A** 33,a) Mischung
to **mix** [mɪks] **IV 1AB** 19 vermischen
(food) **mixer** ['fu:d ˌmɪksə] **II 5A** 61 Mixer
mixture ['mɪkstʃə] **II 5A** 61 Mischung
mobile ['məʊbaɪl] **III 5B** 59 Funk-; beweglich, mobil
model ['mɒdl] **I 6B** 92,2 Modell
modern ['mɒdən] **II 2A** 18 modern
to **modernize** ['mɒdənaɪz] **V 3C** 36 modernisieren, erneuern
mole [məʊl] **II 8C** 108 Maulwurf
mom *(AE)* [mɒm] **III 5A** 58 Mutti, Mama
moment ['məʊmənt] **I 6D** 99,6 Moment, Augenblick
at the **moment** **I 6D** 99,6 im Augenblick
monarch ['mɒnək] **IV 3AB** 49 Herrscher/in, Monarch/in
monarchy ['mɒnəkɪ] **V 3AB** 42 Monarchie, Alleinherrschaft
monastery ['mɒnəstrɪ] **IV 3AB** 48 Kloster
money ['mʌnɪ] **II 2B** 21 Geld
to **monitor** ['mɒnɪtə] **II 7B** 94 überwachen
monster ['mɒnstə] **II 1A** 7 Monster
month [mʌnθ] **I 6A** 91,1 Monat
monument ['mɒnjʊmənt] **V 5AB** 77 Baudenkmal, Monument
mood [mu:d] **V 3B** 33 Stimmung, Laune
moon [mu:n] **II 6D** 86,5 Mond
moorland ['mʊələnd] **III 4C** 54 Moor-/, Heidelandschaft
moor(s) [mʊə] **II 5A** 62,3 Moor, Heide
moped ['məʊped] **V 1C** 15,4 Moped
⟨moral⟩ ['mɒrəl] **VI 3C** 43,6 Moral, sittliche Lehre
moral ['mɒrəl] **VI 1B** 8 moralisch
more [mɔ:] **I FS2** 9 mehr, weitere
more terrible **II 2A** 19 schrecklicher
moreover [mɔ:'rəʊvə] **VI 1A** 6 außerdem, ferner
morning ['mɔ:nɪŋ] **I FS1** 8 Morgen
⟨this morning⟩ **I FS7** 21,9 heute Morgen
in the morning **I FS7** 18 morgens, vormittags
on Saturday morning **I FS11** 30 am Samstag vormittag
mosquito [mə'ski:təʊ] **II 8A** 104,3 Moskito, Stechmücke
most [məʊst] **II 2A** 18 am meisten, die meisten
the most famous **II 2A** 18 der/die/das berühmteste, am berühmtesten
motel [məʊ'tel] **III 7B** 86 Motel
mother ['mʌðə] **I FS4** 12 Mutter
⟨motive⟩ ['məʊtɪv] **V 3D** 40,5 Motiv
motorbike ['məʊtəbaɪk] **V 1C** 15,4 Motorrad
motorway ['məʊtəweɪ] **IV 3C** 41 Autobahn
mountain ['maʊntən] **II 1C** 10 Berg
mouse [maʊs] **II 8C** 108 Maus
mouth [maʊθ] **I 8B** 120,4 Mund
to **move** [mu:v] **I 7C** 110 sich bewegen
to move [mu:v] **I 7A** 102 umziehen
movement ['mu:vmənt] **IV 1AB** 18 Bewegung
movie ['mu:vɪ] **III 7B** 86 Film
movie theater ['θɪətə] **III 7B** 86 Kino
MP *(Member of Parliament)* ['em'pi:] **V 3C** 37,3 Mitglied des Unterhauses im britischen Parlament
m.p.h. *(miles per hour)* ['maɪlz 'pɜ: 'aʊə] **IV 5A** 65 *Maßangabe für Geschwindigkeit*
Mr ['mɪstə] **I FS5** 14 Herr
Mrs ['mɪsɪz] **I FS3** 10 Frau
Ms [mɪz/məz] **III 5B** 60,3 Frau *(auch für Unverheiratete)*
much [mʌtʃ] **I 5A** 78 viel
how **much** **I 6B** 92,3 wie viel
mud [mʌd] **V 3A** 30 Schlamm, Morast
mudguard ['mʌdgɑ:d] **II 4B** 49 Schutzblech
mule [mju:l] **V 4A** 49 Maultier
multicultural [ˌmʌltɪ'kʌltʃərəl] **VI 1C** 14,5 multikulturell
⟨multiculturalism⟩ [ˌmʌltɪ'kʌltʃərəlɪzəm] **VI 1D** 18,5 *das Zusammentreffen verschiedener Kulturen*
multiracial [ˌmʌltɪ'reɪʃl] **VI 3A** 35,4 Vielvölker-
mum [mʌm] **I FS5** 14 Mutti, Mama
murder ['mɜ:də] **IV 5D** 77,10 Mord
to **murder** ['mɜ:də] **V 1B** 11 (er-)morden
murderer ['mɜ:dərə] **V 1B** 12,2 Mörder/in
muscle ['mʌsl] **V 2C** 27,7 Muskel
museum [mju:'zɪəm] **I 4A** 66,1 Museum
music ['mju:zɪk] **II 6A** 78,2 Musik
⟨musical⟩ ['mju:zɪkl] **IV 3C** 45,10 Musical
musician [mju:'zɪʃn] **II 8B** 105 Musiker/in
must* [mʌst] **I 1A** 35,1 müssen
he mustn't* ['mʌsnt] **II 3B** 33 er darf nicht
my [maɪ] **I FS1** 8 mein, meine
mysterious [mɪ'stɪərɪəs] **IV 3C** 41 geheimnisvoll, mysteriös

N

nail [neɪl] **III 3A** 34 Nagel
naive [naɪ'i:v] **III 5D** 67,2 naiv, leichtgläubig
name [neɪm] **I FS1** 8 Name
narrator [nə'reɪtə] **V 5C** 67,1 Erzähler/in
nasty ['nɑ:stɪ] **III 5D** 66 abscheulich, böse, übel
nation ['neɪʃn] **III 2C** 24 Nation, Volk
National Park [ˌnæʃənl 'pɑ:k] **II 6A** 76 Nationalpark
nationality [ˌnæʃə'nælətɪ] **III 6A** 70 Nationalität
native ['neɪtɪv] **III 2AB** 32 Ureinwohner/in, Eingeborene/r
natural resources ['nætʃrəl rɪ'sɔ:sɪz] **V 4A** 48 Bodenschätze
natural ['nætʃərəl] **III 5A** 58 Natur-, natürlich
nature ['neɪtʃə] **V 2A** 18 Natur
nature reserve ['neɪtʃə rɪ'zɜ:v] **III 3B** 37 Naturschutzgebiet
the **Navy** ['neɪvɪ] **III 2AB** 32 die Marine
near [nɪə] **I 7C** 110 in der Nähe
nearest ['nɪərɪst] **II 6A** 79,6 nächste, nächster, nächstes
nearly ['nɪəlɪ] **I FS8** 25,3 fast
neck [nek] **III 7C** 89 Hals, Nacken, Genick
need [ni:d] **V 3A** 30 Notwendigkeit, Bedarf
to **need** [ni:d] **I 6C** 94,1 brauchen
you needn't ['ni:dnt] **II 3B** 33 du musst nicht, du brauchst nicht
negative ['negətɪv] **V 3C** 37,1 negativ
neighbor *(AE)* ['neɪbə] **IV 4A** 51 Nachbar/in
neighborhood *(AE)* ['neɪbəhʊd] **III 5C** 63,3 Nachbarschaft
neighbour ['neɪbə] **I 1A** 36,2 Nachbar/in
neighbourhood ['neɪbəhʊd] **II 6A** 77 Nachbarschaft
neither ['naɪðə] **IV 6C** 83,2 keine/r/s (von beiden)
nephew ['nevju:] **II 1D** 15,6 Neffe
nerve [nɜ:v] **II 8** 111 Nerv(en)
nervous ['nɜ:vəs] **I 7C** 110 nervös
to **nest** [nest] **III 3C** 41,2 nisten
net [net] **II 5C** 68 Netz
never ['nevə] **I 4B** 70,4 nie, niemals
never mind **I 2C** 49,2 macht nichts
nevertheless [ˌnevəðə'les] **VI 1A** 6 nichtsdestoweniger, dessen ungeachtet
new [nju:] **I FS1** 8 neu
a **new one** **II 2B** 21 eine neue (Uhr)
news *(sing.)* [nju:z] **II 2C** 25 Nachricht(en), Neuigkeit(en)
newsagent ['nju:zˌeɪdʒənt] **II 3C** 35 Zeitungsverkäufer/in
newspaper ['nju:sˌpeɪpə] **I FS9** 26 Zeitung

next [nekst] **I 4A** 67,2 danach, als Nächstes
next to ['neks_tʊ] **I 8C** 123 neben
the next day **I 3A** 54,2 am nächsten Tag
next door **I FS7** 18 nebenan
Nez Percé ['nez 'pɜːs] **VI 2A** 20 *Name eines Indianerstammes*
nice [naɪs] **I 5C** 84 nett, schön
niece [niːs] **II 1D** 15,6 Nichte
Nigerian [naɪ'dʒɪərɪən] **VI 1D** 18,4 nigerianisch; Nigerianer/in
night [naɪt] **I FS7** 18 Nacht
night watchman [ˌnaɪt'wɒtʃmən] **IV 5D** 73 Nachtwächter/in
at **night** **I FS7** 18 nachts
nightmare ['naɪtmeə] **III 6C** 75 Albtraum
nine out of ten **II 5B** 63 *Bewertung:* neun von zehn (Punkten)
no big deal [diːl] **III 7A** 84 nichts Besonderes
no [nəʊ] **I FS5** 14 nein
no idea **I FS2** 9 keine Ahnung
no longer [ˌnəʊ 'lɒŋgə] **III 2B** 22 nicht mehr
no one ['nəʊ wʌn] **II 8A** 103 niemand
no use [juːs] **IV 3A** 37,5 keinen Zweck, keinen Sinn (haben)
nobody ['nəʊbədɪ] **I 2B** 46 niemand
to **nod** [nɒd] **IV 5D** 74 nicken
noise [nɔɪz] **I 5A** 78 Geräusch, Lärm
noisy ['nɔɪzɪ] **II 5C** 72,9 laut, lärmend
⟨non-Brits⟩ ['nɒnˌbrɪts] **VI 1D** 18,5 Nicht-Briten
none [nʌn] **II 1D** 15,6 keine
nor [nɔː] **IV 6C** 83,2 noch
normal ['nɔːml] **III 5A** 58 normal, üblich
Norman ['nɔːmən] **IV 1AB** 18 normannisch
north [nɔːθ] **II 6C** 82 (nach) Norden, Nord-, nördlich
northeast [ˌnɔːθ'iːst] **II 6C** 82 Nordosten
northern ['nɔːðn] **IV 6A** 78 Nord-, nördlich, nach Norden
Northerner ['nɔːðənə] **VI 2C** 30,2 Nordstaatler/in
Norwegian [nɔː'wiːdʒən] **IV 1B** 11,6 norwegisch; Norweger/in
nose [nəʊz] **I 8B** 120,4 Nase
not [nɒt] **I FS1** 8 nicht
not … any more **II 3D** 38 nicht mehr
not … anywhere [ˌnɒt 'enɪweə] **III 1A** 10,4 nirgends, nirgendwo
not … at all **I 5C** 85 gar nicht, überhaupt nicht
(*not*) either of them ['aɪðə] **IV 2C** 29,3 weder … noch
not my cup of tea [ˌkʌp_əv_'tiː] **IV 1A** 6 nicht mein Fall, liegt mir nicht
not … until [ˌnɒt ən'tɪl] **III 2B** 22 erst
note [nəʊt] **I 7B** 106,3 Zettel, Notiz; Ton, Note
nothing ['nʌθɪŋ] **II 1D** 12 nichts
⟨nothing better⟩ **I 7C** 113,5 nichts Besseres
notice ['nəʊtɪs] **II 3B** 33 Notiz, Schild
notice board ['nəʊtɪs bɔːd] **III 4B** 49 Schwarzes Brett, Anschlagbrett
to **notice** ['nəʊtɪs] **II 4C** 54 bemerken
novel ['nɒvl] **II 7A** 91 Roman
now [naʊ] **I FS6** 17 jetzt, nun
nowhere ['nəʊweə] **II 8A** 103 nirgendwo
number ['nʌmbə] **I FS10** 28,2 Nummer, Zahl
number plate ['nʌmbə 'pleɪt] **V 3D** 39 Nummernschild

O

to **obey** [ə'beɪ] **V 3AB** 47 gehorchen, befolgen
obvious ['ɒbvɪəs] **VI 3B** 39,4 offensichtlich, nahe liegend
occasional [ə'keɪʒənl] **VI 4B** 53,3 gelegentlich
ocean ['əʊʃn] **II 1C** 11,1 Ozean
o'clock [ə'klɒk] **I FS11** 30 Uhr
⟨odd⟩ [ɒd] **III 7AA** 96 ungerade
of [ɒv; əv] von
a lot of ['lɒt_əv] **I 1A** 35,1 viel/e
a packet of biscuits **I 4C** 71,2 eine Packung Kekse
in front of **I FS6** 17 vor *(örtlich)*
of course [ɒv'kɔːs] **I FS8** 24 natürlich, sicher
off [ɒf] entfernt, weg; vor *(einer Küste)*
off to … ['ɒf tʊ] **II 6A** 76 unterwegs nach
to get off **I 5C** 84 aussteigen *(aus einem Bus/Zug)*
to take off **I 4C** 71,1 ausziehen
offer ['ɒfə] **III 5B** 60,2 Angebot
to **offer** ['ɒfə] **III 5A** 58 anbieten, bieten
office ['ɒfɪs] **II 6A** 77 Büro
tourist office ['tʊərɪst ˌɒfɪs] **III 3A** 36,7 Fremdenverkehrsamt
officer ['ɒfɪsə] **III 2C** 24 Offizier/in, Beamter/Beamtin
official [ə'fɪʃl] **VI 4A** 47,b) Beamte/r
official [ə'fɪʃl] **III 6C** 75 offiziell
offside [ˌɒf'saɪd] **II 5C** 68 (im) Abseits
often ['ɒfn] **I 3A** 54,1 oft, häufig
oh [əʊ] **I FS1** 8 oh
Oh dear! **I FS6** 17 O je! Ach du meine Güte
Oh God! [əʊ 'gɒd] **I 7C** 110 Oh Gott!
oil [ɔɪl] **II 4A** 47 Öl
oil rig ['ɔɪlrɪg] **III 2A** 20 Ölbohrinsel
to go **'oink'** [ɔɪŋk] **II 7B** 95,2 grunzen *(bei Schweinen)*
OK [ˌəʊ'keɪ] **I FS6** 17 ist gut
old [əʊld] **I FS5** 14 alt
old-fashioned [ˌəʊld'fæʃnd] **IV 5C** 70 altmodisch
oldie ['əʊldɪ] **III 7C** 89 *eine alte Platte*
Olympic [ə'lɪmpɪk] **II 2A** 18 olympisch
on [ɒn] **I FS4** 12 auf
on board [bɔːd] **I 8C** 122 an Bord
on business ['bɪznɪs] **III 2A** 21,1 geschäftlich
on duty ['djuːtɪ] **IV 1C** 13 im Dienst
on horseback ['hɔːsbæk] **IV 1AB** 20 zu Pferde
on the left/right **I 1A** 35,3 links/rechts, auf der linken/rechten Seite
on the one/other hand **III 5D** 67,2 einerseits, andererseits
on time **I 4B** 69 pünktlich
on top of [ɒn 'tɒp_ɒv] **I 7C** 110 oben auf
to be on holiday **I 4C** 72,6 Ferien/Urlaub machen
to go on **I FS7** 19,2 weitermachen
on Saturday morning **I FS11** 30 am Samstag vormittag
once [wʌns] **III 3C** 39 einmal
at once **I 3C** 59 sofort
one [wʌn] **I FS10** 28 eins
green ones **II 2B** 21 grüne (Hüte, Äpfel etc.)
one all **II 5C** 68 eins beide *(Spielstand)*
one-sided [ˌwʌn'saɪdɪd] **IV 4D** 59 einseitig
⟨one-way street⟩ **I 7C** 112,3 Einbahnstraße
onion ['ʌnjən] **V 5B** 62 Zwiebel
only ['əʊnlɪ] **I 1C** 39,2 einzig, nur
⟨the only one⟩ **I 7C** 113,5 der, die, das einzige
onto ['ɒntʊ; _tə] **I 2C** 50,6 (hin-)auf
oops! [ʊps] **III 5C** 62 hoppla!
to **open** ['əʊpən] **I FS10** 28,1 öffnen, aufmachen
open ['əʊpən] **I 1C** 40,8 offen
opening ['əʊpnɪŋ] **V 5A** 60 Öffnung, Spalt
to **operate** (*on*) ['ɒpəreɪt] **III 4A** 48 operieren
operation [ɒpə'reɪʃn] **III 4B** 49,3 Operation
operator ['ɒpəreɪtə] **III 4A** 46 Vermittlung; Bediener/in, Operator/in
opinion [ə'pɪnjən] **IV 4D** 60,1 Meinung, Ansicht
opinion poll [ə'pɪnjən 'pəʊl] **VI 3B** 38,b) Meinungsumfrage
opportunity [ˌɒpə'tjuːnətɪ] **III 5B** 59 Gelegenheit, Möglichkeit
opposite ['ɒpəzɪt] **I 1C** 42,5 Gegenteil, Gegensatz
opposite ['ɒpəzɪt] **II 1D** 13 gegenüber(-liegend), entgegengesetzt
optimistic [ˌɒptɪ'mɪstɪk] **V 3B** 34,2 optimistisch, zuversichtlich
or [ɔː] **I FS5** 14,1 oder
orange ['ɒrɪndʒ] **I 4C** 71,2 Apfelsine, Orange
order ['ɔːdə] **III 2D** 26 Befehl; Anordnung, Ordnung
word order ['wɜːd_ɔːdə] **I 4B** 70,4 Wortstellung, Satzstellung
to **order** ['ɔːdə] **III 1C** 16,5 bestellen; befehlen
organization [ˌɔːgənaɪ'zeɪʃn] **IV 6D** 87,3 Planung, Organisation
to **organize** ['ɔːgənaɪz] **IV 3A** 37,5 planen, organisieren
Oriental [ˌɔːrɪ'entl] **VI 1B** 8 orientalisch; Orientale/Orientalin
origin ['ɒrɪdʒɪn] **VI 3A** 33,a) Ursprung
original [ə'rɪdʒənl] **IV 4A** 50 ursprünglich, original
⟨original⟩ [ə'rɪdʒənl] **III 7C** 95,12 original
originally [ə'rɪdʒənəlɪ] **IV 1AB** 20 ursprünglich
orphanage ['ɔːfənɪdʒ] **V 5AB** 75 Waisenhaus
other ['ʌðə] **I 3C** 60 andere, anderer, anderes
the **others** **I 5A** 78 die anderen

otherwise ['ʌðəwaɪz] **V 1A** 7 ansonsten, anderenfalls
Ouch! [aʊtʃ] **II 8A** 103 Aua!
ought to* ['ɔ:t tʊ] **II 8A** 103 sollte
our ['aʊə] **I FS4** 12 unser/e
ours ['aʊəz] **III 1C** 14 unsere, unserer, unseres
to go **out** [aʊt] **I 2C** 49,1 weggehen
to get out **I 1C** 40,6 herauskommen
out of breath [ˌaʊt‿əv 'breθ] **III 3C** 40 außer Atem
over and out **I 2B** 46 Ende der Durchsage *(Funksprache)*
to come out **I 4C** 72,5 herauskommen
to get out of **I 4C** 71,3 aussteigen
to take out **I 2C** 49,2 herausnehmen, herausholen
out [aʊt] **I FS7** 18 draußen, nicht zu Hause
outcast ['aʊtkɑ:st] **IV 5C** 72,6 Ausgestoßene/r
outdoor ['aʊtdɔ:] **II 5A** 60 Frischluft-, im Freien
outlaw ['aʊtlɔ:] **II 2B** 21 Geächtete/r, Vogelfreie/r, Bandit/in
outpost ['aʊtpəʊst] **VI 1C** 12 (militärischer) Vorposten
outside [aʊt'saɪd] **I FS8** 24 draußen; außerhalb, vor
⟨over⟩ ['əʊvə] **I FS11** 32,4 über
over and out **I 2B** 46 Ende der Durchsage *(Funksprache)*
to be over **I 3C** 63,6 vorbei/zu Ende/aus sein
to fall over **I 4C** 71,3 fallen über
over there **I FS9** 26 dort drüben
over to you [tə 'ju:] **I FS1** 8,1 du bist/ihr seid/Sie sind dran
overall ['əʊvərɔ:l] **VI 4A** 47,b) (einteiliger) Anzug, Overall
to **overlook** [ˌəʊvə'lʊk] **IV 6C** 84,5 Aussicht gewähren auf
to **owe** [əʊ] **VI 2B** 25 jmd etw schuldig sein, jmd etw verdanken
own [əʊn] **II 7B** 95,2 eigene, eigener, eigenes
on our own [aʊər‿'əʊn] **III 1B** 11 wir (ganz) allein
owner ['əʊnə] **I 7B** 107,5 Besitzer
ownership ['əʊnəʃɪp] **VI 2A** 19 Eigentum, Besitz
ox, *(pl)* oxen [ɒks, 'ɒksən] **III 6C** 75 Ochse
ozone layer ['əʊzəʊn 'leɪə] **V 1A** 9,7 Ozonschicht

P

⟨p (= penny)⟩ [pi:] **I 6** 101 = penny *(kleinste britische Münzeinheit)*
to **pack** [pæk] **III 7C** 91,3 packen
packet ['pækɪt] **I 4C** 71,2 Packung
paddle ['pædl] **III 2D** 28,3 Paddel
page [peɪdʒ] **I 1A** 36,1 Seite
pain [peɪn] **II 3A** 30 Schmerz
to be a pain [peɪn] **II 5B** 63 einem auf den Wecker gehen
paint [peɪnt] **II 7C** 96 Farbe
to **paint** **I 8B** 120,4 malen
to paint [peɪnt] **II 7C** 96 anstreichen, (be-)malen, lackieren
painter ['peɪntə] **I 7A** 102 Maler/in
painting ['peɪntɪŋ] **III 3A** 34 Gemälde, Bild
pale [peɪl] **III 4B** 49 blass, bleich
pancake ['pænkeɪk] **II 7C** 96 Pfannkuchen
to **panic** ['pænɪk] **III 4C** 51 in Panik geraten
pants *(AE, pl)* [pænts] **V 5C** 66 (lange) Hose
paper ['peɪpə] **I 4C** 75,8 Papier
parade [pə'reɪd] **III 7FE** 107 Parade, Umzug
paragraph ['pærəgrɑ:f] **II 8C** 109,2 Abschnitt, Paragraph
parents ['peərənts] **I FS4** 13 Eltern
park [pɑ:k] **I 3B** 57 Park
coach park ['kəʊtʃ ˌpɑ:k] **III 3B** 37 Busparkplatz
to **park** [pɑ:k] **IV 3B** 40,6 parken
parliament ['pɑ:ləmənt] **IV 3AB** 48 Parlament
Parma ham [ˌpɑ:mə 'hæm] **II 5B** 65,5 Parmaschinken
⟨parody⟩ ['pærədɪ] **III 7C** 95,12 Parodie
parrot ['pærət] **II 4C** 57,7 Papagei
part [pɑ:t] **II 1D** 12 Teil, Rolle
to take part in [pɑ:t] **II 5A** 61 teilnehmen an
⟨to part from⟩ ['pɑ:t ˌfrɒm] **III 4C** 54 sich trennen von
partner ['pɑ:tnə] **III 5C** 63,4 Partner/in
party ['pɑ:tɪ] **I 6B** 92,1 Party, Fete
to **pass** [pɑ:s] **IV 5A** 65 vorbeigehen (an)
to pass *(a test)* [pɑ:s] **II 4C** 53 (eine Prüfung) bestehen
⟨to pass s.th.⟩ [pɑ:s] **III 2D** 29,7 an etw. vorbeigehen
passage ['pæsɪdʒ] **I 1C** 39,3 Gang
passenger ['pæsɪndʒə] **I 2B** 46 Fahrgast, Passagier
passport ['pɑ:spɔ:t] **I 7B** 106,2 Reisepass
past [pɑ:st] **IV 1A** 8,4 Vergangenheit
to go **past*** [pɑ:st] **I 7B** 108,6 vorbeigehen, vorbeifahren
past [pɑ:st] **I 3A** 56,5 nach, vorbei
half past seven **I 3A** 54,1 halb acht
to go past [pɑ:st] **I 7B** 108,6 vorbeifahren
path [pɑ:θ] **II 2B** 21 Weg, Pfad
to **pave** [peɪv] **VI 3A** 36,7 pflastern, den Boden belegen
⟨paved⟩ [peɪvd] **III 1C** 18,9 gepflastert
to **pay** *(for)** [peɪ] **II 2B** 24,6 zahlen, bezahlen
peace [pi:s] **IV 1AB** 19 Frieden
⟨peace of mind⟩ [ˌpi:s‿əv 'maɪnd] **III 3C** 44,9 innere Ruhe, Seelenfrieden
peaceful ['pi:sfʊl] **IV 3AB** 49 friedfertig, friedlich
⟨peak⟩ [pi:k] **III 6C** 76,6 Gipfel
peak [pi:k] **VI 3A** 35,2 Spitze, Gipfel
pearl [pɜ:l] **V 4A** 48 Perle
pedal ['pedl] **II 4B** 49 Pedal
peer ['pɪə] **V 3AB** 43 Gleichrangige/r, Standesgenosse *(des britischen Hochadels)*
pen [pen] **I FS9** 26 Füller, Füllfederhalter
pen pal ['pen,pæl] **III 7A** 84 Brieffreund/in
pence [pens] **II 2C** 25 Pence *(britische Währung)*
pencil ['pensl] **I FS9** 26 Bleistift
pencil case **I FS9** 26 Federmäppchen, Etui
penfriend ['penfrend] **II 4C** 56,5 Brieffreund/in
penguin ['peŋgwɪn] **III 3A** 36,7 Pinguin
⟨penny⟩ ['penɪ] **I 6D** 101 *britische Münze*
people ['pi:pl] **I 3C** 59 Leute, Menschen
per cent [pə'sent] **III 5A** 58 Prozent
per *(year)* [pɜ:] **II 1C** 10 pro (Jahr)
percentage [pə'sentɪdʒ] **V 2D** 29,3 Prozentsatz, Anteil
perfect ['pɜ:fɪkt] **II 7C** 96 perfekt
to **perform** [pə'fɔ:m] **V 5B** 64,3 auftreten, vorführen
performance [pə'fɔ:məns] **IV 2A** 22 Aufführung
perhaps [pə'hæps] **I 1C** 39,3 vielleicht
to **permit** [pə'mɪt] **V 4B** 52 erlauben, gestatten
persecution [ˌpɜ:sɪ'kju:ʃn] **IV 4A** 52,2 Verfolgung
person ['pɜ:sn] **III 5D** 69,8 Person, Mensch
personal ['pɜ:snl] **V 4B** 54,4 persönlich
perspective [pə'spektɪv] **VI 4A** 47,b) Blickwinkel, Perspektive
to persuade [pə'sweɪd] **III 1B** 11 überreden, überzeugen
pet [pet] **I 3C** 59 Haustier; Liebling
philosopher [fɪ'lɒsəfə] **V 3AB** 46 Philosoph/in
philosophy [fɪ'lɒsəfɪ] **V 3AB** 45 Philosophie
phone [fəʊn] **I 7B** 105 Telefon
(phone) call ['fəʊn ˌkɔ:l] **III 4A** 46 Anruf
to **phone** [fəʊn] **I 8B** 120,7 anrufen
photo ['fəʊtəʊ] **I 7A** 102 Foto
to take a **photo** **I 7B** 105 ein Foto machen
to **photograph** ['fəʊtəgrɑ:f] **IV 5C** 70 fotografieren
photography [fə'tɒgrəfɪ] **III 5B** 60,3 Fotografie
phrase [freɪz] **IV 1A** 7,2 (Rede-) Wendung
phrase-book ['freɪzbʊk] **III 2B** 23 Sprachführer
physical education ['fɪzɪkl ˌedʒʊ'keɪʃn] **VI 3C** 40 Sportunterricht, Leibeserziehung
piano [pɪ'ænəʊ] **II 5B** 65,4 Klavier
to **pick up** [ˌpɪk‿'ʌp] **I 3B** 57 aufheben
to pick s.o. up [pɪk‿'ʌp] **IV 2B** 26,3 jmd abholen
picnic ['pɪknɪk] **I 3C** 60 Picknick
picture ['pɪktʃə] **I 1A** 36,1 Bild
picture-book **I 2A** 45,2 Bilderbuch
pie [paɪ] **II 5B** 63 Pastete
piece [pi:s] **I 2A** 44,1 Stück
pier [pɪə] **I 8C** 122 Anlegestelle, Pier
pig [pɪg] **II 7B** 94 Schwein
pilot ['paɪlət] **III 7C** 92,6 Pilot; Lotse
pine tar ['paɪn ˌtɑ:] **II 8C** 108 Kienteer
pineapple ['paɪnæpl] **I 6C** 94,1 Ananas
pink [pɪŋk] **II 5C** 70,4 rosa

pioneer [ˌpaɪəˈnɪə] **III 6C** 75,3 Wegbereiter/in, Pionier/in
pirate [ˈpaɪrət] **II 7A** 93,5 Pirat/in, Seeräuber/in
pit [pɪt] **IV 1A** 6 Grube, Zeche
⟨pitcher⟩ [ˈpɪtʃə] **III 6D** 81 Werfer/in
to **pity s.b.** [ˈpɪtɪ] **V 2B** 22,1 mit jmd Mitleid haben, jmd bedauern
What a **pity!** [ˈpɪtɪ] **III 4C** 53,5 Wie schade!
pizza [ˈpiːtsə] **I 8A** 117,5 Pizza
place [pleɪs] **I 7A** 104,5 Platz, Ort
plague [pleɪg] **III 1A** 8 Pest, Seuche
the **plains** [pleɪnz] **VI 2A** 22,3 die (großen) Ebenen im Zentrum der USA
plan [plæn] **I 4A** 66,1 Plan
to **plan** [plæn] **II 5C** 67 planen
plane [pleɪn] **I 6B** 92,2 Flugzeug
planner [ˈplænə] **V 3A** 31,3 Planer/in
plant [plɑːnt] **III 2AB** 32 Pflanze
recycling plant [ˌriːˈsaɪklɪŋ ˌplɑːnt] **III 3C** 42,5 Recyclinganlage
to **plant** [plɑːnt] **IV 4A** 51 anpflanzen
plantation [plænˈteɪʃn] **VI 2C** 28 Plantage, Pflanzung
plastic [ˈplæstɪk] **I 4A** 67,2 Plastik
plate [pleɪt] **I 6D** 96 Teller
platform [ˈplætfɔːm] **I 4C** 71,1 Bahnsteig, Plattform
play [pleɪ] **II 7A** 91 Schauspiel
role play [ˈrəʊl ˌpleɪ] **I 2B** 48,3 Rollenspiel
to **play** [pleɪ] **I FS9** 26 spielen
to play tricks on [trɪks] **II 6D** 84 jdm Streiche spielen
player [ˈpleɪə] **II 5C** 68 Spieler/in
playground [ˈpleɪgraʊnd] **II 4B** 49 Schulhof, Spielplatz
playing area [ˈpleɪɪŋ ˌeərɪə] **II 5C** 71,7 Spielfeld
⟨pleasant⟩ [ˈpleznt] **III 7FE** 105 angenehm
please [pliːz] **I FS3** 10 bitte
pleasure [ˈpleʒə] **IV 6C** 84,5 Vergnügen, Freude
plenty [ˈplentɪ] **IV 4C** 58,4 Fülle, Überfluß
plot [plɒt] **III 5B** 61,5 Handlung; Grundstück; Verschwörung
plot [plɒt] **III 7FE** 99 Verschwörung
plow (*AE*) [plaʊ] **IV 5C** 70 Pflug
plug [plʌg] **II 4A** 47 Zündkerze
to **plug** [plʌg] **IV 4AB** 64 (ein-)stöpseln
plural [ˈplʊərəl] **I 2A** 45,1 Mehrzahl, Plural
p.m. [ˌpiːˈem] **I 8A** 114 nachmittags, abends
pocket [ˈpɒkɪt] **IV 4C** 57 (Hosen-)Tasche
pocket money [ˈpɒkɪt ˌmʌnɪ] **II 6B** 81,3 Taschengeld
poem [ˈpəʊɪm] **II 8D** 115,7 Gedicht
poet [ˈpəʊɪt] **IV 3AB** 49 Dichter/in
pogrom [ˈpɒgrəm] **VI 3A** 35,3 *Ausschreitungen gegen religiöse oder ethnische Gruppen*
point [pɔɪnt] **III 2A** 21,1 Punkt; Stelle; Grad; Spitze; Zweck
to **point to** [pɔɪnt] **IV 1B** 11,6 zeigen, deuten
point of view [ˌpɔɪnt‿əv‿ˈvjuː] **IV 1AB** 20 Gesichtspunkt, Blickwinkel

7.1 (*seven point one*) **III 6D** 79 sieben Komma eins
poison [ˈpɔɪzn] **II 5B** 63 Gift
poisson aux tomates **II 5B** 63 *Fisch mit Tomaten (französisch)*
Pole [pəʊl] **V 5C** 66 Pole/Polin
pole [pəʊl] **III 6D** 78 Mast; Stange; Pol
police [pəˈliːs] **I FS10** 28,2 Polizei
police car **I 5A** 80,4 Polizeiwagen
police-station [pəˈliːsˌsteɪʃn] **II 3B** 33 Polizeirevier
policeman [pəˈliːsmən] **I 7C** 110 Polizist
to **polish** [ˈpɒlɪʃ] **II 4A** 47 polieren
Polish [ˈpəʊlɪʃ] **V 5B** 64,3 polnisch
polite [pəˈlaɪt] **VI 1C** 13,4 höflich
(political) party [pəˈlɪtɪkl ˈpɑːtɪ] **V 5AB** 74 Partei
political [pəˈlɪtɪkl] **V 2C** 25,2 politisch
politician [ˌpɒlɪˈtɪʃn] **IV 3AB** 47 Politiker/in
politics (*pl*) [ˈpɒlətɪks] **V 3AB** 45 Politik
to **pollute** [pəˈluːt] **IV 6D** 87,3 verschmutzen, verunreinigen
pollution [pəˈluːʃn] **III 6A** 70 (Umwelt-)Verschmutzung
pony [ˈpəʊnɪ] **II 2A** 20,4 Pony
pony-trekking [ˈpəʊnɪˌtrekɪŋ] **IV 3A** 34 längerer Ausritt mit einem Pony
poor [pɔː] **I 7B** 105 arm
pop star [ˈpɒp stɑː] **I 7C** 110 Popstar
pope [pəʊp] **IV 3AB** 46 Papst
popular [ˈpɒpjʊlə] **II 6B** 81,3 beliebt, populär
population [ˌpɒpjʊˈleɪʃn] **III 6A** 71 Bevölkerung; Bewohner, Einwohner
port [pɔːt] **III 2A** 21,1 Hafen
fishing port [ˈfɪʃɪŋˌpɔːt] **III 2A** 21,1 Fischereihafen
to **portray** [pɔːˈtreɪ] **IV 4A** 51 lebendig darstellen, porträtieren
possible [ˈpɒsəbl] **II 1D** 12 möglich
post [pəʊst] **V 5AB** 73 Posten, (Arbeits-)Stelle
postcard [ˈpəʊstkɑːd] **I 7A** 102,2 Postkarte
poster [ˈpəʊstə] **I 8A** 117,6 Plakat
postman [ˈpəʊstmən] **IV 2B** 26,3 Briefträger/in
⟨posy⟩ [ˈpəʊzɪ] **III 4C** 53 Sträußchen
potato(*es*) [pəˈteɪtəʊ] **IV 4AB** 6 Kartoffel(n)
potty [ˈpɒtɪ] **I FS11** 30 Töpfchen
pound [paʊnd] **I FS10** 29,4 Pfund *(Währung)*
⟨to pour⟩ [pɔː] **III 7C** 95,12 gießen
to pour (*down*) [ˈpɔː‿ˌdaʊn] **V 4C** 55 gießen, schütten
poverty [ˈpɒvətɪ] **IV 5B** 66 Armut
power [ˈpaʊə] **III 2AB** 33 Macht, Kraft
power station [ˈpaʊə ˈsteɪʃn] **V 3D** 38 Kraftwerk
powerful [ˈpaʊəfʊl] **II 2A** 19 mächtig
practical [ˈpræktɪkl] **IV 5C** 71,2 handwerklich, praktisch
practice [ˈpræktɪs] **II 5A** 61 Training, Übung
to **practice** (*AE*) [ˈpræktɪs] **IV 4A** 52 (aus-)üben, praktizieren
to **practise** [ˈpræktɪs] **II 4B** 49 üben
prairie [ˈpreərɪ] **III 6C** 76,5 Prärie
to **pray** [preɪ] **IV 3AB** 47 beten

preacher [ˈpriːtʃə] **VI 4A** 47,a) Prediger
precision [prɪˈsɪʒn] **VI 1B** 10,3 Genauigkeit, Präzision
prefect [ˈpriːfekt] **IV 3C** 45,6 Vertrauensschüler/in
to **prefer** [prɪˈfɜː] **II 7A** 92,4 lieber mögen, vorziehen, bevorzugen
prefix [ˈpriːfɪks] **IV 2C** 32,10 Vorsilbe, Präfix
prejudice [ˈpredʒʊdɪs] **VI 3B** 37 Vorurteil
preparation [ˌprepəˈreɪʃn] **V 5C** 66 Vorbereitung
to **prepare** [prɪˈpeə] **V 5AB** 75 vorbereiten
preposition [ˌprepəˈzɪʃn] **I 7C** 113,4 Präposition
prescription [prɪˈskrɪpʃn] **II 3A** 30 Rezept
present [ˈpreznt] **IV 1A** 8,4 Gegenwart
to **present** [prɪˈzent] **III 6C** 75,3 übergeben, überreichen, schenken
present [ˈpreznt] **I 6B** 92 Geschenk
to **preserve** [prɪˈzɜːv] **V 4A** 50,3 beschützen, erhalten
president [ˈprezɪdənt] **I 8C** 124,2 Präsident/in
presidential [ˌprezɪˈdenʃl] **V 5AB** 76 Präsidenten-
press [pres] **III 6B** 73 Presse
pressure [ˈpreʃə] **V 5AB** 78 Druck
prestige [preˈstiːʒ] **VI 1D** 17,2 Ansehen, Prestige
to **pretend** [prɪˈtend] **V 1C** 13 vorgeben, vortäuschen
pretty [ˈprɪtɪ] **II 3C** 35 hübsch
pretty [ˈprɪtɪ] **III 4B** 49 ganz schön, ziemlich
to **prevent** [prɪˈvent] **V 1C** 17,7 verhindern
price [praɪs] **III 7A** 84 Preis
⟨pride⟩ [praɪd] **III 1C** 19,10 Stolz
priest [priːst] **IV 1AB** 18 (katholischer) Priester
primary school [ˈpraɪmərɪ ˈskuːl] **VI 3C** 41 Grundschule
prime minister [ˈpraɪm ˈmɪnɪstə] **V 3AB** 42 Premierminister/in, Ministerpräsident/in
primitive [ˈprɪmɪtɪv] **VI 4C** 58,5 einfach, primitiv
principal [ˈprɪnsəpl] **III 6A** 72,4 Rektor/in; Haupt-, hauptsächlich
principle [ˈprɪnsəpl] **V 3AB** 42 Grundsatz, Prinzip
to **print** [prɪnt] **IV 3AB** 49 drucken
prison [ˈprɪzn] **III 1A** 8 Gefängnis
prisoner [ˈprɪznə] **II 1D** 12 Gefangene/r
private [ˈpraɪvɪt] **IV 3B** 40,6 privat
prize [praɪz] **IV 1A** 6 Preis, Auszeichnung
probably [ˈprɒbəblɪ] **II 7B** 94 wahrscheinlich
problem [ˈprɒbləm] **II 5C** 67 Problem
process [ˈprəʊses] **V 5AB** 76 Verfahren, Prozess
to **produce** [prəˈdjuːs] **VI 2D** 32,1 herstellen, produzieren
product [ˈprɒdʌkt] **VI 1A** 5,1 Erzeugnis, Produkt
production [prəˈdʌkʃn] **V 2A** 19 Produktion, Fertigung
⟨professional⟩ [prəˈfeʃənl] **III 6D** 81 professionell, Profi

profile ['prəʊfaɪl] **II 7A** 91 Steckbrief
programme ['prəʊgræm] **II 8B** 105 Programm
progress ['prəʊgres] **V 2C** 27,7 Fortschritt(e)
prohibition [ˌprəʊɪ'bɪʃn] **V 5C** 69,9 Prohibition, Alkoholverbot
project ['prɒdʒekt] **II 2A** 18 Projekt
promise ['prɒmɪs] **VI 3A** 36,5 Versprechen
to **promise** ['prɒmɪs] **II 4B** 49 versprechen
to **prompt to** [prɒmpt] **VI 2B** 24 zu etw bewegen, zu etw veranlassen
to **pronounce** [prə'naʊns] **IV 1A** 6 aussprechen
pronunciation [prəˌnʌnsɪ'eɪʃn] **IV 3B** 67,3 Aussprache
propeller [prə'pelə] **V 3D** 39,2 Propeller
properly ['prɒpəlɪ] **II 4B** 49 richtig
to **propose** [prə'pəʊz] **VI 1B** 8 vorschlagen, vorhaben
to **protect** [prə'tekt] **III 7C** 92,6 schützen, beschützen
protection [prə'tekʃn] **V 2A** 20 Schutz
protector [prə'tektə] **IV 3AB** 48 Beschützer/in, Schirmherr/in
Protestant ['prɒtɪstənt] **IV 3AB** 47 evangelisch, protestantisch
to **prove** [pru:v] **IV 4AB** 64 beweisen
proverb ['prɒvɜ:b] **V 3D** 41,7 Sprichwort
⟨psychiatrist⟩ [saɪ'kaɪətrɪst] **V 1A** 10,10 Psychiater/in
pub [pʌb] **III 1A** 9 Kneipe, Lokal, Gasthaus
public ['pʌblɪk] **IV 6A** 78 Öffentlichkeit
public baths [ˌpʌblɪk'bɑ:ðz] **II 5A** 60 Hallenbad
public ['pʌblɪk] **IV 5C** 72,6 öffentlich
to **publish** ['pʌblɪʃ] **V 3AB** 46 veröffentlichen
puck [pʌk] **II 5C** 71,7 Puck
to **pull** [pʊl] **I 1C** 40,6 ziehen
pullover ['pʊlˌəʊvə] **I FS11** 30 Pulli
pump [pʌmp] **III 7C** 89 Zapfsäule; Pumpe
to **pump up** [pʌmp] **II 4A** 47 aufpumpen
pumpkin ['pʌmpkɪn] **III 7FE** 98 (Garten-)Kürbis
to **punish** ['pʌnɪʃ] **III 4C** 51 (be-)strafen
pupil ['pju:pl] **II 5A** 60 Schüler/in
⟨puppy⟩ ['pʌpɪ] **III 7FE** 104 *junger Hund*
to **purify** ['pjʊərɪfaɪ] **IV 4AB** 62 reinigen, läutern
purse [pɜ:s] **II 2C** 26,5 Geldbeutel
purser ['pɜ:sə] **III 2D** 29,5 Zahlmeister/in
to **push** [pʊʃ] **I 1C** 40,6 drücken
to **put*** [pʊt] **I FS6** 17 stellen, legen, setzen
to put down **III 5B** 59,1 auflegen; wegtun; zuklappen
to put on **I 4C** 72,5 anziehen
to put together **I 3B** 58,1 zusammensetzen
to put up **II 3D** 38 aufstellen, aufhängen
puzzle ['pʌzl] **I 2A** 44,1 Puzzle

Q

quality ['kwɒlətɪ] **V 5AB** 78 Eigenschaft, Qualität
quarter ['kwɔ:tə] **I 3A** 54,1 Viertel
(*a*) quarter to nine **I 3A** 54,1 Viertel vor neun, dreiviertel neun
⟨quarter pounder⟩ [ˌkwɔ:tə 'paʊndə] **III 7B** 88,6 *Hamburger, der ein Viertelpfund wiegt*
⟨quarter⟩ ['kwɔ:tə] **III 7C** 95,12 25 cents
queen ['kwi:n] **I 7C** 110 Königin
question ['kwestʃən] **I FS3** 11,1 Frage
questionable ['kwestʃənəbl] **VI 1B** 8,1 fraglich, fragwürdig
questionnaire [ˌkwestʃə'neə] **II 1D** 15,5 Fragebogen
queue [kju:] **V 3D** 40,4 Schlange (von Menschen)
to **queue up** ['kju:‿'ʌp] **IV 3B** 38 eine Schlange bilden, sich anstellen
quick [kwɪk] **II 3C** 35 schnell
quiet ['kwaɪət] **I 2C** 50,5 ruhig
to **quit*** [kwɪt] **III 7B** 86 kündigen, aufgeben
quite [kwaɪt] **I 8C** 122 ziemlich, ganz, völlig
quitter (*coll*) ['kwɪtə] **V 5C** 66 Drückeberger, Feigling
quiz [kwɪz] **I 6C** 95,3 Quiz
quotation [kwəʊ'teɪʃn] **VI 1B** 9 Zitat

R

rabbit ['ræbɪt] **II 2A** 20,4 Kaninchen
race [reɪs] **IV 5B** 66 Rasse
to **race after** [reɪs] **III 3C** 40 hinter jmd herhetzen, -jagen
racial ['reɪʃl] **VI 3A** 33,a) rassisch, Rassen-
racism ['reɪsɪzəm] **VI 4A** 48,3 Rassismus
racist ['reɪsɪst] **VI 1C** 13,2 Rassist/in
radio ['reɪdɪəʊ] **I 2B** 46 Radio, Rundfunkgerät
rafting ['rɑ:ftɪŋ] **II 7A** 93,6 Wildwasserfahren
⟨rags⟩ [rægz] **III 1C** 19,10 Lumpen
ragtime ['rægtaɪm] **VI 4C** 58,5 *Musikrichtung*
rail [reɪl] **III 2B** 22 Bahn-
railing ['reɪlɪŋ] **III 2C** 24 Geländer
railroad (*AE*) ['reɪlrəʊd] **VI 2B** 25 Eisenbahn
railway ['reɪlweɪ] **I 4A** 66,1 Eisenbahn
rain [reɪn] **II 6C** 82 Regen
to **rain** **I FS11** 30 regnen
rainforest ['reɪnfɒrɪst] **V 4A** 49 Regenwald
rainy ['reɪnɪ] **II 6C** 83,3 regnerisch
to **raise** [reɪz] **IV 3C** 42 hochheben
rambler ['ræmblə] **III 4C** 54 Wanderer/in
ranger ['reɪndʒə] **II 8A** 104,3 Ranger/in (*Aufseher/in in einem Nationalpark*)
ranger station ['reɪndʒə ˌsteɪʃn] **II 8A** 104,3 Aufseherwache
rap [ræp] **VI 4B** 54,4 *Musikrichtung*
rat [ræt] **II 7C** 96 Ratte
rate [reɪt] **IV 4C** 57 Preis, Betrag
rather ['rɑ:ðə] **IV 1A** 6 eher
to **reach** [ri:tʃ] **III 3C** 40 erreichen, ankommen (an, in)
to **react** [rɪ'ækt] **IV 1C** 14,2 reagieren
to **read*** [ri:d] **I FS11** 30 lesen
to **read s.o.'s mind** [maɪnd] **IV 2A** 22 Gedanken lesen, etw. ahnen
ready ['redɪ] **I 4A** 67,2 fertig
to get ready **I 6D** 96 sich bereitmachen
real [rɪəl] **I 7C** 110 echt
realistic [ˌrɪə'lɪstɪk] **III 5B** 61,5 realistisch, naturgetreu
reality [rɪ'ælətɪ] **IV 3B** 40,5 Wirklichkeit, Realität
realization [ˌrɪəlaɪ'zeɪʃn] **IV 6D** 87,3 Verwirklichung, Realisierung
to **realize** ['rɪəlaɪz] **III 2D** 26 erkennen, sich klar werden
really ['rɪəlɪ] **I 7A** 102 wirklich
not really **I 5A** 78 eigentlich nicht
to **reappear** [ˌri:ə'pɪə] **III 3C** 39 wiedererscheinen, -auftauchen
rear light [rɪə] **II 4B** 49 Rücklicht
reason ['ri:zn] **III 7C** 91,2 Grund; Vernunft
⟨reason⟩ ['ri:zn] **III 7FE** 99 Grund
to **rebel** (*against*) [rɪ'bel] **V 3AB** 44 rebellieren, sich auflehnen (gegen)
rebellion [rɪ'beljən] **V 3AB** 44 Rebellion, Auflehnung
to **rebuild*** [ˌri:'bɪld] **III 1A** 8 wieder aufbauen
⟨to recall⟩ [rɪ'kɔ:l] **III 7FE** 101 sich erinnern an
to **receive** [rɪ'si:v] **IV 6B** 80,3 erhalten, bekommen
recently ['ri:sntlɪ] **IV 1B** 9 kürzlich, vor kurzem
⟨recipe⟩ ['resɪpɪ] **III 7FE** 104 Rezept
reconstruction [ˌri:kən'strʌkʃn] **VI 2D** 32,2 Wiederherstellung, Wiederaufbau
record ['rekɔ:d] **III 6A** 71,1 Rekord
record ['rekɔ:d] **I 6B** 92,2 Schallplatte
record-player ['rekɔ:dˌpleɪə] **I 6B** 92,2 Plattenspieler
to record [rɪ'kɔ:d] **III 6C** 75,3 aufzeichnen, aufnehmen
recreation area [ˌrekrɪ'eɪʃn 'eərɪə] **IV 6A** 78 Erholungsgebiet
rector ['rektə] **III 4C** 51 Pfarrer
recycling [ˌri:'saɪklɪŋ] **V 3D** 39 Recycling, Wiederaufbereitung
recycling plant [ˌri:'saɪklɪŋ ˌplɑ:nt] **III 3C** 42,5 Recyclinganlage
red [red] **I 1A** 35 rot
to **reduce** [rɪ'dju:s] **V 3AB** 45 reduzieren, verringern
giant **redwood** ['dʒaɪənt 'redwʊd] **III 6A** 71 Mammutbaum
referee [ˌrefə'ri:] **II 5C** 68 Schiedsrichter/in
to **reflect** [rɪ'flekt] **V 3D** 38 reflektieren
reform [rɪ'fɔ:m] **V 3AB** 45 Reform, Verbesserung
reformation [ˌrefə'meɪʃn] **IV 3AB** 48 Erneuerung, Reformation
refrigerator [rɪ'frɪdʒəreɪtə] **IV 5C** 72,6 Kühlschrank
refugee [ˌrefjʊ'dʒi:] **VI 3B** 39,4 Flüchtling
to **refuse** [rɪ'fju:z] **IV 6C** 83,4 verweigern
reggae ['regeɪ] **III 1C** 18,8 *westindische Popmusik*
region ['ri:dʒən] **VI 2B** 26,2 Region, Gebiet

regional [ˈriːdʒənl] **V 3A** 30 regional
register [ˈredʒɪstə] **I FS3** 10 Klassenbuch
to **register** [ˈredʒɪstə] **VI 4A** 48,3 *(in die Liste)* eintragen, einschreiben
to **regret** [rɪˈgret] **V 3B** 33 bedauern
regular [ˈregjʊlə] **II 3C** 37,4 regelmäßig
to **rehearse** [rɪˈhɜːs] **II 7B** 94 proben
⟨reindeer⟩ [ˈreɪnˌdɪə] **III 7FE** 100 Rentier
to **relate to** [rɪˈleɪt] **IV 6D** 87,3 sich beziehen auf
what **relation is** … **to** …? [rɪˈleɪʃn] **II 1D** 15,6 Wie ist … mit … verwandt?
relationship [rɪˈleɪʃnʃɪp] **IV 4D** 59 Beziehung
relative [ˈrelətɪv] **IV 6B** 80,2 Verwandte/r
to **relax** [rɪˈlæks] **IV 4A** 50 ausspannen, sich erholen
relaxed [rɪˈlækst] **III 7C** 89 locker, entspannt, ruhig
religion [rɪˈlɪdʒən] **IV 4A** 51 Religion
religious [rɪˈlɪdʒəs] **IV 4A** 52,2 religiös, Religions-
relocation [ˌriːləʊˈkeɪʃn] **VI 2A** 19 Umsiedelung, Verlegung
to **remain** [rɪˈmeɪn] **IV 5C** 71,3 übrig bleiben
remark [rɪˈmɑːk] **VI 2D** 32,1 Bemerkung, Äußerung
to **remember** [rɪˈmembə] **I 7A** 104,6 sich erinnern an
to **remind** [rɪˈmaɪnd] **VI 4B** 53,3 jmd erinnern (an)
to **renovate** [ˈrenəˌveɪt] **IV 3C** 44,4 instandsetzen, renovieren
repair [rɪˈpeə] **III 1B** 11 Reparatur
to **repair** [rɪˈpeə] **I 3B** 57 reparieren
⟨to repeat⟩ [rɪˈpiːt] **V 3D** 40,5 wiederholen
to repeat [rɪˈpiːt] **VI 4A** 49,4 wiederholen
to **replace** [rɪˈpleɪs] **V 3C** 36 ersetzen
to **reply** [rɪˈplaɪ] **II 5C** 68 erwidern, antworten
report [rɪˈpɔːt] **II 6C** 82,1 Bericht
to **report s.th.** [rɪˈpɔːt] **II 4C** 53 (etw.) melden, anzeigen
reporter [rɪˈpɔːtə] **I 3A** 54,1 Reporter/in
to **represent** [ˌreprɪˈzent] **V 5AB** 74 vertreten, repräsentieren
representative [ˌreprɪˈzentətɪv] **V 5AB** 74 Vertreter/in, Repräsentant/in
republic [rɪˈpʌblɪk] **V 3AB** 42 Republik
request [rɪˈkwest] **I 4C** 72,6 (Platten-)Wunsch, Bitte
to **request** [rɪˈkwest] **VI 1B** 8,2 bitten um, ersuchen um
requirement [rɪˈkwaɪəˌmənt] **III 5B** 60,3 Pflichtfach *(AE)*; Bedürfnis, Erfordernis
⟨rescue⟩ [ˈreskjuː] **III 4C** 56 Rettung
to **rescue** [ˈreskjuː] **II 2C** 25 retten, befreien
reservation [ˌrezəˈveɪʃn] **V 4A** 51,5 Reservat
reserve [rɪˈzɜːv] **II 5C** 68 Reserve
nature reserve [ˈneɪtʃə rɪˈzɜːv] **III 3B** 37 Naturschutzgebiet
reservoir [ˈrezəvwɑː] **IV 1B** 9 Reservoir, Talsperre
resident [ˈrezɪdent] **V 4B** 53,2 Anwohner, Bewohner
⟨resolution⟩ [ˌrezəˈluːʃn] **III 7FE** 102 Vorsatz
respect [rɪˈspekt] **VI 2C** 30,2 Respekt
to **respect** [rɪˈspekt] **IV 3AB** 49 achten, respektieren
respectable [rɪˈspektəbl] **VI 4C** 58,5 ehrbar, anständig
responsibility [rɪˌspɒnsəˈbɪlətɪ] **V 1B** 11 Verantwortung
rest [rest] **V 2C** 24 Rest
restaurant [ˈrestərɒnt] **II 5B** 65,5 Restaurant
restaurant-car [ˈrestərɒntˌkɑː] **IV 2B** 26,2 Speisewagen
result [rɪˈzʌlt] **IV 4B** 55,2 Ergebnis, Resultat
to **result** *(in)* [rɪˈzʌlt] **V 2A** 19 zur Folge haben, hinauslaufen (auf)
to **retain** [rɪˈteɪn] **VI 1A** 6 behalten, erhalten
to **retell*** [ˌriːˈtel] **II 8C** 109,2 wiedererzählen
to **return** [rɪˈtɜːn] **IV 3A** 34 zurückkommen, *hier:* erwidern
revenge [rɪˈvendʒ] **IV 5D** 75,4 Rache
revolution [ˌrevəˈluːʃn] **V 2A** 18 Umsturz, Revolution
revolutionary [ˌrevəˈluːʃnərɪ] **VI 2C** 28 revolutionär, Revolutions-
rhyme [raɪm] **I FS10** 28,1 Gedicht
rhythm [ˈrɪðəm] **IV 5B** 69,5 Rhythmus
⟨rhythm'n'blues⟩ [ˈrɪðəm‿n‿ˈbluːz] **VI 4C** 59,6 *Musikrichtung*
rib [rɪb] **V 5C** 68,6 Rippe
rice [raɪs] **II 5B** 63 Reis
rich [rɪtʃ] **II 2A** 20,3 reich
ride [raɪd] **II 3D** 38 Ritt, Fahrt
to **ride*** [raɪd] **I 2A** 44,8 reiten, mit dem Fahrrad fahren
to ride away **I 3C** 59 wegfahren *(auf dem Fahrrad)*
ridiculous [rɪˈdɪkjʊləs] **IV 6D** 85 lächerlich
oil **rig** [ˈɔɪlrɪg] **III 2A** 20 Ölbohrinsel
right [raɪt] **II 2B** 24,6 Recht
right [raɪt] **I 7C** 110 genau
right [raɪt] **I FS3** 11,2 richtig
all right [ˌɔːl ˈraɪt] **III 3A** 35 in Ordnung
on the right **I 1A** 35,3 rechts, auf der rechten Seite
right away [ˌraɪt‿əˈweɪ] **IV 1A** 6 sofort, gleich
⟨rim⟩ [rɪm] **III 1C** 19,10 Rand
rim [rɪm] **V 4A** 49 Rand
⟨ring⟩ [rɪŋ] **III 4C** 53,3 Ring
to **ring*** [rɪŋ] **I 2B** 46 klingeln
to ring up **I 5C** 85 anrufen
to **rise*** [raɪz] **III 2D** 27 sich (er-)heben; ansteigen
to **risk** [rɪsk] **II 7C** 97 riskieren
river [ˈrɪvə] **I 5C** 85 Fluss
road [rəʊd] **I FS4** 12 Straße
Road Safety Officer [ˌrəʊd ˈseɪftɪ ˌɒfɪsə] **II 4B** 49 Verkehrssicherheitsbeamter/beamtin
roar [rɔː] **IV 1C** 13 Schreien, Brüllen, Tosen
to **rob** [rɒb] **II 2B** 24,6 rauben, berauben
rock [rɒk] **III 3C** 40 Stein, Fels
rock-pool [ˈrɒkˌpuːl] **III 3C** 40 Felstümpel
rodeo [ˈrəʊdɪəʊ] **II 6C** 83,4 Rodeo
role [rəʊl] **IV 4A** 50 Rolle, Funktion
role play [ˈrəʊl pleɪ] **I 2B** 48,3 Rollenspiel
roll [rəʊl] **II 3C** 35 Rolle
to **roll** [rəʊl] **II 2B** 21 rollen
roller-skate [ˈrəʊləskeɪt] **III 4C** 55,10 Rollschuh
rollerblade [ˈrəʊləbleɪd] **IV 5B** 66 Rollschuh *(mit 3-5 Rollen hintereinander)*
Roman [ˈrəʊmən] **III 1A** 8 Römer/in, römisch
roof [ruːf] **I 8A** 116,3 Dach
room [ruːm] **I FS11** 30 Zimmer, Platz
⟨rooster⟩ *(AE)* [ˈruːstə] **III 6C** 76,6 Hahn
root [ruːt] **VI 2C** 28 Wurzel
rope [rəʊp] **II 2C** 26,3 Seil
⟨rose⟩ [rəʊz] **III 4C** 53 Rose
rough [rʌf] **III 2C** 24 rau, stürmisch
to swing **round*** [ˌswɪŋ ˈraʊnd] **I 7C** 110 herumschleudern
round [raʊnd] **II 5C** 71,7 herum, rund
round the house **I 5C** 85 um das Haus (herum)
route [ruːt] **III 2B** 23 Strecke, Route
routine [ruːˈtiːn] **IV 2A** 22 Routine, Gewohnheit
royal [ˈrɔɪəl] **VI 1C** 13,4 königlich
rubber [ˈrʌbə] **I FS9** 26 Radiergummi
rubbish [ˈrʌbɪʃ] **III 1B** 12,3 Abfall, Müll; Blödsinn
rucksack [ˈrʌksæk] **III 3C** 39 Rucksack
rude [ruːd] **IV 1C** 13 unverschämt, grob, unhöflich
rugby [ˈrʌgbɪ] **II 5A** 60 Rugby
ruin [ˈrʊɪn] **III 3C** 39 Ruine
to **ruin** [ˈrʊɪn] **III 3B** 37 verderben, zerstören, ruinieren
rule [ruːl] **II 5A** 61,2 Regel
to **rule** *(over)* [ˌruːl‿ˈəʊvə] **IV 1AB** 19 herrschen, regieren
ruler [ˈruːlə] **I FS9** 26 Lineal
ruler [ˈruːlə] **V 3AB** 47 Herrscher/in
run [rʌn] **III 7A** 84 Fahrt, Linie, Strecke
to **run*** [rʌn] **I FS11** 30 laufen, rennen
to run away **I 3B** 57 weglaufen
run-down [ˈrʌndaʊn] **V 1B** 11 baufällig, heruntergekommen
runner [ˈrʌnə] **IV 5D** 73 Läufer/in
runway [ˈrʌnweɪ] **I 7C** 111 Start- und Landebahn
rural [ˈrʊərəl] **IV 6A** 78 ländlich, Land-
to **rush** [rʌʃ] **III 4A** 46 eilen, hetzen, schnell transportieren
to rush after **I 3B** 57 hinterherrennen
Russian [ˈrʌʃn] **V 2B** 23,2 russisch; Russe, Russin
rusty [ˈrʌstɪ] **VI 4A** 47,b) rostig

S

sad [sæd] **III 4C** 52,1 traurig
saddle [ˈsædl] **II 4B** 49 Sattel
safari [səˈfɑːrɪ] **II 5C** 71,8 Safari
safe [seɪf] **II 4B** 52,7 sicher
safety regulation [ˈseɪftɪ ˌregjʊˈleɪʃn] **V 3D** 39,2 Sicherheitsvorkehrungen
to **sail** [seɪl] **III 2D** 26 segeln; ablegen
to go **sailing** [ˈseɪlɪŋ] **II 1B** 8 segeln

sailor ['seɪlə] **III 2AB** 32 Seemann, Segler/in, Matrose
salad ['sæləd] **I 6C** 94,1 Salat
sale [seɪl] **III 3A** 36,7 Ausverkauf; Verkauf
salesman ['seɪlzmən] **III 6C** 75 Verkäufer, Vertreter
salmon ['sæmən] **VI 2A** 23,5 Lachs
salt [sɔ:lt] **II 5C** 72,11 Salz
salty ['sɔ:ltɪ] **VI 4C** 57,4 salzig
the **same** [seɪm] **I 1B** 37,1 der-, die-, dasselbe, gleiche
sanctuary ['sæŋktʃʊərɪ] **III 3C** 40 Station; Zuflucht, Schutzgebiet
sand [sænd] **II 3B** 33 Sand
⟨sands⟩ [sændz] **I 4** 65 Sandstrand
sandwich ['sænwɪdʒ] **I 4C** 71,3 Sandwich, Butterbrot
sarcastic [sɑ:'kæstɪk] **V 1C** 13 sarkastisch, mit beißendem Spott
satanic [sə'tænɪk] **V 2A** 18 teuflisch, satanisch
satellite ['sætəlaɪt] **III 6C** 75 Satellit, Trabant
satire ['sætaɪə] **V 2B** 23,2 Satire
to **satisfy** ['sætɪsfaɪ] **VI 2A** 23,5 zufrieden stellen, befriedigen
saucer ['sɔ:sə] **II 5C** 72,11 Untertasse
⟨sausage⟩ ['sɒsɪdʒ] **I 3** 53 Wurst
sausage ['sɒsɪdʒ] **V 5C** 66 Wurst
savage ['sævɪdʒ] **IV 4D** 59 Wilde/r
to **save** [seɪv] **II 6B** 80 retten
savings ['seɪvɪŋz] **V 1A** 8,3 Ersparnis
to **saw** [sɔ:] **V 3D** 38 sägen
Saxon ['sæksn] **II 2B** 24,6 Sächsin, Sachse; sächsisch
to **say*** [seɪ] **I FS2** 9 sagen, sprechen
saying ['seɪɪŋ] **IV 6B** 80,4 Sprichwort
Scandinavian [ˌskændɪ'neɪvjən] **IV 1AB** 19 Skandinavier/in, skandinavisch
scarf [skɑ:f] **I 2C** 49,3 Schal, Halstuch
scarves [skɑ:vz] **I 2C** 49,3 Schals, Halstücher
scene [si:n] **I FS** 8 Szene
schedule (*AE/BE*) ['skedʒl, 'ʃedju:l] **III 5B** 60,3 Stundenplan *(AE)*; Programm, Zeitplan
school [sku:l] **I FS3** 10 Schule
at school **I FS7** 20,5 in der Schule
comprehensive school [ˌkɒmprɪ'hensɪv] **I 1B** 37,1 Gesamtschule
school-bag ['sku:lbæg] **I FS3** 11,1 Schultasche
⟨school children⟩ **I 1** 34 Schulkinder
school colours **I 1A** 35 Farben von Schuluniformen, -abzeichen usw.
school uniform **I 1A** 35 Schuluniform
to get to school **I 3A** 54,1 die Schule erreichen, zur Schule kommen
to go to school **I 3C** 59 in die/zur Schule gehen
to school [tə 'sku:l] **I 3A** 54,1 zur Schule, in die Schule
science ['saɪəns] **III 5C** 63,2 Naturwissenschaft, Wissenschaft
scientist ['saɪəntɪst] **III 2D** 26 Wissenschaftler/in
to **score** [skɔ:] **II 5C** 68 ein Tor schießen
Scottish ['skɒtɪʃ] **III 3C** 42,5 schottisch
scrapbook ['skræpˌbʊk] **III 2AB** 32 Sammelalbum
scratch [skrætʃ] **II 4B** 49 Kratzer
scratched [skrætʃt] **II 4C** 54 zerkratzt
to **scream** [skri:m] **I 7C** 110 schreien, kreischen
screech [skri:tʃ] **IV 5D** 73 (gellendes) Kreischen
screw [skru:] **II 5C** 70,5 Schraube
script [skrɪpt] **V 2B** 23,2 Drehbuch
scriptwriter ['skrɪptˌraɪtə] **V 4A** 48 Drehbuchautor/in
sculpture ['skʌlptʃə] **IV 3C** 45,7 Plastik, Skulptur
scurvy pl ['skɜ:vɪ] **VI 1A** 7,4 Skorbut
sea [si:] **I 4C** 71,3 Meer
sea level ['si: ˌlevəl] **III 6A** 71 Meeresspiegel
seafaring ['si:ˌfeərɪŋ] **III 2C** 24 seefahrend, Seefahrer-
seal [si:l] **III 3A** 36,7 Seehund
to **search** [sɜ:tʃ] **VI 4B** 53,3 durchsuchen
seasick ['si:sɪk] **III 2A** 21,2 seekrank
to go to the **seaside** ['si:saɪd] **I 4A** 66,1 ans Meer fahren
season ['si:zn] **III 7C** 93,7 Jahreszeit, Saison
seat [si:t] **I 3A** 54,1 Sitz(-platz)
second ['sekənd] **II 1C** 10 Sekunde
secondary school ['sekəndərɪ 'sku:l] **VI 3C** 41 *weiterführende Schule in Großbritannien*
secret ['si:krɪt] **I 1C** 39,3 geheim, Geheimnis
secretary ['sekrətrɪ] **III 6AB** 82 Sekretär/in
section ['sekʃn] **V 5D** 71,1 Abschnitt, Teil
security [sɪ'kjʊərətɪ] **V 1B** 11 Sicherheit
I **see** **I 3A** 54,1 ich verstehe; ach so
to see* [si:] **I 1B** 37,3 sehen
You see, … **I 3A** 54,1 Wissen Sie, …
to **seem to** [si:m] **VI 3B** 39,4 anscheinend, scheinbar
to **seem** [si:m] **V 5A** 61,2 scheinen, den Anschein haben
to **segregate** ['segrɪˌgeɪt] **VI 4A** 48,3 *(nach Rassen, Geschlechtern etc.)* trennen, absondern
segregation [ˌsegrɪ'geɪʃn] **VI 4A** 47,b) (Rassen-)Trennung
selectors [sɪ'lektəz] **VI 1D** 18,4 Auswahlgremium
self-determination ['selfdɪˌtɜ:mɪ'neɪʃn] **VI 1C** 14 Selbstbestimmung
selfish ['selfɪʃ] **III 5C** 62 egoistisch, selbstsüchtig
to **sell*** [sel] **I 5A** 78 verkaufen
⟨semi⟩ (*AE*) ['semɪ] **III 7C** 95,12 Sattelschlepper
⟨semi-detached house⟩ [ˌsemɪdɪ'tætʃt] **I 5** 77 Doppelhaushälfte
Senate ['senɪt] **V 3AB** 46 Senat, Oberhaus *(der amerikanischen Regierung)*
senator ['senətə] **V 5AB** 74 Senator/in
to **send*** [send] **I 2B** 46 schicken
senior (*AE*) ['si:njə] **V 1C** 13 Schüler/in im letzten Schuljahr
sense [sens] **V 3AB** 42 Sinn; Bedeutung *(Wort)*
sensible ['sensəbl] **III 5B** 59 vernünftig
sentence ['sentəns] **I 3B** 58,1 Satz
⟨sentimental⟩ [ˌsentɪ'mentl] **III 7FE** 103 sentimental
separate ['seprət] **VI 4A** 48,3 getrennt, separat
separation [ˌsepə'reɪʃn] **IV 4AB** 63 Trennung
sergeant ['sɑ:dʒənt] **VI 1B** 10,3 Feldwebel
serious ['sɪərɪəs] **IV 2B** 25,1 ernst, ernsthaft
servant ['sɜ:vənt] **IV 4D** 59 Dienstbote/Dienstmädchen
to **serve** [sɜ:v] **III 3B** 37 servieren; dienen, bedienen
service ['sɜ:vɪs] **III 2B** 22 Zufahrts-, Versorgungs-; Dienst
(*church*) service ['sɜ:vɪs] **III 4C** 52 Gottesdienst
to **set*** [set] **IV 2B** 26,2 *hier:* stellen, einstellen
to set off [set‿'ɒf] **IV 6D** 85 aufbrechen
to set up [ˌset 'ʌp] **III 6AB** 82 aufbauen, aufstellen
to set* [set] **II 5C** 72,11 decken
to **settle** ['setl] **IV 1AB** 19 siedeln
settlement ['setlmənt] **VI 1A** 6 Siedlung
settler ['setlə] **IV 4A** 50 Siedler/in
several ['sevrəl] **III 5B** 61,5 mehrere
sexist ['seksɪst] **VI 4B** 54,5 sexistisch, andere aufgrund des Geschlechts benachteiligend
shadow ['ʃædəʊ] **II 1D** 13 Schatten
to **shake*** [ʃeɪk] **II 7C** 97 schütteln
Shall I …?* [ʃæl] **III 3A** 34 Soll ich …?
⟨shame⟩ [ʃeɪm] **III 7FE** 99 Schande
shame [ʃeɪm] **IV 3A** 35 (es ist) schade
shame [ʃeɪm] **V 2C** 24 Schande, Schmach
⟨shamrock⟩ ['ʃæmrɒk] **III 7FE** 105 Klee, Kleeblatt
to **share** [ʃeə] **IV 6A** 78 teilen
shark [ʃɑ:k] **III 5D** 69,9 Hai(-fisch)
she [ʃi:] **I FS2** 9 sie
sheep [ʃi:p] **I 8A** 116,3 Schaf
sheepdog ['ʃi:pdɒg] **II 3C** 36,2a Hirtenhund
sheet [ʃi:t] **VI 4A** 47,b) Bettlaken, Betttuch
Sheriff ['ʃerɪf] **II 2A** 18 Sheriff
she's = she is [ʃi:z] **I FS2** 9 sie ist
to **shine*** [ʃaɪn] **I FS11** 30 scheinen
⟨shiny⟩ ['ʃaɪnɪ] **III 7FE** 101 glänzend
ship [ʃɪp] **III 1A** 9 Schiff
shipbuilding ['ʃɪpˌbɪldɪŋ] **V 2C** 24 Schiffbau
shipping ['ʃɪpɪŋ] **III 2A** 22 Schifffahrt(s-)
shipyard ['ʃɪpjɑ:d] **V 3C** 36 (Schiffs-)Werft
shirt [ʃɜ:t] **I 1A** 35,1 Hemd
to **shiver** (*with*) ['ʃɪvə] **V 5C** 65 zittern, schaudern
shock [ʃɒk] **II 3D** 39 Schock, Schreck
to **shock** [ʃɒk] **IV 5B** 66 erschüttern, schockieren
shoe [ʃu:] **I 1A** 35,1 Schuh
to **shoot*** [ʃu:t] **II 2C** 26 schießen, erschießen
shop [ʃɒp] **I FS4** 12 Geschäft, Laden
shop-assistant ['ʃɒpəˌsɪstənt] **I 6B** 92,3 Verkäufer/in
shoplifter ['ʃɒpˌlɪftə] **IV 5D** 73 Ladendieb/in
shopping centre ['ʃɒpɪŋ ˌsentə] **II 4C** 53 Einkaufszentrum

to go **shopping** **I 6C** 94,1 einkaufen gehen
short [ʃɔ:t] **I FS8** 25 kurz
short cut [ˈʃɔ:t ˌkʌt] **III 1B** 12,2 Abkürzung, Schnellverfahren
shortbread [ˈʃɔ:tbred] **III 3A** 35,3 *schottisches Gebäck*
shorts [ʃɔ:ts] **III 3C** 43,8 Shorts
⟨should⟩ [ʃʊd] **I FS10** 28,3 sollte
you should [ʃʊd] **III 2A** 20 du solltest …
shoulder [ˈʃəʊldə] **IV 2A** 22 Schulter
to **shout** [ʃaʊt] **I 4A** 66,2 rufen, schreien
show [ʃəʊ] **IV 5A** 65 Aufführung, Vorstellung
to **show*** [ʃəʊ] **I 3B** 57 zeigen
shower [ˈʃaʊə] **V 3C** 37,2 Dusche
⟨shrill⟩ [ʃrɪl] **III 7FE** 105 schrill
to **shut*** [ʃʌt] **I 4C** 71,1 schließen
shut **I 1C** 40,7 geschlossen, zu
shuttle [ˈʃʌtl] **III 2B** 22 Pendelzug, -bus
shy [ʃaɪ] **IV 4B** 54 schüchtern
to be **sick** [sɪk] **III 2C** 24 sich übergeben, brechen
I feel sick. [sɪk] **II 3A** 32,5 Ich fühle mich nicht wohl./Mir ist übel.
sick [sɪk] **IV 3AB** 49 krank
side [saɪd] **I 8A** 117,5 Seite
⟨side order⟩ [ˈsaɪd ˌɔ:də] **III 7B** 88,6 Beilage
sidewalk [ˈsaɪdwɔ:k] **IV 5B** 66 Bürgersteig
sight [saɪt] **I 8A** 114 Sehenswürdigkeit
sightseeing [ˈsaɪtˌsi:ɪŋ] **IV 4A** 50 Besichtigung von Sehenswürdigkeiten
sign [saɪn] **III 2D** 26 Zeichen
to **sign** [saɪn] **IV 4A** 52 unterzeichnen, unterschreiben
signal [ˈsɪgnəl] **III 2D** 26 Zeichen, Signal
to **signal** [ˈsɪgnəl] **II 4B** 52,7 (die Richtung) anzeigen
silence [ˈsaɪləns] **III 4C** 51 Schweigen, Stille
silly [ˈsɪlɪ] **I 5B** 81 doof, albern, dumm
⟨silver⟩ [ˈsɪlvə] **III 6D** 80,4 Silber
silver [ˈsɪlvə] **V 3D** 41,7 Silber
similar [ˈsɪmɪlə] **IV 5B** 67,1 ähnlich
simply [ˈsɪmplɪ] **IV 6B** 80,2 einfach, nur
since [sɪns] **II 5B** 63 seit
sinful [ˈsɪnfʊl] **IV 5D** 77,10 sündig, sündhaft
to **sing*** [sɪŋ] **I 4C** 74,4 singen
single [ˈsɪŋgl] **III 7C** 94,9 Einzel-; unverheiratet, einzige/r/s
singular [ˈsɪŋgjʊlə] **I 2A** 45,1 Einzahl, Singular
to **sink*** [sɪŋk] **III 2D** 26 (ver-)sinken, untergehen, versenken
⟨sinner⟩ [ˈsɪnə] **I 7C** 113,5 Sünder/in
sir [sɜ:] **II 4B** 49 *höfliche Anrede für einen Mann/Lehrer*
sister [ˈsɪstə] **I FS4** 12 Schwester
sit-in [ˈsɪtˌɪn] **VI 4A** 48,3 Sitzstreik, Sit-in
to **sit*** [sɪt] **I FS11** 30 sitzen
to sit down **I FS3** 10 sich hinsetzen, Platz nehmen
to sit up [ˌsɪt ˈʌp] **III 4B** 49 aufrecht sitzen; sich aufrichten
site [saɪt] **IV 6C** 84,5 Stelle, Standort, Gelände
sitting-room [ˈsɪtɪŋrʊm] **I 5B** 81 Wohnzimmer
situation [ˌsɪtjʊˈeɪʃn] **V 5C** 68,7 Situation
size [saɪz] **II 4C** 54 Größe
to **skate** [skeɪt] **V 5A** 60 Schlittschuh oder Rollschuh laufen
skateboard [ˈskeɪtˌbɔ:d] **I 8A** 117,6 Skateboard
to go **skateboarding** [ˈskeɪtbɔ:dɪŋ] **I 7A** 103,4 Skateboard fahren
to **ski** [ski:] **IV 5B** 66 Ski laufen
skiing [ˈski:ɪŋ] **II 7A** 93,6 Skilaufen
skill [skɪl] **II 7C** 97 Geschicklichkeit, Fähigkeit
skin [skɪn] **VI 2A** 19 Haut
skirt [skɜ:t] **I 1A** 35,1 Rock
⟨sky⟩ [skaɪ] **IV 6D** 88,5 Himmel
sky [skaɪ] **V 4A** 48 Himmel
skyline [ˈskaɪlaɪn] **I 8C** 123 Skyline
skyscraper [ˈskaɪˌskreɪpə] **I 8A** 114 Wolkenkratzer
slap [slæp] **IV 6D** 85 Schlag, Klaps
⟨slaughter⟩ [ˈslɔ:tə] **III 6C** 76,6 Schlachten, Gemetzel
slave [sleɪv] **V 3AB** 44 Sklave/Sklavin
slavery [ˈsleɪvərɪ] **IV 4D** 59 Sklaverei, Sklaventum
to **sleep*** [sli:p] **I 1C** 39,1 schlafen
sleeping-bag [ˈsli:pɪŋ bæg] **I 6D** 96 Schlafsack
sleeve [sli:v] **III 7C** 91,3 Ärmel; Hülle
⟨sleigh⟩ [sleɪ] **III 7FE** 101 Schlitten
slide [slaɪd] **II 2A** 19 Dia
to **slide*** (*off*), slid [slaɪd, slɪd] **V 3D** 39 schlittern, rutschen
to **slip** [slɪp] **III 2D** 27 rutschen, gleiten
slippery [ˈslɪpərɪ] **V 5C** 66 schlüpfrig, glitschig, glatt
⟨slope⟩ [sləʊp] **III 7FE** 106 Abhang, Hang
to **slow down** [ˌsləʊ ˈdaʊn] **III 4A** 46 langsamer fahren
slow (*slowly*) [sləʊ, ˈsləʊlɪ] **I 8C** 122 langsam
slum [slʌm] **V 3C** 36 Elendsviertel, Slum
small [smɔ:l] **I 1C** 39,4 klein
smart [smɑ:t] **IV 4B** 55,2 gescheit, geschäftstüchtig
smell [smel] **II 5B** 63 Geruch
to **smell*** [smel] **II 5B** 63 riechen
to **smile** [smaɪl] **I 7A** 102 lächeln
smog [smɒg] **III 6A** 70 Smog
smoke [sməʊk] **I 4C** 71,1 Rauch
to **smoke** [sməʊk] **III 7A** 84 rauchen
smuggle [smʌgl] **V 3D** 38 Schmuggel
smuggler [ˈsmʌglə] **V 3D** 38 Schmuggler/in
snack bar [ˈsnæk ˌbɑ:] **II 4C** 54 Imbissstube
snake [sneɪk] **IV 2B** 25 Schlange
⟨to snap (*one's fingers*)⟩ [snæp] **III 7B** 88,6 schnippen (mit den Fingern)
⟨to sneeze⟩ [sni:z] **III 4C** 53 niesen
snobbish [ˈsnɒbɪʃ] **III 5D** 67,2 snobistisch, versnobt
snow [snəʊ] **II 6C** 83,3 Schnee
snowy [ˈsnəʊɪ] **II 6C** 83,3 verschneit
I don't think **so.** **I 6B** 92,2 Das glaub' ich nicht.
so clever **I 3B** 57 so klug
So do I. **I 8B** 118 Ich auch.
so [səʊ] **I FS7** 18 so, also
so that [ˈsəʊˌðət] **III 4A** 46 damit
so did **I 8B** 118 auch
soccer [ˈsɒkə] **IV 4B** 54 Fußball
social life [ˈsəʊʃl‿ˌlaɪf] **IV 2A** 23,2 soziale Beziehungen
social [ˈsəʊʃl] **V 1B** 11 sozial, gesellschaftlich
society [səˈsaɪətɪ] **IV 5C** 70 Gesellschaft
sock [sɒk] **I 1A** 35,1 Socke, Kniestrumpf
soda (*coll, AE*) [ˈsəʊdə] **V 1C** 13 Limo(nade)
to **soften** [ˈsɒfn] **V 5C** 66 weich werden, sanft werden
soldier [ˈsəʊldʒə] **II 2B** 21 Soldat/in
solo [ˈsəʊləʊ] **IV 1C** 13 Solo(-spiel), Einzelauftritt
solution [səˈlu:ʃn] **IV 6B** 80,4 Lösung
to **solve** [sɒlv] **VI 4A** 48,1 lösen, beseitigen
some [sʌm] **I 1C** 40,5 einige, etwas
somebody [ˈsʌmˌbɒdɪ] **I 4C** 72,6 (irgend-)jemand
somehow [ˈsʌmhaʊ] **IV 5B** 66 irgendwie
someone [ˈsʌmwʌn] **I 2C** 50,5 jemand
something [ˈsʌmθɪŋ] **I 3C** 64,9 etwas
sometimes [ˈsʌmtaɪmz] **I FS7** 18 manchmal
somewhere [ˈsʌmweə] **I 8A** 114 irgendwo
son [sʌn] **I 7B** 107,5 Sohn
song [sɒŋ] **I 4C** 74,4 Lied
soon [su:n] **I 2B** 46 bald
as soon as [əz ˈsu:n ˌəz] **III 4B** 49 sobald (wie)
⟨sooner⟩ [ˈsu:nə] **III 4C** 54 eher
the sooner the better [ˈsu:nə] **II 4B** 49 je früher, desto besser
sore [sɔ:] **II 3A** 30 wund, weh
sorry [ˈsɒrɪ] **I FS1** 8 Entschuldigung, tut mir Leid
to be sorry **I 3B** 57 Leid tun
to **sort** (*out*) [sɔ:t] **V 2A** 20 (aus-)sortieren
SOS [ˌes əʊ ˈes] **III 2D** 26 SOS (Notsignal)
soul [səʊl] **VI 4C** 58,5 *Musikrichtung*
sound [saʊnd] **IV 1C** 13 Ton, Klang
to **sound** [saʊnd] **II 1D** 13 ertönen, klingen, sich anhören
soup [su:p] **II 5B** 63 Suppe
source [sɔ:s] **III 6AB** 82 Quelle, Ursprung
south [saʊθ] **I 8A** 117,6 südlich, Süden
south-east [ˌsaʊθˈi:st] **IV 1B** 9 Südosten
souvenir [ˌsu:vəˈnɪə] **II 5B** 66,7 Souvenir
space [speɪs] **IV 4AB** 64 Platz, Raum
Spaghetti Bolognese [spəˈgetɪ ˌbɒləˈneɪz] **II 5B** 65,5 Spagetti Bolognese *(italienisches Nudelgericht)*
Spaniard [ˈspænjəd] **IV 4D** 59 Spanier/in
Spanish [ˈspænɪʃ] **III 2AB** 60 Spanisch, (die) Spanier
to **speak*** [spi:k] **I FS8** 24 sprechen
speaker [ˈspi:kə] **IV 2C** 33,12 Sprecher/in
special [ˈspeʃl] **I 4C** 71 Sondersendung
special [ˈspeʃl] **IV 2A** 22 besonders, speziell

speech [spi:tʃ] **IV 3B** 38 Rede, Ansprache
speed [spi:d] **III 2D** 26 Geschwindigkeit
to **spell*** [spel] **I 1C** 43 buchstabieren
to **spend*** [spend] **II 6A** 76 verbringen
to spend (*money*) [spend] **III 5B** 59 ausgeben
spider [ˈspaɪdə] **II 7A** 91 Spinne
spinning jenny [ˈspɪnɪŋ ˈdʒenɪ] **V 2A** 19,2 Spinnmaschine, ‚Jennymaschine'
spirit [ˈspɪrɪt] **VI 2B** 24 Geist
spiritual [ˈspɪrɪtʃʊəl] **VI 4C** 58,5 *Musikrichtung*
splash [splæʃ] **III 3B** 37 Tupfen, Spritzer; Platschen
split [splɪt] **VI 1A** 6 Spaltung, Teilung
sponge [spʌndʒ] **I FS6** 16 Schwamm
spoon [spu:n] **II 5C** 71,11 Löffel
sport [spɔ:t] **I 6B** 92,2 Sport, Sportart
⟨spotted hog⟩ [ˌspɒtɪd ˈhɒg] **III 6C** 76,6 geflecktes Mastschwein
spray [spreɪ] **III 2C** 24 Gischt; Sprühdose
to **spread*** [spred] **III 4C** 51 (sich) ausbreiten
spring [sprɪŋ] **II 6C** 83,3 Frühling
sprinkler [ˈsprɪŋklə] **II 6D** 84 Rasensprenger, Sprinkler
squad car [ˈskwɒd ˌkɑ:] **IV 5D** 73 Polizeiauto
square [skweə] **I 7B** 108,6 Platz
square dance [ˈskweə ˌdæns] **II 7A** 91 Square Dance *(amerikanischer Volkstanz)*
square meter (*AE*) [ˈskweə ˈmi:tə] **IV 5A** 65 Quadratmeter
squash [skwɒʃ] **IV 4D** 59 Kürbis
⟨squaw⟩ [skwɔ:] **IV 6D** 87,4 Indianerin
to **squeeze** [skwi:z] **III 5D** 67 drücken
Ssh [ʃ] **I 2C** 50,6 Sch(t), Psst
stadium [ˈsteɪdjəm] **IV 5A** 65 Stadion
staff manager [ˈstɑ:f ˈmænɪdʒə] **IV 4B** 55,2 Personalleiter/in, -chef/in
stage [steɪdʒ] **IV 1C** 13 Bühne
⟨stage designer⟩ [ˈsteɪdʒ dɪˈzaɪnə] **IV 2C** 30,6 Bühnenbildner
stained glass [ˌsteɪnd ˈglɑ:s] **III 5B** 59 Buntglas
stairs [steəz] **I 1C** 39,3 Treppe
stamp [stæmp] **I 7A** 102 Briefmarke
to **stamp** [stæmp] **IV 3B** 38 stampfen, trampeln
stand [stænd] **II 6B** 80 Imbissstand
to **stand*** **I 2A** 44,5 stehen
to stand up [ˌstænd ˈʌp] **II 8C** 108 nach oben stehen; aufstehen
⟨standard⟩ [ˈstændəd] **III 1C** 19,10 korrekt; normal, üblich
stanza [ˈstænzə] **II 8D** 115,7 Strophe
star [stɑ:] **II 6D** 87,5 Stern; Star
to **stare at** [ˈsteər‿æt] **II 7B** 94 starren auf
to **start** [stɑ:t] **I 3A** 54,1 anfangen; losfahren
to start ... ing [stɑ:t] **II 7C** 96 anfangen, etw. zu tun
starter [ˈstɑ:tə] **II 5B** 63 Vorspeise
⟨starvation⟩ [stɑ:ˈveɪʃn] **III 6C** 76,6 Hunger(-tod)
starving [ˈstɑ:vɪŋ] **II 5B** 63 sehr hungrig
state [steɪt] **II 6A** 76 Staat; Bundesland
⟨statement⟩ [ˈsteɪtmənt] **V 2C** 26,5 Aussage, Erklärung
statement [ˈsteɪtmənt] **VI 2B** 26,3 Aussage, Behauptung
⟨statement⟩ [ˈsteɪtmənt] **VI 1D** 18,5 Aussage, Behauptung
station [ˈsteɪʃn] **IV 5A** 65 Haltestelle
station [ˈsteɪʃn] **I 2B** 46 Bahnhof
bus station [ˈbʌs ˌsteɪʃn] **I 4C** 71,1 Busbahnhof
statistics (*pl*) [stəˈtɪstɪks] **V 4B** 53,1 Statistik
stative [ˈsteɪtɪv] **VI 4C** 57,4 statisch
statue [ˈstætju:] **I 7A** 103,3 Statue
status [ˈsteɪtəs] **VI 1C** 13,4 Status, (Rechts-)Stellung
to **stay** [steɪ] **I 6B** 92,1 bleiben, übernachten
to **steal*** [sti:l] **II 4C** 53 stehlen
stealer [ˈsti:lə] **IV 3C** 45,7 Dieb/in
steam [sti:m] **I 4A** 66,2 Dampf
steamship [ˈsti:mʃɪp] **V 2A** 19 Dampfschiff, Dampfer
steel [sti:l] **IV 1B** 9 Stahl
steelworks [ˈsti:lwɜ:ks] **IV 1B** 9 Stahlwerk
steep [sti:p] **IV 6D** 85 steil, jäh
to **steer** [stɪə] **III 2C** 24 steuern
stem [stem] **III 7FE** 98 Stiel
step [step] **II 4B** 52,8 Schritt, Stufe
to **step on s.th.** [step] **III 3B** 37 auf etw. treten
stereo [ˈsterɪəʊ] **IV 4B** 54 Stereoanlage
stern [stɜ:n] **III 2D** 27 Heck
stewardess [ˌstjʊəˈdes] **II 6A** 78,4 Stewardess
stick [stɪk] **I 3B** 57 Stock
to **stick***, stuck [stɪk, stʌk] **V 5C** 65 kleben, haften, stecken bleiben
sticker [ˈstɪkə] **IV 3A** 36,2 Aufkleber
still [stɪl] **I FS8** 25,3 (immer) noch
stomach [ˈstʌmək] **II 3A** 32,5 Magen, Bauch
stone [stəʊn] **I 4C** 71,3 Stein
⟨to stoop⟩ [stu:p] **III 7FE** 105 sich beugen
to **stop** [stɒp] **I 5C** 84 aufhören, anhalten
to stop fighting **II 2B** 21 aufhören zu kämpfen
store [stɔ:] **III 7B** 86 Laden, Geschäft *(AE)*; Lager
storm [stɔ:m] **II 6A** 78,2 Sturm
stormy [ˈstɔ:mɪ] **II 6C** 83,3 stürmisch
story [ˈstɔ:rɪ] **I 3C** 62,4 Geschichte
stove [stəʊv] **IV 5C** 72,6 Herd
straight [streɪt] **I 5B** 81 geradewegs
straight on [streɪt‿ˈɒn] **I 7B** 108,6 geradeaus
strange [streɪndʒ] **II 1B** 8 seltsam, fremd
strange [streɪndʒ] **V 3D** 38 fremd
stranger [ˈstreɪndʒə] **IV 5C** 70 Fremde/r
to **strangle** [stræŋgl] **III 6D** 78 erwürgen, erdrosseln
⟨straw⟩ [strɔ:] **III 7FE** 99 Stroh
strawberry [ˈstrɔ:bərɪ] **I 6C** 94,1 Erdbeere
stream [stri:m] **IV 6D** 85 Bach
street [stri:t] **I 5C** 84 Straße
to **stress** [stres] **IV 6C** 84,6 betonen, mit Akzent versehen
stretcher [ˈstretʃə] **III 4A** 46 (Trag-)Bahre
strict [strɪkt] **VI 4A** 48,3 streng, genau
⟨strike⟩ [straɪk] **III 6D** 81 verfehlter Schlag
strike [straɪk] **V 2C** 24 Streik, Arbeitsniederlegung
string [strɪŋ] **I 3B** 57 Schnur, Kordel
strong [strɒŋ] **I 4C** 72,4 stark
structure [ˈstrʌktʃə] **V 4A** 50,2 Struktur, Gebilde
stuck [stʌk] **I 1C** 40,7 eingeklemmt
student [ˈstju:dnt] **III 6A** 72,4 Student/in; Schüler/in *(AE)*
studio [ˈstju:dɪəʊ] **II 7B** 94 Studio
study [ˈstʌdɪ] **V 3A** 32,6 Studium
to **study** [ˈstʌdɪ] **III 1A** 10,4 studieren, lernen; beobachten
stuff [stʌf] **IV 6B** 80,3 Zeug, Kram
stupid [ˈstju:pɪd] **III 4B** 49 dumm, blöd
style [staɪl] **V 3C** 37,1 Stil
subject [ˈsʌbdʒɪkt] **II 5A** 60 Fach
suburb [ˈsʌbɜ:b] **III 1A** 8 Vorort
suburban [səˈbɜ:bən] **V 4C** 55 vorstädtisch
subway (*AE*) [ˈsʌbweɪ] **IV 4C** 58 U-Bahn
to **succeed** [səkˈsi:d] **IV 3A** 37,6 erfolgreich sein, gelingen
success [səkˈses] **IV 4A** 51 Erfolg
successful [səkˈsesfʊl] **II 2A** 18 erfolgreich
such [sʌtʃ] **V 1A** 6 so, solch
suddenly [ˈsʌdnlɪ] **I 6D** 97 plötzlich
to **suffer** [ˈsʌfə] **II 8C** 108 leiden
suffix [ˈsʌfɪks] **IV 2C** 32,10 Nachsilbe, Suffix
sugar [ˈʃʊgə] **II 5C** 72,11 Zucker
to **suggest** [səˈdʒest] **III 3C** 39 vorschlagen, andeuten
suggestion [səˈdʒestʃən] **III 3A** 35,4 Vorschlag
suit [su:t] **VI 4A** 47,b) Anzug, Kostüm
suitable [ˈsu:təbl] **V 3A** 30 geeignet, passend
suitcase [ˈsu:tkeɪs] **I 7B** 105 Koffer
to **sum up** [ˈsʌm‿ˌʌp] **VI 2C** 30,1 zusammenfassen
⟨to summarize⟩ [ˈsʌməraɪz] **VI 3C** 43,6 zusammenfassen
summary [ˈsʌmərɪ] **III 4B** 49,1 Zusammenfassung
summer [ˈsʌmə] **I 8B** 119,3 Sommer
(*summer*) camp [kæmp] **II 8A** 103 (Sommer-)Lager
sun [sʌn] **I FS11** 30 Sonne
sunny [ˈsʌnɪ] **II 6C** 82 sonnig
super [ˈsu:pə] **II 1B** 8 super
⟨superlative⟩ [su:ˈpɜ:lətɪv] **IV 4C** 58,4 höchste Stufe
⟨supermarket⟩ [ˈsu:pəˌmɑ:kɪt] **I 6** 90 Supermarkt
⟨supermarket⟩ [ˈsu:pəmɑ:kɪt] **V 2C** 26,5 Supermarkt
superpower [ˌsu:pəˈpaʊə] **V 2A** 21,5 Supermacht
supervisor [ˈsu:pəˌvaɪzə] **IV 4B** 56,3 Aufsichtsführende/r, Supervisor/in
supper [ˈsʌpə] **IV 3AB** 47 Abendessen
to **support** [səˈpɔ:t] **IV 1A** 6 unterstützen, fördern

to **suppose** [sə'pəʊz] **IV 1A** 6 annehmen, vermuten
supreme [sʊ'pri:m] **IV 3AB** 48 oberste/r, höchste/r
sure [ʃɔ:; ʃʊə] **I 6B** 92,2 sicher
sure enough [ʃɔ:r‿ɪ'nʌf] **IV 6B** 79 wirklich, tatsächlich
to **surf** [sɜ:f] **III 5C** 65,7 wellenreiten, surfen
surgery ['sɜ:dʒərɪ] **II 3A** 30 Praxis
surprise [sə'praɪz] **II 5C** 67 Überraschung
to **surprise** [sə'praɪz] **V 5A** 60 überraschen
surprised [sə'praɪzd] **I 5C** 86,3 überrascht
to **survive** [sə'vaɪv] **III 6D** 80,5 überleben
survivor [sə'vaɪvə] **III 2D** 27,1 Überlebende/r
to **suspect** [sə'spekt] **VI 1C** 12,1 vermuten, den Verdacht haben
swear-word ['sweəwɜ:d] **VI 1C** 13,2 Fluch
sweatshirt ['swetʃɜ:t] **II 5C** 67 Sweatshirt *(Baumwollpullover)*
Swede [swi:d] **IV 4C** 57 Schwede/Schwedin
sweet shop ['swi:tʃɒp] **I 5C** 84 Süßwarenladen
sweet [swi:t] **I 6D** 96 süß
sweets [swi:ts] **I 4C** 74,8 Süßigkeiten, Bonbons
swelling ['swelɪŋ] **III 4C** 51 Schwellung
to **swim*** [swɪm] **I 2A** 44,6 schwimmen
⟨swimmer⟩ ['swɪmə] **III 2D** 30,10 Schwimmer/in
(outdoor) **swimming-pool** ['swɪmɪŋ,pu:l] **II 5A** 60 Freibad
to go **swimming** [gəʊ 'swɪmɪŋ] **I 7A** 103,4 schwimmen gehen
swing [swɪŋ] **VI 4C** 58,5 *Musikrichtung*
to **swing round*** [,swɪŋ 'raʊnd] **I 7C** 110 herumschleudern
Swiss [swɪs] **IV 1B** 11,6 Schweizer-; Schweizer/in
to **switch** [swɪtʃ] **II 6D** 85 vertauschen
to switch on [,swɪtʃ‿'ɒn] **II 5A** 61 einschalten
swollen ['swəʊlən] **II 3D** 39 geschwollen
sword [sɔ:d] **II 1D** 12 Schwert
symbol ['sɪmbl] **III 7FE** 107 Symbol
symbolic [sɪm'bɒlɪk] **VI 4A** 47,b) sinnbildlich, symbolisch
to **synchronize** ['sɪŋkrənaɪz] **V 3B** 33 synchronisieren, zeitgleich ablaufen
synonym ['sɪnənɪm] **VI 4A** 50,5 bedeutungsgleiches oder -ähnliches Wort, Synonym
system ['sɪstəm] **V 2A** 19,2 System

T

T-shirt ['ti:ʃɜ:t] **II 5C** 68 T-Shirt
table ['teɪbl] **I FS10** 29,5 Tisch
tail [teɪl] **III 3C** 39 Schwanz
tailor ['teɪlə] **III 4C** 51 Schneider/in
to **take*** [teɪk] **I 2B** 46 nehmen, bringen, machen
to take a photo **I 7B** 105 ein Foto machen
to take *(a test)* **II 4B** 49 (eine Prüfung) machen
to take care of **II 7B** 94 sorgen für, sich kümmern um
to take cover ['teɪk 'kʌvə] **IV 5D** 75,4 in Deckung gehen
to take for a walk **I 3C** 59 spazierenführen
to take home **I 3A** 54,1 nach Hause bringen
to take off **II 4B** 49 abnehmen, abmontieren; abfliegen; ausziehen
to take out **I 2C** 49,2 herausnehmen, herausholen
to take *(time)* **III 1A** 8 dauern, brauchen
to take to bed **I 3C** 60 ins Bett bringen
to take turns **I FS9** 26 sich abwechseln, etw. abwechselnd tun
takeaway restaurant ['teɪkə,weɪ 'restərɒnt] **V 1A** 8,3 Restaurant mit Straßenverkauf
talented ['tæləntɪd] **II 8B** 105 begabt, talentiert
talk [tɔ:k] **III 5B** 60,3 Gespräch, Vortrag
to **talk to** ['tɔ:k tə] **I 1A** 35,2 sprechen mit
tall [tɔ:l] **III 6A** 71 hoch, groß
tall [tɔ:l] **IV 1C** 12 groß, hochgewachsen
tall story [,tɔ:l 'stɔ:rɪ] **II 8B** 105 Lügengeschichte
to have got a **tan** [tæn] **II 1B** 8 braun sein
tank [tæŋk] **III 4A** 47,3 Tank
tanker ['tæŋkə] **III 3C** 41,2 Tanker
tape [teɪp] **II 3C** 35 Klebeband
tape [teɪp] **IV 1A** 7 Tonband
task [tɑ:sk] **VI 1B** 8 Aufgabe
taste [teɪst] **VI 3C** 43,5 Geschmack, Vorgeschmack
to **taste** [teɪst] **II 5A** 61 probieren, schmecken
tax [tæks] **V 3AB** 43 Steuer
taxi ['tæksɪ] **I FS7** 18 Taxi
taxi driver **I FS7** 18 Taxifahrer/in
tea [ti:] **I 4C** 74,6 Tee
to **teach*** [ti:tʃ] **I 3B** 57 unterrichten, lehren, beibringen
teacher ['ti:tʃə] **I FS1** 8 Lehrer/in
team [ti:m] **II 5B** 63 Team, Mannschaft
team-mate ['ti:m,meɪt] **V 5C** 65 Mannschaftskamerad/in
teamwork ['ti:mwɜ:k] **IV 2A** 24,5 Gemeinschaftsarbeit, Teamarbeit
teapot ['ti:pɒt] **II 5C** 72,11 Teekanne
tear [tɪə] **IV 5D** 73 Träne
to **tear* down,** tore, torn [teə, tɔ:, tɔ:n] **V 5B** 63 abreißen, herunterreißen
to **tease** [ti:z] **IV 3A** 35 necken, auf den Arm nehmen
teaspoon ['ti:spu:n] **II 5C** 72,11 Teelöffel
technology [tek'nɒlədʒɪ] **V 2A** 19 Technologie
teddy ['tedɪ] **I FS7** 20,6 Teddy(-bär)
teen [ti:n] **V 1A** 8,3 Teenager-, Jugend-
teenage ['ti:neidʒ] **V 1A** 8,1 Teenager-, Jugend-
teenager ['ti:n,eɪdʒə] **IV 2B** 25 Jugendliche/r
teeth [ti:θ] **II 3C** 37,4 Zähne
telephone ['telɪfəʊn] **I FS7** 19,4 Telefon
telephone box **II 3D** 39 Telefonzelle
to **telephone** **I 2B** 46 anrufen, telefonieren (mit)
⟨telephoto lens⟩ ['telɪ,fəʊtəʊ 'lenz] **V 4D** 59,6 Teleobjektiv
to **tell*** [tel] **I 2C** 52,5 erzählen, berichten; sagen
telly *(coll)* ['telɪ] **V 1A** 6 Fernseher, ‚Beule'
temperature ['temprətʃə] **II 3A** 30 Fieber, Temperatur
to take s.o.'s temperature **II 3A** 30 bei jdm Fieber messen
to **tend to** [tend] **VI 1C** 13,3 zu etw neigen, tendieren zu
tennis ['tenɪs] **I 7A** 103,4 Tennis
tense [tens] **IV 6C** 82 angespannt
tent [tent] **III 3C** 44,10 Zelt
tepee ['ti:,pi:] **II 8C** 109 (Indianer-)Zelt
term [tɜ:m] **II 5A** 60 Trimester
term [tɜ:m] **V 5AB** 76 Dauer, (Amts-)Zeit
terminal ['tɜ:mɪnl] **III 2B** 22 Endstation, -bahnhof
⟨terraced house⟩ ['terəst] **I 5** 77 Reihenhaus
terrible ['terəbl] **I FS4** 12 fürchterlich, schrecklich; unmöglich
terribly ['terəblɪ] **II 3C** 35 schrecklich
territory ['terətərɪ] **IV 6A** 78 Gebiet, Territorium
⟨in great terror⟩ ['terə] **III 6C** 76,6 erschrocken
test [test] **II 3A** 30 Prüfung, Test, Untersuchung
to **test** **I FS9** 26 prüfen, abfragen
Texan ['teksən] **II 6A** 76 Texaner/in
textbook ['tekstbʊk] **I 1B** 37,2 Lehrbuch
textile ['tekstaɪl] **V 2A** 19 Gewebe, Stoff
Thailand ['taɪlænd] **VI 3B** 39,4 Thailand
(higher) **than** [ðæn] **II 1C** 10 (höher) als
to **thank** [θæŋk] **IV 4C** 58,2 danken
thank you **I FS3** 10 danke schön
thanks [θæŋks] **I 1B** 37,2 danke (schön)
thanks for calling **I 8B** 118 danke für den Anruf
that [ðæt, ðət] **I FS4** 12 dass; der, die, das
that boy **I FS2** 9 der Junge da
that's wrong **I FS8** 24,2 das stimmt nicht
the poor [pɔ:] **VI 4B** 53,3 die Armen
the [ðə, ðɪ] **I FS3** 10 der, die, das; die *(pl)*
the … the … **II 4B** 49 je …, desto (je) …
theatre ['θɪətə] **IV 2C** 27 Theater
their [ðeə] **I FS5** 14 ihr
theirs [ðeəz] **III 1C** 16,3 ihre/r/s
them [ðem] **I 2B** 46 sie, ihnen
then [ðen] **I FS9** 26 dann, danach
theocracy [θɪ'ɒkrəsɪ] **IV 4AB** 64 Theokratie, Herrschaft der Kirche
there [ðeə] dort
over there **I FS9** 24 dort drüben
there are ['ðeər‿ɑ:] **I FS10** 29,5 es gibt, da sind
there is ['ðeər‿ɪz] **I FS7** 18 es gibt, da ist

⟨there'd be⟩ ['ðeəd bɪ] **I FS10** 28,3 es würden sein
these [ði:z] **I 2A** 44,4 diese (hier)
they managed ['mænɪdʒd] **III 7B** 86 es gelang ihnen
they [ðeɪ] **I FS5** 14 sie
they're = they are [ðeə] **I FS5** 14 sie sind
thick [θɪk] **III 5D** 66 dick, dicht
thief [θi:f] **II 4C** 53 Dieb/in
thieves (*pl*) [θi:vz] **II 4C** 53 Diebe/Diebinnen
thin [θɪn] **II 4A** 47 dünn
thing [θɪŋ] **I 3A** 54,1 Sache, Ding
to **think*** [θɪŋk] **I 4A** 67,1 denken, meinen, glauben
to think of **I 5A** 78 denken an
thinker ['θɪŋkə] **V 3AB** 46 Denker/in
thirsty ['θɜ:stɪ] **II 5B** 65,5 durstig
this [ðɪs] **I FS9** 26 dies, das; dieser, diese, dieses
⟨this boy⟩ **I 1** 34 dieser Junge
this morning **II 5** 74,3 heute Morgen
this question **I 1B** 35,3 diese Frage
those [ðəʊz] **I 2A** 44,4 diese dort
though [ðəʊ] **IV 2A** 22 obwohl, obgleich
thought [θɔ:t] **V 4D** 58,2 Gedanke
⟨thoughtful⟩ ['θɔ:tfʊl] **IV 6D** 88,5 nachdenklich
thousand ['θaʊzənd] **II 1C** 10 Tausend
to **thrash** [θræʃ] **VI 1D** 18,3 schlagen, verdreschen
twelve and **three quarters** ['kwɔ:təz] **II 7A** 91 zwölf dreiviertel
throat [θrəʊt] **II 3A** 30 Hals
through [θru:] **I 1C** 39,4 durch, hindurch
to **throw*** [θrəʊ] **I 2C** 50,6 werfen
to throw away **I 5B** 82,2 wegwerfen
thunder ['θʌndə] **II 1D** 12 Donner
Thunderbirds ['θʌndə ˌbɜ:dz] **II 8C** 108 Donnervögel
thunderstorm ['θʌndəˌstɔ:m] **II 6C** 82 Gewitter
thus [ðʌs] **VI 1A** 6 so, folglich
ticket ['tɪkɪt] **I 8C** 112 Karte, Fahrkarte
tide [taɪd] **IV 3C** 43,2 Gezeiten, Tiden, Ebbe und Flut
to **tidy** ['taɪdɪ] **IV 2C** 31,7 aufräumen, in Ordnung bringen
tie [taɪ] **IV 3C** 45,6 Krawatte
to **tie** [taɪ] **I 2C** 50,6 binden
to **tighten** ['taɪtn] **II 2C** 26 anziehen, festziehen
tights [taɪts] **I 1A** 35,1 Strumpfhose
timber ['tɪmbə] **V 4A** 48 (Natur-) Holz
time [taɪm] **I 3A** 56,4 Zeit, Uhrzeit
Have a good time! **I 5C** 84 Viel Spaß!
little time **I 3C** 63,6 wenig Zeit
on time **I 4B** 69 pünktlich
this time **I 4C** 72,4 diesmal
What time is it? **I 3A** 56,4 Wie spät ist es?
four **times** [taɪmz] **II 2A** 19 viermal
timetable ['taɪmˌteɪbl] **I 4B** 70,2 Fahrplan
tin [tɪn] **III 3C** 42,5 Blech, Zinn; Blechdose
tired ['taɪəd] **II 3A** 30 müde
title ['taɪtl] **II 2A** 18 Titel
***to bind up** ['baɪnd ˌʌp] **VI 2D** 31,a) verbinden
to [tu:; tʊ; tə] zu, in
(*a*) quarter to nine [tə 'naɪn] **I 3A** 54,1 Viertel vor neun
(*in order*) to **III 5D** 66 um … zu
over to you [tə 'ju:] **I FS1** 8,1 du bist/ihr seid/Sie sind dran
toast [təʊst] **II 5C** 72,11 Toast
today [tə'deɪ] **I FS8** 23 heute
together [tə'geðə] **I FS4** 12 zusammen
to put together **I 3B** 58,1 zusammensetzen
toilet ['tɔɪlɪt] **II 5C** 71,8 Toilette
tolerance ['tɒlərəns] **IV 4AB** 63 Toleranz
tomato ketchup [təˌmɑ:təʊ 'ketʃəp] **I 6C** 94,1 (Tomaten-)Ketschup
tomato, (*pl.*) tomatoes [tə'mɑ:təʊ] **II 5B** 63 Tomate
tomorrow [tə'mɒrəʊ] **I 6D** 99,6 morgen
ton [tʌn] **III 3A** 35,3 Tonne
tongue [tʌŋ] **IV 1A** 6 Zunge
tonight [tə'naɪt] **II 3B** 34,2 heute Abend
too [tu:] **I FS4** 12 auch
too big **I 1C** 39,4 zu groß
tool [tu:l] **III 2D** 28,3 Werkzeug
tooth [tu:θ] **II 3C** 37,4 Zahn
toothpaste ['tu:θˌpeɪst] **III 7C** 90 Zahnpasta
top [tɒp] **I 8A** 116,3 ganz oben
on top of [ɒn 'tɒp‿ɒv] **I 7C** 110 oben auf
at the tops of their voices **III 1B** 12,3 aus vollem Halse
to be on top **II 5C** 68 das Spiel beherrschen
torch [tɔ:tʃ] **V 3D** 39 Taschenlampe
tornado [tɔ:'neɪdəʊ] **III 6D** 78 Tornado
to **touch** [tʌtʃ] **II 1D** 13 berühren
tour [tʊə] **IV 1B** 11,5 Fahrt, Reise
tourist ['tʊərɪst] **I 8B** 121,8 Tourist/in
tourist office ['tʊərɪst ˌɒfɪs] **III 3A** 36,7 Fremdenverkehrsamt
tournament ['tɔ:nəmənt] **IV 3A** 34 Turnier
towards [tə'wɔ:dz] **I 6D** 97 auf… zu
⟨towed⟩ [təʊd] **III 2AB** 31 geschleppt
tower ['taʊə] **I 8A** 114 Turm
town [taʊn] **II 2A** 19 Stadt
toy [tɔɪ] **I FS7** 20,7 Spielzeug
toy car **I 5A** 78 Spielzeugauto
toyshop ['tɔɪʃɒp] **I 6B** 92,3 Spielwarenladen
track [træk] **VI 2B** 25 Gleis, Schienenstrang
tractor ['træktə] **IV 3A** 35 Traktor
to **trade** [treɪd] **III 2AB** 33 handeln
trader ['treɪdə] **IV 6A** 78 Händler/in
trading post ['treɪdɪŋ 'pəʊst] **VI 1A** 6 Handelsniederlassung
tradition [trə'dɪʃn] **VI 3A** 36,6 (überliefertes) Brauchtum, Tradition
traffic ['træfɪk] **I 8A** 116,3 Verkehr
trail [treɪl] **IV 6C** 84,5 (Trampel-) Pfad, Weg
train [treɪn] **I 4A** 66 Zug
by train **I 4A** 66 mit dem Zug
to **train** [treɪn] **IV 4A** 51 ausbilden
transcontinental ['trænzˌkɒntɪ'nentl] **VI 2B** 25 einen Erdteil durchquerend, transkontinental
to **translate** [træns'leɪt] **II 7B** 95,3 übersetzen
transport ['trænspɔ:t] **V 2A** 19,1 Beförderung, Transport
transportation [ˌtrænspɔ:'teɪʃn] **VI 2B** 25 Beförderung, Transportsystem
trapper ['træpə] **VI 2B** 26,3 Pelztierjäger, Trapper
travel agent ['trævl ˌeɪdʒənt] **I 7A** 104,5 Reisebürokaufmann/-frau
travel costs ['trævl ˌkɒsts] **IV 1C** 16,6 Reisekosten
to **travel** ['trævl] **III 1C** 15,1 reisen, fahren
traveler (*AE*) ['trævlə] **V 4A** 51,6 Reisende/r
traveller ['trævlə] **II 2B** 21,6 Reisende/r
⟨treason⟩ ['tri:zn] **III 7FE** 99 Verrat
treasure ['treʒə] **I 1C** 40,5 Schatz
treat [tri:t] **III 7FE** 98 eine besondere Überraschung
to **treat** [tri:t] **IV 2C** 27 behandeln
treatment ['tri:tmənt] **VI 4A** 49,5 Behandlung
tree [tri:] **I 8A** 117,6 Baum
trend [trend] **VI 3A** 33,b) Tendenz, Trend
to **trespass** ['trespəs] **IV 3B** 40,6 widerrechtlich betreten
trial ['traɪəl] **V 1B** 12,2 Prozess, Gerichtsverfahren
triathlon [ˌtraɪ'æθlən] **IV 3A** 35 Dreisportwettkampf *(Schwimmen, Radfahren, Laufen)*
tribe [traɪb] **III 6AB** 82 Stamm
trick [trɪk] **I 3B** 57 Kunststück, Trick
trip [trɪp] **I 7A** 103,3 Reise
troops pl [tru:p] **VI 1B** 10,3 Truppe/n
to be in **trouble*** ['trʌbl] **III 5C** 64,6 Ärger, Schwierigkeiten bekommen/haben
trousers ['traʊzəz] **I 1A** 35,1 Hose
truck [trʌk] **III 6D** 78 LKW
truck stop ['trʌkstɒp] **III 7A** 84 Fernfahrerraststätte
to **truck** [trʌk] **III 7A** 84 Lastwagen fahren
trucker ['trʌkə] **III 7A** 84 Fernfahrer/in
true [tru:] **I 8C** 122 wahr
trumpet ['trʌmpɪt] **II 5C** 68 Trompete
trunk (*AE*) [trʌŋk] **IV 5D** 76,8 Kofferraum
to **trust** [trʌst] **IV 4AB** 63 (ver-)trauen
truth [tru:θ] **III 1C** 15,2 Wahrheit
to **try** (*to*) [traɪ] **I 6D** 97 versuchen; probieren
tube [tju:b] **III 1A** 8 U-Bahn *(in London)*
tune [tju:n] **IV 1C** 12 Melodie
to **tune** [tju:n] **IV 3B** 38 (ein Instrument) stimmen
tunnel ['tʌnl] **II 1C** 10 Tunnel
turbine ['tɜ:baɪn] **V 3B** 33 Turbine
turkey ['tɜ:kɪ] **IV 4D** 59 Truthahn, Pute/r
⟨turkey⟩ ['tɜ:kɪ] **III 7FE** 100 Truthahn
Turkish ['tɜ:kɪʃ] **IV 1B** 11,6 türkisch
turn [tɜ:n] **I 5A** 78 Runde
it's his turn **I 5A** 78 er ist an der Reihe
to miss a turn **I 5B** 81 eine Runde aussetzen
to **turn** [tɜ:n] **I 7B** 108,6 abbiegen
to turn down **II 5C** 68 leiser stellen

to turn (*green*) **III 2C** 24 (grün) werden
to turn off [tɜ:n‿'ɒf] **IV 2C** 28 ausschalten
to turn on **II 6D** 84 andrehen, einschalten
to turn out [ˌtɜ:n‿'aʊt] **IV 6C** 82 sich herausstellen, sich entpuppen
to turn to [tɜ:n] **IV 2C** 28 sich wenden an, drehen zu
turning-point ['tɜ:nɪŋ ˌpɔɪnt] **IV 5D** 74,2 Wendepunkt
to take **turns** **I FS9** 26 sich abwechseln, etw. abwechselnd tun
TV [ti:'vi:] **I 3C** 60 Fernseher
to watch TV **I 3C** 60 fernsehen
twice [twaɪs] **V 1C** 13 zweimal
to **twist** [twɪst] **III 6D** 78 verbiegen; drehen
type [taɪp] **IV 6C** 84,5 Typ, Sorte
typical ['tɪpɪkl] **I FS5** 14 typisch
tyre ['taɪə] **II 4A** 47 Reifen

U

Ugh! [ʊh] **I 5B** 81,0 I! I gitt!
ugliness ['ʌglɪnɪs] **V 2A** 18 Häßlichkeit
Uhhh? [ɜ:] **II 6D** 84 *Ausdruck der Unsicherheit*
umbrella [ʌm'brelə] **I 7C** 110 Regenschirm
unchanged [ˌʌn'tʃeɪndʒd] **IV 1A** 7,3 unverändert
unchecked ['ʌnˌtʃekt] **V 3B** 33 unkontrolliert, ungeprüft
uncle [ʌŋkl] **I 8B** 120,4 Onkel
uncomfortable [ʌn'kʌmfətəbl] **IV 2C** 28 unbequem
under ['ʌndə] **I FS6** 16 unter
underclass ['ʌndəˌklɑ:s] **V 1B** 11 unterpriviligierte gesellschaftliche Klasse
underground ['ʌndəgraʊnd] **I 7C** 110 Untergrundbahn
to **underline** [ˌʌndə'laɪn] **IV 4D** 61,4 unterstreichen
to **understand*** [ˌʌndə'stænd] **I 4C** 73,3 verstehen
unemployed [ˌʌnɪm'plɔɪd] **IV 1B** 9 arbeitslos
unemployment [ˌʌnɪm'plɔɪmənt] **VI 3A** 34,c) Arbeitslosigkeit
unfair [ˌʌn'feə] **II 5C** 68 unfair
unfortunately [ʌn'fɔ:tʃnətlɪ] **II 2B** 21 leider, unglücklicherweise
unfriendly [ˌʌn'frendlɪ] **IV 4B** 55,2 unfreundlich
unhappy [ʌn'hæpɪ] **I 4C** 71,1 unglücklich
uniform ['ju:nɪfɔ:m] **I 1A** 35 Uniform
union ['ju:njən] **V 2A** 20 Gewerkschaft
unit ['ju:nɪt] **I 1A** 35 Einheit; Lektion
university [ˌju:nɪ'vɜ:sətɪ] **IV 4B** 54 Universität, Hochschule
unknown [ˌʌn'nəʊn] **V 2A** 18 unbekannt
⟨unless⟩ [ən'les] **III 7FE** 107 es sei denn
unlike [ʌn'laɪk] **III 7C** 92,6 im Gegensatz zu; unähnlich
unpopular [ˌʌn'pɒpjʊlə] **IV 6D** 86,1 unbeliebt
unpunctual [ˌʌn'pʌŋktʃʊəl] **IV 4B** 55,2 unpünktlich
unsinkable [ʌn'sɪŋkəbl] **III 2D** 26 unsinkbar
until [ən'tɪl] **I 5B** 81 bis
not ... until [ˌnɒt ən'tɪl] **III 2B** 22 erst
unusual [ʌn'ju:ʒl] **V 5D** 71,2 ungewöhnlich
up [ʌp] **I 1C** 39,4 hinauf
to get up **I 3A** 54,1 aufstehen
to look up **I 4A** 66,2 aufblicken
to pick up **I 3B** 57 aufheben
to ring up **I 5C** 85 anrufen
to sit up **I 2C** 50,7 aufrecht sitzen, sich aufrichten
to wake s.o. up **I 3C** 59 jdn aufwecken
to wash up **I 5B** 81 abwaschen
upon [ə'pɒn] **VI 1A** 5 auf, an
upper deck [ˌʌpə'dek] **I 8C** 122 Oberdeck
upset [ʌp'set] **III 3B** 37 gekränkt, ärgerlich
upstairs [ˌʌp'steəz] **I FS6** 17 nach oben
urban ['ɜ:bən] **V 3C** 35 städtisch, Stadt-
urgent ['ɜ:dʒənt] **V 5C** 66 eilig, dringend
us [ʌs] **I 2A** 44,5 uns
use [ju:s] **V 2A** 19 Gebrauch, Anwendung
to **use** [ju:z] **I 5A** 78 benutzen, verwenden
useful ['ju:sfʊl] **I 5A** 78 nützlich
user ['ju:zə] **V 5AB** 75 Benutzer/in
as **usual** [əz 'ju:ʒʊəl] **II 5C** 67 wie üblich
usually ['ju:ʒʊəlɪ] **I 4B** 70,3 normalerweise, gewöhnlich

V

vacancy ['veɪkənsɪ] **III 7C** 94,9 freies Zimmer; freie Stelle
vacation (*AE*) [və'keɪʃn] **III 7C** 89 Ferien, Urlaub
valley ['vælɪ] **IV 1B** 11 Tal
van [væn] **I FS4** 12 Lieferwagen
vandalism ['vændəlizm] **V 3C** 36 Vandalismus, Zerstörungswut
vanity ['vænətɪ] **VI 3D** 45 (persönliche) Eitelkeit
vegetable(*s*) ['vedʒtəbl] **II 5B** 63 Gemüse
verb [vɜ:b] **I 7A** 103,3 Verb
⟨verse⟩ [vɜ:s] **III 1C** 19,10 Strophe
⟨verse⟩ [vɜ:s] **VI 4C** 59,6 Vers, Strophe
⟨verse⟩ [vɜ:s] **IV 6D** 88,5 Vers, Strophe
very ['verɪ] **I FS7** 18 sehr
vet [vet] **II 3C** 35 Tierärztin/arzt
veto ['vi:təʊ] **V 5AB** 74 Einspruch, Veto
vice-president [ˌvaɪs'prezɪdənt] **V 5C** 65 Vizepräsident
victim ['vɪktɪm] **III 4C** 52 Opfer
Victorian [vɪk'tɔ:rɪən] **V 2C** 27,8 viktorianisch
video ['vɪdɪəʊ] **II 5C** 68 Video
view [vju:] **I 8A** 114 Ansicht, Aussicht
village ['vɪlɪdʒ] **I 3A** 54,1 Dorf
villager ['vɪlɪdʒə] **III 4C** 51 Dorfbewohner/in
violence ['vaɪələns] **VI 2D** 32,3 Gewalt
violet ['vaɪələt] **IV 6C** 82 Veilchen
violin [ˌvaɪə'lɪn] **IV 3A** 36,4 Geige
virtual reality goggles ['vɜ:tʃʊəl rɪ'ælətɪ 'gɒglz] **IV 4AB** 64 *Brille für Virtuelle-Realitäts-Anwendungen*
⟨vision⟩ ['vɪʒn] **III 7FE** 105 Vision
vision ['vɪʒn] **V 3AB** 46 Wunschbild, Phantasievorstellung, Vision
visit ['vɪzɪt] **III 1B** 11 Besuch
to **visit** **I 7A** 102 besuchen, besichtigen
visitor ['vɪzɪtə] **II 2B** 21 Besucher/in
Visitors' Centre ['vɪzɪtəz'sentə] **II 2B** 21 Touristenzentrum, Besucherzentrum
vital ['vaɪtl] **IV 5D** 77,10 (lebens-) wichtig
vocabulary [vəʊ'kæbjʊlərɪ] **I FS9** 27,2 Wortschatz
voice [vɔɪs] **I 2C** 50,5 Stimme
at the tops of their voices **III 1B** 12,3 aus vollem Halse
volleyball ['vɒlɪbɔ:l] **II 5C** 71,7 Volleyball
voluntary ['vɒləntərɪ] **V 3A** 31,3 freiwillig, unentgeltlich
vote [vəʊt] **V 3AB** 45 (Wahl-)Stimme, Votum
to **vote** [vəʊt] **V 1C** 15,4 abstimmen, wählen
voucher ['vaʊtʃə] **II 6B** 80 Gutschein, Bon
voyage ['vɔɪɪdʒ] **III 2AB** 32 Seereise

W

to **wag** [wæg] **III 3C** 39 wedeln
⟨wage-slave⟩ ['weɪdʒ ˌsleɪv] **III 4C** 54 Lohnsklave/-sklavin
wagon ['wægən] **III 6C** 75,4 Wagon, Planwagen, Fuhrwerk
to **wait** [weɪt] **I FS7** 20,5 warten
to wait for **I FS11** 32 warten auf
waiter ['weɪtə] **II 5B** 65,5 Kellner
waitress ['weɪtrɪs] **II 5B** 65,5 Kellnerin
to **wake up*** [ˌweɪk 'ʌp] **I 4C** 71,1 aufwachen
to wake s.o. up **I 3C** 59 jdn wecken
walk [wɔ:k] **I FS11** 30 Spaziergang
to take for a walk **I 3C** 59 spazierenführen
to **walk** [wɔ:k] **I 4B** 69,1 zu Fuß gehen
to go for a **walk** **I FS11** 30 spazieren gehen
walkman ['wɔ:kmən] **I 7B** 106,2 Walkman
wall [wɔ:l] **I FS11** 30 Mauer, Wand
garden wall **I 3C** 59 Gartenmauer
wallet ['wɒlɪt] **II 2B** 21 Brieftasche
to **waltz** [wɔ:ls] **IV 3B** 38 Walzer tanzen
⟨to wander⟩ ['wɒndə] **III 1C** 19,10 bummeln, schlendern
to **want** [wɒnt] **I 3A** 54,2 wollen, mögen
war [wɔ:] **III 2AB** 32 Krieg
warden ['wɔ:dn] **III 3B** 38,3 Aufseher/in
warehouse ['weəhaʊs] **IV 5D** 73 Lager(-haus)
warm [wɔ:m] **I 4C** 72,5 warm
to **warn** [wɔ:n] **III 4A** 46 warnen, verwarnen
warrior ['wɒrɪə] **IV 4B** 56,4 Krieger/in

to **wash** [wɒʃ] **I 3C** 59 waschen
to wash up **I 5B** 81 spülen, abwaschen
washing machine ['wɒʃɪŋ məˌʃiːn] **III 7B** 86 Waschmaschine
to do the **washing up*** [ˌwɒʃɪŋ'ʌp] **III 3A** 36,6 abspülen
waste [weɪst] **V 3A** 30 Abfall, Müll
wasteland ['weɪstlænd] **V 3C** 35 Brachland
watch [wɒtʃ] **I 5C** 85 (Armband-)Uhr
to **watch** [wɒtʃ] **I FS11** 30 zuschauen
to watch TV **I 3C** 60 fernsehen
⟨watchdog⟩ **I 7C** 112,3 Wachhund
water ['wɔːtə] **I FS6** 16 Wasser
water melon ['wɔːtə ˌmelən] **II 8A** 104,2 Wassermelone
water-pistol ['wɔːtəˌpɪstl] **I FS6** 17 Wasserpistole
watertight ['wɔːtətaɪt] **III 2D** 26 wasserdicht
wave [weɪv] **III 2C** 24 Welle
to **wave** [weɪv] **II 5C** 68 winken, schwenken
wax [wæks] **I 7C** 101 Wachs
waxwork ['wækswɜːk] **I 7C** 110 Wachsfigur
way [weɪ] **I 1C** 39,4 Weg
the wrong way **I 1C** 40,7 (in) die falsche Richtung
to know one's way about **III 1B** 11 sich auskennen, sich zurechtfinden
way of life [ˌweɪ‿əv 'laɪf] **III 1A** 9 Lebensstil, -art
we [wiː] **I FS3** 10 wir
weak [wiːk] **III 3C** 40 schwach
wealth [welθ] **V 2C** 24 Reichtum, Vermögen
wealthy ['welθɪ] **IV 3AB** 49 wohlhabend, reich
to **wear*** [weə] **I FS11** 30 tragen, anhaben
weary ['wɪərɪ] **VI 4A** 47,b) müde, erschöpft
weasel ['wiːzl] **II 8C** 108 Wiesel
weather ['weðə] **II 1B** 8 Wetter
What will the weather be like? **II 6C** 82,1 Wie wird das Wetter?
weaver ['wiːvə] **V 2A** 20 Weber/in
we'd like to ... [wiːd] **I 7A** 104,5 wir möchten
⟨wedding⟩ ['wedɪŋ] **III 7FE** 106 Hochzeit
wedding ['wedɪŋ] **V 5C** 65 Hochzeit
week [wiːk] **I 3C** 63,7 Woche
⟨weeks upon weeks⟩ [ə'pɒn] **III 6C** 76,6 wochenlang
weekend [ˌwiːk'end] **IV 3A** 37,5 Wochenende
to **weigh** [weɪ] **II 1C** 10 wiegen
to **welcome** ['welkəm] **III 2AB** 33 begrüßen, willkommen heißen
welcome ['welkəm] **I FS** 7 willkommen
you're welcome **I 7A** 104,5 Bitte.
welfare ['welfeə] **V 3AB** 46 Wohl, Wohlergehen
to feel **well** **I 6D** 97 sich wohl fühlen
well [wel] **I FS7** 18 also; gut
⟨wellington (*boot*)⟩ ['welɪŋtən] **III 7FE** 106 Gummistiefel
Welsh [welʃ] **IV 1A** 6 Walisisch, walisisch, (die) Waliser
we're = we are [wɪə] **I FS3** 10 wir sind
west [west] **II 6C** 82 (nach) Westen, West-
west [west] **I 8A** 117,6 westlich
West Indian [ˌwest‿'ɪndɪən] **III 1A** 9 westindisch, Westinder/in
western ['westən] **IV 4C** 57 *hier:* Film über den amerikanischen Westen
westward ['westwəd] **VI 2B** 24 nach Westen, in westlicher Richtung
wet [wet] **II 1B** 8 nass
wharf [wɔːf] **V 5B** 64,3 Kai
what [wɒt] **I FS1** 8 was
What a pity! ['pɪtɪ] **III 4C** 53,5 Wie schade!
what colour is **I 1A** 36,2 welche Farbe hat
⟨What do I care?⟩ **III 7FE** 104 Was geht mich das an?
What time is it? **I 3A** 56,4 Wie spät ist es?
What's for lunch? **II 5B** 63 Was gibt's zum Mittagessen?
What's the matter? **I 4A** 66,2 Was ist (los)?
what about **I FS7** 18 was ist mit
whatever [wɒt'evə] **V 4A** 48 was (auch immer), egal was
wheat [wiːt] **V 5A** 60 Weizen
wheel [wiːl] **II 4B** 49 Rad; Steuer
to **wheel** [wiːl] **III 4A** 47,2 schieben; fahren
when [wen] **I 4C** 71,1 als, wenn, wann
where [weə] **I FS3** 10 wo, wohin
wherever [weər'evə] **III 4C** 51 wo (auch) immer
whether ['weðə] **III 2B** 22 ob
which [wɪtʃ] **II 6B** 80 der, die, das ...
which? [wɪtʃ] **II 5B** 63 welche, welcher, welches
for a **while** [waɪl] **III 4C** 51 (für) eine Weile, eine Zeit lang
while [waɪl] **I 8C** 122 während
whisk(*e*)y ['wɪskɪ] **III 7C** 90 *alkoholisches Getränk*
to **whisper** ['wɪspə] **II 1D** 12 flüstern
whistle ['wɪsl] **II 5C** 68 Pfeife
to **whistle** ['wɪsl] **II 5C** 68 pfeifen
white [waɪt] **I 1A** 35,1 weiß
whitewater ['waɪtˌwɔːtə] **V 4A** 51,5 gefährliches Wasser
who [huː] **I FS7** 18 wer; der, dem, den, die *(Relativpronomen)*
whole [həʊl] **IV 2A** 22 ganz, komplett
whom [huːm] **IV 1A** 8,5 wem; wen
to **whom it may concern** [tə 'huːm ɪt ˌmeɪ kən'sɜːn] **V 4B** 52 *Anrede im Brief, wenn der Adressat nicht bekannt ist*
whose [huːz] **II 6B** 80 deren, dessen
whose? [huːz] **I 7B** 105 wessen?
why [waɪ] **I 1A** 35,3 warum
wide [waɪd] **III 6A** 70 breit, weit, umfangreich
wide awake [ˌwaɪd ə'weɪk] **III 7C** 89 hellwach
widow ['wɪdəʊ] **IV 3AB** 47 Witwe
wife [waɪf] **II 1D** 15,6 Ehefrau
Wild West Show [ˌwaɪld 'west 'ʃəʊ] **II 6D** 87,5 Wildwestspektakel
wild [waɪld] **II 6D** 85 wild
wilderness ['wɪldənɪs] **IV 4D** 59 Wildnis, Wüste
wildlife ['waɪldlaɪf] **V 4A** 48 wildlebende Tiere
will [wɪl] **IV 6B** 80,4 Wille, Wunsch
⟨will⟩ [wɪl] **III 7FE** 105 Wille
will have done* **III 3B** 37 werde ... gemacht haben
I will be doing... **III 3B** 37 Dann mache ich ... (werde ich ... machen)
to **win*** [wɪn] **I 5A** 78 gewinnen
wind [wɪnd] **I 4C** 72,4 Wind
at the **window** ['wɪndəʊ] **I FS6** 16 am Fenster
windsock ['wɪndˌsɒk] **III 6D** 78 Luft-, Windsack
wing [wɪŋ] **II 3B** 33 Flügel
⟨winner⟩ ['wɪnə] **I 7C** 113,5 Sieger/in
winter ['wɪntə] **II 5A** 60 Winter
to **wipe** [waɪp] **IV 5C** 71,3 (ab-)wischen, reinigen
to wipe out [waɪp‿'aʊt] **IV 4A** 52 ausrotten, vernichten
wish [wɪʃ] **VI 1B** 10,4 Wunsch
to **wish** [wɪʃ] **II 5A** 61 wünschen
witch [wɪtʃ] **III 7FE** 98 Hexe
with [wɪð] **I FS5** 14,1 mit
without [wɪ'ðaʊt] **II 4B** 49 ohne
⟨wolf, wolves (*pl*)⟩ [wʊlf, wʊlvz] **VI 3C** 43,6 Wolf
woman ['wʊmən] **I FS5** 14 Frau
women (*pl*) ['wɪmɪn] **I 2A** 44,9 Frauen
to **wonder** ['wʌndə] **III 1B** 11 sich fragen, überlegen
wonderful ['wʌndəfʊl] **I 5C** 84 wunderbar
wood [wʊd] **II 8A** 103 Holz; Wald
wooden ['wʊdn] **IV 3AB** 46 Holz-, hölzern
woof [wʊf] **I 7A** 102 Hundebellen
wool [wʊl] **VI 1A** 5,1 Wolle
word [wɜːd] **I FS3** 11,2 Wort
word order ['wɜːd‿ɔːdə] **I 4B** 70,4 Wortstellung, Satzstellung
work [wɜːk] **II 4A** 47 Arbeit
to **work** [wɜːk] **I 1B** 38,3 arbeiten, funktionieren
to work out [wɜːk] **II 6C** 83,4 ausrechnen
worker ['wɜːkə] **V 2A** 20 Arbeiter/in
workshop ['wɜːkʃɒp] **III 5C** 62 Kurs, Workshop; Werkstatt
world [wɜːld] **II 1C** 10 Welt
worm [wɜːm] **II 3B** 33 Wurm
⟨worn out⟩ [ˌwɔːn 'aʊt] **III 1C** 19,10 abgetragen
worried ['wʌrɪd] **II 3A** 30 besorgt
Don't **worry.** **II 3A** 30 Keine Sorge!
to worry about s.th. ['wʌrɪ] **II 3A** 30 sich Sorgen machen (um etw.)
worse [wɜːs] **II 2C** 25 schlimmer, schlechter
worship ['wɜːʃɪp] **IV 4AB** 63 Verehrung, Anbetung
to **worship** ['wɜːʃɪp] **IV 4AB** 64 verehren
worst [wɜːst] **II 2B** 24,6 schlimmste, schlimmster, schlimmstes
worth [wɜːθ] **III 5B** 60,2 wert
Would you ...?* [wʊd] **III 3A** 34 Würdest du ...?
Would you like ...? [wʊd] **II 5B** 65,5 Möchtest du ...? Möchten Sie ...?
wound [wuːnd] **VI 2D** 31,a) Wunde
wow [waʊ] **I 8C** 122 Mensch!
to **wrap** [ræp] **II 3C** 35 wickeln
wrecking (*AE*) ['rekɪŋ] **V 5B** 63 Abriss, Abbruch
wrist [rɪst] **V 5C** 68,6 Handgelenk
to **write*** [raɪt] **I 3A** 55,2 schreiben

writer ['raɪtə] **III 6C** 76,7 Schriftsteller/in
creative **writing** [kri:'eɪtɪv 'raɪtɪŋ] **III 5B** 60,3 dichterisches Schreiben
wrong [rɒŋ] **I FS8** 24,2 falsch
that's wrong **I FS8** 24,2 das stimmt nicht

Y

Yahoo! [jə'hu:] **II 6C** 83,5 Hurra!
to **yawn** [jɔ:n] **I 8C** 122 gähnen
yd. (*yard*) [jɑ:d] **IV 3B** 40,6 *Maßeinheit (91,4 cm)*
yeah! [jeə] **II 1B** 8 ja
year [jɪə] **II 1B** 8 Jahr
yellow ['jeləʊ] **I 1A** 35 gelb
yes [jes] **I FS4** 12 ja
yesterday ['jestədeɪ] **I 8A** 114 gestern
yet [jet] **II 4A** 47 schon; doch
not … yet **II 4A** 47 noch nicht
⟨yet⟩ [jet] **III 3C** 44,9 doch
yoghurt ['jɒgət] **II 7C** 96 Joghurt
⟨yoke⟩ [jəʊk] **III 6C** 76,6 Gespann
⟨in days of yore⟩ [jɔ:] **III 7FE** 105 in alten Zeiten
you [ju:; jʊ; jə] du, dir, dich; ihr, euch; Sie, Ihnen
over to you **I FS1** 8,1 du bist/ihr seid/Sie sind dran
you are **I FS3** 10 du bist, ihr seid, Sie sind
you bet [bet] **I 8B** 118 Und ob!
you guys (*AE*) [gaɪz] **II 8B** 105 ihr Jungs
young [jʌŋ] **II 1C** 11,3 jung
youngster ['jʌŋstə] **IV 5D** 73 Jugendliche/r
your [jɔ:] **I FS1** 8 dein/e, euer (eure), Ihr/e
you're welcome **I 7A** 104,5 Bitte.
you're = you are [jɔ:] **I FS3** 10 du bist
yours [jɔ:z] **III 1C** 16,3 deine; euere; Ihre/r/s
Yours sincerely, ['jɔ:z sɪn'sɪəlɪ] **V 3A** 30 Mit freundlichen Grüßen (*als Briefschluss*)
youth [ju:θ] **IV 2A** 23,2 Jugend
youth hostel ['ju:θˌhɒstl] **IV 2A** 23,3 Jugendherberge
Yuk! [jʌk] **II 6B** 80 Igitt!

Z

zipper ['zɪpə] **IV 5C** 71,2 Reißverschluss
zoo [zu:] **I 8A** 116,3 Zoo

List of names

Boys' names

Jacob ['dʒeɪkəb] **VI 2A** 20
Kim [kɪm] **VI 4A** 49,5
Leroy ['li:rɔɪ] **VI 4A** 49,5
⟨Ravi⟩ ['rævɪ] **VI 1D** 18,5
Travis ['treɪvɪs] **VI 3D** 46,2
Verrall ['verɔ:l] **VI 1C** 12

Girls' names

Anna Mae ['ænə 'meɪ] **VI 4C** 57,1
Meredith ['merədɪθ] **VI 2B** 26,3
Zachary ['zækərɪ] **VI 2B** 26,3

Surnames

Dole [dəʊl] **VI 3C** 42
Fallow ['fæləʊ] **VI 3D** 45
Hawkins ['hɔ:kɪnz] **VI 4C** 57,1
Lamb [læm] **VI 3D** 46,1
Reed [ri:d] **VI 4A** 47,b)
Rifkin ['rɪfkɪn] **VI 3D** 46,1

Geographical names

Afghanistan [æf'gænɪstæn] **VI 1B** 10,4
Alabama [ˌælə'bæmə] **VI 4A** 47,a)
Arkansas ['ɑ:kənsɔ:] **VI 4A** 48,3
Barbados [bɑ:'beɪdɒs] **VI 1A** 6
Battant ['bætənt] **VI 3B** 39,4
Bering Strait ['berɪŋ 'streɪt] **VI 2A** 22,3
Biafra [bɪ'æfrə] **VI 1D** 18,4
Britannia [brɪ'tænjə] **VI 1A** 5
Cambodia [kæm'bəʊdjə] **VI 3B** 39,4
Cape of Good Hope ['keɪp‿əv‿'gʊd‿'həʊp] **VI 1A** 6
Cuba ['kju:bə] **VI 3B** 37,a)
Falkland Islands ['fɔ:klənd 'aɪləndz] **VI 1A** 5
Georgia ['dʒɔ:dʒjə] **VI 4A** 48,3
Gettysburg ['getɪzbɜ:g] **VI 2D** 31,b)
Ghana ['gɑ:nə] **VI 1A** 6
Gibraltar [dʒɪ'brɔ:ltə] **VI 1C** 14
Harlem ['hɑ:ləm] **VI 4A** 50,6
Havana [hə'vænə] **VI 3A** 34,b)
Hong Kong [ˌhɒŋ'kɒŋ] **VI 1C** 14
Hungary ['hʌŋgərɪ] **VI 3A** 35,3
Jamestown ['dʒeɪmztaʊn] **VI 1A** 6
Kenya ['kenjə] **VI 1A** 6
Malaya [mə'leɪə] **VI 1C** 14
Montana [ˌmɒn'tænə] **VI 2A** 20
Montgomery [mənt'gʌmərɪ] **VI 4A** 47,a)
Nebraska [nɪ'bræskə] **VI 2B** 25
Nigeria [naɪ'dʒɪərɪə] **VI 1A** 6
Pakistan [ˌpɑ:kɪ'stɑ:n] **VI 1A** 6
Promontory ['prɒməntrɪ] **VI 2B** 25
Quebec [kwɪ'bek] **VI 1C** 14,6
Rhodesia [rəʊ'di:zjə] **VI 1C** 14
Roanoke Island ['rəʊəˌnəʊk 'aɪlənd] **VI 1A** 6
Saigon [saɪ'gɒn] **VI 3A** 34,b)
Sandwich Islands ['sænwɪdʒ 'aɪləndz] **VI 1A** 7,4
St. Kitts [snt'kɪts] **VI 1A** 6
Sudan [su:'dɑ:n] **VI 1C** 14
Tasmania [tæz'meɪnjə] **VI 1A** 7,4
Tennessee [ˌtenə'si:] **VI 2C** 30,3
the Commonwealth ['kɒmənwelθ] **VI 1A** 6
Versailles [veə'saɪ] **VI 1C** 14
Vietnam [ˌvjet'næm] **VI 3B** 37,a)

Other names

Aeneas [i:'ni:æs] **VI 1B** 9
Alex Haley ['ælɪks 'heɪlɪ] **VI 2C** 28
⟨Big Mama Thornton⟩ ['bɪg 'mæmə 'θɔ:ntən] **VI 4C** 59,6
Bismarck ['bɪzmɑ:k] **VI 1B** 10,4
Bob Dylan ['bɒb 'dɪlən] **VI 2A** 19
Census Bureau ['sensəs 'bjʊərəʊ] **VI 3A** 33,a)
Central Pacific ['sentrəl pə'sɪfɪk] **VI 2B** 25
Chanrithy Oak [tʃæn'rɪθɪ 'əʊk] **VI 3B** 39,4
EEC (*European Economic Community*) ['i:i:'si:] **VI 1C** 14
George V [dʒɔ:dʒ] **VI 1C** 14,5
Harrow ['hærəʊ] **VI 3C** 41
Henning ['henɪŋ] **VI 2C** 30,3
Henry David Thoreau ['henrɪ 'deɪvɪd θɔ:'rəʊ] **VI 2B** 24
Horace M. Greeley ['hɒrɪs 'em 'gri:lɪ] **VI 2A** 19
⟨James Thurber⟩ ['dʒeɪmz 'θɜ:bə] **VI 3C** 43,6
John Wilkes Booth ['dʒɒn 'wɪlks 'bu:ð] **VI 2D** 31,a)
Khmer Rouge ['kmeə 'ru:ʒ] **VI 3B** 39,4
Ku Klux Klan ['ku:klʌks'klæn] **VI 2D** 32,3 *Geheimorganisation, die nach dem Bürgerkrieg gegründet wurde mit dem Ziel die Vorrechte der Weißen in Amerika zu erhalten*
Kunta Kinte ['kʊntə 'kɪntə] **VI 2C** 28
Langston Hughes ['læŋstən 'hju:z] **VI 4A** 50,6
LL Cool J ['el‿'el‿'ku:l‿'dzeɪ] **VI 4B** 54,4
Lord Palmerston ['lɔ:d 'pɑ:məstən] **VI 1B** 8
Louis Farrakhan ['lu:ɪ 'færəkən] **VI 4B** 54,5
Louisiana [lu:ˌi:zɪ'ænə] **VI 2B** 25
Mahatma Gandhi [mə'hɑ:tmə 'gændi:] **VI 1C** 14
Marquess of Queensberry ['mɑ:kwɪs‿əv‿'kwi:nzbərɪ] **VI 1B** 11
Martin Luther King ['mɑ:tɪn 'lu:θə 'kɪŋ] **VI 4A** 47,a)
⟨M.C. Hammer⟩ ['hæmə] **VI 4C** 59,7
Murray Fisher ['mʌrɪ 'fɪʃə] **VI 2C** 30,3
Napoleon Bonaparte [nə'pəʊljən 'bəʊnəpɑ:t] **VI 2B** 25
Nelson Mandela ['nelsn mæn'delə] **VI 1B** 8,2
Red Cross ['red 'krɒs] **VI 3B** 39,4
Rosa Parks ['rəʊzə 'pɑ:ks] **VI 4A** 47,a)
Rudyard Kipling ['rʌdjəd 'kɪplɪŋ] **VI 1B** 9
Ruppert High ['rʌppət 'haɪ] **VI 3D** 46,1
the Prairie Belt ['preərɪ 'belt] **VI 2A** 22,3
⟨Trina Johnson⟩ ['tri:nə 'dʒɒnsən] **VI 4C** 59,7
Union Pacific ['ju:njən pə'sɪfɪk] **VI 2B** 25
Victoria [vɪk'tɔ:rɪə] **VI 1A** 6
Virgil ['vɜ:dʒɪl] **VI 1B** 9
Wal-Mart ['wɔ:lˌmɑ:t] **VI 4A** 47,b)
Walter Wingfield ['wɔ:ltə 'wɪŋfi:ld] **VI 1B** 11
W.C. Handy ['hændɪ] **VI 4C** 57,4
William Ewart Gladstone ['wɪljəm 'ju:ət 'glædstən] **VI 1B** 10,4
William Webb Ellis ['wɪljəm 'web 'elɪs] **VI 1B** 11
Winchester ['wɪntʃɪstə] **VI 3C** 41
Yankee ['jæŋkɪ] **VI 2B** 26,2

List of irregular verbs

infinitive	past tense	past participle	German
be [iː]	was (were)	been [iː/ɪ]	sein
beat [iː]	beat [iː]	beaten [iː]	schlagen
become [ʌ]	became [eɪ]	become [ʌ]	werden
begin [ɪ]	began [æ]	begun [ʌ]	beginnen
bend [e]	bent [e]	bent [e]	(sich) biegen, beugen
bet [e]	bet [e]	bet [e]	wetten
bind [aɪ]	bound [aʊ]	bound [aʊ]	(ver)binden
bite [aɪ]	bit [ɪ]	bitten [ɪ]	beißen
bleed [iː]	bled [e]	bled [e]	bluten
blow [əʊ]	blew [uː]	blown [əʊ]	blasen
break [eɪ]	broke [əʊ]	broken [əʊ]	(zer)brechen
bring [ɪ]	brought [ɔː]	brought [ɔː]	(her)bringen
build [ɪ]	built [ɪ]	built [ɪ]	bauen
burn [ɜː]	burned [ɜː] burnt [ɜː]	burned [ɜː] burnt [ɜː]	(ver)brennen
buy [aɪ]	bought [ɔː]	bought [ɔː]	kaufen
catch [æ]	caught [ɔː]	caught [ɔː]	fangen
choose [uː]	chose [əʊ]	chosen [əʊ]	(aus)wählen
come [ʌ]	came [eɪ]	come [ʌ]	kommen
cost [ɒ]	cost [ɒ]	cost [ɒ]	kosten
cut [ʌ]	cut [ʌ]	cut [ʌ]	schneiden
deal [iː]	dealt [e]	dealt [e]	sich befassen, austeilen
dig [ɪ]	dug [ʌ]	dug [ʌ]	(aus)graben
do [uː]	did [ɪ]	done [ʌ]	tun
draw [ɔː]	drew [uː]	drawn [ɔː]	zeichnen, ziehen
dream [iː]	dreamed [iː] dreamt [e]	dreamed [iː] dreamt [e]	träumen
drink [ɪ]	drank [æ]	drunk [ʌ]	trinken
drive [aɪ]	drove [əʊ]	driven [ɪ]	fahren
eat [iː]	ate [e]	eaten [iː]	essen
fall [ɔː]	fell [e]	fallen [ɔː]	fallen
feed [iː]	fed [e]	fed [e]	füttern
feel [iː]	felt [e]	felt [e]	(sich) fühlen
fight [aɪ]	fought [ɔː]	fought [ɔː]	(be)kämpfen
find [aɪ]	found [aʊ]	found [aʊ]	finden
fly [aɪ]	flew [uː]	flown [əʊ]	fliegen
forget [e]	forgot [ɒ]	forgotten [ɒ]	vergessen
forgive [ɪ]	forgave [eɪ]	forgiven [ɪ]	vergeben, verzeihen
freeze [iː]	froze [əʊ]	frozen [əʊ]	(er)frieren
get [e]	got [ɒ]	got [ɒ]	bekommen
give [ɪ]	gave [eɪ]	given [ɪ]	geben
go [əʊ]	went [e]	gone [ɒ]	gehen
grow [əʊ]	grew [uː]	grown [əʊ]	wachsen, anbauen
hang [æ]	hung [ʌ] hanged [æ]	hung [ʌ] hanged [æ]	(auf)hängen (er)hängen
have [æ]	had [æ]	had [æ]	haben
hear [ɪə]	heard [ɜː]	heard [ɜː]	hören
hide [aɪ]	hid [ɪ]	hidden [ɪ]	verstecken
hit [ɪ]	hit [ɪ]	hit [ɪ]	treffen
hold [əʊ]	held [e]	held [e]	halten
hurt [ɜː]	hurt [ɜː]	hurt [ɜː]	verletzen, schmerzen
keep [iː]	kept [e]	kept [e]	behalten
know [əʊ]	knew [juː]	known [əʊ]	wissen

infinitive	past tense	past participle	German
lead [i:]	led [e]	led [e]	führen
learn [3:]	learnt [3:] learned [3:]	learnt [3:] learned [3:]	lernen
leave [i:]	left [e]	left [e]	(ver)lassen
lend [e]	lent [e]	lent [e]	leihen
let [e]	let [e]	let [e]	lassen
lie [aɪ]	lay [eɪ]	lain [eɪ]	liegen
lose [u:]	lost [ɒ]	lost [ɒ]	verlieren
make [eɪ]	made [eɪ]	made [eɪ]	machen
mean [i:]	meant [e]	meant [e]	bedeuten, meinen
meet [i:]	met [e]	met [e]	(sich) treffen
misunderstand [æ]	misunderstood [ʊ]	misunderstood [ʊ]	missverstehen
pay [eɪ]	paid [eɪ]	paid [eɪ]	bezahlen
put [ʊ]	put [ʊ]	put [ʊ]	setzen, stellen, legen
quit [ɪ]	quit [ɪ], quitted [ɪ]	quit [ɪ], quitted [ɪ]	aufgeben, verlassen
read [i:]	read [e]	read [e]	lesen
ride [aɪ]	rode [əʊ]	ridden [ɪ]	reiten
ring [ɪ]	rang [æ]	rung [ʌ]	läuten
rise [aɪ]	rose [əʊ]	risen [ɪ]	sich (er)heben
run [ʌ]	ran [æ]	run [ʌ]	laufen, rennen
say [eɪ]	said [e]	said [e]	sagen
see [i:]	saw [ɔ:]	seen [i:]	sehen
sell [e]	sold [əʊ]	sold [əʊ]	verkaufen
send [e]	sent [e]	sent [e]	schicken
set [e]	set [e]	set [e]	setzen, stellen
shake [eɪ]	shook [ʊ]	shaken [eɪ]	schütteln
shine [aɪ]	shone [ɒ]	shone [ɒ]	scheinen
shoot [u:]	shot [ɒ]	shot [ɒ]	schießen
show [əʊ]	showed [əʊ]	shown [əʊ]	zeigen
shut [ʌ]	shut [ʌ]	shut [ʌ]	schließen
sing [ɪ]	sang [æ]	sung [ʌ]	singen
sink [ɪ]	sank [æ]	sunk [ʌ]	(ver)sinken, untergehen
sit [ɪ]	sat [æ]	sat [æ]	sitzen, sich setzen
sleep [i:]	slept [e]	slept [e]	schlafen
slide [aɪ]	slid [ɪ]	slid [ɪ]	schlittern, rutschen
speak [i:]	spoke [əʊ]	spoken [əʊ]	sprechen
spell [e]	spelt [e], spelled [e]	spelt [e], spelled [e]	buchstabieren
spend [e]	spent [e]	spent [e]	verbringen, ausgeben
spread [e]	spread [e]	spread [e]	(sich) ausbreiten
stand [æ]	stood [ʊ]	stood [ʊ]	stehen
steal [i:]	stole [əʊ]	stolen [əʊ]	stehlen
stick [ɪ]	stuck [ʌ]	stuck [ʌ]	kleben, haften
swim [ɪ]	swam [æ]	swum [ʌ]	schwimmen
swing [ɪ]	swung [ʌ]	swung [ʌ]	schwingen
take [eɪ]	took [ʊ]	taken [eɪ]	nehmen, (hin)bringen
teach [i:]	taught [ɔ:]	taught [ɔ:]	unterrichten
tear [eə]	tore [ɔ:]	torn [ɔ:]	(ab)reißen
tell [e]	told [əʊ]	told [əʊ]	erzählen, sagen
think [ɪ]	thought [ɔ:]	thought [ɔ:]	denken, glauben
throw [əʊ]	threw [u:]	thrown [əʊ]	werfen
understand [æ]	understood [ʊ]	understood [ʊ]	verstehen
wake [eɪ]	woke [əʊ]	woken [əʊ]	(auf)wecken, (auf)wachen
wear [eə]	wore [ɔ:]	worn [ɔ:]	tragen *(Kleidung)*
win [ɪ]	won [ʌ]	won [ʌ]	gewinnen
write [aɪ]	wrote [əʊ]	written [ɪ]	schreiben

⟨Useful phrases in class⟩

What you can say to your friends or to the teacher

• What's this in English/German? What does … mean?	Was heißt dies auf Englisch/Deutsch? Was bedeutet …?
• Can I ask a question, please? How do you do this exercise? Can/Could you help me, please? I don't understand this word/sentence. Pardon? Could you write it on the board, please? What must we do for homework?	Kann ich bitte eine Frage stellen? Wie macht man/geht diese Übung? Können Sie/Kannst du mir bitte helfen? Ich verstehe dieses Wort/diesen Satz nicht. Wie bitte? Können Sie es an die Tafel schreiben? Was haben wir als Hausaufgabe auf?

What you can say when you talk about stories, poems, songs, etc.

• This story is good/great/interesting/exciting/terrific/sad/awful/funny. I think it's terrible/boring/good/fantastic. I find it … . I like it./I enjoyed it. Why didn't you like it?	Diese Geschichte ist gut/großartig/interessant/spannend/klasse/traurig/schrecklich/komisch. Ich meine, sie ist schrecklich/langweilig/gut/fantastisch. Ich halte sie für … ./Ich finde sie … . Mir gefällt sie./Sie hat mir Spaß gemacht. Warum hat sie dir nicht gefallen?
• It's OK but I have read better ones.	Sie ist ganz nett, aber ich habe schon bessere gelesen.
I didn't like it much. I prefer … .	Mir hat sie nicht so gut gefallen. Ich mag lieber … .
• The text/song is divided into … parts.	Der Text/das Lied ist in … Abschnitte unterteilt.
The first part is about … . I'd suggest the following headings for each part.	Der erste Abschnitt handelt von … . Ich würde für die Abschnitte folgende Überschriften vorschlagen.
The turning-point in the story is in line …/part … . To understand this we have to look at … .	Der Wendepunkt in der Geschichte ist in Zeile …/Abschnitt … . Um dies zu verstehen, muss man … anschauen.
• There are some details in the text which show that … . The author gives the information in a direct/an indirect way. The main points are … . It's my impression that … . In line … it says … .	Im Text sind einige Details, die zeigen, dass … . Der Autor gibt die Information sehr direkt/indirekt. Die Hauptgesichtspunkte sind … . Ich habe den Eindruck, dass … . In Zeile … heißt es … .

• The story reminds me of … . This story/song/poem makes me feel … .	Die Geschichte erinnert mich an … . Diese(s) Geschichte/Lied/Gedicht macht mich … .
• The main/minor characters are … . The characters in the story (don't) change. At first … . Later … .	Die Haupt-/Nebenfiguren sind … . Die Charaktere in der Geschichte ändern sich (nicht). Zuerst … . Später … .

What you can say when you discuss things

• What do you think? How do you feel about it? I'm not sure. In my opinion … . I find all this stupid/very interesting.	Was ist deine Meinung? Was hältst du davon? Ich bin nicht sicher. Meiner Meinung nach … . Ich halte dies alles für blöd/sehr interessant.
• I think she/he is right/wrong. That's wrong, I'm afraid. I think she/he has got it all wrong. No, I don't believe that. That's not the same at all. How do you know? What makes you think that? You can't be sure. I suppose … .	Ich denke, sie/er hat recht/unrecht. Das stimmt nicht, fürchte ich. Ich glaube, sie/er hat es ganz falsch verstanden. Nein, das glaube ich nicht. Das ist überhaupt nicht das Gleiche. Woher weißt du das? Wie kommst du darauf? Man kann sich nicht sicher sein. Vermutlich … .
• I wonder why … . I suppose … . It's surprising to hear that … . I didn't know that … . I find it hard to believe that … . I hadn't imagined that … .	Ich frage mich, warum … . Ich vermute/Vermutlich … . Es ist erstaunlich zu hören, dass … . Ich habe nicht gewusst, dass … . Für mich ist es schwer zu glauben, dass … . Ich hatte mir nicht vorgestellt, dass … .
• I don't agree with you. I'm for/against it. I think we should find out the facts first. Yes, that's a much better idea. On the one/other hand … .	Ich stimme dir nicht zu. Ich bin dafür/dagegen. Ich meine, wir sollten erst einmal die Tatsachen herausfinden. Ja, das ist eine viel bessere Idee. Einerseits/andererseits … .
• I don't understand. Could you explain that again? Oh, I see. How stupid of me. But unfortunately/luckily … .	Ich verstehe das nicht. Vielleicht kannst du das noch mal erklären. Aha, ich verstehe. Wie dumm von mir. Aber unglücklicherweise/glücklicherweise … .
• I'd like to make a suggestion: Why don't we …? We have to be careful, I suppose. That's why it's important to … .	Ich möchte gern einen Vorschlag machen: Warum … wir nicht …? Wir müssen wohl vorsichtig sein. Deshalb ist es wichtig zu … .

THE UNITED STATES OF AMERICA
CT = Connecticut
DE = Delaware
MA= Massachusetts
MD = Maryland
NH = New Hampshire
NJ = New Jersey
RI = Rhode Island
VT = Vermont
35 major highways
4⁰⁰ time zones, compared with Central European Time 12⁰⁰ (noon)
0 500 1000 km
0 300 500 Miles
CANADA
USA
MEXICO
THE BAHAMAS
PACIFIC OCEAN
ATLANTIC OCEAN
Gulf of Mexico
Brit. Columbia
Alberta
Saskatchewan
Manitoba
Ontario
Québec
New Brunswick
Washington
Oregon
California
Idaho
Nevada
Utah
Arizona
Montana
Wyoming
Colorado
New Mexico
North Dakota
South Dakota
Nebraska
Kansas
Oklahoma
Texas
Minnesota
Iowa
Missouri
Arkansas
Louisiana
Wisconsin
Illinois
Michigan
Indiana
Ohio
Kentucky
Tennessee
Mississippi
Alabama
Georgia
Florida
South Carolina
North Carolina
Virginia
West Virginia
Pennsylvania
New York
Maine
VT
NH
MA
CT
RI
NJ
MD
DE
Rocky Mountains
Sierra Nevada
Appalachians
Columbia R.
Colorado R.
Rio Grande
Arkansas R.
Missouri R.
Mississippi R.
Ohio R.
St. Lawrence R.
Lake Superior
L. Michigan
Lake Huron
Lake Erie
L. Ontario
Niagara-F.
Vancouver
Seattle
Tacoma
Portland
Salem
Spokane
Lethbridge
Great Falls
Butte
Billings
Boise
Reno
San Francisco
Santa Cruz
Monterey
Salinas
Las Vegas
Los Angeles
San Diego
Tijuana
Hawaii 3600 km
Promontory
Salt Lake City
Phoenix
Tucson
Casper
Cheyenne
Denver
Rapid City
Santa Fe
Albuquerque
El Paso
Winnipeg
Fargo
Bismarck
Pierre
Sioux Falls
Omaha
Wichita
Enid
Oklahoma City
Fort Worth
Frisco
McKinney
Farmersville
Dallas
Fredericksburg
New Braunfels
San Antonio
Westphalia
Houston
Weimar
Hochheim
Nordheim
Duluth
Minneapolis
St. Paul
Des Moines
Kansas City
Hannibal
St. Louis
Little Rock
Stuttgart
Memphis
Oxford
Birmingham
Baton Rouge
New Orleans
Rhinelander
Oshkosh
Baraboo
Milwaukee
Chicago
Galesburg
Gary
Indianapolis
Louisville
Nashville
Knoxville
Lexington
Cincinnati
Sault Ste. Marie
Grand Rapids
Holland
Detroit
Cleveland
Pittsburgh
Gettysburg
Toronto
Buffalo
Fairport
Ottawa
Montreal
Québec
Houlton
Portland
Boston
Cape Cod
Hopkinton
New York
Philadelphia
Baltimore
Washington D. C.
Richmond
Jamestown
Charlotte
Atlanta
Charleston
Jacksonville
Kennedy Space Center
Fort Lauderdale
Miami
Miami Beach
Pacific Time
Mountain Time
Central Time
Eastern Time
300
400
500
600
700
Alaska
Yukon R.
Bering Strait
St. Lawrence I.
Fairbanks
Anchorage
Whitehorse
CANADA
Alaska Time
Pacific Time
Mountain Time
Bering Sea
Aleutian Islands
100
200
0 500 1000 km
0 200 400 600 Miles
Hawaii-Aleutian Time
1⁰⁰
Kauai
Hawaii
Honolulu
Maui
Hawaii
0 200 Miles